# HORARY ASTROLOGY

## PLAIN
## &
## SIMPLE

# Horary Astrology Plain & Simple
## A Review by Bruce Scofield

This book by Anthony Louis is the most thorough presentation of traditional horary astrology I have seen for a long time. As indicated by the subtitle, it is based on at least two thousand years of astrological divination technique found in the writings of some of the greatest astrologers in history: Ptolemy, Dorotheus, Bonatus, Lilly, Jones, and others.

The author's knowledge of the history of his subject is remarkable and commendable. There is much to be gained from familiarity with history in any field, but especially so in astrology, which suffers today in part because its roots are deeply buried in the past. Louis is a good historian. He has read the relevant sources. He understands them (something that many historians of science do not), is critical of them, and freely relates when the old techniques prove dubious in modern practice.

In many respects this book can be considered a manual of the Western astrological tradition and, with its emphasis on principles, will admirably serve the general learning needs of beginners, whatever their interest in astrology, as well as any text, old or new, I can think of. Louis relies on both ancient and modern horary authorities to sort through contradictions in the literature and present a coherent methodology for analysis. The use of case studies is a vital part of any book on horary astrology, and the cases in this text are especially varied. His section on finding lost objects is particularly thorough.

Louis is a practicing psychiatrist. His knowledge of psychology adds a great deal to his study and I wish more people from other fields would write on astrology. Throughout the book he maintains a critical and objective attitude toward the subject, using only the techniques that can actually be demonstrated in practice. What's missing—and this is what makes the book so refreshing—is the astrological cheerleading, the warped interpretations of history and over-confidence in the "correctness" of certain traditions. In addition, he enlivens what might be a necessarily tedious read with odd and delightful observations, humor, witticisms and puns.

In summary, this book is well written, superbly organized, and very readable (quite a feat for a book about one of the most technical branches of traditional astrology). Horary has a lot of specialized terminology, but Louis is at pains to explain it all, providing many examples along the way. Here is a work that is likely to remain on the bookstore shelves for many years—sophisticated, diligent, destined to become a classic.

—Bruce Scofield
Amherst, Massachusetts

# About the Author

Anthony Louis is a psychiatrist with training in Freudian analysis. It was his interest in symbolism that led to his in-depth study of the history and practice of astrology, and his background in the classics and Latin that enabled him to research the original sources of Western horary astrology. An empirical thinker, he is unwilling to accept astrological rules and practices that are not backed up by hard evidence.

Louis has contributed numerous articles to publications such as *American Astrology, The Horary Practitioner, The Ascendant,* as well as Llewellyn's *Astrological Calendar* and *Sun Sign Book.* He has also written a computer program for Geomancy—another time-honored method of astrological divination, and is the author of *Tarot Plain and Simple.*

Below is Anthony Louis' natal chart. He was born on September 3, 1945, 9:04 A.M. EDT, 73W03/41N33. His Sun in the 11th house conjoins a traditional astrological degree—11° Virgo.

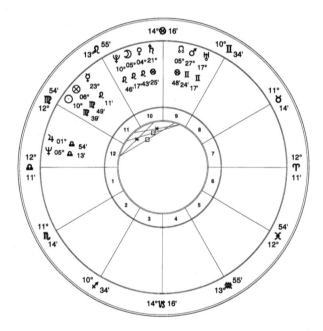

# To Contact the Author

If you would like to contact the author or would like more information about this book, please write to him in care of Llewellyn Worldwide. We cannot guarantee that every letter will be answered, but all will be forwarded. Please write to:

Anthony Louis
c/o Llewellyn Publications
P.O. Box 64383, Dept. K401-4
St. Paul, MN 55164-0383, U.S.A

Please enclose a self-addressed, stamped envelope for reply or $1.00 to cover costs. If ordering from outside the U.S.A., please enclose an international postal reply coupon.

# ANTHONY LOUIS

# HORARY ASTROLOGY

## PLAIN

## &

## SIMPLE

## FAST

## &

## ACCURATE

## ANSWERS

## TO

## REAL

## WORLD

## QUESTIONS

1998 • LLEWELLYN PUBLICATIONS • ST. PAUL, MN 55164-0383 U.S.A.

FIRST EDITION
First Printing, 1998

Cover design: Tom Grewe
Editing and book design: Ken Schubert

**Library of Congress Cataloging-in-Publication Data**

Louis, Anthony, 1945–
    Horary astrology plain & simple : fast & accurate answers to real
world questions / Anthony Louis. -- 1st ed.
        p.  cm.
    Includes bibliographical references.
    ISBN 1-56718-401-4 (trade paper)
    1. Horary Astrology.   I. Title.
  BF1717.5.L69   1998
133.5'6--dc21                                   97-52798
                                                    CIP

**Publisher's Note**

Llewellyn Worldwide does not participate in, endorse, or have any authority or responsibility concerning private business transactions between our authors and the public. All mail addressed to the author is forwarded but the publisher cannot, unless specifically instructed by the author, give out an address or phone number.

Llewellyn Publications
A Division of Llewellyn Worldwide, Ltd.
P.O. Box 64383 Dept. K401-4
St. Paul, MN 55164-0383, U.S.A.

Printed in the United States of America

# TABLE OF CONTENTS

# INDEX OF ASTROLOGICAL CHARTS

# Index of Figures

# Index of Tables

# Foreword

Fashions change in astrology, as in everything else, and for many years the horary art was out of style. It's easy to understand why. With its emphasis on psychology and humanistic themes, twentieth-century astrology has seen horary as hopelessly fatalistic, rigid, old-fashioned, event-oriented fortune telling.

Those descriptions are true, but times change, and now horary astrology is enjoying a renaissance. What was once fatalistic and event-oriented is now practical and realistic. People who lead hectic lives want down-to-earth, sensible advice about real life problems, but answers to their questions are often hard to find in natal charts. And while psychological counseling has its place, someone who wonders whether to expand a business appreciates a fast and accurate answer.

Horary is the branch of astrology that answers people's questions—which can be anything from, "Will I win the election?" to "Will my son get married this year?" to "Where did I put my diamond ring?" and a thousand other topics. If the question asks when, where, or whether, it's a candidate for horary. The more elusive why is difficult, but in some case horary charts describe background conditions as well.

A horary chart is a horoscope, but instead of representing a person's birth, it symbolizes the birth of a question. A question is "born" when first articulated, that is, when it is asked aloud or in writing, especially if it's asked of another person, such as an astrologer. The question's horoscope is drawn for the day, time, and place of its birth.

There is definitely something spooky about horary charts. Why should the planets' positions at a particular moment describe the answer to a question someone poses at that moment? Natal astrology is hard enough to understand, but horary art goes beyond what our intuition tells us about the workings of planetary cycles. In addition, it completely ignores the concept of free will, which explains its fall from favor.

Perhaps the answer lies in Carl Jung's concept of synchronicity. Jung conjectured that many things are connected by an acausal connecting principle—a connection we cannot see, measure, or understand, but which operates all the time and which explains the coincidences that make our lives interesting. You lose your watch, you wonder where it is, and at 3:45 on a Sunday afternoon you phone your astrologer to say, "It's driving me crazy, I can't find my watch. Where is it? Will I get it back?" Your astrologer draws the chart, phones you back, and says, "Look in an upstairs closet along the northeast wall close to the floor"—and there it is.

Why did you wait until that particular moment to ask the question? Horary artists would say that you waited until the arrangement of signs, luminaries, and planets coincided with the answer. There are times when specific, pressing, clear questions well out of us, when they demand to be asked. We probably are, at those moments, responding to something far beyond us; we are probably manifesting Dr. Jung's theory.

Anthony Louis has spent many years studying these connections, and he brings to the art of horary a refreshing blend of skeptic, scholar, and experimentalist. He has taken the time to study authorities from long ago, when horary astrology flourished, and from today, and his experiments have tested his theories in real life.

His findings make very interesting reading. This is an exciting time in the history of horary astrology, for there are many approaches to the subject, and they differ wildly in theory and practice. We students of horary face bewildering choices. In addition to studying modern authors such as the late Barbara Watters and Ivy Goldstein-Jacobson, who are easily the most influential and widely read American authorities of recent years, we can now study the works of William Lilly, the subject's grand master, to whose writings we have recently gained access. Some of us have turned to the seventeenth century and accepted Lilly as our final authority, while others branch out in futuristic directions. Anthony Louis balances the old and the new while adding his own observations.

Any horary book worth its while brings theory to life with examples, and this book is no exception. Every question has its story, and the stories are often dramatic.

No matter what your approach to horary, whether modern or ancient or something in between, there is much to study, ponder, and test—and we are all the richer for it.

—Carol Wiggers, Q.H.P.
Issaquah, WA

*Readers may contact Carol A. Wiggers regarding her publication at:*
*JustUs & Associates, 1420 N.W. Gilman, Suite #2154, Issaquah, WA 98027-7001 USA*
*Telephone: (425) 391-8371*
*Fax: (425) 392-1919*
*e-mail: cwiggers@halcyon.com.*

# Preface

Horary is the art of astrological divination. Its roots lie in the ancient omen litera-ture of Babylon that gave rise to all branches of astrology. It is not possible to date exactly the origin of horary astrology, but we can locate its underlying principles in the fifth century before Christ. Astrology could not exist until humans had to struggle with the concept of their future. The early nomads lived a day-to-day existence and did not trouble themselves with long-range planning. Only with the advent of the agricultural rev-olution in Mesopotamia around 8000 B.C. did the ability to predict the future become a matter of human survival.

The calendar was invented to predict changes in climate and the availability of water for crops—in short, to ensure a good harvest. Early observers began to note correlations between events in nature and human activity. Correspondences were drawn between worldly events and just about any natural phenomenon—the flight of birds, the livers of sacrificial animals, and most importantly the movements of heavenly bodies. But none of these observations could be recorded until the invention of cuneiform writing by the Sumerians in 3300 B.C.

In Babylon during the second millennium before Christ, hundreds of years of astrologi-cal correspondences were recorded on a series of tablets called the *Enuma Anu Enlil*. The information on these tablets formed the ancient database from which modern astrological theory developed—raw data waiting for the theoretical glue that would be provided by the early Greek philosophers. Most notably, Pythagoras of Samos (560–480 B.C.), a Greek philosopher, mystic and mathematician, provided the link between Babylonian astrologi-cal omen lore and modern astrological philosophy. Pythagoras and his followers, like many modern astrologers, believed in the transmigration of souls. Pythagoras taught that every-thing could be understood in terms of numbers. He discovered that the vibrating strings of musical instruments produced harmonious tones only when the lengths of the strings were ratios of whole numbers. He talked about similar ratios among the celestial spheres of the planets producing the "harmony of the spheres."

When applied to the horoscope, the Greek theory of music became the basis for the classical "major" astrological aspects, which display the same ratios of whole numbers as the harmonious tones. Horary—or for that matter, modern astrology—could not exist until a mathematical theory of aspects was developed, and it was the Pythagoreans who provided the philosophical rationale. The early Greek thinkers also invented the conceptual zodiac, a mathematical model of twelve equal thirty-degree signs patterned after the actual constellations. The earliest known horoscope using this modern mathematical astrology dates from around 409 B.C. Most likely, horary astrology originated in the period between this date and the life of Pythagoras.

The basic premise behind horary astrology is that a question, like a person, comes into the world at a particular significant moment. A horoscope cast for the birth of an inquiry is called a horary chart. An analysis of that chart reveals the circumstances surrounding the question and its eventual outcome.

The principle of cosmic sympathy underlies horary analysis. In other words, a parallel exists between the universe and the human mind. The planets, signs, and houses of the horoscope are symbols that reflect human thought and events of human life. If the astrologer can decipher the symbolic meaning of the chart, he or she can understand the significance of the matter at hand and foresee its eventual resolution. Horary is primarily an astrology of the twelve houses of the horoscope.

The person asking the question is always shown by the 1st house. The matter asked about belongs in one of the twelve houses. Each house has a planetary ruler. The fundamental axiom of horary astrology is this: The first major aspect between the rulers of the two essential houses determined by the question will show the outcome of that question. Usually the two significant houses are the 1st, which governs the person asking the question (the querent), and the house that rules the matter inquired about (the quesited). Of course, life is rarely simple and many factors can modify the answer given by the basic aspect between significators.

This book represents a substantial revision of my 1991 text *Horary Astrology: The History and Practice of Astro-Divination*. Since the time of the first publication, I have become more impressed with traditional techniques. In addition, I have come to understand more clearly the meanings of some of the terms used in classical horary astrology. In this revision I have tried to remain open-minded about the various schools of horary astrology while at the same time presenting a coherent system that works, as demonstrated by the case examples. Horary is an intricate and complex branch of the celestial science. My goal throughout has been to present the material in a clear and user-friendly manner that will make this ancient science fully accessible to the modern reader.

Let me credit those who most influenced my understanding of horary. I cut my eye-teeth on horary with the 1943 text *Problem Solving by Horary Astrology* by Marc Edmund Jones. Studying Jones led me back to the ancient Greek and Latin texts, the thirteenth-century guide by Guido Bonatus and, of course, *Christian Astrology* by the master himself, William Lilly. Lilly's 1647 book remains the bible of the art. I also owe a debt of gratitude to the lectures on horary by contemporary astrologers Joan McEvers and Bobbye

Bratcher-Nelson. Their clarity of thought and presentation are models to emulate. British astrologer Sue Ward's researches into Lilly's original manuscripts were especially enlightening. *The Horary Practitioner,* edited by Carol Wiggers, Sue Ward, and C. J. Puotinen, has made available a wealth of material on traditional horary methods. I would have been lost in trying traditional techniques without the superb computer program Horary Helper by Allen Edwall. Project Hindsight, inspired by Rob Hand, Robert Schmidt, and Rob Zoller, has made crucial astrological classics available to the modern world. Bruce Scofield has been a model of scholarship and dedication to the celestial art. Finally, I must thank the readers of the first edition who wrote with their questions, corrections, criticisms, and suggestions for improving the text.

Writing and revising this book has been great fun. As such, it was a 5th house activity. In the process I have learned much about astrology and made the acquaintance of several excellent horary astrologers who all have their own unique ways of practicing the art. I hope I have conveyed my enthusiasm for horary along with what I have learned. I make no claim to have all the answers. On the other hand, I am a serious and devoted student who freely admits he has much to learn from his own charts and from the experience of other astrologers. Any feedback or constructive criticism can be sent to me through the publisher.

Although a novice at astrology could read and understand this text, it has been written for the intermediate astrologer. A basic understanding of the signs, planets, aspects, and houses will add immensely to the reader's appreciation of this material. My aim has been to bring clarity, order, historical accuracy, and reasonableness to the muddled horary universe. Whatever your background, may your venture into horary be as enjoyable and enlightening as it has been for me.

—Anthony Louis
November 1996

# ACKNOWLEDGMENTS

First, I must thank my wife, Linda, and my sons, David and Aaron, for their patience and support while I was writing and revising this manuscript. I hope I was not too much of an absent husband and father when I went off to horary land.

Next, I must express gratitude to the many astrologers, colleagues, and friends who helped shape the present volume in direct or indirect ways. Joan McEvers gave generously of her time, advice, and horary questions. Without Joan's inspiration this book would never have been written.

Bruce Scofield reviewed the text and gave his imprimatur that I was not too far afield in my historical approach to horary. Irish astrologer Maurice McCann sent many letters across the Atlantic to point out errors and suggest helpful corrections for the revised edition.

The folks at *The Horary Practitioner* kindly offered their time and knowledge of horary. Carol A. Wiggers graciously agreed to write a foreword. C. J. Puotinen reviewed the definitions of horary terms and made many helpful suggestions. Sue Ward engaged in a lively correspondence across the Atlantic that kept me on my toes.

Computer programmer and astrologer Allen Edwall helped to clarify the meanings of some of the traditional horary terms and techniques. I would have been lost without the accuracy and information in his wonderful computer program Horary Helper for Windows. No horary astrologer should be without it.

Special thanks go to Diana K. Rosenberg for her thoughtful review of the compendium of fixed stars that appears in the appendix. Indirect thanks should also go to Robert Hand for his scholarly lectures and his encyclopedic grasp of astrology that served as the model I tried to emulate.

My friends Michael Cunningham and Luis Alvarado both read the manuscript carefully for content, grammar, and style. Their comments helped make the text more readable, and I thank them for their gifts of time, encouragement, and friendship.

Jill Dotlo invited me to her horary study group, where I met several astrologers dedicated to learning the art. The lively discussions helped clarify my thinking about some vexing horary principles.

The editor at Llewellyn of the first edition, Tom Bridges, was a delight to work with. His keen eye and sense of balance and proportion also helped shape this book. I feel a sense of loss that our work together has drawn to a close. Best of luck to Tom in all his future endeavors. I am also very grateful to Ken Schubert who edited the current edition with such great care and professionalism.

Finally, I wish to thank anyone whose name I have inadvertently omitted in the above listing, and also all who contributed horary questions to the text, especially my friend Sara, who allowed me to put into print one of the more painful episodes of her life.

*There are more things in heaven and earth, Horatio, than are dreamt of in your philosophy.*
—Shakespeare, *Hamlet*

*O Swear not by the moon, the inconstant moon, that monthly changes in her circled orb.*
—Shakespeare, *Romeo and Juliet*

*The heavens declare the glory of God And the firmament sheweth his handiwork.*
*Day unto day uttereth speech, And night unto night sheweth knowledge.*
*There is no speech nor language, Where their voice is not heard.*
—Psalm XIX

*To every thing there is a season, and a time to every purpose under heaven.*
—Ecclesiastes 3:1

*There are many who do not presume either to bathe, or to dine, or to appear in public, until*
*they have diligently consulted the status of Mercury and the*
*aspects of the Moon according to the rules of astrology.*
—Ammianus Marcellinus (fourth century historian)

*Mortal as I am, I know that I am born for a day, but when I follow the serried multitude of*
*stars in their circular course, my feet no longer touch the earth; I ascend to*
*Zeus himself to feast on ambrosia, the food of the Gods.*
—Claudius Ptolemaeus of Alexandria

# CHAPTER ONE

# How I Got Hooked on Horary

Astrology is part of the warp and woof of Western culture. No one can avoid at least a superficial exposure to it. Words like *saturnine, martial, mercy, consider, disaster, jovial, influenza, aspect, mercurial,* and *venereal* all derive from astrology and permeate our language. Although astrology has been an avocation for over thirty years, I must confess that I am a skeptical astrologer. My accurate predictions repeatedly astound me, and I feel disappointed but never too surprised when I am wrong.

My first contact with astrology came when I was nine years old and my family was visiting an amusement park in Rye, New York. We came upon a machine filled with little scrolls that purported to tell your future for the coming month. My father put in a dime and out popped his monthly horoscope. On one side of the scroll was a description of his Gemini Sun sign. To my amazement, the scroll described my father to a tee. He loved to talk and was always taking short trips in his car to visit friends. The scroll said he might work in the transportation industry, and in fact he was a helicopter mechanic. Being a typical Gemini, he was always collecting things. Years later my stepmother would complain lovingly that all he did was "talk, talk, talk" and that he was forever bringing home "junk" which she, as a Scorpio, felt compelled to throw in the garbage. So many of the scroll's statements were accurate that I began to wonder if my father had rigged the machine. Years later, my wife would wonder if I rigged the outcome of horary questions. I realized my father had no prior connection with the machine, and my interest in astrology was born.

As an adolescent, I read whatever I could find on the subject. The local library had the works of Evangeline Adams, which I voraciously devoured. One prediction of hers especially impressed me. In her 1931 book *Astrology for Everyone,* Adams forecast the United States' entry into World War II. How did she know this? Adams noticed that, starting in 1776, each time Uranus was in the sign Gemini, which ruled the United States Ascendant, this country had been involved in a war. In 1776 there was the Revolutionary War and in 1860, the Civil war. In 1931 she wrote: "In the year 1942, Uranus once again enters the sign Gemini and unfortunately Saturn and Mars will also be in conjunction with it....This unusual configuration certainly portends another period when this country will be plunged into war." Evangeline Adams died in 1932, ten years before her prediction came to pass.

Other than the books of this outstanding woman, there was little else on astrology in the local library. As I began to look for other sources of information, I stumbled on *Dell's Horoscope Magazine*. When Dell made a special offer of a free natal horoscope with a paid subscription, I took them up on it. The quality of the free horoscope was disappointing. It was general and vague. Some of it was true, but much of it was inaccurate.

The skeptic in me gained ascendancy. I grew disillusioned with astrology and began to wonder if the predictions themselves did not cause their own outcomes. That is, did people born under different Sun signs act in certain ways precisely because they knew how astrologers expected them to behave? I gave up astrology for the next few years, but not before learning the basics of chart interpretation and how to cast a natal horoscope. Besides, I was about to start college and my interests lay elsewhere.

In college, I majored in mathematics with a minor in physics. I loved the liberal arts and took as many philosophy and religion courses as I could. My interest in the classics had begun in high school where I studied Latin, and my knowledge of Latin helped me research the medieval horary texts for this book. In 1967, I went to New York City to begin a doctoral program in mathematics. This was to be a turning point in my interest in astrology, for I met another devotee of the art. She was a fellow graduate student in the literature department. She knew a lot about theoretical astrology, but had trouble with the math.

Early one day I was helping my new friend calculate a natal chart. To thank me, she looked at my chart and told me I would have a visit from an old friend that very evening. It was not possible, I informed her, because it was the middle of the week and I wasn't expecting any visitors. I forgot all about her prediction and went to my classes. Later that evening, I was studying at home when the doorbell rang. I answered the door to find an old friend from college standing there. He happened to be driving through New York and took a chance at finding me in. Suddenly, I remembered the prediction my astrologer friend made that morning. I was back into astrology. I had to know how she could make so accurate a prediction, and I wanted to be able to do it myself. I began to collect natal data from all my friends and to give them written predictions based on transits for the coming year. In exchange, I asked them to tell me how accurate I was at forecasting events. I made many mistakes, but with feedback and experience I became accurate a good part of the time.

Let me illustrate what I mean by an accurate prediction. My sister-in-law, Barbara, an apartment dweller, wanted to buy a house. In March of 1987 she asked me to look at her chart to see when a move was likely. I studied her chart for an indication of a major move. I could find none until a year and a half later when, on December 7, 1988, Saturn would conjoin her natal Jupiter in her 4th house. Barbara searched for real estate and made an offer on a house in June 1988. Because she planned to close on the house in August, she informed me that my prediction was off by several months. I looked again at her chart and told her I could find no indication of a closing in August. We both agreed that time would tell. As it turned out, there were numerous petty delays and the closing had to be postponed until the end of November. Barbara finally moved on December 4, three days before the date I had given her in writing a year and a half earlier!

To get back to my story, circumstances beyond my control caused me to interrupt my graduate studies. Having completed a Master's degree, I taught high school mathematics for the next three years. When I returned to graduate work in 1971, I chose to study medicine. I specialized in psychiatry and had further training in Freudian psychoanalysis. I was fascinated by the workings of the mind and the symbolic language of the unconscious. All the while astrology—another symbolic system—continued as a hobby. Despite a busy schedule, I devoted time to it whenever I could. Astrology and psychoanalysis have a lot in common. Both arts regard the client as an individual with his or her unique personal history and world view. It is the symbolic interpretations of both astrology and psychoanalysis that fascinate me most.

Those familiar with astrological symbolism will feel at home with the following ideas from Freud's *The Interpretation of Dreams*. Freud noticed that his patients in psychoanalysis often had dreams about the treatment process. They would not dream about the therapy directly, rather in symbolic, disguised forms. For example, patients would dream about journeys in modern vehicles whose speed reflected their thoughts about the progress of the treatment. They referred to their unconscious by dreams about subterranean regions. Sometimes these same regions stood for the female body or the womb.

The following is a typical quote from Freud's dream book: "'Down below' in dreams often relates to the genitals, 'up above,' on the contrary, to the face, mouth, or breast. Wild beasts are as a rule employed by the dream-work to represent passionate impulses of which the dreamer is afraid, whether they are his own or those of other people." The experienced astrologer will see how close chart interpretation is to Freudian dream analysis.

Let me give an example from a woman in psychoanalysis. Early in the treatment, before I knew a lot about the client's early life, she reported the following dream:

> I enter a very large room, like a ballroom. Across the room is my old boyfriend from high school. We dance and I enjoy it very much. Then my husband enters the large hall. I feel like I have to make a choice between my husband and my old boyfriend.

On a manifest level, the dream refers to some recent difficulties the woman had been having with her husband. I am struck, however, by her emphasis on the large room. I get an image of this woman as a little girl alone, feeling abandoned, in a normal-sized room that seems very large to a child, and I say, "Could the large room refer to some experience you had as a child, a feeling of being all alone or deserted? Perhaps someone important to you died when you were very young?"

My client is visibly shaken and close to tears. She recounts how, when she was two years old, her mother gave birth to a baby girl who died two days later. Her mother became depressed after the death and my client felt alone and abandoned as if she lost both her baby sister and her mother at the same time. Understanding the symbolism of dreams is similar to interpreting the symbols in an astrological chart.

I approach horary the way I approach psychoanalysis. In either case, there is a mystery to be solved. Under ideal circumstances, I remain firm in my conviction that, with persistent cooperation and mutual understanding, the client and I can gain perspective on the conflicts involved. If we work diligently enough, we will gradually appreciate the client's world view, how it developed, why it is maintained so rigidly, and how it might more flexibly adapt to reality. In the course of this process, the client learns to take responsibility for the course of his or her own life.

Like the psychoanalyst, the horary astrologer must remain firm in the conviction that, with persistent effort and understanding, he or she can find the answer in the chart. Not everyone can become a horary astrologer, just as not everyone can become a psychoanalyst. According to Dane Rudhyar, "The safe and sound practice of horary astrology requires a basic knowledge of its technique; but it demands also of the practitioner a deep sense of psychological values, and as deep a sense of responsibility to humanity as a whole and to God Who is the personification of this universal intelligence."

The horary chart depicts a cross-section of a particular moment in time. It captures in symbolic form some vexing concern of the querent. Like the client in psychoanalysis, each horary chart is unique. If the astrologer can penetrate the meaning implicit in the chart, he or she can appreciate the nature of the querent's concern and its likely outcome. As in psychoanalysis, the responsibility for the final decision lies with the querent and not with the stars. Horary art is no substitute for sound judgment and personal maturity.

Let me return to my narrative. Around 1970, I came across an advertisement about horary astrology. A teacher in Brooklyn was collecting questions for his class. In return for sending him an inquiry, he promised to return the class's answer in the mail. I no longer remember what question I asked. I mailed it and forgot about it. Two months later I got back my original question with a simple "No" in quotes beneath it. By then the matter had run its course and "No" was the right answer. I thought it was interesting that the horary students got it right. But the skeptic in me said they had a fifty-fifty chance anyway. A toss of the coin might have been as accurate.

Nonetheless, this first experience with horary planted a seed. It seemed silly to think that the universe would trouble itself with my petty concerns. I later came across a passage from a nineteenth-century English occultist, Francis Barrett, who expressed the same opinion. In an 1801 book titled *The Magus, or Celestial Intelligencer,* Barrett commented about horary:

> *...our astrologers in most of their speculations seek without a light, for they conceive*
> *every thing may be known or read in the stars: if an odd silver spoon is but lost, the inno-*
> *cent stars are obliged to give an account of it; if an old maiden loses a favorite puppy,*
> *away she goes to an oracle of divination for information of the whelp. Oh! vile credulity,*
> *to think that those celestial bodies take cognizance of, and give in their configurations*
> *and aspects, continued information of the lowest and vilest transactions of dotards, the*
> *most trivial and frivolous questions that are pretended to be resolved by an inspection*
> *into the figure of the heavens.*

Francis Barrett notwithstanding, what if there were something to horary? Over the next several years I read some on horary and experimented with a few charts. I felt frustrated that the authorities contradicted each other. I didn't have the time or energy to sort it all out, so I consoled myself with Barrett's attitude that horary is nonsense. Like Barrett, I looked with disdain on the art.

Then in the summer of 1987 I had an experience that changed every
Sara was visiting for a few days. She had been trying to get pregnant for th
was having difficulty and had suffered a miscarriage. Incidentally, Sara's Sun
degrees of Sagittarius and Saturn had been transiting this area of the zodiac for
ous year. I remembered Evangeline Adams' warning that women often have a h
with pregnancy when Saturn passes over their natal Sun.

At the beginning of that summer, Sara actually did get pregnant. Since she'd ha
much reproductive difficulty in the prior year, she was worried about the new pregnan
On the day of her visit Sara told me she had felt something change inside her body on the
previous day. My first reaction was that my friend was "being neurotic" and that everything would be fine.

"Isn't there some kind of chart you can do?" asked Sara, who is not an astrologer. I was
reluctant, but she insisted. I had the preconceived notion that Sara had nothing to worry
about when I agreed to cast a horary chart. Still a novice at horary, I pulled out my books
and sat down with her to read the chart. I wanted Sara to see the reasoning behind the
answer so she wouldn't feel I was just trying to assuage her.

Sara's question was, verbatim, "Is this baby healthy?" From our discussion, my understanding of the question was: "Did something happen to the pregnancy in the past day or
two, and will the baby be born healthy?" Sara asked the question on Thursday, 8/6/87 at
9:30 P.M. EDT at 73W01, 41N19. Thursday is a Jupiter day, and as you will see Jupiter rules
the child's health in this chart. (See Chart 1 on page 22, Chapter Two.)

The next few paragraphs may seem a bit technical. Don't worry if you don't fully understand them. The ideas presented here will become second nature by the time you finish this
book. At the time I cast the chart I used the Placidus house system. I now use either the
Koch or the Regiomontanus house systems in horary work.

The 1st house of the horary chart always represents the querent—the person asking the
question—Sara, in this case. The 5th house is the house of children and is where we locate
Sara's child. Health problems are shown by the 6th house. But since we are concerned
about the child's health, we must count six houses starting at the fifth of children. Five, six,
seven, eight, nine, ten. So the 10th house represents the child's health.

The 1st house stands for Sara and her physical body. Jupiter (expansion) is intercepted at
29° 28' Aries in the 1st house—apt symbolism for something growing inside her body. The
sign Cancer rules the 5th house of children so the Moon rules the child. The 5th house also
contains Mercury at 0° 19' Leo, making it a co-ruler of the child. Jupiter rules the cusp of
the 10th house of the child's health. In the 10th house are Neptune retrograde at 5° 40'
Capricorn and the Moon at 10° 21' Capricorn. Jupiter rules the baby's 6th house of health,
with Neptune and the Moon as co-rulers.

The fact that Mercury (the baby) had just completed a square to Jupiter (the baby's
health) immediately disturbed me. The square occurred on the very day that Sara noticed
a change inside her body. Squares mean obstacles and problems. Had the fetus suffered a
health problem the previous day? Jupiter ruling the baby's health is fortunate because
Jupiter is benefic and strong in the 1st house. But two factors weakened Jupiter. It was
intercepted in the 1st house and was in the last degree of Aries. Intercepted planets are not

ntly imply a crisis or change of state as the planet pre-
next.

by's health was not a good sign either. Maybe the
of the baby's health, would give a positive answer.
r rulers of the baby. No information there. The
gn is a square to Jupiter, again showing health
n a panoramic way the ultimate outcome—an

of the matter is the 4th house of the person under con-
ing about the baby in the 5th house. The 4th house of the 5th is
the chart. Scorpio in on the Eighth cusp and Pluto, the modern ruler of
lies at 7° 16' Scorpio in the 8th house. Pluto is strong in his own sign and house.
Clearly Sara is worried about death. Pluto, Scorpio, and the 8th house are all natural rulers
of death. Mercury (the baby) is applying with an orb of five degrees to a square with Pluto.
The baby is facing death. The five-degree orb suggests Sara may learn something about the
question in roughly five days. Time is hard to judge accurately in horary work. In addition,
Mars, which rules the radical 8th house of death, lies in Leo in the unfortunate 6th house
of the radical chart. The Moon in Capricorn applies to a quincunx (150°) of Mars, an
aspect associated with stress and illness.

Try as hard as I might, I could find no favorable indications about the baby's health. I
tried to reassure Sara that I was just a novice at horary. Maybe there was some horary rule
I didn't know that would change the answer. I urged her to ignore our reading of the
horary chart. She replied that the chart merely confirmed what she already suspected.

As part of her prenatal care, Sara had scheduled a chorionic villa sampling for Wednesday, August 12. When Sara's doctor repeated the sonogram on that date, he could detect no
fetal heartbeat. The doctor estimated that the fetus had been dead about a week. In terms
of the horary chart, the fetus had died on the same day that Mercury squared Jupiter, and
Sara learned this news six days after we read the chart. Let me review the chronology of the
events related to Sara's question:

July 29: Sonogram shows a healthy fetus.

August 5: Sara feels "different" about the state of her body and worries something has gone
wrong with the pregnancy.

August 6: Horary chart is unfavorable for the health of the fetus.

August 12: Repeat sonogram shows no fetal heartbeat. Fetus has been dead about a week.

When Sara called me with the news, I shuddered. The correspondence between the
horary chart and the unfolding of events was uncanny. I felt as if we had tapped into a
powerful force within the universe and that we should tread lightly. This eerie yet reverent
feeling prevented me from doing horary charts for several months. I pondered Sara's chart
for a long time. Finally I overcame my trepidation and read every horary chart I could get
my hands on. As I compared each new chart to my experience with Sara's chart, I came to
realize an important truth about horary: Earnest questions produce straightforward

charts of profound accuracy. Trivial questions produce silly charts with contradictory indications. Horary works best when you need it most.

In researching this book I learned that I was not alone in discovering this aspect of horary. Almost a century ago Alan Leo wrote, "It is important to remember that no questions should be asked, nor any horary figure cast, unless the mind is truly serious and quite anxious concerning the matter on which the information is sought. Otherwise, disappointment and erroneous judgment will certainly result." I caution the reader to heed Alan Leo's advice.

The experience with Sara's chart inspired me to read widely both in horary itself and in the history of Western astrology. I wanted to master the technique and see how it developed through the ages Still my skepticism persists. Could my accuracy, however detailed and precise, be the result of chance? It seems unlikely, even if I have a fifty-fifty chance of being right with "yes/no" questions. And why do I sometimes get the wrong answer when I use the same principles to arrive at my conclusions?

I stand in good company in getting wrong answers to horary questions. Munkasey, for example, reported that his personal research into financial astrology showed that "about three times in four astrology will accurately answer the astrological trend or direction of the market." He found that horary astrology was about 75% accurate in answering specific questions about buying particular stocks at a certain date and time. Munkasey recommended, however, that one devote at least seven years to studying horary before using it to make financial decisions.

A second personal experience pierced another hole in my skepticism. I had noticed over the years that when I made predictions based on transits to my natal chart, the timing was always slightly off. About ten years ago, I rectified my chart to a birth time five minutes earlier. Since then, the transits have triggered events like clockwork. My birth certificate says that I was born at 9:09 A.M. EWT. My rectified chart changes the birth time to 9:04 A.M., five minutes earlier. It made sense that the nurse who did the recording might have been late in recording the exact time. The clock in the delivery room might have been a few minutes fast. I despaired of ever knowing the true time of my birth.

Then, in the summer of 1989, my stepmother, forever cleaning out my father's junk, tackled the trunks in the attic. She found a notebook in which my father had recorded the birth times of all his children. Unknown to me, he had been present at each birth and kept his own records. When she told me this news on the phone, I got excited. But then she couldn't remember where she put the book! I asked her if she recalled what time my father had jotted down for my birth. She thought it said five in the morning. My heart sank. How could I be four hours off in my rectification? Finally, she found the book. She was right about the five, but it wasn't 5:00 A.M.—it was 9:05 A.M.! There, preserved in my father's script, was the time within a minute of the rectification I had made using time-honored astrological principles. Maybe there is something to this stuff after all.

I hope by now you are interested enough to want to read on. By the time you finish this book, you should be able to interpret a horary chart. In doing so, you will need to come to terms with the confusion and contradictions found in horary practice. The best way I have found to do this is to study its development. Throughout the text I have tried to show how the ideas originated, why the contradictions exist, and what decisions the modern horary astrologer must make to practice the art. For further details on the history of astrology and traditional techniques, I recommend *Classical Astrology for Modern Living* by J. Lee Lehman.

---

### HISTORICAL INTERLUDE
### PTOLEMY AND THE MUSIC OF THE SPHERES

The Greek astronomer Claudius Ptolemy (A.D. 127-145) is regarded as the father of modern astrology. Ptolemy's *Tetrabiblos* (four books) on astrology summarized all the available knowledge on the subject and became a bible for future generations of astrologers. Ptolemy was influenced by the numerology of the Greek philosopher Pythagoras who sought mathematical harmonies in the universe and developed a mathematical theory of music.

Ptolemy combined the Greek theory of music with his knowledge of astrology to produce a theory of astrological aspects between signs of the zodiac. He recognized four traditional ("major") aspects among zodiac signs: the sextile, square, trine, and opposition. It made no sense to speak of a sign conjoining itself, but Ptolemy wrote that the planets could be related "by bodily conjunction or through one of the traditional aspects."

Why only four major aspects among signs? Because these aspects repeat the same harmonic ratios of the musical scale. The important ratios in Greek music were 1:1, 1:2, 1:3, 2:3, and 3:4. Two signs in opposition "meet on a straight line" and have a type of 1:1 correspondence. A square has a 1:2 relation with an opposition. Similarly, a sextile and a trine have a 1:3 and a 2:3 relation with an opposition, respectively. Finally, the ratio of a square to a trine is 3:4. Because the four traditional aspects have the same mathematical harmony as the Greek musical scale, Ptolemy spoke of the "music of the spheres," and this became the basis for all future work in astrology.

# CHAPTER TWO

# A Method of Horary Analysis

This chapter outlines a method for analyzing horary charts derived from the astrological literature and my own experience with horary charts. The remaining chapters will flesh out this outline and add further details from the horary literature. To illustrate the technique we will again consider the chart for Sara's baby from Chapter One. Next we will review a less serious question of Sara's which shows a variation on the horary theme. This chapter concludes with three event charts—the October 1989 San Francisco earthquake, the May 1996 Everglades crash of ValuJet Flight 592, and finally the explosion of TWA Flight 800—to show how horary methods can aid in event analysis.

My approach resembles but also differs from the methods of the astrologers from whom I learned horary. I have tried all the rules and included them here only if I have examined actual horary charts in which the rules proved reliable. The exceptions are those rules or conditions which have not appeared in my own charts but which other astrologers have documented with convincing case examples. I continually turn to Lilly when I get stuck on a chart, but Marc Edmund Jones is the writer who most fundamentally influenced my thinking. What attracted me to Jones was the way he thought about doing horary. Jones advised his students to learn basic principles first. The difficult aspects of the subject then follow naturally. If the students master the fundamentals, they don't need to memorize trivial facts. By understanding the basics, they can avoid blindly following rules they do not understand solely on the authority of the ancients. Like Jones, my goal in writing this book is to teach the reader to think like a horary astrologer.

Marc Edmund Jones accepted the idea of cosmic sympathy, the philosophical heart of astrology. Life is organic. A concordance exists between the changing relationships of the planets and the workings of the human mind. For Jones, the horary chart puts the astrologer in touch with a significant moment in the life of a person. The horary figure is a snapshot of a focal point for the querent in the space and time. It captures the essential qualities of that moment when the querent conveys to the astrologer a need to put his difficulty into cosmic perspective.

Jones taught that everything in horary astrology "depends, fundamentally, upon the correct selection of a pertinent point of experience in time and space, as the basis for analysis." This tenet raises a practical question: how do you recognize the proper time and place to cast the chart? Some astrologers say you must use the time and location of the person who asks the question. They argue that this approach gives the querent control over the matter.

Giving querents control over their lives is a noble ideal, but Jones takes a different tack. Because the querent has struggled with the problem for some time, Jones argues that what makes the moment significant is the very act of consulting an outside expert—the horary astrologer. The horary chart maps the point at which these two minds meet in space and time. In taking this position, Jones is following a centuries-old tradition. The medieval astrologer Guido Bonatus advised horary artists to consider "in what climate thou [the astrologer] receivest the question, for judgment must be varied as the ascensions of countries and climates differ." William Lilly also followed this method. Like Lilly and Jones, I also use the location of the astrologer and the time when the astrologer first understands the question as the proper point in space-time to cast the chart.

Jones' approach captures the spirit of Lilly's advice that "if a person apply to an astrologer, the figure must be taken for the exact time he first speaks on the subject; or, if it be by letter, when it is first read and understood by the artist." The moment that the astrologer understands the question is the time to cast the chart. The astrologer's effort to penetrate the querent's concern converts an ordinary question into a horary one. Again, to quote Jones: "The hour and minute when the astrologer understands the situation is the point of impact on his consciousness, and is the proper basis for the astrological wheel he will employ in suggesting a solution for any difficulty." Another way to arrive at the same conclusion is to view the horary chart as a horoscope cast for the birth of an idea.

What if the astrologer asks herself or himself a horary question? In this case, Jones says the correct time to cast the chart is "when an individual first realizes that a given matter, or phase of the matter is critical." It may be the time when the astrologer notices a "welling up in consciousness of an overlooked or hitherto unsuspected consideration," or the moment when he or she decides to do a horary analysis.

William Lilly, for instance, asked himself a question about whether to buy the houses of Mr. B. As both querent and astrologer, Lilly cast the chart for the time he found his mind "most perplexed and solicitous about it." Lilly loved the house and couldn't wait to buy it. If you study his analysis of the chart, you will find that he appears to have fudged part of the interpretation to make it come out the way he wanted. Though generally correct in his interpretation, some of Lilly's analysis is an exercise in astrological legerdemain. It's hard to remain objective when acting as your own astrologer. I will review the houses of Mr. B. in a later chapter.

Lilly advised that the proper time to cast a chart is "when you feel most anxious about any matter, and first form a resolution to erect a figure on the subject." Such a chart will reflect your mind's attempt to solve the problem. For fans of *Star Trek*'s Mr. Spock, the horary chart is like a Vulcan mind-meld with the universe. To quote Jones again, "What a horary chart measures is the contents of a given mind." Jones borrowed this idea from C. C. Zain (1931) who stated that the horary chart "pictures the relation of the various mental factors within the unconscious mind of the person asking the question." Zain believed that the horary chart mapped "three distinct, but sympathetically related, things." First, the chart shows the positions of the planets at the time the querent first clearly formulated the question. Second, the chart shows the simultaneous mental factors within the mind of the querent. And, finally, the chart reveals the various factors that comprise the matter at hand.

Equating a horary chart with the contents of a human mind allows a more fundamental understanding of the "considerations before judgment." Some modern astrologers refer to these as "strictures against judgment" because they advise us to proceed with caution in reading the chart. Classical horary astrology paid special attention to four considerations before judgment that, if present, warn that the chart might not be "radical" or "fit to be judged." Jones maintained that these warnings (strictures, considerations) exist because "intelligence must have a mechanism for protecting itself against its own wishful thinking." In other words, a "stricture" or a "consideration before judgment," having the nature of Saturn, protects us from self-deception and compels us to face reality.

According to Jones, if such a warning appears in a horary chart, the conscious mind may have chosen the incorrect moment as judged "from some deeper frame of reference." Some hidden factor, or some more profound consideration that currently eludes the querent's awareness, may play a role in the question. In such cases the astrologer will have to tell the querent that the chart may not be able to answer the question as stated because some more basic matter is at issue. Judicious discussion with the querent may then produce a more suitable horary question, one more conducive to the resolution of the crisis and the personal growth of the querent.

## AN OUTLINE FOR HORARY ANALYSIS

Now let me present the method I typically follow in horary analysis. These steps are offered as guidelines rather than rigid rules to follow. I cannot agree more strongly with Marc Edmund Jones that "the wise investigator of horary art will ultimately set up his own rules and standards." This statement may dismay the beginning horary astrologer, but I believe it to be a sound approach to the art. If you meet the Buddha on the road, kill him.

Some charts require a departure from this method and a measure of creativity on the part of the astrologer. Every chart is unique and no one method can cover all contingencies. One must learn to think like a horary astrologer to be able to deal with questions that deviate from the norm. As Emerson said, "A foolish consistency is the hobgoblin of little minds."

### Keep Accurate Records

Keep a notebook to record all your horary questions, their horoscope charts, and their outcomes. Review your notebook regularly. Pay special attention to your mistakes, because your errors will teach you the most about horary. Lilly followed this method to become a master of the art. He advised all beginners to "first write down their judgments on each figure at full length, and afterwards contract their opinions into a narrow compass." Lilly added, "It is well to enter every figure in a book for farther reference, and to remark and register such things as have occurred according to their predictions or otherwise; by which they will be able to correct their future judgments."

Always record the querent's question verbatim. Be sure to write down your own understanding of the question if it differs from or clarifies that of the querent. Note the date and time, whether A.M. or P.M., standard or daylight savings time, the location and coordinates, and the day of the week. Don't forget the A.M. and P.M.—this is a common omission.

Horary astrologers who use Lilly's technique should also note the planetary hour of the question as a test of the validity of the chart. For example, the hour ruler should agree with the Ascendant in specific ways (more about this in a later chapter).

## Cast the Chart

I erect the figure for the time and place where I first understand the question. You may wish to experiment with charts erected both for your location and for that of the querent. If the querent's coordinates prove more reliable, by all means use them. I am too self-centered to use someone else's coordinates, and, besides, my mind does not function that way. I'm sure, however, that if Mother Teresa were to do horary, she would use the other person's coordinates to erect the figure and get good results. In the modern world with our ability to talk by phone simultaneously over great distances, a relationship chart cast for the midpoint in space and time between the astrologer and the client may also produce a valid horary figure.

Nowadays most astrologers rely on a computer. I tend to use the Koch or Regiomontanus house systems unless I am studying someone else's chart already cast in a different system. I decided to use Koch in all my work because astrologers whom I respect, like Robert Hand, use the Koch system and it has proven reliable in practice. Lilly used Regiomontanus, and students of classical horary will want to follow his example. Placidus is also popular. Each practitioner should experiment with different methods of house division and use the one that best fits how his or her mind functions. Leave it up to the universe to bring you the questions that match your system. Forcing yourself on the cosmos (or on other people, for that matter) rarely works out.

## Eyeball the Chart for Validity, Descriptiveness, and "Fit"

The Sun tells the time. Is the Sun in the proper house for the time of day? The Sun rises at the Ascendant, peaks at the MC at noon, sets at the Descendant, and is at the IC at midnight. If the Sun is in the 3rd house, it's between midnight and about 2 A.M. when the bars are closing in many localities. Except for inebriates, not many people ask horary questions at this hour. Occasionally an intoxicated person will call when the Sun is in the 3rd house (transportation) to ask for help in finding his car. Only a fool would take such a call. Besides, it would be unethical to help a person drive while drunk.

See if the chart "fits" the querent and the question. The chart must tell the story to be valid. This is a test for "radicality." You can judge "fit" by answering the following questions.

- Does the Ascendant describe the querent and the situation? Lilly was a stickler for insisting that the Ascendant and its ruler physically describe the querent before proceeding with his analysis of the chart.

- Do the houses or the signs of the lights (Sun and Moon) have some bearing on the matter at hand? Do the houses of the lights, those with Cancer and Leo on their cusps, pertain to the issue? The house placement of the Moon, in particular, frequently bears a direct relation to the question on the querent's mind. The moon shows where the mind is.

- Does the most recent past major aspect made by the Moon reflect some recent event in the life of the querent? Does the planet the Moon last conjoined describe the general tone of the situation?

For example, my former editor Tom at Llewellyn asked a horary question about a manuscript that was giving him difficulty. The Moon's most recent past aspect was a square to Mercury, having occurred in the last two hours. Mercury represents manuscripts and the square from the Moon accurately described the frustration he was feeling with the written material (not this text, of course). Mercury and the 3rd house also rule comings and goings, and Tom was feeling overwhelmed by a move to a new office building.

Something more remarkable occurred in connection with Tom's question. Just as he finished stating the question, someone walked into his new office to tell him that a car had smashed into the building that he just moved out of. Mercury rules cars and transport, and the square from the Moon also signifies a transportation accident before the time of the question.

Back to determining fit. If a classical consideration before judgment is present, does it describe the querent or some fundamental aspect of the situation? Does it warn you that a different question is on the querent's mind? Is the querent sincere and in genuine need of an answer? Just what does it tell you about the matter?

If most or all of the above hold true, then the chart is most likely valid, "radical," or fit to be judged. The basic principle is that the astrological symbolism must match the conditions surrounding the question. The chart must tell the story. Some astrologers refer to a chart that "fits" as bearing the signature of the horary question.

## Check the Considerations Before Judgment

Are any of the classical considerations present? If so, do they describe the situation or the querent, and thereby render the chart radical? In a later chapter I will present a chart for the question "Will Mayor Ed Koch win the primary?" to illustrate this point. Some of the classical considerations are:

- **Less than three degrees, or more than twenty-seven degrees rising.** Less than three degrees rising implies a very new or premature question. It may be too early to tell, especially if the rising sign is one of short ascension (Capricorn, Aquarius, Pisces, Aries, Taurus, or Gemini for charts north of the equator). For a matter in its inception, an early Ascendant may perfectly describe the situation.

    More than twenty-seven degrees implies that the question may be too late. The querent is perhaps undergoing a change of circumstance at the time of the question. The querent may have turned to the astrologer as a last resort after seeking counsel from numerous others. If a late Ascendant matches the querent's age, it may be simply describing the querent. If a planet from the querent's natal chart conjoins the Ascendant (within one degree), this may also be an indication of a radical chart and an important matter for the querent.

- **Moon in the Via Combusta (15° Libra to 15° Scorpio).** The "burning way" or "combust path" is a malefic and unpredictable burning influence of the nature of Mars, Saturn, and Uranus. It often refers to matters of illness, damage, danger, fear, confinement, or death. It can literally refer to burning as from a fever or in a fire.

- **A Void of Course Moon.** The modern definition is that the Moon is void of course when it will not complete (perfect) any major aspects before leaving its current sign. Lilly defined the Moon as being void on its course when it travels without being in orb of applying to a major aspect with any other planet. Nothing functions when the Moon is void of course. Matters seldom go handsomely forward. Some astrologers believe that because nothing will come of the matter, there may be nothing to worry about, or little the querent can do to alter the situation.

  If void of course, is the Moon in Cancer, Taurus, Sagittarius, or Pisces? According to Lilly, the Moon is able to perform when void in these signs. Lilly took this rule from Guido Bonatus' aphorism #64, which relates to the Moon occupying the signs of dignity of the benefic planets, Venus and Jupiter.

  If the Moon is void of course, do the significators apply to a major aspect before the Moon leaves its sign? Is this aspect strong enough to overcome the void of course Moon?

- **Moon in late degrees.** Lilly says that the Moon in the last degrees of a sign, especially Gemini (the fall of Jupiter), Scorpio (the home of Mars), or Capricorn (the home of Saturn) may render a chart unsafe to judge. The last degrees of signs are the terms (an essential dignity) of the malefics.

- **Saturn in the 7th.** Does Saturn lie in the 7th house and thereby restrict the astrologer? Some modern astrologers believe that Pluto in the 7th house acts like Saturn. Is the ruler of the 7th house, which signifies the astrologer, afflicted?

## Locate the Question and Identify the Significators and Natural Rulers of the Matter

Locating the question is the crux of horary analysis. One must understand what the twelve mundane houses mean and how they functionally relate to the querent. Always remember that rulerships depend on the role the matter plays in the life of the querent and not simply on a word you look up in a dictionary. Rulership lists can be useful in prodding your mind to come to the right conclusion, but such lists act more like a thesaurus than a dictionary. It helps to list all the ruling planets systematically so you won't neglect important information in the chart.

- **What planet or planets rule the querent?** In traditional horary astrology, the planets that signify the querent are the rulers of the Ascendant, the Almuten(s) of the Ascendant, the rulers of any sign intercepted in the 1st house, and any planets occupying the 1st house. When there is more than one planetary significator, the planet that best describes the querent should be considered primary.

The Moon always co-rules the querent, but the Moon is a primary ruler of the querent only when Cancer is on the Ascendant or when the chart demands the Moon must represent the quesited rather than the querent. Bonatus also used the planet the Moon last aspected as a co-ruler of the querent.

The Almuten of a house is the planet that has the most essential dignity at the cusp of that house. The Almuten of the Ascendant and of the quesited's house may be primary significators, especially if they are stronger than the rulers of those houses. More about this in a later chapter.

- **What planet or planets rule the quesited?** The quesited is the matter or person inquired about. The quesited's significators are the ruler of the sign on the cusp of the focal house, the Almuten of the cusp of the focal house, the ruler of any sign intercepted in the focal house, and any planets in that house. The planet ruling the focal cusp is usually the primary significator. Bonatus also used the planet which the Moon will next aspect as a co-ruler of the quesited. He viewed the Moon, by aspect, as having last aspected the planet signifying the querent and as next aspecting the planet representing the quesited. In addition, each matter usually has a natural planetary significator (Venus for love, Mercury for writing, etc.). When there is more than one planetary significator, the planet that best describes the quesited should be taken as primary.

- **Derived houses.** It is often necessary to use derived houses when the querent asks a question about someone else. Sara's question about her baby is a good example. Sara's inquiry was not about herself, which would be a first house matter. Instead, Sara asked about the baby, a 5th house matter, and about the baby's health, a 10th house (sixth from the fifth) issue. We had to use derivative houses to answer Sara's question.

- **What is the natural ruler of the matter at hand?** Most issues have a natural planetary ruler. I will review the meanings of the planets in detail later in the book. See Table 1 (page 16) for some of the common natural rulerships of the planets. Understanding the nature of the planets is essential for determining the natural rulers of each matter. Sometimes the natural ruler will answer the question when the house cusps do not. In addition, natural rulers will confirm the answer given by the houses.

- **What house in the chart most clearly focuses the matter?** This is important for locating the question and for the Jones' house-and-its-opposite technique. According to Jones, the aspect between the planet ruling the focal house and the planet ruling its opposite should give the answer to the horary question. In practice I have not found this rule to be reliable, but the reader may wish to experiment with Jones' technique. Table 2 (pages 17–18) covers some of the common matters ruled by the houses.

## Table 1: Some Rulerships of the Planets

**SUN:** Authority, officials, life force, health, success, men, prominent people, superiors, employers, executives, illumination, power, ego, persons worthy of trust, men ages thirty-five to forty-five.

**MOON:** Mother, women in general, the public, moods, fluctuations, changes, feelings, receptivity, liquids, fugitives, runaways, short trips, removals, lost objects, things connected with liquids or the sea.

**MERCURY:** Writing, communication, transport, books, letters, messages, questions, buying and selling, contracts, bargaining, trips, travels, neighbors, literary or intellectual activity, young people, students, office workers, secretaries, salespersons, tradespersons, tricksters.

**VENUS (the lesser benefic):** Love, gifts, money, harmony, alliances, relationships, marriage, values, resources, movable goods, lost objects, social affairs, young women, the mother, wife, pleasures, the arts, luxury items.

**MARS (the lesser malefic):** Sex, war, aggression, energy, haste, combat, butchers, surgeons, cuts, assertiveness, leadership, weapons, fire, iron, accidents, quarrels, danger, injury, men ages twenty-five to thirty-five.

**JUPITER (the greater benefic):** Expansion, good fortune, luck, higher education, abundance, long journeys, prophecy, gambling, success, professionals, the wealthy, lawyers, judges, horses, foreigners, middle-aged men.

**SATURN (the greater malefic):** Obstacles, limitations, loss, restrictions, gravity, falls, seriousness, hardness, delays, aging, old people, debts, poverty, real estate, construction, time, inertia, austerity, tribulations, karma, death, loneliness, solitary people, plumbers, the father.

**URANUS:** Breaks, accidents, separations, divorce, surprises, awakenings, electricity, the New Age, strikes; according to Barbara Watters: "sudden, unpredictable, violent, or fateful" events.

**NEPTUNE:** Dissolution, confusion, absentmindedness, spirituality, lack of clarity, fog, undoing, drugs, alcohol, deception, poetry, illusion, unreality, mysticism, seclusion.

**PLUTO:** Powerful forces, sexuality, penetration, the underworld, rebirth, transformation, transition, the unconscious, death, and Barclay adds "ejection."

**PARS FORTUNA (a point, not a planet):** Money, income, possessions, lost objects, good luck, substance, treasure.

## Table 2: Some Matters Ruled by the Houses

**1ST HOUSE:** The querent, a missing person unrelated to the querent, the self, health, length of life, physical description of the querent, the body, the head, appearance, disposition, personality, new arrivals, beginnings, accidents, condition of a vehicle, new projects, personal interests, initiative, efforts to get ahead. The joy of Mercury.

**2ND HOUSE:** Substance, resources, movable goods, lost objects, money, income, values, personal worth, possessions, potential wealth or poverty.

**3RD HOUSE:** Communication, news, siblings, neighbors, neighborhood, elementary education, close kin or relations, cousins (generically), visits, short trips, cars, roads, studies, writing, letters, messages, teachers, mail carriers, reports, rumors, gossip. The joy of the Moon.

**4TH HOUSE:** Father, home, family, domestic issues, end of the matter, lost and recovered wealth, buried treasure, foundations, security, land, real estate, buildings, non-movable goods, houses, farms, wells, mines, resources of the earth, ancestry, old age, elders, the grave.

**5TH HOUSE:** Children, creative self-expression, hobbies, speculation, gambling, lotto, stocks, risk-taking, excitement, contests, elections, recreation, fun, recreational sex, love affairs, romance, pregnancy, pleasure, feasts, entertainment, education, agents of the querent, ambassadors, the father's movable goods. The joy of Venus.

**6TH HOUSE:** Illness, sickness, tedious jobs, drudgery, detailed work, coworkers, pets, small animals ("up to the size of a goat"), servants, employees, service, appliances, paternal aunts and uncles, lodgers, tenants, everyday duties, food, hygiene, climate control, adjustments for proper functioning, toil, healing and healers. The joy of Mars.

**7TH HOUSE:** The mate, partner, spouse, significant other, a person with whom the querent has dealings but whose relation is not specified by another house, opponent, competitor, open enemy, rival, astrologer of the querent, any personal counselor or advisor, thief, runaway, fugitive, sibling's children, marriage, partnerships, divorce, lawsuits, place you would remove to, legal contracts and agreements, dealings with the public.

**8TH HOUSE:** Death, procreative sex, surgery, injury, transformation, rebirth, restructuring, other people's money, other people's movable goods, psychoanalysis, the occult, penetration, probing, refuse, taxes, debts, mortgages, loans, money owed to the querent, insurance, joint money, wills, gifts from others, legacies, estate of the deceased, investigation, the personal unconscious.

**9TH HOUSE:** Long-distance travel or interests, foreign countries and people, in-laws, higher education, lecturing, religion, clergy, the church, philosophy, prophecy, forecasting, horary astrology, publishing, broadcasting, advertising, professional classes, insurance adjusters, voyages, legalizing ceremonies, the court system, lawyers, the law, weddings, science, systematic organized thought, divination, dreams and visions, legal proceedings, exploration. The joy of the Sun.

---

### Table 2 (continued): Some Matters Ruled by the Houses

**10TH HOUSE:** Mother, authority, superiors, the boss, the government, structure, career, profession, employer, monarch, ruler, president, judge, executive, promotions, fame, rank, honor, status, success, achievement, credit, reputation, prestige, public office, officials, career moves, important jobs, employment, worldly position. The Sun and Jupiter do well here.

**11TH HOUSE:** Friends, groups, clubs, socializing, counseling, relationship with humanity, unbonded relationships, legislators, legislation, hopes and wishes, ambition, comfort, relief, praise, trust, income from career, resources of the person in authority, the mother's movable goods, humanitarian activities; according to Bruce Scofield, one's business clients.

**12TH HOUSE:** Seclusion, undoing, personal failings, hospitalization, confinement, jail, bondage, prisoners, captives, slaves, restriction, fears, punishment, self-undoing, the collective unconscious, widowhood, institutions, retreats, clandestine affairs, secret dealings, secrets, poetry, drugs and alcohol, invalids, maternal aunts and uncles, sorrows, unseen dangers, disappointments, hidden limitations, suicide, murder, assassination, charity, animals (larger than a goat). The joy of Saturn.

---

### Identify the Major Positive or Negative Indicators

I find these fixed stars and degrees helpful to consider, using a one-degree orb.

- The malefic degree Serpentis (19° Scorpio) conjunct a significant planet or point. Serpentis is considered very destructive by some, but I have seen charts with a prominent Serpentis where everything worked out fine. Use this with caution.

- Caput Algol, at 26° 10' Taurus in the year 2000. Quite malefic. Losing one's head. Danger of fire. Beware if Algol is prominent in a chart.

- Spica at 23° 50' Libra in the year 2000. Extremely benefic. Success.

- Saturn retrograde in the 1st house. Retrograde Saturn in the 1st may destroy the question or confirm a negative outcome. A lost object may return in damaged condition. A strong chart can overcome this so don't take it as an absolute.

- Alcyone of the Pleiades, just entering 0° 00' Gemini in the year 2000. The weeping sisters give you something to cry about.

- Part of Fortune conjunct a significant planet or point. Quite benefic. Good financially.

- Nodal Degrees. Significant planets or points in any sign in the same degree (regardless of minutes) as the Moon's Mean Nodes. A Nodal Degree suggests the workings of fate—the matter is out of the querent's hands. For example, the Ascendant of the chart for epicenter of the October 1989 San Francisco earthquake is in the same degree as the Moon's Mean Nodes but in a different sign.

## Determine the Cosmic State (Planetary Standing) of the Significators

Are they strong or weak? Is my daddy bigger than your daddy? Consider whether they are:

- Besieged
- Peregrine
- Combust the sun
- Under the sunbeams
- Cazimi
- Intercepted
- In fall or detriment (debility)
- Afflicted by a malefic
- Angular
- Accidentally dignified by house
- Swift in motion
- Stationary or Retrograde
- Conjunction with fixed stars
- Conjunctions with antiscions or contrascions of significators
- In aspect with a relevant Arabic Part
- Other considerations

The literature tells of dozens of such considerations that affect planetary strength. In a later chapter I will discuss a handful of modifying factors that make theoretical sense or seem to have empirical justification.

## Consider the Aspects the Significators Form Among Themselves

According to Jones, "The first aspect made by a significant planet is the normal basis of judgment." The planets are the players, the aspects the script, the signs the costumes, and the houses the fields of action. Think of the planets concretely as people or things inquired about. The applying aspects tell you how they will behave toward one another. Like Santa Claus, the astrologer—by considering planetary strengths and aspects—"sees if you are sleeping, he sees if you're awake, he sees if you've been bad or good," etc. Here are some of the factors:

- No aspect, no action.
- If there is no applying aspect, check for translation and collection of light.
- Sextile or trine: A positive relationship.
- Square or opposition: A negative relationship.
- Squares: Obstacles and frustration.
- Oppositions: Separation and opposing forces.
- Conjunctions: A coming together. Can be positive or negative depending on the planets involved.

- Mutual receptions: quite helpful, a way out.
- List minor aspects, including quincunxes. I use one-degree orbs for minor aspects.
- Quincunxes imply necessary adjustment or reorganization.
- Quincunxes often relate to 6th and 8th house issues, or imply that something is out of joint.
- Semi-squares (45°) and sesqui-quadrates (135°) act like baby squares and cause irritations and annoyances.
- A semi-sextile (30°) with mutual reception can be quite positive.
- What is the first major aspect to occur between significators? This first aspect usually determines the outcome of the matter. Other aspects may contribute to or modify the answer given by the first one.
- What do the aspects mean in this unique chart?
- What answer would you give to the question based on these aspects? Do weak significators hinder the action promised by the aspect?

## Cross-check the Basis of the Judgment

As in the rest of astrology, you should confirm your interpretation in more than one way to be sure of your answer. If you find three or more indications of the same judgment, you can be confident you have a correct interpretation. Contradictory indications in a chart may mean that the querent was confused, did not ask the question really on his or her mind, or selected the wrong place and time to seek horary advice. It may also mean the matter is too complicated to give an adequate answer on the basis of the horary chart. Idle or trivial questions produce muddled charts.

It often helps to consider the 4th house as the end of the matter. The 11th house represents the querent's hopes, and a fortunate aspect between the Ascendant ruler and the 11th ruler suggests a positive outcome. Positive aspects between significators and relevant house cusps can also support other indications in a chart.

There are also many secondary methods that give confirmation. The most popular are the Arabic Parts and Significant Degrees, the Fixed Stars, and the Antiscions or Solstice Points. I will devote a full chapter to these ancillary methods.

## Identify the Modality of the Cross that Appears on the Angles

If mixed, state the mix. Cardinal signs act quickly and assertively. Fixed signs are stubborn and entrenched. Mutable signs are flexible, adaptable, and often unstable. Sara's baby's chart has mutable angles, suggesting some instability in the situation. Mixed crosses start one way and end another.

## Consider Special Factors that Might Affect the Judgment

Are any of the following present? If so, how do they affect your answer? Do they confirm other findings in the chart? (I will discuss these further in another chapter.)

- Parallels or contraparallels of declination between significators
- Refranation
- Hindrance, frustration, or impedition
- Fixed stars; Arabic parts; retrograde Mercury
- Critical degrees
- Moon conjunct sun
- Moon sextile or trine Sun without frustration
- Collection of light
- Solstice points (Antiscions) and Contrascions
- Planets or points rising in the 1st house
- Midpoint contacts

## Check All of the Aspects Made by the Moon

The Moon's most recent aspect before the question shows an event recently past. According to Bonatus, the planet most recently aspected by the Moon (major aspects only) is a co-ruler of the querent. The Moon's most recent conjunction before the question colors the nature of the Moon. All the aspects the Moon will make before leaving its sign show how the circumstances will progress and give a global view of the future of the situation. Bonatus uses the planet the Moon next aspects (Ptolemaic aspects only) after the question as a co-ruler of the quesited. The Moon's final aspect shows in a general way how matters will end.

You can answer most questions by following the above sequence of steps. The remaining chapters will clarify the more obscure parts of this outline. I will now present three cases to illustrate this method of analysis.

# THREE CASE STUDIES: PRINCIPLES IN ACTION

## Case One: Sara's Baby

This is the same example referred to in Chapter One. My friend Sara was worried about her pregnancy and asked this question on a Thursday, a Jupiter day. The chart was done using Placidus houses. Sara asked me to cast a chart to determine the health of the baby. I spent time with her explaining the nature of horary astrology. During this time I was aware of her concern, but she had not yet formulated it as a horary question. There came a point in our discussion at which she said, "Okay, I'm ready to ask a question. Is this baby healthy?" Only then did I check the clock for an accurate time. At that moment I knew that she understood what horary could do and I understood the meaning of her question. Such a discussion with a client is a useful way to formulate the question and select the proper time to cast the chart. See Chart One on page 22.

Eyeballing Sara's chart to check for validity and fit, we see that the Sun is at the beginning of the 6th house, as it should be at 8:30 P.M. A 6th house Sun suggests a question

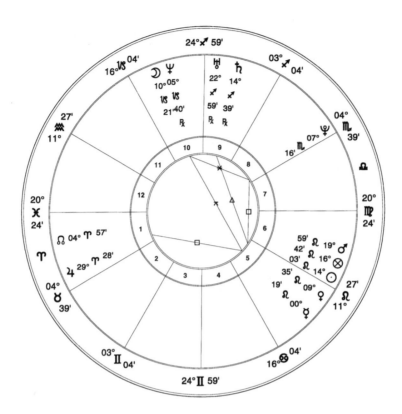

Chart 1:  Sara's Question About her Baby's Health
August 6, 1987, 9:30 PM EDT, 73W01, 41N19 Placidus Houses

about health or work. Mercury (natural ruler of questions) is in the 5th house of children. The Moon is in the 10th house of career and the health of children. Cancer is on the 5th house cusp of children, and Leo governs the 6th house of health. The chart fits the question. It would also "fit" a question about some speculative or creative activity involving work or career.

The Ascendant rules the querent. With Pisces ascending, Jupiter and Neptune rule Sara. With Jupiter in the 1st house, again this planet rules Sara. Aries is intercepted in the 1st house and so Mars also rules Sara. This is a night chart, making Mars Almuten (most essentially dignified planet) at the 20° Pisces Ascendant.

Because the question is about Sara's baby, we must use derivative houses. The 5th house governs pregnancy and children. Cancer is on the 5th cusp, making the Moon ruler of the baby. In addition, Venus and Mercury occupy the 5th house and become co-rulers of the baby. The Moon is also Almuten of the 5th house.

What house rules the baby's health? The 6th of any house governs the sickness of that house. The 6th of the 5th house is the 10th house of the figure. Sagittarius is on the cusp of the 10th, so Jupiter rules the baby's state of health. Jupiter is also Almuten of the 10th. Neptune and the Moon are in the 10th and they become co-rulers of the baby's health. No classical considerations before judgment exist. An intercepted Jupiter in the first house describes the querent because the first house represents Sara's body and Jupiter shows the fetus growing in her womb (intercepted). The chart is radical and fit to judge.

This chart emphasizes Jupiter because Jupiter governs the day (Thursday) and rules both Sara and the baby's health. What is the cosmic state of Jupiter? Mixed. Its placement in first house Aries strengthens it. But an interception in Aries weakens Jupiter, and its placement in the impatient 29th degree of a cardinal sign shows a crisis about to break. Jupiter is also in the terms of Saturn in Aries, another negative influence.

Since Sagittarius is on the 10th cusp (where Jupiter rules and is Almuten), Jupiter is the primary ruler of the baby's health. With Cancer on the 5th cusp (where the Moon rules and is Almuten), the Moon is the primary significator of the baby. The Moon's last aspect before changing sign will be a square to Jupiter, suggesting a negative outcome. The aspect between the primary rulers says, "No, the baby is not healthy."

Because of the gravity of the question, we should confirm this negative conclusion. The baby's 4th house is the 8th house of the chart. Scorpio is on the 8th cusp and Pluto occupying Scorpio in the 8th shows the end of the matter for the baby. The 8th house of the radical figure is Sara's house of death. The ruler of the baby's end in Sara's house of death is ominous. The co-ruler of the baby, Mercury, will shortly square Pluto, again suggesting death.

If we consider the Jones' house-and-its-opposite method, the 5th house rules the pregnancy and its opposite house, the 11th, rules the immediate outcome. The Moon governs the 5th house and Saturn, the 11th. The Moon and Saturn are applying mutually to a semisextile, which is an unfavorable aspect in matters of health.

In matters this serious, we would look for as much confirmation as possible before predicting death. Arabic parts, fixed stars, and solstice points are useful for further confirmation. The Part of Death has this formula: (Longitude of Ascendant) + (Longitude on 8th cusp)—(Longitude of Moon). In this chart the Part of Death is at 14° 41' Sagittarius and is almost exactly conjunct retrograde Saturn at 14° 39' Sagittarius. If I had used a different house system, the Part of Death would have different coordinates.

Recall that Saturn rules Jupiter by term and Jupiter rules the baby's health. This connection places the health of the baby in contact with the Part of Death. With Capricorn on the 11th cusp, Saturn governs Sara's hopes and wishes and joins them to the Part of Death. With Aquarius on the 12th cusp, Saturn and Uranus rule Sara's sorrow. Saturn also rules the death of the baby because the natural 12th is the 8th house of death for the 5th house child. Saturn's placement on the Part of Death confirms the death of the baby, the mother's sorrow, and the demise of her hopes and wishes.

In addition, Saturn rules the immediate outcome of the pregnancy and is dispositor of the Moon, which rules the baby and the pregnancy. Saturn's conjunction with the Part of Death again shows that the pregnancy will end in the death of the fetus. We see another confirmation in the solstice point of Mercury, co-ruler of the baby. Solstice points often represent turning points in the life of the querent. Mercury is at 0° 19' Leo and its solstice point is 29° 41' Taurus, conjunct the fixed star Alcyone of the Pleiades, the weeping sisters. This pregnancy is a turning point in Sara's life and will cause her to weep.

## CHART 2: "WHAT HAPPENED IN THE PAST TWO WEEKS?"

As a counterpoint to the previous example, I will present another question of Sara's, one with a lighter touch. I live in Connecticut and Sara lives in New York City. My wife and I are close friends with Sara and her husband, and we visit each other frequently. On Thursday, October 5,1989, my wife telephoned Sara to plan a visit with her in New York on Saturday. Sara asked to speak to me because she had a horary question.

When I picked up the phone, Sara said in a flat voice, "I'm talking like this because I don't want to give anything away. Something happened in the past two weeks. Can you do a chart to tell me what it is?" I accepted the challenge and noted the exact time: 10:39 P.M. EDT. I cast Chart 2A for this time. I understood her question to be, "What is my question?" It was Thursday, a Jupiter day. Sara, a native of Sagittarius, seems to have a liking for Jupiter days. I didn't have time to look at the chart Thursday evening. I also had a busy day on Friday, and it didn't occur to me until late that evening that I hadn't looked at Sara's question. I wanted to get it done before Saturday morning, when we planned to be in New York.

Actually what happened was that Friday evening I suddenly felt compelled to study Sara's chart. I noted the time. It was 10:53 P.M. EDT on October 6,1989. This urge was so strong that I decided to look at a chart for that moment as well. I set Chart 2B for the time of my urge to read her chart and discover its secret. It was on Friday, a Venus day. I turned on the

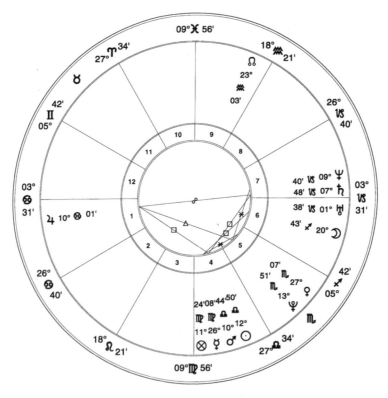

Chart 2A: "What happened in the past two weeks?"
October 5, 1989, 10:39 PM EDT, 73W01, 41N19 Koch Houses

computer and ran off both charts. I was immediately struck by the remarkable similarity between them.

In looking at Chart 2A, I decided that it had to be good news because Jupiter was rising in the first house and the question came on a Jupiter day. Some financial gain possibly. The Moon's most recent conjunction to Venus would confirm this. Did she win Lotto? Then I remembered her old chart with Jupiter in the first. Could she be pregnant again? That would be truly Jupiterian. In addition, Jupiter rules the 6th house of work and service in this chart. Maybe she came into money related to her work.

I next looked at the positions of the Sun, Moon, Mercury, Leo, and Cancer, to get a general sense of the "fit" of the chart. The Sun in the 4th could mean a conception but more likely has to do with domestic matters or real estate. The Moon in the 6th suggests a matter related to health or work. Leo on the 3rd cusp suggests a letter, a short trip, or something to do with a sibling. Since Cancer is on the cusp of the 1st and 2nd houses, it links the querent at the Ascendant to the 2nd house of income and possessions. Finally Mercury, natural ruler of questions, is in Virgo in the 4th, again stressing 4th and 6th house issues—domestic matters, health, and work.

I came up with a list of possibilities but I wasn't satisfied that I had narrowed it down enough. I wanted to impress Sara with a precise reading on Saturday morning. Then I noticed Saturn in the 7th with Capricorn on the 7th cusp. A consideration before judgment!

Chart 2B: My Urge to Look at Sara's Chart
October 6, 1989, 10:53 PM EDT, 73W01, 41N19 Koch Houses

The astrologer was impeded by Saturn and might have trouble answering this one. A 7th house Saturn is a real challenge to the astrologer, as these charts were proving. Furthermore, Saturday is a Saturn day, which would add to my difficulty in making the judgment.

Next I compared the two charts. They were almost identical. But wait a minute….In my "urge" chart, Mercury (the question) is exactly conjunct the Part of Fortune. That must be significant. But what does it mean? Sara's secret must involve good fortune, confirmed by Jupiter in the first, and probably financial good fortune since Pars Fortuna has a special connection with the second house. In addition, Friday was a Venus day, suggesting a gift or general good fortune, and the Moon's last conjoined Venus in Chart 2A, Venus being the goddess of love and money. Maybe Sara did win Lotto. The Moon was about to conjoin Uranus in the Thursday chart, implying a sudden or unexpected future event.

Again I thought back to her old question in which Mercury ruled the baby. Sara had been able to get pregnant again after losing that baby and now had a wonderful, healthy son. Maybe Mercury ruled her son. Maybe he came into money or a family inheritance, which the 4th house sometimes shows. At the time I did not notice that Mercury also governed the 12th house of the chart. Sara is a psychologist who works with emotionally troubled clients (shown by the 12th). Mercury also rules Sara's secret because the 12th house locates secrets and mysteries.

It was past midnight now and I put the charts away for the next day. I hadn't been as thorough as I usually would be, but this horary chart was all in fun and didn't require the same diligence that the chart about the baby's health demanded. I did not look at the charts again till I arrived at Sara's the next morning. "Well, did you find out what happened?" asked Sara. I went over the possibilities described above. She smiled with amazement and said, "You're mostly right except for the part about real estate and domestic concerns. It definitely has to do with money, income, my job, inheritance, and good luck." Sara's husband shook his head disdainfully. A true skeptic, he likes to tease me about my interest in the art and Sara for her gullibility.

Sara then explained that one of her clients, who owed her a large amount of money— thousands of dollars for years of psychotherapy, came into an unexpected inheritance consisting of a health insurance policy the client's late mother had taken out for her. Sara's client was unaware until recently that her mother's bequest would cover the cost of her past treatment that she had been unable to pay. It was money owed Sara that she had written off and never expected to receive.

My understanding of Sara's inquiry had been, "What is Sara's secret question?" In my "urge" chart, Mercury—natural ruler of questions and ruler of the 12th house of secrets— exactly conjoins the lot of fortune. The Mercury/Pars Fortuna conjunction shows Sara's question coming together with a lot of fortune. Amazing how this astrological symbolism works!

Still the 4th house emphasis puzzled me. I read the 4th house as real estate and domestic concerns. Sara said she had been thinking about buying office space for quite some time, not just the past two weeks, and nothing special had happened in that regard. She was also planning to use the money to pay off bills, some of them domestic. Neither of these explanations seemed to fit the 4th house prominence in the chart. So I was partly right, but, after all, I was working against Saturn in the 7th house on his own day of the week.

Saturn in the 7th house often shows that the astrologer will experience a delay in understanding the chart and may need to consult another astrologer for help in judgment. Several weeks after analyzing Sara's chart, I was reading the aphorisms of Guido Bonatus as background for this book. In saying #122, Bonatus tells us to consider "whether the Part of Fortune be in the first 10 degrees of the 4th house, with the Moon's North Node, the Moon, Venus and Jupiter, and they be direct—for that signifies the native shall be lucky in discovering and finding out hidden treasure ... and if only the Part of Fortune be there not afflicted, a small quantity." With Saturn in the 7th house impeding my judgment, I had omitted the symbolism of the 4th house as the location of buried treasure.

Reading Bonatus prompted me to do a little research through the ancient Latin and Greek texts. Early in the fourth century, Firmicus Maternus said the 4th house "shows us family property, substance, possessions, household goods, anything that pertains to hidden and recovered wealth." Undoubtedly the 4th house emphasis in Sara's chart pertains to "hidden and recovered wealth." From now on I will consider this meaning of hidden and recovered wealth when I interpret the 4th house.

## CHART 3: THE 1989 SAN FRANCISCO EARTHQUAKE

On September 17, 1989, at 5:04 P.M. PDT, an earthquake of magnitude 6.9 on the Richter scale devastated areas in and around San Francisco. It happened on Tuesday, a Mars day. The violence of the quake fits the symbolism of Mars. According to the *New York Times,* the epicenter was about ten miles northeast of Santa Cruz and fifty miles southwest of San Francisco. Checking a map, I located the epicenter at 121W53/37N07. The worst human toll was at the Nimitz Freeway in Oakland where the concrete upper deck collapsed, crushing motorists on the lower deck during rush hour. Chart 3 shows the horoscope for this disaster.

This is an event chart, not a horary chart. Nonetheless, we can apply horary principles to the chart to aid in understanding its dynamics. In fact, you will find that learning horary astrology will sharpen your understanding of other branches of the celestial art.

Chart 3 for the epicenter of the quake has 22° 51' Pisces rising. Common (mutable) signs occupy all the angles, forming a mutable cross, which suggests an unstable, rapidly changing situation. (The chart for Sara's baby also had a mutable cross.) The Moon's North Node is at 22° 26' Aquarius in the 12th house of sorrow, and the South Node is at 22° 26' Leo in the 6th house of illness. The Ascendant is in the same degree as the Moon's Mean Node and almost exactly quincunx the Moon's South Node. Nodal degrees can signify a fatality or catastrophe, and quincunxes imply necessary restructuring. The Moon's South Node is of the nature of Saturn, ruler of structure, gravity, falls, and solidity. These are the first clues that we are looking at a disaster chart.

Gemini is on the cusp of the 4th house, making Mercury the ruler of the end of the matter. Jupiter, the Ascendant ruler, has recently completed a succession of oppositions to Uranus, Saturn, and Neptune in the 10th. The Stock Market plunge of Friday, October 13, 1989, also occurred during this period of Jupiter's oppositions to outer planets.

Mercury in the 7th has recently completed squares to Uranus and Saturn, and is about to square Neptune and then Jupiter. As Mercury makes these two squares, it translates the

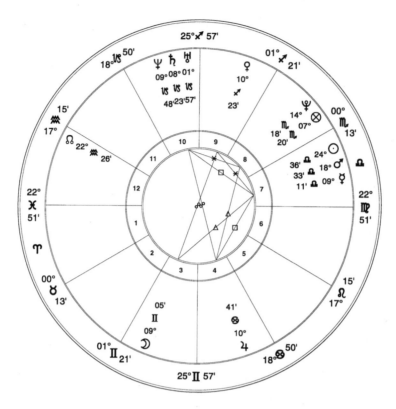

Chart 3: The 1989 San Francisco Earthquake
October 17, 1989, 5:05 PM PDT, 121W53, 37N07  Koch Houses

light from Uranus and Saturn to Neptune and Jupiter. In doing so it reactivates the past Saturn/Neptune conjunction and Jupiter's past oppositions to Uranus and Saturn. In squaring Neptune and then Jupiter in quick succession, Mercury translates the light from Neptune to Jupiter and stirs up the recent opposition of these two heavy planets. Like the little trouble maker he is, Mercury instigates trouble among the giants.

The Moon will also trine Mercury, quincunx Neptune, and semi-sextile Jupiter in quick succession, further activating this complex in the chart. Earlier in the day the Moon completed a quincunx to Uranus and then to Saturn and carries with it the quality of "necessary readjustment by powerful forces" as it approaches its quincunx to Neptune.

What does this all mean? Mercury ruling the "end of the matter" will square the two co-rulers of the Ascendant which themselves are in opposition. This is a high energy, separative, and difficult situation, occurring on a Mars day. In horary, the 4th house rules the earth and damage from earthquakes. In this chart Mercury rules the 3rd, 4th, and 7th houses. The 3rd house rules transportation and the 7th, the people. The 10th house governs structure and in this chart contains Uranus, Saturn, and Neptune who are all powerfully located in an angle.

If we look at the "fit" of the chart, we see the Moon in the 3rd house of transportation, the Sun and Mercury in the 7th house of the people, Cancer on the 5th cusp of sporting events and children, Leo on the 6th cusp of illness and control of the environment. These meanings fit the event.

Another tenet of horary astrology is that all the aspects the Moon makes before leaving its sign show the conditions surrounding the event. The Moon in this chart is in Gemini, the sign of travel and the local environment. The list of aspects that occurred between the Moon and the planets before the Moon changed sign includes a prominence of quincunxes. In addition, there was a square of Mercury to the midpoint of the Saturn/Neptune conjunction shortly before the quake.

Barbara Watters considered the quincunx to be a Uranian aspect because its action is often "sudden, unpredictable, violent, or fateful." Because the quincunx relates to being six or eight houses apart, it connotes 6th house illness or 8th house death. Quincunxes combined with squares and oppositions are especially malefic. The aspects in the list suggest a transportation accident of major proportions. I would not have predicted an earthquake from this list or from the event chart. If, however, this were the chart for a horary question, "Will there be an earthquake?" I would give an unequivocal "Yes" answer.

In horary questions, the last major aspect of the Moon is an indicator of the general outcome. In this chart the Moon's final Ptolemaic aspect is a trine to the Sun. This trine will go a long way to ameliorate the otherwise malefic configurations in the chart. Indeed, the October 30, 1989, issue of *Newsweek* talked about "San Francisco's relative good fortune" in what could have been a far worse disaster. In particular, we should note that the Moon's own sign Cancer rules the 5th house of sporting events and the Sun is the natural ruler of the 5th house. The beneficial trine between the Moon and the Sun suggests good fortune for those at the world series game that was about the start when the earthquake struck.

The local space astrology of this event is fascinating. If one draws lines along the surface of the earth from the epicenter of the quake through the 10th house planets, these "planetary lines" pass through Oakland and San Francisco where most of the damage occurred. In particular, the Saturn line passes directly through the Nimitz Freeway, where the deaths due to falling concrete (Saturn) took place. These planetary lines concentrate the energy of the opposition between Jupiter and the Saturn/Neptune conjunction in Oakland along the Nimitz Freeway. I have found repeatedly in local space charts that Saturn/Neptune aspects reveal malfunction and flaws in structure. With Uranus also opposing Oakland on the map, it is no surprise astrologically that this area was so hard hit. For readers interested in learning more about local space astrology, I recommend *Planets in Locality* by Steve Cozzi.

## CHART 4: DEATH IN THE EVERGLADES

On May 11, 1996, at about 2:25 P.M. EDT, ValuJet Flight 592 plunged into the Florida Everglades about 15 miles northwest of the Miami Airport (Chart 4). Judging from the map of the accident shown in *Time* magazine (May 20, 1996), I estimated the coordinates to be about 80W40 and 26N00. This chart is cast with Regiomontanus houses in deference to William Lilly. We can use horary principles to study an event chart for the moment of this grim accident, which killed everyone on board.

ValuJet Flight 592 took off from the Miami Airport about 2:05 P.M. EDT, just as Pluto lay exactly on the IC (end-of-the-matter 4th cusp) in Miami. Pluto, the modern ruler of Scorpio,

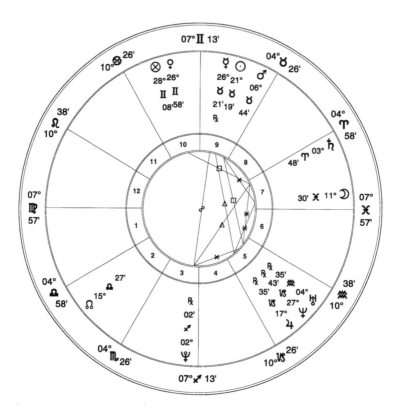

Chart 4: ValuJet Flight 592
May 11, 1996, 2:25 PM EDT, 80W40, 26N00 Regiomontanus Houses

symbolizes power, violence, death, the underworld, and uncontrollable forces. At the time of takeoff the early degrees of Virgo were rising. At 2:20 P.M. the fixed star Hyades (5° 46' Gemini) was at the MC directly overhead the aircraft, which was trying to return to Miami because of a fire on board. Hyades is associated with violence, imbalance, and shipwrecks.

At 2:25 P.M. the Ascendant was almost 8 degrees of Virgo, making Mercury both ruler and Almuten of the first house. Lilly used the Ascendant ruler to symbolize a ship lost at sea (CA, p.162) and so Mercury signifies Flight 592. Mercury is the most debilitated planet in this chart, receiving a score of -11 (negative 11) in Lilly's point system. Mercury is peregrine, retrograde, combust the sun, and closely conjunct the malefic fixed star Caput Algol—a star traditionally associated with fires, violence, decapitation, and death. Because the Sun is Almuten of the 8th house of death and also ruler of the unfortunate 12th house, the combustion of Mercury by the Sun in the 9th of flights is especially dangerous. Mercury also conjoins the contrascion of Uranus, the modern planet associated with accidents and sudden unexpected happenings. Lilly says that contrascion contacts are equivalent to squares and oppositions, that is, it acts like a Mercury square or opposition to Uranus in this chart.

The lesser malefic Mars closely conjoins the Regiomontanus 9th cusp of flights and long-distance travel. Mars is also conjunct the malefic fixed star Hamal at 7° 36' Taurus—a star of the nature of Mars and Saturn, often associated with violence, injury, and misfortune. In the Koch house system, the 9th cusp lies at 8° Taurus, and the malefic star Hamal lies on the midpoint of Mars and the 9th Koch cusp. As usual, the Koch houses also give meaningful results in event and horary analysis.

The greater malefic Saturn closely conjoins the 8th Regiomontanus cusp (death) and also lies almost exactly on the Point of Death at 3° 21' Pisces (Mars + Saturn—MC). In her book on horary astrology Barbara Watters attributed the Point of Death to Charles Emerson, and I have found it to be extremely accurate in horary charts about death.

Venus, ruler of the 9th house of flights and the most dignified planet in this chart, is in the final degrees of Gemini in the terms of the lesser malefic Mars. Venus will soon conjoin Pars Fortuna, which is not especially strong in the final degrees of Gemini (where it loses 2 points for being in the terms of Mars). The dispositor of the Part of Fortune is Mercury, which is the most debilitated planet in the chart. Venus is also within orb of a dissociate square of Saturn.

The closest midpoint contact in this chart is Sun = Uranus/Ascendant (a dangerous environment, an accident). According to Lilly, houses 6, 8, and 12 are the most unfortunate places in the horoscope. This midpoint configuration is significant because Sun rules the 12th house of undoing and is Almuten of the 8th house of death. Uranus is the modern ruler of Aquarius on the cusp of the unfortunate 6th, and the Aquarius Ascendant signifies the flight itself.

## Chart 5: Explosion in the Sky: TWA Flight 800

After a delay of more than an hour, TWA Flight 800 took off at 8:19 P.M. EDT, Wednesday, July 17, 1996, from Kennedy Airport with a destination of Paris, France. It ascended to cruising altitude and was traveling along the southern coast of Long Island, about 50 miles from Kennedy Airport, when it suddenly disappeared from radar about 8:39 P.M. about ten miles offshore at 13,700 feet. About 8:40 P.M. eyewitnesses described seeing an "explosion," a "fireball" or "a second sunset" over Moriches Inlet, Long Island. The 747 jumbo jet then broke into flaming pieces, crashed, and exploded again in the ocean twelve miles south of Moriches Inlet, Long Island. By 8:50 P.M. nine rescue ships and helicopters were on their way to the crash site. See Chart 5 for the takeoff from Kennedy.

With Capricorn rising, Saturn rules the flight. On this day Saturn is making a station and turning retrograde. It is no surprise astrologically that the flight was delayed. In the *Astrologer's Guide* (p. 34), Bonatus wrote that anything begun while the significator is "in his first station, going to be retrograde...will not be accomplished." In a note to this Bonatus text, Lilly commented that the retrograde station shows "dissolution and destruction." Furthermore, Saturn is debilitated, being peregrine (without essential dignity), in its fall in Aries, and conjunct the malefic South Node of the Moon. Saturn, the significator of the flight, rules the 1st and 2nd houses and is Almuten of the 1st, 2nd, 9th (with Venus), and 12th houses. As such, Saturn links the aircraft (1st) with financial issues (2nd), flying/long-distance travel (9th), and secret enemies/self-undoing (12th).

The Ascendant conjoins Neptune and the fixed star Terebellum, a star of the nature of Venus and Saturn (the Almutens of the 9th house of flying). Terebellum has been long associated with despair, violence, murder, and prejudice. This fixed star figures prominently in

Chart 5: TWA Flight 800 Takeoff
July 17, 1996, 8:19 PM EDT, 73W48, 40N38  Regiomontanus Houses

the charts of Iraq and its leader Saddam Hussein. Foramen, a fixed star often found in ship-wreck charts, lies on the Regiomontanus 9th cusp of flight and distant travel.

Two of the modern malefics, Neptune and Uranus, are both retrograde and rising in the 1st, close to the Ascendant. Neptune rules dissolution and Uranus governs accidents and sudden happenings. The sun has just set and closely opposes Neptune on the Ascendant. Mars (fires) applies to a quincunx with Neptune. Recall that Barbara Watters considered the quincunx a Uranian influence, symbolizing sudden, violent events. In addition, Mars exactly conjoins the fixed star Al Hecka (at 24° 43'Gemini in1996), a star of the nature of Mars and traditionally linked to aggression and accidents.

Uranus is retrograde and will conjoin the Ascendant in 7 degrees. Mercury (natural ruler of flight and ruler of the unfortunate 6th and 8th houses) has just passed an opposition with Uranus. The separating Mercury/Uranus opposition suggests that whatever caused the plane to explode may already have been operating when the plane took off.

At the time of the explosion (about 8:40 P.M.), the plane was flying east and slightly south toward Neptune and Uranus and almost exactly on the local space lines of the Mercury/Uranus and the Sun/Neptune oppositions. At that time the fixed star Caput Algol at 26° 07' Taurus lay exactly on the end-of-the-matter 4th cusp. Lilly considered Caput Algol the most malefic of the fixed stars and its symbolism includes beheading, fires, violence, murder, criminality, and horror.

By 8:50 P.M. as the rescue vessels were racing toward the crash site, the Ascendant had moved to 7° Aquarius. The fixed star Praesaepe (at 7° 17' Leo in 1996) of the nature of the Moon and Mars lay on the Descendant. This star traditionally signifies injury, murder, tragedy and fires, and was called by Allen "the exhalation of piled up corpses." In addition, another shipwreck star, North Asellus (at 7° 29 Leo in 1996), was on the Descendant, indicating what the rescuers would find.

On Tuesday, November 18, 1997, the FBI, after a long investigation, announced that they could find no evidence of terrorism or any criminal cause for the explosion. Most likely the accident was due to some kind of mechanical malfunction. On the day of this FBI announcement, the solar arc directed Moon (Almuten of the 4th cusp of endings) of the Flight 800 Takeoff chart was exactly semi-square "natal" Saturn (Ascendant ruler of the Takeoff chart). In addition, the Ascendant of the original chart had just conjoined "natal" Neptune by secondary progression.

HISTORICAL INTERLUDE
REGIOMONTANUS

Johann Muller (June 6, 1436–July 6, 1476), developed the house system that William Lilly used in doing horary astrology. His pseudonym Regiomontanus is a Latin form of the name of Konigsberg, the city where he was born.

Regiomontanus was a child prodigy who became a famous mathematician and astronomer. He assisted in translating the works of Claudius Ptolemy from their original Greek. In 1475 Pope Sixtus IV summoned Regiomontanus to Rome to begin the reformation of the Julian calendar. The pope appointed him bishop of Regensburg, but before he could assume that position he either died of the plague or was poisoned by his enemies. As a result, the Western world would have to wait another century for calendar reform.

Regiomontanus was an expert is spherical trigonometry and used his talents to develop an astrological house system which divides the Celestial Equator into segments, then projects those divisions back onto the ecliptic to demarcate the house cusps.

# CHAPTER THREE

# Some Basic Concepts of Horary Astrology

This chapter begins a systematic review of horary concepts with a focus on how to analyze the chart. First, a word of advice from the scholastic philosopher William of Occam (1285–1349). Confronted with colleagues debating how many angels could dance on the head of a pin, Occam suggested cutting to the heart of a matter. He said that "entities [explanatory assumptions] should not be multiplied beyond what is needed"—a principle now known as Occam's razor. A colloquial translation would be, "Cut the crap," or "Keep it simple." A wise horary astrologer does not use factors in the chart beyond those needed to answer the question.

Horary astrology is the art of answering a question based on analysis of a horoscope for the birth of the question. The analysis proceeds step by step, following specific rules that have proven their worth over centuries. Nonetheless, different systems and, at times, contradictory methods of horary analysis exist. Each practitioner must find an approach that reflects his or her own mental process and use it consistently. Most importantly, the beginner should avoid hit-or-miss, intuitive approaches. An orderly, sequential series of steps produces the most reliable results.

The word *horary* derives from the Latin word *hora*, meaning hour. Horary questions are questions of the hour, or specifically, of the moment that the meaning of the question registers in the mind of the astrologer. Such inquiries are usually matters of pressing personal concern that demand immediate answers. Other questions, such as Sara's challenge in the previous chapter, are more for fun and yield entertaining results. In fact, my interest in astrology continues because I enjoy it so much.

Natal astrology deals with the long-term climate and overall trends of a person's life. Horary astrology, on the other hand, is more like a weather forecast. This analogy suggests that certain horary answers may hold true only for a limited period of time. When the weather front passes, you may need a new forecast. Horary astrologers differ, however, on whether they use a time limit for horary charts.

Some horary astrologers assert that the querent may not ask the same question twice under similar circumstances. This rule reflects the traditional wisdom that horary charts will not give valid answers to repeated frivolous inquiries. If you don't like what the initial chart reveals, you cannot keep asking the same question at different times, hoping to eventually get the answer you desire.

William Lilly did allow his querents to ask about the same matter again, provided they were sincere in the inquiry and the initial chart gave an equivocal, indecisive answer. Lilly writes: "When the testimonies of Fortunes and Infortunes are equal, defer judgment, it's not possible to know which way the balance will turn; however, defer you your opinion till another question better inform you."

Once a querent asks a question, the horary astrologer answers it on the basis of a horoscope for the time the astrologer understands the inquiry. To be certain he or she understands the matter, the astrologer must discuss the issue with the querent. The time and place where the astrologer first comprehends the querent's concern is the proper birth time of the question. The horary chart for that moment reveals the symbolic system of the astrologer's mind as it grapples with the querent's concern.

## On Different Systems of Horary Analysis

Horary astrology became popular because people wanted to ask questions of the stars but did not have accurate birth data. Many of the rules we use today derive from Lilly's seventeenth-century text *Christian Astrology*. Lilly, in turn, took his rules from the astrologers of the Middle Ages and ancient Greece, who borrowed from earlier and often contradictory sources.

Most horary texts after Lilly have simply copied his rules with little thought and even less originality. As a result, the horary branch of astrology withered after the mid-1600s. Notable exceptions are the books by Marc Edmund Jones in 1943, by Barbara Watters in 1973, by Sylvia DeLong in 1980, by Derek Appleby in 1985, and by Olivia Barclay in 1990. In addition, the 1960 text *Simplified Horary Astrology* by Ivy M. Goldstein-Jacobson is a valuable compendium of rules and tidbits about the art. Simmonite's 1850s work contains valuable descriptions of the quesited according to decanates and facets.

As mentioned, several systems of horary analysis are now in use, and some of these use contradictory and competing methods that can confuse the novice. In this book I have tried to synthesize various schools of thought into an orderly, logical method that works. Where there are differences in the literature I point them out and show how I deal with the issue. In the tradition of Ptolemy and Lilly, I have included only those rules that are theoretically sound and confirmed in my own experience. Readers should test the rules for themselves rather than take my word that they work.

Astrology reflects the historical period in which it is practiced. A rule that was sound centuries ago in a desert climate may not be viable today. The same Sun that brings life to the Eskimo may parch the Arab to death. The idea of a planet being weakened by being close to the Sun is an example of such cultural variance. Some astrologers find this rule helpful while others see no value in it. The symbolism of the Sun may vary with one's culture or position on the globe.

As research into horary astrology continues, some of the rules may need changing. Horary, like all astrology, is an empirical science. It establishes correspondences between the state of the heavens and the affairs of men—as above, so below. As we gain more experience, we will be able to fine-tune some rules and abandon others. The novice at horary will need to keep an open mind and test the various horary rules to decide which ones to keep. The only absolute in horary is that there are no absolutes. The horary rules are really guidelines that are reliable in most instances. Experience is the best teacher. Every practitioner must devise a system of his or her own that is consistent, dependable, and reflects the way his or her mind functions.

This last point may seem odd, but I believe it is the crux of what makes a horary system work. Based on how his or her mind functions, each astrologer will develop a potentially different, though equally effective, system for horary analysis. Joan McEvers, for example, is a native of Aquarius. She takes a detached, abstract, air-sign approach. Like all horary astrologers, McEvers regards the selection of the proper houses as crucial. She sets up a system of clear, abstract rules in which squares and oppositions between the rulers of the querent and quesited give "no" answers; and trines, sextiles, and conjunctions mean "yes." She does not worry about one significator leaving its sign in ephemeris time before the aspect becomes perfect. In McEvers' system, if an aspect will reach symbolic perfection, regardless of actual ephemeris movement of the planets, then the nature of that aspect gives the answer. Her method is different from mine, but we usually arrive at the same answers. Her lectures on horary are wonderful, and she has written a book detailing her approach.

The following example illustrates the difference between our systems. On Sunday, February 3, 1974, a friend of Joan McEvers asked the question "Is my house going to burn down the end of this month?" The time was 2:58 P.M. PST in Canoga Park, California. (See Chart 6, p.38.)

The chart fits the concern of the querent. It is a Sunday and the Sun, a fire planet, is in the 8th house of death and destruction along with Mercury (questions). The Moon, ruling the querent, is in the 12th house of worry and sorrow and describes the state of the querent. Capricorn is on the 7th cusp, and its ruler Saturn, symbolizing the astrologer, joins the querent, symbolized by the Moon, in the 12th. They are worrying together, and Saturn will give the astrologer a hard time in answering this question.

Saturn rules the Capricorn 7th cusp and is retrograde in the 12th house. A retrograde 7th ruler warns the astrologer to look out for a possible error. This retrograde 7th ruler played itself out in an interesting way here. Joan McEvers copied the figure by hand to a blank horoscope wheel and mailed it to me. She listed the time of the chart as 3:58 P.M. PST. When I ran that time through the computer, the chart was an hour off. I called her to check the time and discovered that she had inadvertently written 3:58 when she meant to write 2:58.

Back to the question. Apparently McEvers' friend had read her monthly forecast in *Horoscope* magazine predicting a fire in her house. She became alarmed and asked a horary question. The chart disturbed both McEvers and her friend, as shown by Saturn and the Moon in the 12th. The Moon, ruling the querent, will oppose Venus, ruler of 4th cusp representing the home that might burn. The two retrograde malefics, Pluto and Uranus, in the 4th house become co-rulers of the property. The querent's Moon will

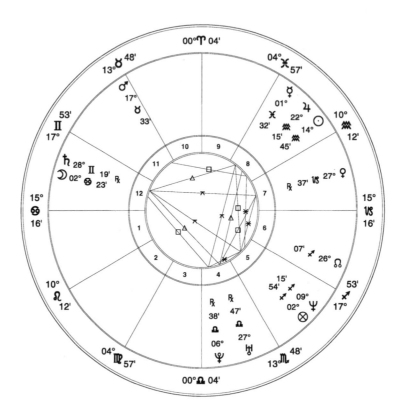

Chart 6: "Is my house going to burn down at the end of this month?"
February 3, 1974, 2:58 P.M. PST, 118W10, 34N20  Koch Houses

square both these retrograde significators. It looks pretty bad. Maybe we should call the fire department right now! Why wait till the end of the month?

McEvers pondered this chart for quite some time. She took it to other horary astrologers who also interpreted that the house would burn. But February came and went without incident, and today the house is still standing. No fire ever occurred. A lesser mortal might have abandoned horary astrology. McEvers, instead, persisted in trying to understand the meaning of the chart. Like a good Aquarius, she abstracted from the situation and hit upon the cornerstone of her method. McEvers deduced that squares and oppositions mean "no," and trines, sextiles, and conjunctions mean "yes." In this chart and in the McEvers system, the squares and oppositions between the querent's ruler and the property's ruler mean a "no" answer to the original question. The answer is, "No, the house will not burn down."

I approach the same chart differently and arrive at the same conclusion. Because the question is about the home and whether it will burn, I use derivative houses. Real estate belongs in the 4th house. Libra is on the 4th cusp and Venus is the primary significator. Pluto and Uranus in the 4th are secondary rulers of the property.

Since I know of no traditional mundane house for "burning down," I would use Mars as the natural ruler of fires. Lilly relied on the symbolism of Mars to predict the fire of London. If I wanted to use a mundane house, I would use the 8th house of the 4th which is the natural 11th house of the chart. Any 8th house represents the injury or death of its first house occupant.

The chart confirms my localization because Mars is in the 11th house of the figure. It is helpful to let the chart be your guide. Taurus is on the 11th cusp so Venus becomes the ruler of both the home and its demise. Mars in the 11th is the secondary ruler of the death of the home. Because Mars rules fires and Venus is already the primary ruler of the property 4th, I use Mars as the primary ruler of the "burning down" of the house.

What aspect will Venus make to Mars? Venus is retrograde at 27° 48' Capricorn. Mars is direct at 17° 49' Taurus. They are mutually applying to a trine which will become exact, ephemeris time, on February 23, 1974. Instead of showing a fire at the end of the month, the ruler of the property is making the most favorable aspect possible to the ruler of fires. My answer is, "No, the house will not burn down." The ruler of fire looks with favor upon the home at this time. A square or opposition here would have alarmed me.

In reading over this story, I wondered if the basic horary question here is not whether the house will burn but whether the statement in *Horoscope* magazine was true. If I had interviewed the querent at the time, I might have rephrased the question to read, "Is the forecast (rumor) true?" I don't place much stock in Sun sign forecasts and regard them as rumors at best.

We locate rumors in the 3rd house. With Virgo on the cusp, Mercury becomes the ruler of the forecast. Mercury is also the natural ruler of reports and communication. Mercury lies in the 8th house as befits a rumor about death and destruction. The end of the matter for the rumor is the 4th of the 3rd, which is the 6th house of the figure. Sagittarius is on the 6th cusp and Jupiter rules the outcome of the rumor, its dismissal to certainty. Mercury and Jupiter make no aspect in this chart. No aspect, no action. Nothing will come of the rumor. It is false. The house will not burn by the end of the month.

We see here two different horary systems and three different approaches to the same chart. They all produce the same answer so long as we are consistent and proceed step by step, according to the method we have chosen. Horary is like that.

## HORARY AS HOUSE-CENTERED & MOON-CENTERED ASTROLOGY

Horary is essentially an astrology of the twelve houses of the horoscope. Horary technique answers questions through the mundane houses. The first step in horary analysis is to place the question in the proper house. This is not a static looking up of a word in a rulership dictionary. On the contrary, assigning house rulership requires a dynamic understanding of the querent's relationship to the issue at hand. The ruler, or sometimes the Almuten (most essentially dignified planet at the house cusp), of the house governing the querent's concern becomes the primary significator of the matter. Any planets in that house, or the ruler or Almuten of a sign intercepted in that house, become co-rulers or secondary significators.

There are two crucial steps in horary astrology. First, one must take the correct moment to ask the question and cast the chart. I would like to dispute here the method used in some horary classrooms to gather questions. Some teachers cast a chart for a predetermined time during the class and then solicit questions from the students. This method will not normally produce authentic horary inquiries because the time is chosen arbitrarily rather than when the querent is "most solicitous" about the matter.

Classroom questions may be useful for demonstrating the rules, but the student must be aware that the answer will be no better than chance under these circumstances. Joan McEvers, for example, told me that she once attended a horary workshop with Barbara Watters. Ms. Watters answered questions posed by the students, using a chart cast for a particular moment during the class. Joan kept a log of Ms. Watters' answers and found them all to be wrong! Since the late Barbara Watters was a competent astrologer, I conclude that her method of obtaining questions was at fault. The skeptic will conclude from this example that horary is nonsense after all.

You cannot coax, cajole, solicit, or compel the querent to give you a horary question. Legitimate questions come to the astrologer in their own proper time when the querent feels a pressing need to seek outside help with a matter. Such circumstances are the breeding ground for horary inquiries. You cannot force anyone to seek horary advice, just as you cannot force anyone to engage in psychotherapy. Seek and ye shall not find. Let the universe bring its questions to you. Or, to paraphrase *Star Wars*, let the force be with you.

The second crucial step is to locate the proper house to represent the matter asked about. If you assign the incorrect house, you will most likely get the wrong answer. Or, more correctly, your answer will be no better than chance.

Why are the mundane houses the crux of horary analysis? Precisely because the house cusps are the most rapidly changing factors in the horoscope. Every twenty-four hours each degree of the zodiac passes over the Ascendant. On average, a new degree rises every four minutes. Because the house cusps move so rapidly, they symbolize the ever-changing concerns of us humans. According to John and Peter Filby, "House division is an important astrological concept, as it is the only factor which alters in a short space of time. Without this division, the relationship of man to his environment would be difficult to ascertain."

Besides the house cusps, the other rapidly changing astrological factor is the Moon, which spends only slightly over two days in each sign and moves about one degree every two hours. In astrological symbolism, the most rapidly changing factors in a chart govern the ephemeral conditions of daily life and thought. If we liken the horary chart to a cosmic clock, the house cusps become the clock's second hand and the Moon, its minute hand. The changing house cusps together with the Moon stand for the fluctuation of the world at large.

The Moon has a special significance in horary as an indicator of the general or trivial conditions that surround a question. She serves as a secondary significator of the querent and of the question when the primary significators fail to provide an answer. The Moon is a backup when the house rulers are not useful. Sue Ward considers the Moon to be a "general significator in all questions." She adds that the Moon "usually shows the events and activities relating to the matter" and as such "can often show timing."

Because of the Moon's rapid motion, many horary astrologers assign her to all change and activity in the chart. The Moon rules the tides of the oceans and of men. All the aspects the Moon makes before leaving its sign will show the general outcome of a question or event begun while the Moon is in that sign. The most recent aspect the Moon made before the question shows what led up to the question. The last aspect to which the Moon will apply before it changes sign reveals the general but not necessarily the specific outcome. As the Moon goes, so the flow of life goes; but it is the aspects made by the primary house rulers (significators) that show the specific outcome. Unlike horary astrologers who rely primarily on the Moon, I regard the more quickly changing house cusps as primary. In my system the Moon is secondary but important.

## SOME BASIC DEFINITIONS OF TERMS USED IN HORARY

### Querent and Rulers of the Querent

The querent is the person who asks the question. The primary significator of the querent is the planet ruling the Ascendant. Any planets in the first house and the ruler of an intercepted sign in the first house become secondary rulers of the querent. The Almuten (the planet with the most essential dignity) of the Ascendant and of any intercepted sign in the 1st house may also be a significator. The Moon is always a secondary or co-ruler of the querent and of the question. Aspects involving primary rulers are more significant than aspects involving secondary rulers.

### Quesited and Rulers of the Quesited

In horary astrology it is useful to keep matters as simple as possible. To this end, I call the person asking the question the "querent" and the matter of concern the "quesited" or simply the "question." The quesited is the person or the matter asked about and is ruled by the proper house. For example, relationship questions are ruled by the 1st and 7th houses, financial questions by the 2nd and 8th, travel questions by the 3rd and 9th, and so on.

The primary ruler of the quesited is the planet ruling the sign on the cusp of the house that locates the matter. Lee Lehman takes the Almuten (the planet with the most essential dignity at the house cusp) as the primary ruler when the Almuten has more dignity than the planet ruling the house cusp. Secondary rulers (co-rulers) are any planets within the focal house and the ruler of any sign intercepted in the house of the quesited. Bonatus also uses the planet with which the Moon next makes a major aspect as a co-ruler of the quesited. As with the querent, aspects involving the primary ruler of the quesited carry more weight than aspects involving the secondary rulers.

### Derived Houses

If a question involves something belonging to or related directly to the querent, then the usual house system holds for interpreting the chart. When the querent asks about someone else's belongings or relationships, we use a system of derived houses. To determine derivative houses, we regard the house representing the person or matter asked about as a new first house. In other words, we begin counting derivative houses from the house of the quesited as the new 1st house.

We have already seen several examples of derived houses. If the question is about a child's book, the 5th house of the figure rules the child. The child's book is ruled by the 3rd house of the 5th, which is the 7th house of the chart. Similarly a child's illness is ruled by the 10th house, which is the 6th house of the natural 5th house of children.

If the question is about a sibling, the new first house is the natural 3rd house of the chart. The natural 4th house becomes the derivative 2nd house, the natural 5th house becomes the derivative 3rd house, and so on. With practice, deriving houses becomes automatic.

The arithmetic of finding the derivative house is to take the number of the house of the quesited, add the number of the derived house you are looking for, and subtract one. The answer will be the number of the natural house of the figure that corresponds to the derivative house you want. For example, if the quesited is a co-worker, the house of the quesited is the 6th. If you want the 8th house of surgery of the co-worker, you add 6 + 8 - 1 = 13. If the answer is greater than 12, you subtract 12; thus 13 - 12 = 1. The first house of the natural chart is the 8th house of the quesited co-worker shown by the 6th.

For fun, I will take an example from the movie *Spaceballs* by Mel Brooks. When Lonestar confronts Dark Helmet toward the end of the film, Dark Helmet says to him, "I am your father's brother's nephew's cousin's former roommate."

"What does that make us?" asks Lonestar.

"Nothing," replies Dark Helmet.

Let's see what astrology has to say about their relationship. Where would we locate the querent's father's brother's nephew's cousin's former roommate? The querent is in the 1st, his father is in the 4th. The father's brother is in the 3rd of the 4th, which is the 6th. The father's brother's nephew is the father's brother's sibling's child. The father's brother's sibling is in the 3rd of the 6th, which is the 8th. The child of that sibling is the 5th of the 8th, which is the 12th.

So far we have gotten to the nephew. The nephew's cousin is the 3rd of the 12th, which is the 2nd. The 3rd is the generic house of cousins. If you know the lineage, you can locate a cousin more specifically in the 4th (mother's sibling's child) or the 10th (father's sibling's child).

Since we don't know if the cousin is paternal or maternal, we use the 3rd house of generic kin. Finally, the roommate is in the cousin's 7th, that is, the 7th of the 2nd, which is the 8th house of the natural figure. Unrelated other people with whom one has dealings are found in the 7th. We conclude that Dark Helmet bears an 8th house relationship to Lonestar. The symbolism of the 8th as the house of death fits because at this very moment in the movie Dark Helmet is trying to kill Lonestar.

If you followed the above example, pat yourself on the back. You're well on your way to becoming a horary astrologer.

## WHAT IS A VALID HORARY QUESTION?

Not all musings are legitimate horary questions, and astrologers disagree on which inquiries they will subject to horary analysis. Many ideas occur to us daily. They become matters of horary analysis only when they are issues of pressing personal concern and we enlist the aid of an astrologer. Each practitioner needs to decide which types of questions to accept in his or her practice.

Most astrologers believe that a horary question must represent a concern or crisis, however minor, in the life of the querent. They feel that horary analysis will not yield dependable results for matters over which the querent has no responsibility or personal concern.

On the other hand, what seems trivial or irrelevant to the astrologer may be a matter of import to the querent.

According to Jones, the most pertinent horary questions are those related to the outcome of a specific current decision or action. Horary technique will not answer static questions like "What is the color of my hair?" A question such as "What will be the outcome of coloring my hair?" will yield accurate results if it matters to the querent. Jones suggested phrasing horary inquiries in the form, "What will be the result or outcome of doing something or making a decision about some specific matter?" Such phrasing takes advantage of the principle of cosmic sympathy, that the motions of the planets parallel the flow of the affairs of men. Even so, you may not be able to phrase all questions in this form.

Another group of widely accepted horary questions relates to lost or stolen items. Such questions include "Who stole my watch?" and "Where is my runaway child?" The astrologer can use the chart to describe the thief or locate the missing person or thing.

Although a horary chart may be able to answer a question such as "Will I ever marry?" it is usually better to use natal methods for such an inquiry. Many natal astrologers, however, decline to answer this question with a simple yes or no. They prefer to counsel the querent about factors in the natal chart that show difficulties in relationships so that marriage might become possible. The issue is more one of ethics and philosophy than technique.

Some modern astrologers feel that a horary interpretation will not hold true indefinitely and therefore impose a fixed time limit. William Lilly did not use a time limit for horary inquiries. He took questions as they came. For example, he answered a question posed by a woman on June 22, 1635, at 9:30 A.M. in London, "Will I ever have children?" Lilly responded, "I declared, positively, that she never would have any children, according to the rules of the science." (See Chart 7, p. 44.)

Lilly reasoned as follows. At the time the woman asked about having children, the barren sign Virgo was rising. The woman's ruler Mercury was in the terms of Saturn at 24° Gemini, a somewhat barren sign. Capricorn ruled the 5th house cusp of children. Saturn, primary ruler of the pregnancy 5th house, was retrograde at 29° Sagittarius in the 4th house of conception.

The woman's ruler Mercury was approaching an opposition to Saturn, significator of the 5th house pregnancy. Saturn was retrograde in the 4th house of conception and simultaneously applied to an opposition with Mercury. The malefic Moon's South Node conjoined the Ascendant, a symbol of the querent's body. All these were strong arguments of barrenness.

Furthermore, the Moon (pregnancy) in the last degree of Virgo is applying (by dissociate aspect) to a square with the Sun (vitality, new life) in the first degree of Cancer. Lilly did not consider this Moon to be void of course because it was within orb of squaring the Sun once it changed signs. In addition, Venus (ruler of the 6th house of the health of the 5th house fetus and dispositor of the Part of Children (Pars Filiorum at 21° 16' Libra in Lilly's original chart) is conjunct the malefic fixed star Caput Algol and is also quincunx the Part of Children which she disposes.

Lilly regarded the Moon (the querent) squaring Saturn (6th ruler of illness) to signify the sickly state of the woman. Of note, the Moon lies in Virgo and Saturn in Sagittarius, both

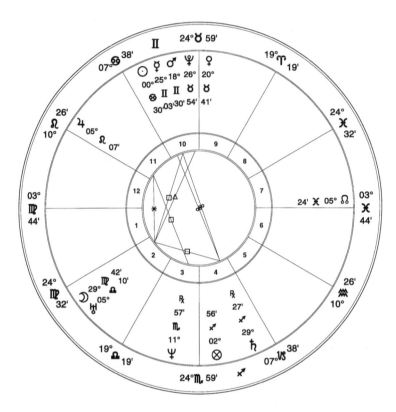

Chart 7: "Will I ever have children?"
June 22, 1635, 9:30 A.M. GMT, 00W10, 51N30 Regiomontanus Houses

signs of long ascension. In other examples, Lilly would have stretched this square into a trine and given it a positive interpretation.

While Lilly shows technical skill in answering the question, one must wonder about the psychological impact of his pronouncement on the querent. When a horary chart gives a clear-cut "no" with an indefinite time limit, is it ethical to reveal the answer? Avoiding questions without a time limit may be the route to follow. I usually refuse to answer such questions. If I am wrong—and astrologers do make mistakes more often than they are willing to admit—I have incorrectly dashed the querent's hopes for life.

Since the accuracy of horary analysis depends on proper placement of the question around the horoscope wheel, the phrasing of the question is critical. When possible, state the concern in terms of traditional house rulerships. Where mundane house rulerships don't seem to apply, you can use the natural planetary ruler of the matter.

The astrologer may need to help the querent phrase the question. Horary astrology can only answer the exact question asked and intended, no more and no less. Once the astrologer and querent have committed to the wording (and meaning) of a question, they cannot go back and alter it. Nor can they expect to derive answers to afterthoughts or new questions about the matter from the original chart.

An example may help clarify some of these points. A friend of mine asked whether a ceremony honoring a certain film maker would take place in London. I cast the chart and gave a "no" answer. I was wrong. The symposium occurred as scheduled and the film maker received his accolades. Only when I reviewed the question with my friend did I learn that he really wanted to know if he would be able to travel to London to be present at the ceremony. The answer to that question was "No." He was unable to leave New York and spend time in London. I had not truly understood the question he was asking. The question I did answer was of no direct personal concern or responsibility to the querent. This may sound like I'm a sore loser or a Monday morning quarterback, but I prefer to think I got the wrong answer because I didn't follow the basic rules of horary technique.

This example also shows why the astrologer should write down his understanding of the question for later reference. In addition, the astrologer should also record his or her steps in locating the question and interpreting the chart. Failure to keep accurate records is a common mistake. Put it in writing and you will proceed step by step to a correct answer. You will also be able review your mistakes and add to your knowledge.

## A SOMEWHAT ATYPICAL HORARY QUESTION

Chart 8 illustrates a somewhat unusual yet legitimate horary question. My friend Don called long distance on Sunday evening, October 15, 1989, to ask the advice of the stars in finding a new secretary for his office in Maryland. It was 10:22 P.M. EDT when he asked, "Would you do a chart to tell me how to get an office secretary?"

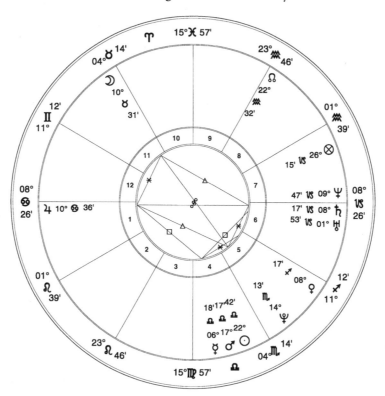

Chart 8: "Tell me how to get an office secretary"
October 15, 1989, 10:22 P.M. EDT, 73W01, 41N19  Koch Houses

I wrote down the question word for word along with the exact time. The rest of my week was busy, and I didn't have a chance to look at his chart until Thursday. Saturn on the 7th cusp warned that I might have difficulty reading the chart. It also showed my delay in looking at the chart.

I decided to approach the chart as if I were looking for a missing person. I located the secretary in the 6th house, which rules employees and those who serve. With Saturn and Uranus in the 6th, I knew she would be a serious, well-organized, and unusual person. There might also be some unexpected delay in finding her.

Sagittarius is on the 6th cusp, making Jupiter the primary ruler of the sought after secretary. Jupiter at 10° 36' Cancer in the first house is just two degrees away from conjoining the Ascendant at 8° 26' Cancer. To me this meant that within two days (by Tuesday) something definite would happen regarding the secretary. It was already Thursday, and I wanted to kick myself for not reading the chart sooner. I should have returned Don's call before Tuesday to alert him that something positive would happen on that date.

I was certain something good was coming because Jupiter is exalted in Cancer and strong in the first house. Since the Ascendant rules Don and Jupiter represents the secretary, she was coming to Don on Tuesday. With Jupiter in Cancer, I expected her to be fat. With Jupiter so near the Ascendant, I thought she would come from the east (Ascendant) and then north because Cancer is a northern sign. Jupiter can also symbolize people of foreign background or those who come from a distance.

Because Don wanted advice on how to find a secretary, I also looked to the benefic Venus and the Lot of Fortune. Venus was in the 5th house. This puzzled me. Would he find a secretary through a child? Pars Fortuna was in the 7th. I would advise him to ask his partners for a lead in finding this person. When I called Don on Thursday night, I told him my findings almost word for word as I have written them above. He chuckled and said, "I'm amazed. There's a woman we really want for the position and she fits the description."

The woman under consideration comes from New York City, east and north of Maryland at some distance. She heard about the job through Don's ex-wife and former "partner." She is planning to move to the Washington, D.C. area to attend law school (Jupiter), but she is looking for work because she is pregnant (5th house) and will not start school for a year. She is organized and serious (Saturn) and has many unusual interests (Uranus). She was supposed to be interviewed on Tuesday but had to reschedule. Don interviewed her on Friday, the day after our phone call. He was so impressed with her qualifications that he offered her a job, and she accepted it. He has been very pleased with her performance.

## What the Astrologer Does with the Question

By now you should have a good sense of what the astrologer does with a question that comes at a moment of pressing concern for the querent. By way of review, he or she has a threefold task. First, the astrologer must discuss the matter with the querent to be sure he or she knows what the querent is asking. This active process of understanding the question converts it into a matter for horary analysis. The astrologer should keep a written record of the question word for word, his understanding of it, and the steps he took to solve the puzzle.

The astrologer's second task is to locate or "focalize" the question in one of the twelve mundane houses. This process is akin to focusing the light of the Sun with a magnifying glass so it comes to an intense point of concentrated energy capable of starting a fire. The astrologer's skill at focalizing the matter separates the novice from the professional.

The final task of the astrologer is to analyze the focalized question through a step-by-step procedure to arrive at the answer. There are many systems in horary. I outlined my method in the previous chapter and will detail it throughout the text. Consistent use of a reasonable system is the secret of success.

For questions with yes or no answers, the astrologer has a fifty-fifty chance of being correct without casting the chart. The astrologer should tally his or her answers and their accuracy. If the accuracy rate is less than fifty percent, the astrologer is using an incorrect technique. He or she is either accepting inappropriate questions or using faulty rules for analysis. Any horary method should be at least as accurate as a weather forecast, which it so closely resembles. A score of eighty to ninety percent correct deserves an "A."

## AN EXAMPLE OF A FOCALIZED QUESTION

Chart 9 is an example of a focalized question. On Saturday evening, July 6, 1996, I could not find the hand-held remote controller for the TV in our bedroom. After a careful search

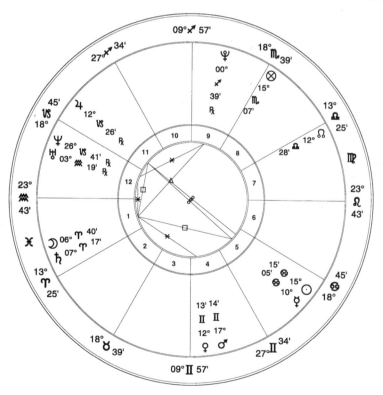

Chart 9: "Where is the missing TV clicker?"
July 6, 1996, 10:24 P.M. EDT, 73W04, 41N16 Regiomontanus Houses

of the room, I asked my wife and my two sons if they had seen it. They had not. I went to the computer to look at a horary chart (set for 10:24 P.M. EDT, 73W04, 41N16) for the question, "Where is the missing TV clicker?" Aquarius (sign of electronics) rises, as fits a question about a television. I am signified by Saturn (traditional ruler of Aquarius) and co-ruled by the Moon. The missing object is shown by Mars, which is both the ruler of the 2nd house (possessions) and the dispositor of Pars Fortuna (one's goods and fortune). Mars lies in Gemini in the angular 4th house. The horary rule is that when the significator in an angular house (1, 4, 7, or 10), the missing object is in the home and should be easy to find. Moon (me) will sextile Mars (the clicker) in 11 degrees from an angular house and cardinal sign. Will I get the clicker back in 11 minutes?

Moon and Sun are in mutual reception by sign/exaltation. The Sun rules the 7th (the spouse), so maybe my wife will find the clicker for me. As I was analyzing the chart, my wife entered the room with the TV clicker. Where did she find it? Under my twelve-year-old son Aaron's bed. The 5th house rules one's children. Gemini is on the cusp of both the 4th and 5th houses, connecting the missing TV clicker (Mars) in the 4th with my son in the 5th. Mercury (my son) is the dispositor of Mars (the clicker) in Gemini, and Mercury will conjoin the Sun (7th ruler, my wife) in 5 degrees in a cardinal sign, suggesting 5 minutes. Furthermore, the radical 4th is the 12th (bedroom) of the 5th (child) and, had I been a smart enough astrologer, I would have looked under Aaron's bed to find the clicker before my wife did (and she without the aid of astrology).

Why Aaron's bedroom and not my older son David's room? Perhaps because Aaron is an Aquarius, the sign ascending in the horary. David is a Taurus, ruled by Venus, which is approaching a conjunction with Mars, the clicker. If my wife had not found it, there is a good chance that David would have. Then again, my wife (7th, the Sun) is a Taurus (ruled by Venus) so it was doubly indicated in this chart that she would find the missing object.

# CHAPTER FOUR

# The Radical Chart and the Considerations Before Judgment

Radix is a word from the Latin, meaning root. Something is radical when it is basic, fundamental, and goes to the root of the issue. For obvious reasons, the astrologer must work with a radical chart to make accurate interpretations. In natal astrology, one can tell if a chart is radical by judging it against the personality and life of the native. In horary astrology, one measures radicality by the fit of the chart to the querent and the situation.

How can one tell if the horary chart is radical? Horary texts are replete with rules about how to make this judgment. There are so many rules, in fact, that the novice may fail to see the forest for the trees. The bottom line is that a chart is radical if and only if it fits the querent and the question at hand. The chart must describe the situation and tell the story.

A chart is never radical if you erect it for the wrong time and place. A quick way to gauge timing is to check the position of the Sun, which acts like an hour hand in the horoscope wheel. The Sun is at the Ascendant at Sunrise, at the MC at noon, at the Descendant at Sunset, and at the IC at midnight. A glance at the position of the Sun will tell you the time of day, which should match the time of the question.

To get a global sense of whether the chart fits the question, I look at the positions of the Sun, Moon, and Mercury. The Sun and the Moon are the major lights in the sky and symbolize those aspects of the chart that are most visible or apparent. The house and sign positions of the lights should have some obvious bearing on the question. The same holds true, to a lesser extent, of the houses ruled by the lights, that is, the houses with Leo or Cancer on the cusp. Finally, Mercury is the natural ruler of questions, and his position in the chart should reflect something about the matter. If these conditions hold true, you know you are getting warm and the chart is probably radical. Sara's question in Charts 2A and 2B illustrates how to use these global indicators to analyze the chart.

Once you have a general sense of the chart, consider the Ascendant and the planets signifying the querent to see whether their natures match those of the querent and the situation. The 1st house refers to the conditions surrounding the question and represents the person making the inquiry. The 1st house ruler and Almuten, the sign on its cusp, and any planets in the 1st describe the querent. The Moon is always a co-ruler of the querent and of the situation prompting the horary question. According to Bonatus, the planet from which the Moon most recently separated by aspect also co-rules the querent. Lilly tried this rule of Bonatus but found it did not work in his charts.

Benefics in the 1st house support a favorable answer if other factors in the chart concur. Jupiter and Venus are respectively the greater and lesser benefic planets. The Moon's North Node and the Part of Fortune are benefic points. When any of these fortunate planets or points are rising, good things are coming and the querent is in a positive frame of mind. The Moon's North Node in the 1st is favorable and implies that a lost item will be found (Lilly, CA, p. 468). Venus ascending brings favor and the finer things in life. Jupiter rising is fortunate and protects the querent regardless of the outcome of the question. I used this principle in Chart 2A to tell Sara she had come into good fortune.

Bonatus included the Sun and the Moon among the benefics. A rising Sun suggests that a matter of importance or some honor in store for the querent. Because the Moon rules change, Luna in the 1st house denotes fluctuations, uncertainty, and insecurity in the matter. The Moon rules the public, and some publicity may accompany the outcome. Mercury rules trivia, and a first house Mercury suggests a trivial matter that may involve documents, writing, or short trips.

Malefics in the 1st house support an unfavorable answer to the question if the rest of the chart supports a "no." Mars and Saturn are the traditional malefic planets, and the Moon's South Node is a malefic point. When a woman asked Lilly if she would ever have children, the Moon's North Node in the 1st house (physical body) was evidence of her inability to conceive (CA, p. 239). Retrograde Saturn in the1st house is particularly nasty and will mess up matters unless major positive factors intervene. According to Lilly, "If Saturn be in the Ascendant, especially retrograde, the matter of that question seldom or never comes to good." In an otherwise favorable chart, retrograde Saturn in the 1st will damage but not destroy the final outcome. Some modern astrologers include the outer planets Uranus, Neptune, and Pluto among the malefics. Since by temperament I usually expect the worst, I am among those who accept five malefic planets. Mars and Saturn are evil on a personal level, and the outer planets refer to forces beyond personal control.

Mars, the god of war, in the 1st house indicates strife or conflict for the querent. Saturn rising implies the question is a matter of serious concern and brings delays and limitations. With Saturn in the 1st, the querent may be depressed, worried, fearful, or in ill health. Uranus in the first suggests an anxious or agitated querent and brings the unexpected and unpredictable. With Uranus prominent, conditions are unstable and disruptions or separations occur. A 1st house Neptune shows a querent who is vague, confused, self-deceived, unrealistic, or close to tears. Pluto in the first signifies complications and profound changes over which the querent has little control.

Having looked at the Ascendant and the 1st house, next look for any of the classical considerations before judgment. Modern astrologers refer to these considerations as "strictures" because the older texts warn that the chart may not be "fit to be judged" when they are present. A stricture, however, does not automatically mean a non-radical chart. Strictures are of the nature of Saturn and often warn the astrologer to be discreet in answering the question. A stricture may describe the situation and confirm a reliable chart. Occasionally strictures signify that the querent did not ask the question he or she really intended, or somehow misrepresented the information. For example, a criminal might ask, "Will I be able to go abroad next week?" when he really wants to know if the police will catch him. In this case a stricture cautions the astrologer about the trick question.

## THE CLASSICAL CONSIDERATIONS BEFORE JUDGMENT

The history of astrology refers to many considerations before judgment, but traditional horary astrologers have paid special attention to four of them. When present, these considerations may imply it is not the proper moment to do an astrological analysis of the question. As Appleby puts it, "This form of divination is self-regulating."

Anyone familiar with psychological testing will be at home with the idea of considerations before judgment. For example, the Minnesota Multiphasic Personality Inventory (MMPI) is a true-false questionnaire designed to measure personality variables. It asks questions such as "I like mechanics magazines" or "I believe I am being plotted against." The questions are grouped into different scales that measure personality variables such as depression, anxiety, paranoia, and so on. In addition, the MMPI has "validity" scales to tell the psychologist whether the subject is lying or being too defensive. These validity scales tell whether the other test results reliably describe the person who took the test. Considerations before judgment in astrology are like the validity scales on the MMPI. They can tell us whether the chart fits the situation or is the result of improper timing or an insincere effort on the part of the client.

The idea of strictures grew out of the experience of astrologers. In the mid-1200s Guido Bonatus, whose writings Lilly carefully studied, had a flourishing practice of horary and electional astrology. Bonatus restricted his horary practice to "matters of honest importance," and refused to answer questions based on "trifling occasions, or light sudden emotions, much less on matters base or unlawful." He noticed that clients sometimes came to "tempt or ensnare" him, or to "put a trick on him." It was as if they had said to themselves, "Let us go to such an astrologer and see if he can tell us the truth or not." Sometimes the querent might "on a sudden think of something, and so ask, as it were, by-the-bye; wherein it is a thousand to one but mistakes happen" in interpreting the horary chart.

Guido asked himself, "How shall I know whether the querent came out of a solid intention, or only to try me?" To answer this question, he studied the charts of those who were trying to ensnare him, and in doing so, he discovered the idea of the non-radical Ascendant. Bonatus reported that "if the Ascendant then happened very near the end of one sign and the beginning of another, so that it seemed as between both, I said they did not ask seriously, or that they came to try me; and I have had many thereupon confessed what I said to be true and began to think that I knew more than before they believed."

Bonatus did not specify what he meant by the Ascendant being "very near the end of one sign and the beginning of another." He used his judgment and experience to decide. By

Lilly's time astrologers had specified the non-radical Ascendant to be between 27 degrees of one sign and three degrees of the next. This area of non-radicality spans six degrees—six out of thirty—which means that one in five charts will have a non-radical Ascendant.

I can only guess that this specificity came about because some anxious student pestered the teacher for a definitive rule to avoid thinking about the chart. Can't you imagine a student asking, "What about 26°59'59"? Is that a radical Ascendant?" Bonatus never intended it as a rule, only as a guideline, to help detect impostors. In the spirit of Bonatus, I view the horary strictures as guidelines and not absolutes. The following example shows a stricture that is not a stricture.

Chart 10 is for the question, "Will Mayor Ed Koch win the primary tomorrow in New York City?" On September 11, 1989, which was Monday, a Moon day, I was listening to the radio on the way to work. The newscaster reported that it was the beginning of the countdown for the Democratic primary race between Ed Koch and David Dinkins. The race was too close to call. I noted the time to be 7:34 A.M. EDT. When I got home that evening, I put up the chart on the computer and told my wife that the incumbent mayor Koch was going to lose.

The most striking feature of the chart is the "non-radical" Ascendant with zero degrees rising. How non-radical can you get? Bonatus is on target because I did "on a sudden think of something, and so ask, as it were, by-the-bye." But simply because I asked "by-the-bye," am I not allowed to read the chart? I was sincere in asking the question. Shouldn't the chart contain a valid answer?

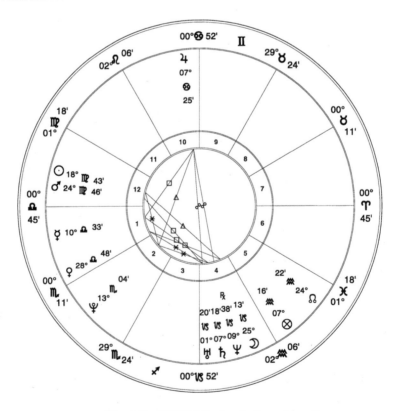

Chart 10  "Will Ed Koch win the primary?
September 11, 1989, 7:34 A.M. EDT, 73W01, 41N19  Koch Houses

Bonatus does not mention it, but I have found that a non-radical Ascendant often means the matter is none of the querent's business. In this case, it is none of my concern whether Koch or Dinkins wins the primary. I am simply curious and have no direct involvement or responsibility in the matter. Perhaps the non-radical Ascendant is nature's way of telling me to mind my own business—"it's not nice to fool with mother nature."

Marc Edmund Jones taught that the chart will contain a reliable answer if the consideration before judgment describes some fundamental aspect of the situation. Here 0° Libra rising fits exactly the beginning of the countdown in a race that is evenly balanced (Libra) and too close to call. For the astrologer who uses his or her brain rather than rote memorization, the chart is radical after all.

In addition, the Ascendant describes the state of the querent—me in this case. Zero degrees rising fits my state of mind, exactly as Bonatus described it. I had heard the news broadcast and "on a sudden" thought of asking the horary question a split second later. The matter had no time to gestate in my mind. In other words, 0° ascending concords with my question, which came suddenly into existence and had no time to develop before I popped the horary question. That is a radical Ascendant!

In the first edition of this text, I followed the method of Joan McEvers and assigned Aries on the 7th house cusp and Mars to Mayor Koch. According to March and McEvers (Vol. IV, p. 5, 1994): "If the question pertains to another person, especially by name, that individual is represented by the 7th house." Libra on the 1st cusp and Venus are the significators of his opponent Dinkins. I assumed that whichever significator was stronger would show who would win the primary. Mars (Mayor Koch) is weak because he is cadent (the 12th house is Koch's 6th house), combust (within 8 1/2 degrees of the Sun), and in the same degree as the Moon's Mean Nodes. Planets in nodal degree suggest a fatality or crisis in the matter. Koch will probably lose the primary. Venus (Dinkins) is strong because she is angular (1st house) and dignified in her own sign, Libra. Dinkins is stronger than Koch and will probably win. Cardinal angles imply a quick resolution, and it was a given that we would know the outcome within twenty-four hours.

Since writing the first edition of this text, I have become more interested in traditional methods and would now read this chart in a more classical manner. The person in power is shown by the 10th house of sovereigns. Since Cancer rules the 10th and Jupiter lies therein, both the Moon and Jupiter represent Mayor Koch. His opponent occupies the opposite 4th house with its Capricorn cusp and with Uranus, Saturn, Neptune, and the Moon within. Dinkins' primary significator is Saturn since the Moon already rules Koch and the outer planets are not used as primary significators in traditional horary.

If the Moon represents Koch, it is of little help because the Moon in this chart has no essential dignity (is peregrine). The Moon is also in Capricorn, the sign of its detriment. Since Capricorn rules Dinkins' cusp, Koch is at the mercy of Dinkins. The Moon's final aspect is a square to Venus, which rules the radical 1st house, which is the end-of-the-matter 4th house of Koch. This Moon/Venus square suggests defeat.

If Jupiter represents Koch, it is a close race. Jupiter is strong in Cancer where it is exalted and in the angular 10th house. In fact, according to Lilly's point system, Jupiter is the strongest planet in this chart. Saturn, however, is also strong, lying in Capricorn which it rules and in the angular 4th house. Saturn is the dispositor of the Part of Fortune and forms a favorable semi-sextile with Pars Fortuna. Of special importance is the fact that Saturn is stationary direct, and Saturn has made its station almost exactly opposite Jupiter. Stationary planets are extremely powerful, especially when they are turning direct, and this fact probably gives Dinkins the edge. Jupiter (Koch) is in partile opposition (within 17' of exact) to the greater malefic Saturn and is applying to an opposition of Neptune, the modern planet of dissolution. On Tuesday, September 12, 1989, Dinkins won the primary.

## THE FIRST CONSIDERATION: A NON-RADICAL ASCENDANT

Having shown that a non-radical Ascendant is not always non-radical, I will now present the party line on the non-radical Ascendant. The basic principle according to Jones is this: "If the Ascendant of a chart lies in the first or last three degrees of a zodiacal sign, the matter at issue is taken as not centered thoroughly enough in one given area of experience to afford a reliable judgment." In other words, more than twenty-seven degrees of one sign and less than three degrees of the next rising is an "index to the proper maturity of the inquiry." In the interest of clarity, I will break the non-radical Ascendant into two parts as follows.

### Less Than Three Degrees Rising

Traditionally less than three degrees of a sign on the Ascendant means the question is premature and cannot be answered with certainty. According to Zain, "the question is undergoing gestation and in not completely formed." The querent may need more information, or matters may not have progressed enough to determine the outcome. Further developments may make the inquiry irrelevant. If new information fundamentally changes the situation, the querent may ask a second time. Another possibility is that a more basic question is on the querent's mind, and careful interviewing of the querent will reveal a deeper issue worthy of horary analysis. Finally, for the paranoid among us, the querent may be trying to trick or ensnare us with the inquiry.

According to Jones, zero to three degrees rising signifies a "premature matter, or something as yet without definite form." Jones continues that sometimes the non-radical Ascendant "will prove to be an accurate description of the issue or situation which is the basis of the inquiry." For example, the first three degrees may signify concern over "some spontaneous notion" or "an enterprise just about to be launched." In Chart 10 my question was a spontaneous notion about the Democratic primary, an enterprise about to be launched the following day.

### More than Twenty-Seven Degrees Rising

If more than twenty-seven degrees of a sign rise on the Ascendant, the question may be obsolete or out of date. Matters may have gone too far for the querent to affect the outcome. The inquirer may be too late in asking because the matter has already been decided, and there may be nothing the querent can do about it. According to Zain, "The question as formulated has been outgrown by new conditions, and these as yet have not been fully grasped by the unconscious mind." Jones says the last three degrees ascending suggest a "proposition long neglected, or a potentiality which has thinned out and so lost its vitality." On the other hand, Jones feels this stricture can accurately describe "some long-delayed or drawn-out affair, or a matter long under consideration." If so, the chart is radical.

With late degrees rising, the querent may have already asked everyone under the Sun and may finally be asking the astrologer simply to confirm a course of action already undertaken. For example, a young woman might ask if she should marry her boyfriend after they have been secretly wed. Sometimes the querent is late in asking the question because he or she has consulted another astrologer or advisor and been disappointed with the results. Late degrees may also denote an insincere client who is trying to trick the astrologer.

Note that Jacobson regards twenty-nine degrees of any sign as a critical degree or crisis point showing impatience to move into the next sign or a new area of experience. According to Jacobson, a significator at twenty-nine degrees is "at the end of his rope or patience: discouraged." In addition, as Dorotheus pointed out, the malefic planets Mars and Saturn rule the terms at the ends of signs and render the final degrees unfortunate.

Lilly reported several exceptions to the rule of the non-radical Ascendant. He said if the first or second degrees of a sign ascend, you could still judge the chart if "the querent be very young, and his corporature, complexion, and moles or scars on his body, agree with the quality of the signs ascending." If twenty-seven or more degrees rise, "It is not safe to give judgment, except the querent be in years corresponding to the number of degrees ascending, or unless the figure be set upon a time certain, viz. any event happening, such as a man went away or fled at such a time precisely; here you may judge, because it is no propounded question."

Lilly had a fascination with the moles and scars on people's bodies and used them to impress his clients and to judge whether a chart was radical. He gave a detailed description of all the marks on his own body in discussing the house of Mr. B and seemed to enjoy telling his clients about the most intimate parts of their anatomy according to the stars. Who knows how far he went with this line of investigation? He did marry his first employer's widow, after all.

One gets the impression from *Christian Astrology* that William Lilly used the chart's description of the querent as his fundamental method to test the radicality of the chart. To describe the querent, Lilly considered the following factors: the sign ascending and the ruler of the Ascendant, the Moon and its sign, any planets in the 1st house, and any planets aspecting either the Ascendant or the Moon. He also considered the sign containing the Ascendant ruler and any 1st house planets, the dispositors of these planets, and the terms of the zodiac in which the planets fell. Fortunately, Just Us & Associates publishes Lilly's method of physical descriptions in a handy booklet titled *A Handbook of Physical Descriptions* by Adrienne Warren.

Some horary astrologers have noted a special exception to the non-radical Ascendant stricture, namely, when a natal planet of the querent is at the exact degree and minute of the Ascendant in the horary chart. In this case, they consider the question to be of special importance to the querent. All these exceptions make the same point. If the stricture describes the querent and the situation, the chart is radical and contains an answer to the horary question. Otherwise, the stricture suggests an insincere or trivial question, and the astrologer should proceed with caution.

Chart 11 illustrates some of the above ideas. On Friday, 7/21/89, a Venus day, at 8:20 A.M. EDT, at 72W50/41N27, I asked, "Should I buy the computerized test?" The question referred to a computer program that I had already ordered. The advertising for the program said it was a psychological test like the MMPI that could run from an IBM computer and be used with clients in the office. The ad promised that the program was as good as the MMPI in clinical practice for only a fraction of the cost. This last statement caused me to have some doubt about my order and I decided to ask a horary question.

We see immediately in Chart 11 that 29° 44' of Leo is rising—a non-radical Ascendant. The question is obsolete because I have already placed the order and it's too late to affect the outcome. I am looking for a confirmation of a decision already made. In a sense it's a trick question because I asked "Should I buy?" rather than "Should I have bought?" Twenty-nine is a critical and unfortunate degree, implying impatience, a crisis, and disappointment. In the fixed sign Leo with a fixed cross in the chart, things are entrenched and will be hard to alter. Now I am thinking I made a bad decision.

There is no consensus about certain modern astrological rulerships. I use the 3rd house to rule computers and computer programs because I view them as vehicles of thought and communication. I regard Mercury (communication) and Uranus (modern gadgets) to be

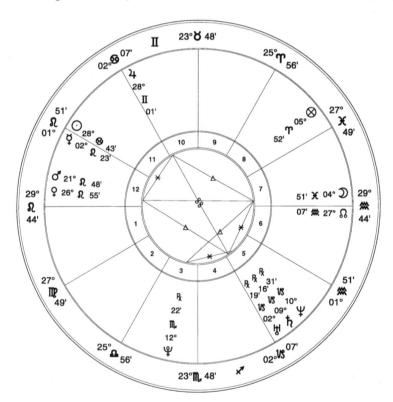

Chart 11: "Should I buy the computerized test?
July 21, 1989, 8:20 A.M. EDT, 72W50, 41N27  Koch Houses

natural rulers of computer-related items. In Chart 11, 25° 56' Libra on the 3rd house cusp makes Venus the ruler of the computer program. Pluto retrograde at 12° 20' Scorpio in the 3rd house is a co-ruler. I am now disturbed to see the 3rd house cusp and the co-ruler Pluto in the Via Combusta (see below). My computer program is awash in the venom of the Scorpion, and I am likely to feel the sting.

Venus, primary ruler of the computer program, occupies the 12th house of sorrow and self-undoing. She is in the company of Mercury (natural ruler of computer programs) and Mars (dispositor of co-ruler Pluto, and of the Lot of Fortune). My lot will be sorrow and disappointment. Uranus, the other co-ruler of the computer program, is retrograde in the fifth house of fun, and besieged between venomous Pluto and depriving Saturn. The matter will be no fun for me.

Finally, with Leo on the Ascendant, my primary ruler is the Sun. Here the Sun makes no aspects and is void of course (see below), showing that I have made an ineffectual decision. No aspects, no action. I should not have bought the computer program.

My co-ruler, the Moon at 4° 50' Pisces, occupies the 7th house of the other person, the seller of the software. I am at the seller's mercy. The Moon will trine retrograde Pluto in the 3rd (the computer program), and then quincunx Mars, ruler of the 4th house end-of-the-matter, and Venus, ruler of the software. The trine would ordinarily be helpful but Pluto is ineffectual in the Via Combusta. The two quincunxes imply adjustments and reorganization. Things will not go smoothly.

What was the outcome? The program arrived without the advertised diskette for my portable computer. I wrote to the company for a replacement. When that arrived, it did not work. To this date I have never been able to get the program to function on my portable computer. I did, however, manage to get a working copy from the diskette onto the office computer. I tried the test with a new patient at the clinic. His test results said he was suffering from a mild depression. The test report was dangerously misleading because that same evening the patient became seriously suicidal and needed hospitalization. His depression was severe; he did not respond to medication, and eventually required electro-convulsive therapy. As Jones would say, the electric current caused a reshuffling in the psychological aggregation of the self and fit the symbolism of the Via Combusta. Needless to say, I also felt the scorpion's sting and never used the computer program again.

## The Second Consideration: The Void of Course Moon or Significator

There is a disagreement among horary astrologers about the definition of "void of course." Modern astrologers regard the Moon (or a planet) as void of course when it will not complete (perfect) any major Ptolemaic aspects before leaving its sign. There are only five major or Ptolemaic aspects: the conjunction, sextile, square, trine, and opposition.

This modern definition is similar to the Dariot's sixteenth-century explanation: "Void or without course is when a planet doth not apply to any other during the time that he tarrieth in that sign and then he is said to have his course and motion void." The modern definition is more stringent because it requires that a void planet not perfect (complete) an aspect while it tarries in a sign, whereas Dariot only requires that the void planet not apply to any other while it remains in a sign. In his practice Gadbury, a contemporary of Lilly, seemed to use the modern definition and called the Moon void of course if she was applying to aspect but had to change signs to perfect the application.

British astrologer Sue Ward has shown that Lilly used yet another definition of void of course. According to Lilly (CA, p.112), "A planet is void of course, when he is separated from a planet, nor doth forthwith [immediately, at once], during his being in that sign, apply to any other." Notice that Lilly writes "apply" rather than "perfect" an aspect. In a similar vein, the classical astrologer Firmicus Maternus refers to the void of course planet as traveling in an aspect vacuum, meaning that it is currently traveling devoid of applying to any major aspect.

A careful study of Lilly's idea will show that it differs significantly from the modern definition of void of course. Lilly considered a planet to be "separated" from another when the two planets had already completed (perfected) an aspect and they were at least six minutes beyond being exactly in aspect. (He allowed up to sixteen minutes of arc for the Sun and the Moon.) Two planets are "applying" to one another when they are within orb of forming an exact aspect and are approaching that aspect. Rephrasing Lilly's definition, we see that a planet or the Moon is void of course whenever it has separated from a planet with which it had been in aspect and is not within orb of applying to any Ptolemaic aspect with another planet.

The void of course state means, in Lilly's usage, not within orb of applying to a major aspect with another planet. Being void can occur anywhere in a sign, and the void planet can then advance to become within orb of a major aspect before leaving the sign. A planet or the Moon at the end of a sign will not be void of course if it is within orb of a major aspect that will become exact when it moves to the next sign. Lilly, for example, reports the question of a woman who asked "when her husband, who is imprisoned, shall be delivered" (Lilly, CA p. 471). In the chart for this inquiry, the Moon is at 29° 10' Aquarius, but is not void because she is within orb of applying to a sextile with Saturn at 0° 36' Taurus. This sextile will become exact when the Moon leaves Aquarius, enters the next sign, and reaches 0° 36' Pisces. In this example, the Moon would be considered void using the modern definition of the term.

Another example from *Christian Astrology*, "If the Presbytery shall stand?" (Chart 12) will further clarify Lilly's definition. On p.439, Lilly writes: "We have the Moon [at 13 ° Libra] separating from Venus [at 9° Aries] in the eighth, then going to be *vacua cursus* [void of course], afterwards she squares with Mars [at 25° Cancer], then with Jupiter [at 28° Cancer]" (CA, p. 440). The distance from the Moon to Mars is 25° minus 13°, or 12°, which is out of classical orb for a Moon-Mars square. The most generous traditional orb for a Moon-Mars aspect is 10 degrees. Hence the Moon is void of course for a little while between 13° and 15° of Libra because she is not within orb of applying to any major Ptolemaic aspect until she reaches 15° Libra, where she is within orb of squaring Mars.

There is no doubt about what Lilly meant, because he repeats himself on p. 442: "The Moon, in plain language, (after a little being void of course), runs hastily to the square of Mars and Jupiter; intimating, the Commonality will defraud the expectation of the Clergy, and so strongly oppose them, that the end thereof shall wholly delude the expectation of

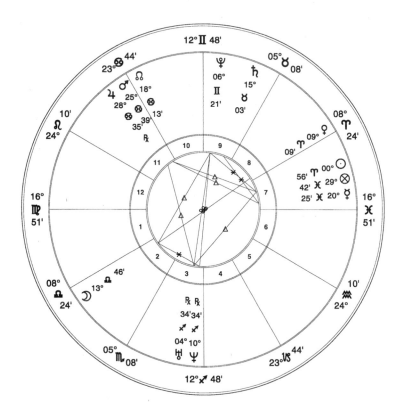

Chart 12: "If the Presbytery shall stand?"
March 21, 1647, 4:50 P.M. GMT, 00W10, 51N30  Regiomontanus Houses

the Clergy." In this example, the Moon went a little void of course before squaring Mars (strife) and Jupiter (ruler of end-of-the-matter 4th house), and Lilly used the brief void period and the aspects the Moon applied to thereafter to form his interpretation.

Lilly said that "all manner of matters go hardly on (except the principal significators be very strong) when the Moon is void of course; yet sometimes she performs if void of course, if in Taurus, Cancer, Sagittarius, or Pisces." Apparently the Moon does well in her own sign Cancer, in her exaltation sign Taurus, and in the signs of the great benefic Jupiter, that is, Sagittarius and Pisces. According to Guido Bonatus, if the Moon "be in Cancer, Taurus, Sagittarius, or Pisces, it signifies good in the matter, although she be joined to the Infortunes and not to the Fortunes; nor does she, being void of course, prejudice so much in those places as elsewhere, provided she be not Combust, for then they will advantage her little or nothing." The Moon is combust when too close to the Sun.

Bonatus was bleak in describing the void of course Moon. To him, the void of course Moon "signifies an impediment to the thing in question, it will not come to a good end; but the querent shall be forced to desist with shame and loss." Or if it is accomplished it shall be with "much labor, sorrow, and trouble, unless the Lord of the Ascendant or significator of the thing, shall be in very good condition, and then it may be hindered, but not wholly frustrated." On the other hand, the void of course Moon is a "good time for drinking, bathing, feasting, etc., and to use ointment for the taking away of hair, especially if she be in Scorpio." Makers of depilatories, take note.

One astrological tradition holds that a void of course Moon in Gemini, Scorpio, or Capricorn (the signs opposite Sagittarius, Taurus, and Cancer) is an especially negative influence that invalidates the chart. Regarding the void of course Moon, Lilly wrote, "You shall seldom see a business go handsomely forward when she is so." Another meaning of a void of course Moon is that nothing will occur, or nothing will come of the matter. Zain writes that a void of course Moon means "the matter is seldom brought to maturity." The Moon rules the changes of daily life—if it makes no major aspects there will be no significant changes. The Moon rules function and when it makes no aspects nothing functions. When the Moon is void of course, things remain static in the situation that gave rise to the horary question. Circumstances change only when the Moon leaves the "aspect vacuum" and again applies to a major aspect with another planet.

Some horary astrologers, like Ivy Jacobson and Alphee Lavoie, feel that the void of course Moon means the querent has nothing to worry about. Lavoie says that with a void of course Moon often "the conclusion has already manifested ... the querent has the answers, knows the outcome, but doesn't want to accept things the way they are. So he phones, hoping that the astrologer will tell him what he wants to hear, thus delaying in confronting the issue." In this case the void of course Moon represents the querent's idle musings and the "what if" syndrome.

Sometimes a question asked under a void of course Moon is moot in the legal sense, hypothetical, or of no real concern to the querent. It may be "nothing to worry about" because there is nothing the querent can do about the matter. The circumstances prompting the question may change unexpectedly, or the question may be about a situation that, unknown to the querent, no longer exists.

Jones felt the void of course Moon showed the querent was "playing with life" or "toying with reality" so that it would be "extraordinarily difficult to help him." According to Jones, "unless this planet makes a vital aspect before leaving the sign in which it is found, the querent or the key person in the inquiry is revealed as not completely or 'honestly' participating in the affair at hand."

The void of course Moon is not a completely negative influence. If the chart otherwise strongly indicates an event, it may still occur but with some delay or difficulty. If the question is about a lost object or person, the void of course Moon often suggests that the person or object will return.

When significators are void of course, they have a similar meaning. The person signified will be ineffectual in the matter.

### The Third Consideration: Saturn in 7th, or the 7th Cusp or Its Ruler Afflicted

The 7th house represents any personal consultant, lawyer, physician, or person hired to advise the querent. In horary practice the 7th house represents the astrologer who is trying to answer the question. Saturn in the 7th, or the 7th cusp or its ruler afflicted, suggests that the astrologer may have difficulty interpreting the chart. He or she may make mistakes in calculation or judgment. Zain warns that when the 7th house is "much afflicted it is often better not to give judgment; for it shows dissatisfaction with the judgment given by the Astrologer and possible trouble for him."

Saturn rules delays, and his presence in the 7th house suggests the astrologer may suffer a delay, sometimes of years, in understanding the chart. A personal blind spot may impair the astrologer's ability to give an objective reading. Since Saturn symbolizes time, the astrologer's timing may be off. An emotionally cold planet, Saturn may show that the astrologer's rapport with the querent is poor. The astrologer may be insensitive to the emotional state of the querent. According to Lilly, "Saturn in the 7th either corrupts the judgment of the astrologer, or is a sign the matter propounded will come from one misfortune to another." Similarly, Lilly reports that if "the lord of the 7th unfortunate, or in his fall, or in terms of the infortune, the artist shall scare give a solid judgment." He adds that when the 7th cusp is afflicted or the 7th ruler is retrograde or impeded in a question that does not involve the 7th house, then "the judgment of the astrologer will give small content."

Jacobson feels that a 7th house Pluto, ruler of complications, acts like Saturn in the 7th.

## The Fourth Consideration: Moon in the Via Combusta

This is perhaps the least understood of the four classical considerations, and many astrologers simply ignore it. Lilly regarded the Via Combusta as the section of the zodiac from 15° Libra to 15° Scorpio. In Latin, *Via Combusta* means "the burned path" or "the fiery way." In ancient times the Via Combusta corresponded to the path of the Sun containing the constellation Scorpio and malefic fixed stars of the nature of Mars (fire) and Saturn (hindrance). Because of precession, these fixed stars have now advanced about thirty degrees in the tropical zodiac from the time of Ptolemy. Some astrologers argue that because these malefic stars no longer occupy the burning way, we should no longer use this consideration in modern astrology.

In the first century, Dorotheus wrote that the Moon in the "burned path" was "corrupted" and ineffectual. He quoted ancient Babylonian and Egyptian sources as referring to the Via Combusta as the "path which the learned call the burned path [the burned path is the middle of the equator, which is Libra and Scorpio]" meaning the region from mid-Libra to mid-Scorpio. Interestingly, Dariot's 1583 text defines the "burnt way" as the area "from the 13th degree of Libra unto the 9th degree of Scorpio."

There remains the puzzle of how the Via Combusta became the region from 15° Libra to 15° Scorpio. My guess is that the "learned" ancient astrologers used Libra and Scorpio because of the burning of the harvest Moon, the dangerous fixed stars in those signs, and the malefic symbolism of Scorpio. In addition, early astrology was purely observational, and unfortunate events must have occurred predictably when the Moon was in the Via Combusta.

Modern astrologers may not appreciate that the ancient sign Scorpio originally spanned what we now call Libra and Scorpio. The claws of the scorpion occupied Libra, and the body of the scorpion rested in Scorpio. Manilius wrote: "When autumn's Claws begin to rise, blessed is he that is born under the equilibrium of the Balance." The modern sign Libra (the balance) received its name because it marked the autumnal equinox, which split the day into evenly balanced twelve-hour parts. The original Greek name for Libra was

*Chelae*, the Claws of Scorpio. Ptolemy used both names, Chelae (claws), and Libra (yoke or balance), to refer to this sign.

Realizing that anyone caught in the claws of the scorpion is not free, the Greek astrologer Stephanus (A.D. 621) commented that "rising Libra brings servitude to all men." Stephanus was making a pun on the Greek word for Libra which means "yoke." Although the astrological glyph for Libra looks like the scales of justice, it originally depicted a yoke of the sort put around the necks of oxen that draw plows through the field. The little loop on top of Libra's glyph is the hole for the head of the ox. The Greeks had yet another yoke for people to put over their necks and shoulders to carry a pair of buckets, one at either end. The buckets hanging from the human yoke resembled the scales in the glyph of Libra.

Libra came to symbolize marriage because the husband and wife are joined together in the "yoke" of matrimony. Using the Scorpionic symbolism of Libra, cynical astrological misogynists may see marriage as the wife catching the husband in her claws. Only in modern times is marriage seen as the egalitarian relationship symbolized by the balanced scale of Libra. In English the word *yokefellow* still refers to a partner, an associate, or a spouse (yokemate).

The claws of the Scorpion filled the section of sky beginning at 15° of Libra. The mouth of the Scorpion began at the end of Libra, and the Scorpion's body extended to about 15°. The tail of the scorpion occupied the remainder of his sign. The Via Combusta corresponds to the claws and body of the ancient sign Scorpio and has the nature of Mars—god of fire, injury, war, and death. At the center of the Via Combusta is the mouth of the scorpion. A planet passing through the Via Combusta is caught in the Scorpion's claws and stung by its fiery venom—not a fortunate place to be. A significator so placed is ineffective to act in the querent's behalf. Only a sadist would enjoy the sting of the scorpion.

Jones understood this negative Scorpionic symbolism when he wrote that the "meaning of the Moon in the Via Combusta is an unsettled state of affairs that resists judgment, and that involves a perverse self-satisfaction in the confusion." According to Jones, the burning way represents a "chaotic reshuffle in the psychological aggregation of self, or a species of cosmic fluctuation." Perverse self-satisfaction and chaotic reshuffle are good key words for this region of the zodiac.

As usual, Jones tells us when we are able to read a chart with a Via Combust Moon. If the horary question is "an attempt to put such a chaotic condition to advantage, or to make some use of a baffling re-alignment in the general situation," then the chart can be read as radical. In the case of the computerized test above, the seizure (a chaotic electrical discharge in the brain) which relieves profound depression is "an attempt to put a chaotic condition to advantage."

For several years Barbara Watters tried to ignore the Via Combust Moon, but she found that it acted consistently like the Moon conjunct Uranus, and she went back to observing the stricture. In Watters' experience, events took sudden, unpredictable, and contrary turns when the Moon was in contact with the ancient Scorpion. She found that the Via Combust Moon signified events related to war, violence, accidents, disasters, the sudden death of persons controlling the question, and the destruction of the property asked about. Sounds a lot like Scorpio and the 8th house, doesn't it?

In a similar vein, Sue Ward pointed out that the Moon in the Via Combusta often occurs in charts that deal with illness, death, fear, and issues like imprisonment or hidden matters. For example, in chart 13, Lilly's chart about "Whether man or wife shall die first?" (CA, p. 415) the Moon is Via Combust at 8° Scorpio in the radical 2nd house (the 8th of the 7th), suggesting that the wife is ill and approaching death. In addition to the Moon being Via Combust, the malefic Saturn is in his fall in Aries in the 7th of the wife. Seventh ruler Mars (the wife) occupies the cadent 9th in Gemini. Mercury, the dispositor of Mars, rules the unfortunate radical 12th (which is the 6th of illness of the 7th), and Mercury is debilitated by being retrograde and in his fall in Pisces.

In chart 14, Lilly's chart about "If bewitched?" (CA, p. 468) the Moon is Via Combust at 6° Scorpio and the querent was ill, fearful of being bewitched, and suffering from a vene-real disease and possible damage to his reputation. Lilly regarded bewitching to be a 12th house matter and looked to the ruler of the 12th to answer the question. In this chart Saturn occupies the 12th and the Moon is about to oppose Saturn, raising the possibility of witchcraft. Lilly decided that the querent was not bewitched because Mercury, which rules the querent with Gemini rising, is trine Jupiter, the greater benefic, and is trine Mars, the ruler of the 12th. In addition, Saturn is far from the Ascendant (the querent) and Venus, the lesser benefic, also occupies the 12th. Furthermore, after leaving the Via Combusta and opposing Saturn, the Moon will trine Mercury (the querent) which lies "above the earth, ascending towards the Meridian" (MC).

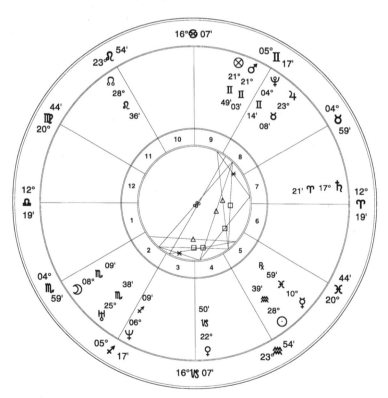

Chart 13: "Whether man or wife shall die first?"
February 16, 1645, 9:22 P.M. GMT, 00W10, 51N30 Regiomontanus Houses

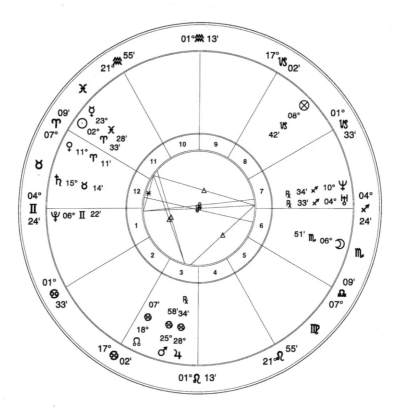

Chart 14: "If bewitched?"
March 23, 1647, 8:12 A.M. GMT, 00W10, 51N30  Regiomontanus Houses

Some astrologers believe that they should not read the chart when the Moon is in the Via Combusta because things will not work as planned. Fortunately, Spica, the most benefic fixed star, is passing through the Via Combusta area. The star Spica, at 23° 50' Libra in the year 2000, offers an oasis of good fortune in an otherwise parched and burning land. Like the other fixed stars, Spica moves slowly forward in the tropical zodiac about one degree every seventy-two years. Any planet conjunct Spica within one degree orb participates in its success and good fortune.

According to Ptolemy, Spica has a nature "like that of Venus and, in a less degree, that of Mars." You might wonder how a Martian fixed star can be so helpful. In this case, the Mars side of Spica makes her at home in the body of the Scorpion so the Venus side can be truly gracious. As Bonatus puts it, "Venus takes off the fury of Mars," and here Spica takes off the fury of the burning way. She soothes the sting of the scorpion.

## USING PLANETARY HOURS TO DETERMINE WHETHER A CHART IS RADICAL

Following tradition, William Lilly noted the planetary hour and whether its ruler harmonized with the horary Ascendant. According to the ancients, for a horary chart to be valid, the planet that rules the hour should agree with the horary Ascendant in one of three ways:

- The same planet should rule both the hour and the sign ascending,

- The same planet should rule both the hour and the triplicity of the sign ascending, or

- The planets that rule the hour and the Ascendant should be of the same nature (e.g., hot and dry, cold and moist, etc.).

Some traditional astrologers also accept a chart as radical if the Moon closely aspects the planet ruling the hour, or if the hour ruler closely aspects the 1st cusp (Ascendant).

Irish horary astrologer Maurice McCann reviewed Lilly's charts in *Christian Astrology* and found that ten of Lilly's horary charts did not meet the classical criterion that the planetary hour ruler accords with the Ascendant in one of the three ways listed above. In other words, about a third of the time Lilly's horary charts in *Christian Astrology* did not fulfill these criteria. McCann's data suggest that Lilly was not particularly concerned about planetary hour agreement in judging a chart.

Horary astrologer Sue Ward, one of the editors of *The Horary Practitioner*, objected to McCann's findings by pointing out the existence of mitigating factors in eight of these ten "non-radical" charts. Such factors included the following: the hour ruler might be angular, might lie in the house of the quesited, might be the natural or accidental ruler of the matter, or might be trine the Ascendant or trine the ruler of the triplicity. Taking these extenuating factors into consideration, Sue Ward showed that only two charts (CA, p. 238 and p. 395) did not meet the planetary hour criteria for being radical.

Interestingly, both of the charts that Sue Ward felt did not meet the planetary hour criteria are cast twelve years apart (a Jupiter return) with Jupiter at 5° Leo and ruling the hour of the question. In Lilly's chart on p. 238 (CA, "If the querent should ever have children?"), the Moon lies at the end of Virgo and is within orb of a sextile to Jupiter. In Lilly's chart on p. 395 (CA, "Money lost, who stole it?"), Jupiter at 5° Leo is applying to a square of the 8° Scorpio Ascendant in signs of long ascension. Lilly believed that squares in signs of long ascension got stretched out and acted like trines. In addition, both the hour ruler Jupiter and the Ascendant ruler Mars occupy Leo in this chart. From these two examples, it appears that Lilly regarded the Moon sextile the hour ruler, and the hour ruler square the Ascendant in signs of long ascension, as further mitigating factors. If so, all of Lilly's horary charts show some type of agreement between the planetary hour ruler and the Ascendant.

Before moving on the other considerations before judgment, let's look more closely at Lilly's chart from p. 395. See Chart 15. The question is asked on a Moon day during a Jupiter hour.

To find the thief Lilly notes the location of the peregrine planets, that is, planets that have no essential dignity, which in this chart are the Sun, Moon, Mercury, and Jupiter. Lilly's experience had shown him that a peregrine planet in the 1st house most commonly signifies the thief. If there is no peregrine planet ascending, Lilly next looked for peregrine planets in the 10th, 7th, 4th, and finally the 2nd house, in that order for the thief. In this chart only Mercury is both peregrine and occupies an angle (the 7th house). Mercury thus signifies the thief. Mercury has just completed a square to Ascendant ruler Mars, this square symbolizing the recently completed theft.

Lilly went on to describe the thief as fifteen to sixteen years old and male, because Mercury squares Mars and conjoins Saturn— both masculine planets. Saturn rules the 3rd and

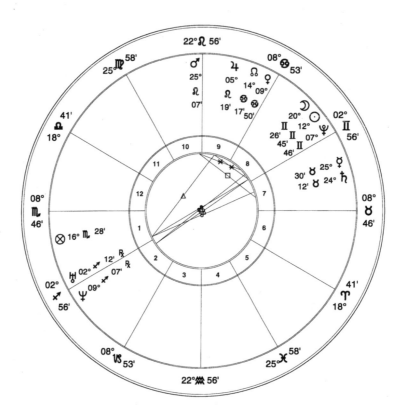

Chart 15: "Money lost, who stole it?"
June 3, 1647, 4:54 P.M. GMT, 00W10, 51N30  Regiomontanus Houses

4th houses, indicating to Lilly that the boy is a neighbor's child. The money is represented by 2nd house ruler Jupiter and by Mars, the dispositor of Pars Fortuna. The querent's co-ruler, the Moon, will sextile Mars within four degrees. From this Lilly concluded that the querent would get his money back within four days (days because Mars is angular, close to the MC, and both Moon and Mars are fast in motion). Apparently the querent "believed not a word I said," but Lilly stuck to his guns and, sure enough, the money returned three days later.

Although Lilly does not mention it, there is other evidence in this chart for the return of the money. The same planet Mars rules both the querent (Scorpio rising) and the Part of Fortune (the money). Jupiter rules the 2nd house of the querent's money and will square the Ascendant (the querent) in about three degrees in signs of long ascension, suggesting that the money will return in three days because in classical horary astrology a square in signs of long ascension behaves like a trine.

## OTHER CONSIDERATIONS PRIOR TO JUDGMENT

Lilly listed several other considerations before judgment which later astrologers did not elevate to the level of the four classical strictures. Lilly took these rules from Guido Bonatus and from Dorotheus of Sidon. I will list the key ones here for easy reference.

## The Moon in late degrees of a sign, especially Gemini, Scorpio, and Capricorn.

Dorotheus points out that the late degrees of the signs are the terms of Mars or Saturn, and the Moon is not at home with either of the malefics. Gemini is the unfortunate 12th house of the Moon's own sign Cancer. Capricorn, the sign of Saturn and detriment of the Moon, is the opposing 7th house of Cancer. Scorpio, the home of lecherous Mars, is a bad place for a virtuous Moon to hang out.

## "If the Lord of the Ascendant be combust, neither the question propounded will take, nor the querent be regulated."

When the querent's significator is near the Sun (combust), the matter will not come to pass, and the querent will be unhappy with the astrologer's judgment. Olivia Barclay warns that a combust Ascendant ruler may mean the astrologer has been misinformed or given too little information.

## "When the testimonies of the fortunes and infortunes are equal, defer judgment: it is not possible to know which way the balance will turn."

Lilly developed an elaborate point system for scoring the strengths of the planets. I will present his system in a later chapter. While these numerical scores are helpful, one must take into account all the factors to judge a horary chart.

## Lord of the Hour Agreement.

According to Lilly, the astrologer may take the question as radical "or fit to be judged, when the Lord of the hour at the time of proposing the Question and erecting the Figure, and the Lord of the Ascendant or the first house, are of one Triplicity, or be one, or of the same nature." To the horror of my traditional colleagues, I generally ignore this rule. Students should test it and decide for themselves.

## Saturn in the 1st or 7th.

If Saturn "be in the Ascendant, especially retrograde, the matter of that question seldom or never comes to good; Saturn in the 7th either corrupts the judgment of the astrologer, or is a sign that the matter propounded will come from one misfortune to another" (Lilly).

## What is the state of the Astrologer?

Fortunately, the horary chart warns the astrologer when he or she is not in a state to judge adequately. In addition to the considerations before judgment, the planetary standing of the astrologer's significator further reveals the astrologer's state of mind. If the planet ruling the astrologer is weak by being in hard aspect to Saturn, cadent, retrograde, intercepted, and so on, then the astrologer may have difficulty interpreting the chart. Appleby found that when the 7th house ruler was retrograde, circumstances often prevented him from delivering his judgment to the querent.

Lilly included several warnings that the "judgment of the astrologer will give little content, or nothing please the querent." These included: the cusp of the 7th house afflicted; the ruler of the 7th retrograde or impedited; Saturn in the 7th; or, the ruler of the 7th house unfortunate, in his fall, or in terms of the malefics.

Chart 16 is one of my favorite horary examples and illustrates many of the ideas in this chapter. In the spring of 1989 I heard an audiotape of a horary lecture by Joan McEvers. When she mentioned she had misread a chart that continued to puzzle her, I wrote to her for a copy. In 1978 Joan McEvers' son asked a horary question, "Should we buy the stained glass business?" on Saturday, September 9, 1978, at 1:30 P.M. PST 116W46/47N41. It was a Saturn day, and Saturn rules crystalline structures.

The Ascendant is radical at 17° 45' Sagittarius, making Jupiter her son's significator. The Moon is his co-ruler. The houses ruling business are the 10th and possibly the 6th. Taurus on the 6th cusp and Libra on the 10th cusp give Venus primary rulership of the business. Mars in the 10th is a co-ruler of the stained glass business. Mars is also a natural ruler of furnaces and of glass making.

There is no aspect between her son's primary ruler Jupiter and the two rulers of the business, Venus and Mars. No aspect, no action. He should not buy the business based on primary rulers. The Moon as her son's co-ruler will sextile Mars. If he grasps this opportunity, he can succeed in the business. McEvers did not notice this sextile when she first read the chart and told her son not to go ahead with the deal. Like many children, Joan's

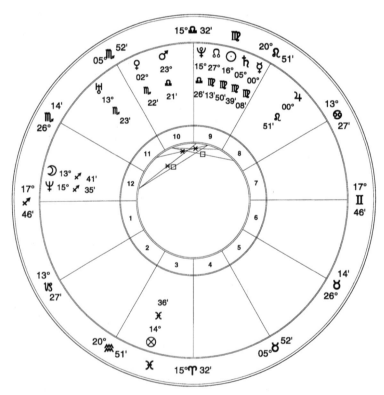

Chart 16: "Should we buy the stained glass business?"
September 9, 1978, 1:30 P.M. PST, 116W46, 47N41  Koch Houses

son disregarded his mother's advice and bought the business anyway. He has been extremely successful. Why did Joan have trouble reading the chart? And why has the business been so successful?

To answer the first question, we must look at the 7th house, which stands for the astrologer. Gemini on the seventh cusp shows Mercury as the planet ruling Joan McEvers. This fits because she is a writer and likes to communicate. Mercury is in Virgo, which is intercepted in the ninth house of predictions, and in four degrees Mercury will conjoin Saturn (delays, hindrances). Mercury (Joan McEvers) is also under the beams of the Sun, a somewhat weakening influence.

The cosmic state of Mercury suggests that the astrologer will experience difficulty or delay in interpreting this chart and may need to consult with another astrologer to come up with the right answer. Planets in intercepted signs have trouble expressing themselves. Saturn inhibits the action of planets whom he conjoins. The conjunction of the 7th house ruler with Saturn has the same effect as Saturn in the 7th house and impairs the astrologer's ability to read the chart.

I was able to shed light on this chart ten and a half years after Joan erected it. The timing of my involvement is shown by a comparison of the horary figure with my natal chart. My natal Sun is at 10° 39' Virgo, and I obtained a copy of the chart when horary Mercury at 0° 8' Virgo had progressed (at one degree per year) to conjoin my natal Sun. Because of this chart, I (Sun at 10° 40' Virgo) first contacted (conjunction) Joan McEvers (Mercury). This is another of those astonishing coincidences that keeps me interested in astrology.

Why was the business so successful? For many reasons. Neptune is a natural ruler of glass and probably of stained glass, though I can find no ancient source to support this rulership. The Moon, co-ruler of her son, will conjoin Neptune (stained glass) within two degrees. He will soon come together with stained glass. The 10th cusp and the two rulers of the business, Mars and Venus, are in the Via Combusta. That's pretty bad. But wait a minute. Mars is at home in the claws of the Scorpion. The Via Combusta would ordinarily emphasize the sadistic side of Mars, were he not conjunct Spica, the most benefic fixed star of all. In this chart Mars at 23° 22' Libra is approaching Spica at 23° 27' Libra in 1978. They are a mere five minutes of arc away from an exact conjunction. The Venus side of Spica tames the perverse nature of Mars and puts his fiery energy to good use, as in the making of stained glass. Mars conjoining Spica promises the stained glass business will be a smashing success.

But doesn't Venus, the primary significator of the business, mess things up by passing through the Via Combusta? Ordinarily yes, but in this chart Mars and Venus are in mutual reception. Venus is in Scorpio ruled by Mars and Mars is in Libra ruled by Venus. The mutual reception puts Venus in contact with Spica and amplifies her beneficence. As Bonatus says, "reception abates all malice," and "Venus takes off the fury of Mars." Furthermore, what better place for Mars, ruler of glass furnaces, and Venus, ruler of the business, than in the burning way. The significators of the business in the Via Combusta suggest the chart is radical because the question is a matter related to combustion.

Several months after sending the above interpretation to Joan McEvers, I came across one of the sayings of Guido Bonatus that applies to this case. It was uncanny. In aphorism #107 Bonatus advises the horary astrologer to consider "whether Mars be in the 2nd or in the 10th, and well-disposed; for it denotes that the native or querent shall gain a fortune or estate by those persons that deal or work in iron or fire, as smiths, furnace men, glass men, etc." I am not making this up. Seven centuries ago Bonatus really said McEvers' son would make a fortune working with fire, furnaces, and glass. Amazing!

---

### HISTORICAL INTERLUDE
### PTOLEMY AND THE PLANETARY RULERSHIPS OF THE SIGNS

The Greek astronomer Claudius Ptolemy (A.D. 127–145) knew that when the Sun entered the sign Cancer it was at its northernmost declination and appeared to stand still (the summer "sol-stice"). This was the hottest time of the year in the northern hemisphere, and it was natural to associate the summer signs of Cancer and Leo with the two lights in the sky. Because Cancer is feminine and Leo masculine, the Moon came to rule Cancer and the Sun, Leo. To preserve the harmony of the spheres, Ptolemy assigned planetary rulerships to the signs so that the distances of the planets from the Sun paralleled the distances of the zodiac signs from Cancer and Leo.

Thus, Mercury, the next planet from the Sun, rules Gemini and Virgo, the two signs that adjoin Cancer and Leo. Venus, the next planet after Mercury, governs Taurus and Libra, the two signs that adjoin Gemini and Virgo. And so the pattern continues until we reach Saturn, the furthest visible planet from the Sun, which rules Aquarius and Capricorn, the two signs most distant from Cancer and Leo. (See Figure 7, page 159.)

# CHAPTER FIVE

# Aspects and Orbs in Horary

When I first started doing horary, I did not pay close attention to the orbs of aspects. Instead, influenced by Joan McEvers and Marc Edmund Jones, I followed the modern rule that planets, by and large, may not leave their original signs in the horary chart to complete an aspect. Instead of orbs, I used the teaching of Jones that "the first aspect made by a significant planet is the normal basis of judgment." Over the past several years I have been impressed by the teaching and research of Sue Ward, Carol Wiggers, C. J. Puotinen, Robert Zoller, Robert Hand, and the scholars of ARHAT. As a result, I now pay more attention to orbs in horary.

## ORBS IN HORARY: EXACT, PERFECT, PARTILE, AND PLATIC ASPECTS

"Orb" comes from the Latin *orbis,* meaning circle. According to the modern definition, the orb of an aspect is the number of degrees during which the aspect between two planets remains in effect. In classical astrology, the orbs belong to planets rather than to aspects. To understand the traditional meaning of orbs, we must first consider the classical ideas of exact, perfect, partile, and platic aspects. Let me define these concepts.

### Exact Aspect

An aspect is "exact" when the centers of the aspecting bodies are exactly as far apart as specified by the aspect (to the nearest degree, minute, and second). For example, Venus at 9° 25' 17" Leo is exactly trine Jupiter at 9° 25' 17" Aries.

### Perfect Aspect

An aspect is "perfect" when there are points on the bodies of the aspecting planets that lie exactly as far apart as the angular distance specified by the aspect. Lilly allowed planets a radius of three minutes of arc, and the lights (Sun and Moon) a radius of almost seventeen minutes. A perfect aspect is exact within an "orb" of the sum of the radii of the two aspecting planets. For example, Venus at 9° 28' Leo is in perfect trine with Jupiter at 9° 23' Aries because they are only five minutes apart and some point on the body of Venus lies exactly trine some point on the body of Jupiter. Also, the Moon at 17° 40' Cancer is "in perfect trine" with the Sun at 17° 24' Pisces (Lilly, CA, p.391) because there exists a point on the Moon's body that is exactly 120 degrees from some point on the Sun's body.

## Partile Aspect

According to Lilly, "When two planets are exactly so many *degrees* (italics mine) from each other as make a perfect aspect: as if Venus be in 9 degrees of Aries and Jupiter in 9 degrees of Leo, this is a partile trine; so the Sun in one degree of Taurus and the Moon in one degree of Cancer make a partile sextile" (CA, p. 106). An aspect is partile (from the Latin *pars* for part) when the aspecting planets occupy the same numerical degree of their respective signs. The idea behind partile aspects is that each sign of the zodiac is divided into thirty special "parts" called degrees. When planets are in partile aspect, the degrees of the zodiac occupied by the aspecting planets are exactly as far from one another as specified by the aspect. For example, Venus at 9° 01' Leo is in partile trine with Jupiter at 9° 59' Aries because they are both in 9 degrees of their respective signs. For casting horary charts, Lilly used "whole degrees without sensible error" for the positions of the planets. In partile aspects, the planets share in the aspect formed by the zodiac degrees in which they lie.

## Platic Aspect

An aspect is platic (from the Greek *platys*, meaning broad or flat) when it is within orb and the aspecting planets occupy different degrees of their respective signs. The planets are within orb of forming an aspect, but the degrees in which those planets lie do not form that exact aspect. Platic aspects are more broad-based than partile ones. For example, Venus at 9° 01' Leo is in platic trine with Jupiter at 1° 59' Aries because they are in orb but occupy different degrees of their respective signs.

Lilly did not share the modern preoccupation with being precise to the nearest degree, minute, and second. Partile aspects are exact to the degree, disregarding minutes and seconds. In erecting charts for horary questions, Lilly advised (CA, p. 44) that "the place of the planets ought to be rectified to the hour of the setting of the figure, especially the place of the Moon, because of her swift motion; in the planets you need not be scrupulous, but take whole degrees without sensible error." In charts of nativities, Lilly was more careful in his calculations: "in nativities, you are to have the places of them [the planets] exactly to degrees and minutes; and above all the motion of the Sun to minutes and seconds."

The degree of the zodiac where the aspect becomes partile resembles the epicenter of an earthquake. The force of a quake, or of an aspect, radiates out from the degree of exactitude (epicenter) over an orb of influence, a concentric circle extending in all directions. In traditional horary, the radius of this circle is called the moiety (see below). Aspects gradually decrease in power as the planets move farther away from the aspect's "epicenter" or degree of exactitude. For example, if two planets are 5° apart, most astrologers consider them within orb of a conjunction. Two planets are exactly conjunct when they are exactly zero degrees apart and share the same degree of longitude on the ecliptic. The influence of the conjunction is felt up to ten degrees around the zero degree point of exactitude.

Orbs are important in natal astrology because people rarely have partile aspects in their birth charts. By using orbs, the astrologer can determine which aspects are likely to manifest in the life of the native. In horary practice, I follow the movements of the planets in the ephemeris, starting with the planetary positions at the birth of the question. When aspects become exact in the ephemeris, events related to the inquiry occur according to the nature of the aspects.

Table 3 presents the ranges of the traditional orbs of the planets. Lilly reported two sets of orbs for the planets. In choosing which orb or moiety (half the orb) to use, Lilly wrote: "I sometimes use the one, and sometimes the other, as my memory best remembereth them, and this without error" (CA, p. 107). Table 4 shows the typical combined moieties of planetary pairs in aspect in traditional horary.

| Table 3: Lilly's Table of Orbs of the Planets | | |
|---|---|---|
| **Planet** | **Orb** | **Moiety ($\frac{1}{2}$ Orb)** |
| Sun | 15° or 17° | 7.5° or 8.5° |
| Moon | 12° or 12.5° | 6° or 6.25° |
| Mercury | 7° | 3.5° |
| Venus | 7° or 8° | 3.5° or 4° |
| Mars | 7° or 7.5° | 3.5° or 3.75° |
| Jupiter | 9° or 12° | 4.5° or 6° |
| Saturn | 9° or 10° | 4.5° or 5° |

| Table 4: Combined Moieties of Planetary Pairs in Aspect | | | | | | | |
|---|---|---|---|---|---|---|---|
| **Planet & its Orb:** | **Sun** (15–17°) | **Moon** (12–12.5°) | **Mercury** (7°) | **Venus** (7–8°) | **Mars** (7–7.5°) | **Jupiter** (9–12°) | **Saturn** (9–10°) |
| **Sun (15–17°)** | * | | | | | | |
| **Moon (12–12.5°)** | 13.5–14.75 | * | | | | | |
| **Mercury (7°)** | 11–12 | 9.5–9.75 | * | | | | |
| **Venus (7–8°)** | 11–12.5 | 9.5–10.25 | 7–7.5 | * | | | |
| **Mars (7–7.5°)** | 11–12.25 | 9.5–10 | 7–7.25 | 7–7.75 | * | | |
| **Jupiter (9–12°)** | 12–14.5 | 10.5–12.25 | 8–9.5 | 8–10 | 8–9.75 | * | |
| **Saturn (9–10°)** | 12–13.5 | 10.5–11.75 | 8–8.5 | 8–9 | 8–8.75 | 9–11 | * |

**Note:** In Table 4, the numbers in parentheses refer to the range of orbs given to the planets, the numbers in the table refer to the sum of the moieties of the two planets involved in the aspect. For example, Venus and Saturn are "within orb" when they are at most eight (or nine) degrees apart, depending on which set of orbs you use for the planets.

Unlike modern astrologers, who attribute orbs to aspects, Lilly assigned each planet an orb of influence. The planetary orb is an imaginary sphere of light surrounding the planet with the planet at the center of that sphere. The rays of the planet within this sphere (orb) are powerful enough to influence other heavenly bodies by contacting their spheres of light (rays) through conjunction or Ptolemaic aspect; the rays of the two planets are blended according to the nature of the aspect.

In classical astrology, half the orb (the radius of the sphere) is called the moiety, meaning "half-measure." Thus, Jupiter has an orb of 12 degrees and a moiety of 6 degrees. Jupiter's moiety tells us that the light surrounding Jupiter (orb) is potent enough to form aspects when it contacts the light of another planet within a distance (radius) of 6 degrees from Jupiter's body (longitude position along the zodiac).

To visualize this, picture Jupiter as a point (or more accurately a dot with a diameter of six minutes of arc) at the center of a twelve-degree wide sphere of "Jupiterian light." Jupiter's orb is 12° and his moiety 6°. Similarly, Saturn lies at the center of a 10° wide ball of "Saturnian light" with a moiety (radius) of 5°. Jupiter and Saturn come into contact (conjunct) just as their distance apart decreases to 11° (the sum of their two moieties). At that distance the conjunction begins to take affect. See Figures 1 and 2.

Strictly speaking, the planets are not points but bodies in their own right. Lilly allowed about six minutes of arc for the diameter of a planet's body on the Celestial Sphere, so that even after an aspect became exact the departing bodies of the planets would overlap a little during separation. Because the bodies of the Sun and the Moon occupy just over half a degree of arc in the sky, Lilly allowed about seventeen minutes of arc past exactitude for separation from the Sun or the Moon. For example, Lilly states that the Moon at 17° 40' Cancer is "in perfect trine" with the Sun at 17° 24' Pisces (CA, p. 391). Here the Moon is sixteen minutes past the exact trine of the Sun, but their bodies are still in contact. The following schematics illustrate these ideas about the bodies of planets in perfect aspect:

**Two planets:** <—3'—> (P1) <—3'—><—3'—> (P2) <—3'—>

Here, P1 is the center of the first planet and P2 is the center of the second planet. Each planet has a diameter of 6 minutes and a radius of 3 minutes of arc. The planets are in perfect aspect until their centers are more than 6 minutes of arc apart. The planets separate from perfect aspect when the center of the faster planet gets more than 6 minutes away from the center of the slower planet.

**Sun and Moon:** <—17'—> (Sun) <—17'—><—17'—> (Moon) <—17'—>

Here, the bodies of the Sun and Moon overlap until they are almost thirty-four minutes apart. The Sun and Moon remain in perfect aspect until their centers are more than thirty-four minutes apart.

**Planet and Sun:** <—3'—> (P) <—3'—><——17'——> (Sun) <——17'——>

Here, the bodies of the planet (P) and the Sun (or Moon) overlap and the aspect remains perfect until they are almost twenty minutes apart.

To repeat, Lilly considered an aspect between planets to be separating when the center of the faster planet moved more than six minutes of arc away from the center of the other planet. In other words, the planets are separating from aspect when the bodies of the two planets no longer overlap at the angle specified by the aspect. The sum of the radii of two planets is six minutes of arc. The Sun and the Moon have larger diameters than the planets on the celestial sphere. Lilly used about thirty-four minutes of arc for the diameter of the lights, and this figure accords with modern calculations.

For example, the Sun has a diameter of 865,400 miles and on average a distance of 93,000,000 miles from the earth. If we place the Sun on a circle with the earth as its center, the radius of that circle is 93 million miles, and its circumference is $2\pi$ times the radius. The percent of the sky that the Sun occupies is the diameter of the Sun divided by the circumference of its "orbit" around the earth, namely, 865,400 divided by $2\pi$ times 93 million = 0.00148 of a 360 degree circle = 0.533 degrees = 32 minutes of arc. The Arabs had observed the diameter of the sun to be almost thirty-four minutes of arc and defined a planet as Cazimi (in the heart of the Sun) when the center of the planet was no more than seventeen minutes (the Sun's radius or half its diameter) away from the center of the Sun. Within seventeen minutes of arc the center of the planet remains in contact with the body of the Sun.

A similar calculation for the Moon, which has a diameter of 2,160 miles and an average distance from the earth of 240,000 miles, shows that the Moon on average occupies thirty-one minutes of arc (that is 360 degrees times 2,160 divided by $2\pi$ times 240,000).

The temporal sequence of aspects as they occur in the ephemeris parallels the temporal unfolding of the outcome of the question. According to modern authors, the only restriction is that, when applying to a major aspect with another planet, a significator may not leave the sign that it originally occupies in the chart. Lilly allowed planets to perfect aspects in the next sign provided they were in orb in the previous sign. Aspects that are in orb but will perfect only after the planet changes sign often indicate a significant change in the querent's circumstances.

Some modern horary astrologers (McEvers, for example) disregard orbs and allow all significators and the Moon to perfect all the aspects they can before leaving their signs. In this sense, the signs of the zodiac are large orbs of influence. The signs of the zodiac are natural boundaries because each sign represents a different area of experience. When a planet

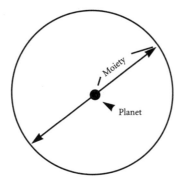

Figure 1: Orb of a Planet (Sphere of Influence)

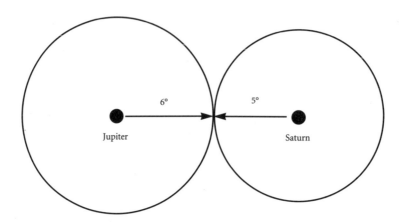

Figure 2: Jupiter and Saturn Becoming Conjunct

moves into a new sign, it enters a new situation and becomes less related to the original circumstances surrounding the question. This idea of signs as discreet areas of experience also gave rise to the notion of critical degrees marking the cusps between signs or between other divisions of the zodiac.

Generally, the first Ptolemaic aspect between primary significators acts as the major indicator of the outcome of the question. Other aspects may clarify or modify the answer given by the first aspect between significators. Translation or collection of light can intervene to bring about a favorable outcome when the first major aspect is a square or an opposition. If a potential aspect becomes perfect only after one or both significators have entered the next sign, that aspect may refer to an event removed from the original situation prompting the question.

For example, I once received a call from a woman in Seattle, Washington, who asked whether she would marry. It was the weekend after Valentine's Day, 1992, and she must have had love on her mind. See Chart 17. The horary chart has Libra rising, as fits a chart about marriage. The Ascendant ruler Venus (the querent) is at the end of Capricorn and will conjoin Mars (ruler of the prospective husband—Aries 7th cusp) only after both Venus and Mars enter the next sign. Because of the closely applying conjunction between the 1st and 7th rulers, I said she would marry—but only after a change of circumstances (because Venus must change signs to perfect the conjunction with Mars). A couple of years later I received a letter updating me on her circumstances. She had not done well professionally in Seattle (notice Moon ruling the 10th of career and posited in the 10th opposing the restrictive planet Saturn). For career reasons she had moved to Denver, Colorado, where her career went smoothly and she was also able to marry, as the chart had indicated, after a change of circumstances. In this chart, the Uranus/Neptune conjunction posited on the 4th cusp is also suggestive of a major change in the domestic environment.

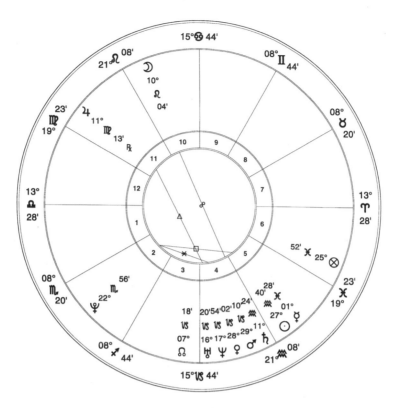

Chart 17: "Will I marry?"
February 16, 1992, 9:15 P.M. EST, 73W01, 41N19 Regiomontanus Houses

## A CLASSICAL EXAMPLE HIGHLIGHTING ASPECT PRINCIPLES

On October 29, 1645, around 6:53 P.M., in London, a woman asked Lilly "when her husband, who is imprisoned, will be delivered?" (See Chart 18, p. 78.) Lilly's analysis was brief and to the point: "This question belongs to the 12th house [of prisoners]; Jupiter Lord of the 7th signifies the Lady's husband, in Cancer Retrograde, lately, or the day before, in Trine with the Sun, the Moon applying to a Sextile of Saturn, Retrograde, then to a trine of Jupiter, with a most forcible Reception; from hence I made not many words, but told the Lady, she should neither care to make Friends to his Majesty or any else for delivery of her Husband, for I was assured he either was or would within three days be discharged of his imprisonment, by means of a Solar man, Commander, who would release him and furnish him with what was convenient for his necessity." The woman's husband had been released the day before she asked the question "by an honest Parliament-Colonel, who plentifully relieved him with Money."

The Moon at 29° 10' Aquarius is void of course in the modern sense. A contemporary astrologer might interpret that nothing would come of the matter because the void of course Moon means question is moot—her husband had already been released from prison. Lilly, however, does not consider this Moon void of course because she is within orb of a sextile with Saturn and a trine with Jupiter. Lilly's practice is consistent with Bonatus'

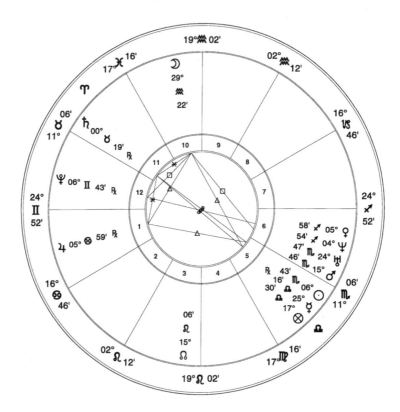

Chart 18: "When her husband, who is imprisoned, shall be delivered?"
October 29, 1645, 6:53 P.M. GMT, 00W10, 51N30  Regiomontanus Houses

definition that the Moon is void of course "when not joined to [within orb of] any planet by body or aspect." Because the Moon is applying within orb to major aspects, Lilly allows her to leave Aquarius and enter Pisces to perfect the sextile with Saturn and then the trine with Jupiter.

The Moon lies in Aquarius in the sign of Saturn (traditional ruler of Aquarius). Saturn lies in Taurus in the exaltation of the Moon. The Moon and Saturn are in mutual reception. When the Moon passes into Pisces, it enters the Saturn face (decan) of Pisces. The mutual reception, now by sign and face, persists and reinforces the meaning of the sextile between the Moon and Saturn.

Of note in this example is the principle of Bonatus that the planet the Moon will next aspect co-rules the person inquired after. Here the next aspect is the sextile to a retrograde Saturn, which will occur in 1° 26'. Thus, according to Bonatus, Saturn becomes a co-ruler of the husband, and his retrograde status means the husband will return. Lilly generally ignored this rule of Bonatus because he felt it did not work in his charts.

In this example Bonatus appears right on target. If Lilly had followed the rule of Bonatus and paid more attention to the Moon/Saturn sextile, he could have told the woman that Moon at the very end of Aquarius (void in the modern sense) and the backward moving Saturn, mutually applying to a sextile in 1° 26', meant that her husband had already gained his freedom within the past day and a half (measuring time backward because of the retrograde Saturn and Moon void in the modern sense).

Substituting a degree for a day, the 1° 26' needed to perfect the sextile between the Moon and Saturn corresponds to about thirty-four hours in the past. I say "in the past" because Saturn is retrograde (moving backward) and the void of course Moon, by modern definition, is in a symbolically backward situation. The Moon is never actually retrograde but it can have retrograde equivalents, like being slow in motion or void of course. Although Lilly only reports the time of the husband's release as occurring the day before the question (asked about 7 P.M.), the chart suggests the husband's release took place about 9 A.M. (thirty-four hours earlier) on the previous day. Unfortunately, there is no way to verify my conjecture about the timing of his release.

As mentioned, Lilly allows the Moon to trine Jupiter after changing signs because she is already in orb of aspecting Jupiter at her current position. The Moon will enter Pisces, ruled by Jupiter, and Jupiter lies in Cancer, ruled by the Moon—a "most forcible reception." Jupiter rules the 7th house of the husband, and Jupiter retrograde (moving backward) means the husband will return. Jupiter is strong in the first house and exalted in Cancer, these dignities showing the husband's good condition. Jupiter's presence in the first house (of the querent) confirms his return to his wife.

Interestingly, Bonatus gave us a rule about when to use a conjunction that a planet perfects shortly after leaving its sign, suggesting that Bonatus did not judge aspects that perfected after a sign change except in certain circumstances. According to Bonatus, "When one planet applies to the Conjunction of another, if he be near the end of the same sign wherein he is himself, or that other to whom he applies; so that he will pass out of that sign before the Conjunction is perfected; and... if he be joined with him in the following sign to which he is changed, ... then the cause is perfected if that planet confers anything on him in that sign wherein he is so joined to him; that is, if any reception happen, unless the said planet, or he to whom he applies, be first joined to another; for then the business comes to nothing, and will not be perfected." Bonatus is right on target in this example.

In summary, the horary chart contains potential aspects which will perfect in the course of time. The order in which those aspects become exact, ephemeris time, before the planets leave their signs is the order in which events will unfold for the question. The transits show the course of events. Lilly also allowed aspects to perfect after the planets change signs, provided they are within orb of perfection prior to the sign change.

## TRADITIONAL VERSUS MODERN RULERSHIPS

Horary astrology developed before the discovery of the three outer planets, Uranus, Neptune and Pluto. Traditionally horary astrologers used only the seven classical planets that could be seen with the naked eye. Modern astrologers have tried to incorporate the more recently discovered planets into horary art, with mixed results. According to Sue Ward, the modern planets (Uranus, Neptune, Pluto) are without orbs because they cannot be seen and are not surrounded by "rays" or globes of light that constitute orbs of influence.

Although it may go against the grain of those versed in natal astrology, I use the seven traditional planets as rulers. I tried using the modern rulerships but came across charts where the traditional rulerships gave a more definitive answer. Such experiences caused me to re-institute using the seven classical planets. I do not ignore the newer planets. I simply give them secondary status unless the chart compels me to consider them primary. By way of review, in traditional astrology the Sun rules Leo, the Moon rules Cancer, Mercury rules Gemini and Virgo, Venus rules Taurus and Libra, Mars rules Aries and Scorpio, Jupiter rules Sagittarius and Pisces, and Saturn rules Capricorn and Aquarius.

What about the three outer planets? They are useful as co-rulers and as primary significators of forces beyond personal control. The closer a planet is to the sun, the more it affects the individual. The Sun, Moon, Mercury, Venus, and Mars are the most personal of the planets. Jupiter and Saturn extend into the social realm. Uranus, Neptune and Pluto have transpersonal significance beyond the control of any individual. They symbolize powerful social, spiritual, or natural forces, and concretely may symbolize the products of modern technology.

Because horary astrology deals with personal questions over which the querent has some control, it makes sense to limit rulerships to the most personal of the planets. The three outer planets can serve as secondary rulers of their respective signs and often show conditions that have an impersonal or universal quality. The outer planets also refer to modern conditions that did not exist in the ancient world.

Uranus is the modern co-ruler of Aquarius, Neptune the modern co-ruler of Pisces, and Pluto the modern co-ruler of Scorpio. If the nature of the question dictates, the astrologer can use common sense to assign the outer planets as primary rulers of particular matters.

A question such as "Should I undergo psychoanalysis?" falls more naturally to Pluto (psychological probing) than Mars if Scorpio defines the cusp of the quesited. Uranus more accurately symbolizes computer technology than Saturn when Aquarius locates the question. Neptune is a more apt symbol for film making than Jupiter when Pisces governs the quesited. The astrologer's judgment and experience rather than slavish devotion to a rulership book is the key to choosing the appropriate significator.

## THE ASPECTS ARE THE GUTS OF THE CHART

To paraphrase Shakespeare: All the horary chart is a stage, and all the planets and lights are merely players. The planets ruling the querent and quesited are the key actors. The house cusps identify what department of life they represent. The signs show in which circumstances the planets find themselves. The aspects are the script that tells the players how to act toward one another. In other words, the aspects are the guts of the horary chart. If the significators make no aspects, generally no action takes place. No guts, no glory. No aspects, no action. When neither the rulers nor the co-rulers make any aspects, you need to tell the querent nothing will take place in the matter.

By following the sequence of aspects as they occur between the key players in the chart, you can see how events will develop until the final outcome. The nature of each aspect shows the type of action. The first aspect to occur between the two primary significators is the normal basis of judgment. The aspects act as the script that directs the significators on how to relate to one another. The aspects between the planetary rulers determine the outcome of the question. A conjunction brings the querent and quesited together cooperatively. Trines and sextiles show mutual harmony and a helping hand between the two.

Oppositions reveal them moving apart because they cannot agree. Squares show the querent and quesited grating at each other, frustrating and blocking each other's activity. Once you understand the script, you can predict the final curtain.

## APPLYING ASPECTS ONLY

The horary chart contains potential aspects between significators. By following these potential aspects to their completion, we can determine the outcome of the question. Applying aspects are those in which the faster planet is approaching the exact angular relationship to a slower planet as specified by the aspect. If the faster applying planet is in direct motion, it is in an earlier degree than the slower planet which it approaches. If the faster planet is retrograde, it can approach the slower planet from a later degree by backward motion. In this latter case, both planets are approaching each other by mutual application.

Applying aspects signify future events. In horary astrology we use applying aspects because horary deals with the future course of a specific act or decision. Separating aspects are those that have already occurred, and the planets are moving away from the angle defined by the aspect. We use separating aspects when we want to know what led up to the question. We saw the usefulness of separating aspects in the chart for Sara's baby. The recently completed square between Mercury (the baby) and Jupiter (ruler of the baby's 6th house of illness) coincided with Sara's awareness that something had gone wrong the previous day, and in fact identified the time of the baby's death.

## PLANETS' SPEED: FASTER PLANETS APPLY TO SLOWER ONES

In conventional astrology, the faster planet always applies to a slower one. Mohammed goes to the mountain; the mountain does not come to Mohammed. When describing aspects, we always name the faster planet first. Thus, the Moon applies to Mercury, but Mercury does not apply to the Moon unless Mercury is retrograde and approaches the Moon in apparent backward motion. The approximate average daily speeds of the planets are listed here in order from fastest to slowest.

In Table 5, note that the mean values (not the average daily motions) of the fastest and slowest times used by Lilly are for Mercury 1° 23' and for Venus 1° 12' (See Clark, *The Horary Practitioner,* 1996 Special Edition, p. 15).

Bear in mind that these are only average daily speeds and planets may move faster or slower than at the rates listed. When a planet is stationary, it appears to be standing still; when retrograde, it has an apparent backward motion. In these cases, you can follow the planetary motion in an ephemeris to determine whether the stationary or retrograde planet is approaching an aspect with another planet. In addition, Pluto sometimes travels inside the orbit of Neptune, and Pluto then moves faster than Neptune with reference to the earth. In this century Pluto is within the orbit of Neptune from January of 1979 until March of 1999. As with retrograde planets, it is easiest to follow the aspects of these outermost planets in an ephemeris.

| Table 5: Average Daily Motions of the Planets | | |
|---|---|---|
| Planet | Geocentric Average Daily Motions (degrees/day) | Heliocentric Orbit: Planetary "Year" (in Earth time) |
| Moon | 13° 10' 36" | 27 days 7 hrs. 43 min. |
| Mercury | 0° 59' 08" | 88 days |
| Venus | 0° 59' 08" | 225 days |
| Sun | 0° 59' 08" | n/a |
| Mars | 0° 31' 27" | 687 days |
| Jupiter | 0° 04' 59" | 11.9 years |
| Saturn | 0° 02' 01" | 29.5 years |

## THE FIVE PTOLEMAIC OR MAJOR ASPECTS

Traditionally horary astrology has relied on the five major aspects described by Ptolemy. The Ptolemaic aspects are the conjunction (0°), sextile (60°), square (90°), trine (120°), and opposition (180°). The conjunction, sextile and trine favor a positive outcome. The square and opposition bring obstacles and problems.

The conjunction brings the significators into a close relationship with one another. It fosters cooperation, brings the querent and quesited together, and unites whatever the planets signify.

The sextile gives the querent an opportunity to bring a matter to perfection. The querent will need to grasp the opportunity to make it a reality. Sextiles require more effort than trines. The 3rd and 11th houses are in sextile relationship to the 1st.

The trine represents a fortunate relationship between significators. They will work toward a common good. The accomplishment of a desired task will be easy. Trines imply good luck and success without much effort. The 5th and 9th houses are trine the 1st.

The opposition is a negative, disappointing, separative aspect. When the significators apply to a 180° aspect, they are at odds, pulling apart, or on opposite sides of the fence. If the rulers of two people are in opposition, those individuals are in conflict and moving away from one another. The 7th house is opposite the first. A planet in the sign opposite the one it rules is in its "detriment."

The square is also a negative influence and suggests problems and obstacles to overcome. Squares are high-energy aspects so sometimes the matter will perfect but in a way the querent will regret. Squares show frustrations, difficulties, losses, and the need to exert much effort to accomplish anything. They represent stress and strain between the significators. The 4th and 10th houses are square the 1st.

The meanings of the aspects have remained stable for centuries. Firmicus Maternus in the mid-300s A.D. had the following to say about them. The opposition is "always an unfavorable and threatening sign." The trine is a "prosperous and fortunate aspect." The square is a "threatening sign full of adverse influence." Finally, "sextile aspects are the same as the trine, but less powerful."

Lilly used the technique that, in signs of long ascension, sextiles got stretched out and acted like squares, and squares got stretched out and acted like trines. In signs of short ascension squares got shrunk to favorable sextiles and trines shrunk into squares. This horary legerdemain sometimes got him out of jams in his interpretations. More about this in a later chapter.

## QUINCUNXES: OUT OF JOINT

Quincunx literally means five-twelfths (Latin: *quinque*—"five," and *uncia*—"twelfth part"). That's five-twelfths of a circle. One twelfth is 30° and 5 x 30° = 150°. Many astrologers regard the quincunx (150°) as a major aspect in natal astrology. Some horary astrologers give it almost Ptolemaic status and regard it as negative. Ptolemy called signs in quincunx (five signs apart) "inconjunct" or "disjunct," which colloquially means "out of joint."

The quincunx aspect implies something is out of joint and the querent will need to adjust it. Some facet of the situation will require restructuring, re-negotiation, or alteration. The querent may need to lend support, financial or otherwise, to a person involved in the question. The quincunx relates naturally to the sixth and eighth houses, each being five houses from the first. Quincunxes suggest sixth and eighth house issues such as illness, service, distress, drudgery, surgery, injury, death, taxes, or joint finances. The Moon's quincunxes with the malefics were prominent in the October 1989 San Francisco earthquake chart. While quincunxes do not qualify as traditional major aspects, they can often be informative in a horary chart.

## THE USEFULNESS OF QUINCUNXES IN HORARY: AN EXAMPLE

On June 23, 1990, at 11:58 A.M. EDT at 73W01, 41N19, my sister-in-law asked, "Will I need to buy a new air conditioner? Can I fix the one I have? What's wrong with it?" See Chart 19.

The chart has 20° Virgo rising, so Mercury at 21° Gemini in the 10th rules the querent. Air conditioners are shown by the 6th house (appliances), which has 21° Aquarius on the cusp. The rulers of the air conditioner are Saturn, retrograde at 23° Capricorn, and Uranus, retrograde at 8° Capricorn.

Because Mercury (the querent) is mutually applying to a quincunx with Saturn (the air conditioner), I told her that the air conditioner could be fixed or adjusted (quincunx). The retrograde status of the air conditioner's rulers showed its debilitated state. Saturn suggested an obstruction of some kind. The trine of Mercury to the 6th cusp supported a favorable outcome.

The repairman discovered that some debris from her roof (which had been repaired over the winter) had fallen into the air conditioner, obstructing its fan (Uranus). She suffered two days of discomfort as a result (Mercury was two degrees from the quincunx to Saturn). The quincunx exactly described her relationship to her air conditioner.

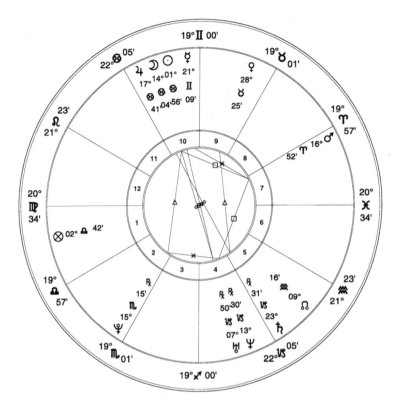

Chart 19: "Will I need to buy a new air conditioner?"
June 23, 1990,11:58 A.M. EDT, 73W01, 41N19  Koch Houses

## Parallels and Contraparallels of Declination

Two planets are "parallel of declination" when they are at the same declination, that is, the same angular distance above or below (north or south of) the Celestial Equator. When two planets are equidistant above or below the equator but one is north and the other south, they are "contraparallel."

Declination measures planetary position north or south of the equator. In contrast, the measure of distance above or below the Ecliptic is "celestial latitude" and should not be confused with declination. Celestial latitude refers to the ecliptic; declination refers to the equator. The ecliptic and the equator are at a 23.5° angle from one another, the so-called obliquity of the ecliptic.

Parallels have become popular in modern times. In the Newcastle edition of Lilly's text, Zadkiel added the line that the parallel "is the most powerful of all aspects but is not generally used in horary astrology." Many would disagree that the parallel is so powerful, and only the school of Ivy Jacobson seems to use parallels in horary work.

Instead of using parallels, William Lilly paid attention to antiscions and contra-antiscions (or contrascions). Antiscions are the two points on the Ecliptic that are at the same distance east or west of the Summer or Winter Solstice, points where the sun has the same declination. By definition, the Sun is parallel to its antiscion degree. Contrascions are the two points on the Ecliptic, the same distance east or west of the Spring or Autumn Equinoxes, where the sun has equal but opposite declination north or south of the Celestial Equator. By definition, the Sun is contraparallel to its contrascion degree. According to Lilly, a conjunction of a benefic planet to an antiscion is "equal to a sextile or a trine." Lilly also felt that a conjunction to a contrascion is "of the nature of a square or opposition."

In his seminal first-century work on "interrogations," Dorotheus does not refer to parallels of declination, but he does mention aspects in latitude (north and south of the Ecliptic rather than the Celestial Equator). Unlike modern astrologers who act as if the world is flat, Dorotheus pictured the horoscope in three dimensions. For Dorotheus planets could conjoin along the zodiac circle or in celestial latitude above or below the ecliptic.

For example, in his chapter on fugitive slaves, Dorotheus writes, "If the Moon conjoins with Mars in longitude, then beating and imprisonment will reach the runaway at that hour in this running away of his. If the Moon is conjoining with Jupiter in latitude while Jupiter aspects Mars, then it indicates that misfortune will reach the runaway because of the Moon's conjoining with Mars and fear of death will be immoderate in him, but he will escape from this death because of Jupiter's aspect of the Moon." Here the Moon and Mars conjoin on the ecliptic, which indicates a beating (Mars) for the fugitive (Moon); but because the Moon (the slave) lies at the same Celestial Latitude as Jupiter (good luck), the slave escapes death.

My impression is that those who use parallels of declination are the followers of Ivy Jacobson. She regards the parallel and contraparallel of declination as similar to the conjunction and uses a one-degree orb. According to Jacobson, if a parallel exists between significators, "the thing is as good as done now." She feels that a parallel can "save" the Moon from being void of course (making no Ptolemaic aspect before leaving sign). Jacobson says that if the Moon is void of course "but is parallel Fortuna, she still will bring the matter to perfection." In Jacobson's way of thinking, the Moon is "only zodiacally void of course" when parallel to Pars Fortuna. To find the declination of the Part of Fortune, one looks up the declination of the sun when it occupies the same degree of the zodiac as the Part of Fortune.

Unlike Jacobson, I restrict the definition of the void of course Moon to the five major Ptolemaic aspects; otherwise, for me, the Moon is in an aspect vacuum. I can find no classical references that support her use of parallels of declination to "save" the Moon from being void of course. To be honest, I have not tested her theory. Readers will have to try Jacobson's ideas and see for themselves.

## MUTUAL RECEPTIONS

Mutual receptions are potent forces in horary astrology. Bonatus says "reception abates all malice." I receive you when I invite you into my home. Planet A receives planet B when B enters one of the essential dignities of A, that is, when B is in A's home sign, exaltation, triplicity, term, or face. Don't worry about these concepts now; I will explain essential dignity in the next chapter.

Two planets are in "mutual reception" by sign when each planet is in the sign ruled by the other. I am staying at your house and you are staying at mine. Remember that astrology was originally an anthropomorphic theory. Each planet owns certain regions of the zodiac. If I want something from Jupiter, I cannot get it from a territory owned by Mars. I must go to one of Jupiter's dignities because that's where he keeps his goods.

There can also be mutual reception by any combination of essential dignities. Mutual reception by ruling sign is the strongest. Some astrologers believe that mutual receptions give the planets exchange status. In other words, you can read the planet back in its own sign, exaltation, triplicity, term, or face, as the case may be. Ivy Jacobson says that when you read planets back in their own dignity they stay in the same degree they originally occupied in the chart. Others, such as Olivia Barclay, allow the planets to exchange degrees when they exchange signs.

## ALL THE MOON'S ASPECTS AND MUTUAL RECEPTIONS

As the fastest moving body, the Moon represents the general climate and routine changes surrounding the question. The aspects the Moon has made in the same sign before the time of the question signify events that led up to the question. The planet the Moon most recently passed over, no matter how far back in the chart, colors the character of the Moon and influences its role in the question. All the aspects the Moon will make before changing sign show the future developments of the matter. The final aspect the Moon will make before changing sign shows the general conditions of the outcome of the matter. The specific outcome is shown by the significators. The astrologer should consider all the aspects and mutual receptions the Moon makes before it changes sign.

Some astrologers overemphasize the significance of the Moon in horary. I agree with Jones that the role of the horary Moon is secondary and adjunctive. Jones describes the Moon as "the special distributor of the more trivial indication in any given reference; i.e., the public panorama, experience in general." He adds that the Moon "shows the particular emphasis of that which, while pertinent, is essentially trivial. This includes normal necessary activities, the passing touch with other people collectively, and the ebb and flow of emotional, reflex and physiological reactions to the general rhythm of the world." The nature of the last aspect of the Moon correlates with the answer to the specific horary question about 50% of the time—a frequency accounted for by chance alone! The system I follow for horary analysis puts the Moon in the back seat. What drives the chart are the aspects between the rulers of the significant houses.

## WHEN TO CONSIDER MINOR ASPECTS

Although there are dozens of minor aspects, the three most commonly used in horary are the semi-sextile (30°), semi-square (45°), and sesquiquadrate (135°). Keep in mind that major aspects indicate major events, and minor aspects show minor ones.

The semi-square and sesquiquadrate resemble the square in their effect. The semi-sextile relates signs that adjoin one another; that is, signs with a 2nd or 12th house relationship. Because the 2nd house governs the querent's substance and money, the semi-sextile is helpful in financial matters. On the other hand, because the 12th house rules the querent's confinement, sorrow, hospitalization, grief, and undoing, the semi-sextile without reception is unfortunate in health-related questions, especially if the faster planet is approaching the slower one from a 12th house direction.

The horary astrologer can use minor aspects when the major or semi-major (quincunx, reception, parallel for those so inclined) aspects provide insufficient information. They are helpful as confirmations of other indications in the chart. I have found minor aspects reliable under the following conditions. Obviously the more of these conditions that apply, the stronger the influence of the minor aspect.

- The minor aspect is nearly exact within one degree of orb.
- The planets making the minor aspect are dignified or exalted by house or sign.
- The planets making the minor aspect are in mutual reception.
- One or both significators making the minor aspect are closely conjunct a benefic fixed star such as Spica (23° 50' Libra in 2000) or the Part of Fortune.

## THE USEFULNESS OF MINOR ASPECTS IN HORARY: AN EXAMPLE

On the morning of Friday the 13th in July of 1990, my friend and colleague, Luis, told me that he was worried that his car loan might not be approved. I noted the time and location to be 9:43 A.M. EDT, 72W50/41N27, when I asked the horary question, "Will Luis get the loan?" See Chart 20.

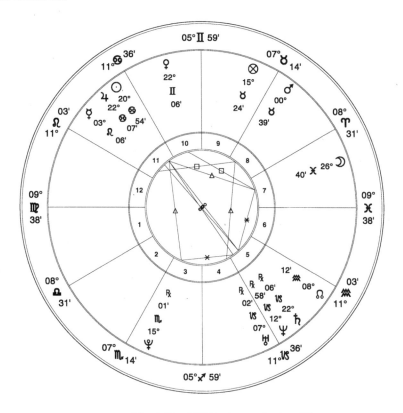

Chart 20: "Will Luis get the loan?"
July 13, 1990, 9:43 A.M. EDT, 72W50, 41N27  Koch Houses

Virgo is rising, and so I am represented by Mercury, which is in the 11th house of friends, and my question concerns a friend. The chart appears radical. With Pisces on the 7th cusp of the named other person (using McEvers' method of horary), Jupiter and Neptune rule Luis, as does the Moon, which inhabits the 7th house. The loan is signified by the 8th from the 7th, or the 2nd house of the radix. Libra is on the 2nd cusp, so Venus rules the loan. Venus also rules Friday, the day of the question.

Venus (loan) applies to an almost exact semi-sextile (a financial aspect) with Jupiter (Luis). The loan is fast approaching Luis. The Moon, though void of course, is in Pisces, where it can still function. The Moon is also in mutual reception with Jupiter, and this supports a favorable outcome.

After reading the chart, I encouraged Luis to call the credit union. He telephoned shortly after 10 A.M. EDT and was told at 10:07 A.M. that the loan had been approved. The semi-sextile between Venus and Jupiter became exact (according to the ephemeris) at 10:09 A.M. EDT, two minutes after he learned of the loan's approval!

## Mutual Application

When one planet is direct and the other retrograde, they can apply to each other to make an aspect. Because each planet is moving toward the other, we call this condition "mutual application" and regard it as a potent force in bringing an event to pass. An aspect carries more weight if it occurs by mutual application.

Chart 21 is an example of two mutual applications in a single chart. On September 14, 1996, British astrologer Sue Ward posted a note on the Internet that the manager of a local "off license" (place to buy alcohol) was missing his timid fluffy red cat. Sue found the following note in her door and cast a chart for the time (6:42 P.M. BST) when she understood the question: "Have you found our cat? Large ginger tabby/spotty male called Ed [Red Ed — get it?]. Wearing a yellow collar ... Reward is offered."

I wrote to Sue that I thought the cat would return in a day or two. The querent has several rulers: Jupiter (Pisces rising), Saturn retrograde in the 1st, and Venus—Almuten of Ascendant. Saturn retrograde in the 1st raises some concern about the outcome. The cat is shown by the 6th house with a Cancer cusp so the cat ruler is the Moon primarily (Moon also naturally rules strays), but also Venus and Mars which occupy the 6th. Moon is Almuten of 6th. The Sun also rules the cat because Leo is intercepted in the 6th.

The Moon is void of course by Lilly's definition so I suspected that the cat had wandered off and was wandering aimlessly in a westerly direction (Libra, 7th house). With Moon in the 7th in Libra (disposed by Venus, Almuten of 1st), I thought there was a good chance the cat would return. The 7th house emphasis suggested that the spouse or partner of the owner has or would find the cat. Because the cat was red, I thought Mars might describe the cat. If Mars in 6th is the cat, Mars is mutually applying to a trine of Saturn in 1st (the manager and owner of the cat), so the cat may return rather quickly.

The cat was spotted by a neighbor east of its home (not west as the chart suggested) and returned home five days later on the morning of September 19 with some injuries to its legs and tail (as suggested by Saturn retrograde in the 1st house). Note that the Sun (the cat)

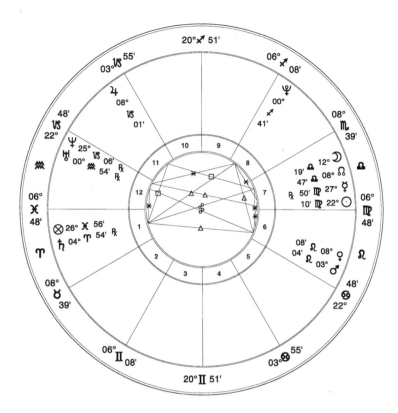

Chart 21: "Have you found our cat?"
September 14, 1996, 6:42 P.M. BST, 00E34, 51N31 Regiomontanus Houses

and Mercury (ruler of the 3rd of neighbors and the 7th of the manager's spouse) are mutually applying to a conjunction in five degrees (symbolizing five days).

## DEXTER (WAXING) AND SINISTER (WANING) ASPECTS

Dexter means "on the right-hand side of" and sinister means "on the left-hand side of." When astrologers actually looked at the night sky, they observed that when two planets traveling direct were separating from a conjunction, the faster planet would "cast its rays" to the right of itself, thereby forming a dexter aspect. In this case the faster planet was waxing with respect to the slower one. Because waxing or "increasing in light" were considered beneficial, dexter aspects were regarded as stronger than sinister ones.

A sinister aspect occurs when the faster planet casts its rays to the left of itself to form the aspect. If the faster planet is direct in motion, it is approaching an eventual conjunction with the slower one and is thus waning or decreasing in light. The ancients regarded waning or sinister aspects as less potent than waxing or dexter ones.

Confusion arose because many contemporary "authorities" did not understand what the ancient texts meant by dexter and sinister, that is, what was on the left or right side of what. Several modern texts actually reverse the traditional meanings of dexter and sinister. In addition, what is dexter (on the right) in the northern hemisphere is sinister (on the left) in the southern hemisphere. I think astrology would be better off by replacing dexter with "waxing," and sinister with "waning." See Figure 3.

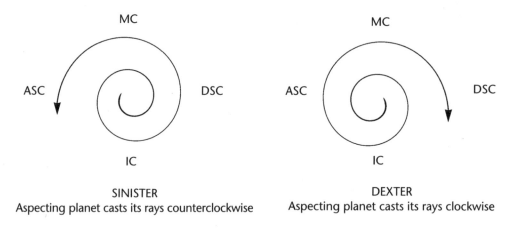

SINISTER
Aspecting planet casts its rays counterclockwise

DEXTER
Aspecting planet casts its rays clockwise

Figure 3: Sinister and Dexter Aspects

## ASPECTS TO HOUSE CUSPS

Lilly used aspects to the cusp of the house ruling a person to derive information. For example, the chart on page 452 of Lilly's *Christian Astrology* (Dec 8, 1642; Tz = 0; 9.20 A.M.; 51N30, 0W10) deals with the status of Prince Rupert, signified by the 10th house or 10° Scorpio on the MC. The Moon is at 10° Cancer, and Jupiter is at 10° Pisces. Lilly writes: "I must confess, at first finding the Moon in Cancer to cast her Trine Sinister to the cusp of the 10th, I judged the person of the man would be in no great danger ... and verily Jupiter doth also cast his Trine Dexter to the cusp of the 10th house, whereby I judged that we should not destroy his person." Sometimes a significator's aspect to a house cusp, especially a conjunction, will show the timing of an event.

## TRANSLATION OF LIGHT: AN ASTROLOGICAL BUCKET BRIGADE

Translation of light can either restore the action of a separating aspect between significators, or can intercede before a difficult aspect between significators becomes exact. Suppose, for example, that the primary significators have recently formed a major aspect that would have brought the matter to perfection if only the planets were still applying. Translation of light can come to the rescue.

Translation means that a planet that is faster than both significators can carry the light from one primary significator to another, reactivating a recent past aspect or interposing a favorable connection before a square or opposition can take place. It's like an astrological bucket brigade or the passing of a baton in a relay race. In the first instance, the significators were in aspect, they have passed that aspect, and a planet faster than both brings them into connection again. In the second instance, the significators are applying to an unfavorable square or opposition, but the faster third planet favorably connects their lights before the

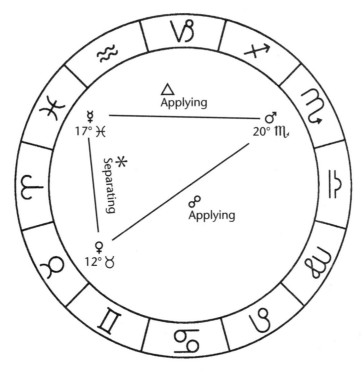

Figure 4

Example of translation from Bonatus: Venus and Mars are the primary significators. Mars is at 20° Scorpio, Venus at 12° Taurus, and Mercury at 17° Pisces. The faster third planet Mercury separates from sextile to Venus, who receives Mercury in her exaltation Pisces. Mercury carries the light of Venus to Mars, which Mercury is about to trine, creating a favorable connection between the primary significators. By transferring the light of Venus to Mars, Mercury allows a favorable outcome, which would otherwise be denied because Venus opposes Mars.

difficult aspect becomes exact. Study Figure 4 for an example from Bonatus of translation of light. Let me give an anthropomorphic example to illustrate these ideas of translation of light. Suppose you need both your uncle and your grandfather to sign a document. You go to grandpa's house and discover that your uncle has recently visited your grandfather but has already left. You obtain your grandfather's signature and leave in search of your uncle. If you're fast enough, you can catch up with your uncle and get him to sign also. Because you move faster than both your elders, you can transport the document from one to the other and bring them into contact again.

A variation on this theme would be that, left to their own devices, your uncle and grandfather would never sign the document. Instead, they would be in opposition and might even square off against one another. Being younger and faster, you approach both your uncle and grandfather separately and use your charm (sextiles and trines) to get each of them to sign the document individually, thus bringing the matter to perfection.

A footnote to the aphorisms of Bonatus says that translation of light occurs "when a planet separates from one that is slower than itself, and overtakes another either by conjunction or aspect." The classical definition requires that the significator from which the faster planet separates must receive the translating planet in one of its essential dignities. In other words, the faster planet must start out in a segment of the zodiac governed (through one of the dignities) by the first significator so that it can carry the light of the first significator with it to the second one. As in a relay race, the translating planet must accept the baton from a member of its own team, not from an unrelated team.

Many modern astrologers do not require reception by essential dignity and allow the faster planet to aspect both significators in turn, rather than separating from one and applying to the other. The modern definition is this: a third planet faster than both significators and in an earlier degree, must aspect each of them in turn to translate the light and restore the potency of the separating aspect that exists between significators.

To translate the light of an aspect, the translating planet must be moving faster than both significators. Naturally this role often falls to the Moon or Mercury, the two fastest bodies in the tropical zodiac. These two bodies take on the coloring of any planets they aspect. We saw in the San Francisco earthquake chart how Mercury, having completed squares to Uranus and Saturn, and applying to squares with Jupiter and Neptune, translated the light and reactivated the various conjunctions and oppositions among these heavy planets. The Moon played a similar role in the earthquake chart as it translated the light among the various heavy planets, recharging their previous malefic connections.

Translation of light is easy to miss if you don't look for it. The trick is this: if the two primary significators are applying to a square or an opposition, or have recently made a favorable aspect that you wish you could use to answer the question, see whether a faster planet can create a favorable connection by translating the light from one significator to the other. A third planet translation the light implies that a third party will voluntarily enter the situation to help in its completion.

## COLLECTION OF LIGHT: THE ASTROLOGICAL STOREHOUSE

In translation of light, a faster (lighter) third planet can reactivate an aspect that recently occurred between significators but is now over, or can interpose a positive connection between significators before a stressful aspect between them becomes exact.

In collection of light, a slower (heavier) third planet can establish a contact between significators that are not applying to a favorable major aspect needed to perfect the matter. It may be that the significators will not form a major aspect or else will oppose (or square) one another, denying perfection of the matter. Perfection is still possible, however, if a slower third planet stores up the energies of the two faster significators in a weightier spot in the zodiac.

Suppose the two primary significators make no favorable Ptolemaic aspect before leaving their signs, but it would be nice for the outcome if they did. Suppose further that each significator applies to a major aspect with a third planet slower than both and in a later degree. The slower third planet can act like a toll collector, or, better yet, a lightning rod that draws and stores the energy from both significators to make it available to perfect the matter.

In the classical definition of collection of light, each significator must receive the slower third planet in at least one of its essential dignities. In other words, the heavier third planet must be in the sign, exaltation, triplicity, term, or face of the primary significators. Symbolically the heavier third planet represents a third party to whom both persons can turn for help in bringing the matter to perfection.

Bonatus gives the example of a night chart with the Sun and Jupiter as primary significators. Jupiter lies at 15° Sagittarius, the Sun at 14° Gemini, and weighty Saturn at 18° Aries. Saturn lies in Aries, the exaltation of the Sun, so the Sun receives Saturn through its exaltation. Jupiter receives Saturn through his triplicity because Jupiter rules the fire triplicity (Aries) by night. Jupiter applies to a trine of Saturn, and the Sun applies to a sextile of Saturn. The problem is that the Sun and Jupiter are applying to an opposition—a separative aspect that will not allow perfection of the matter. Saturn, however, being in a later degree than both the Sun and Jupiter, is able to collect both their lights just after the Sun and Jupiter form an opposition, thus bringing the matter to perfection. Symbolically, Saturn signifies a third person who facilitates a fortunate completion.

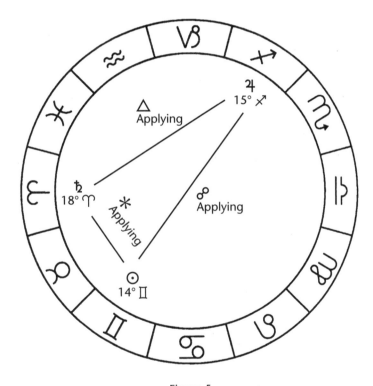

Figure 5

Example of Collection of Light from Bonatus: The Sun and Jupiter are the primary significators. Jupiter is at 15° Sagittarius, the Sun at 14° Gemini, and Saturn at 18° Aries. The heaviest planet Saturn lies in Aries, the exaltation of the Sun, so the Sun receives Saturn through its exaltation. Jupiter receives Saturn through his triplicity because Jupiter rules the fire triplicity (Aries) by night. Jupiter applies to Saturn by trine, and the Sun applies to Saturn by sextile. The Sun and Jupiter are applying to an opposition—a separative aspect that implies non-accomplishment. However, just after Sun opposes Jupiter, the heavier third planet Saturn will collect the light of both the Sun and Jupiter and favorably reunite them, allowing the matter to come to perfection. Symbolically, Saturn signifies a third person who can bring the matter to a fortunate completion.

Like translation, collection is easy to miss if you don't look for it. You should check for collection when the two significators make no favorable aspect but you wish that they did. If the two primary rulers make no aspect between themselves, or apply to a square or opposition, ask if they will each favorably aspect an even slower planet; if so, that slower third planet can collect their lights and bring the matter to perfection. Study Figure 5 for an example from Bonatus of collection of light.

## AN ILLUSTRATIVE EXAMPLE OF MORE ADVANCED CONCEPTS

The following case illustrates many of the concepts in this chapter. Joan McEvers had included this question when she sent me the one about her son's stained glass business. It was a second question whose horary chart puzzled her. See Chart 22.

McEvers is the querent. On June 24, 1987, at 10 A.M. PST, 116W46/47N41, she asked, "Will I get the job with Llewellyn?" Ordinarily I would interview the querent to find out more about the type of job and the circumstances surrounding the question. Because I was working with only the verbatim question, I had to approach this chart cold. The only thing I knew was that Llewellyn is a publisher of astrological books, including this one. I also had a bias that Llewellyn would be foolish not to hire someone of McEvers' stature.

There are no classical considerations before judgment. Virgo rising, ruled by Mercury (writers), fits the querent. Mercury ruling both the Ascendant and the MC links the 1st and

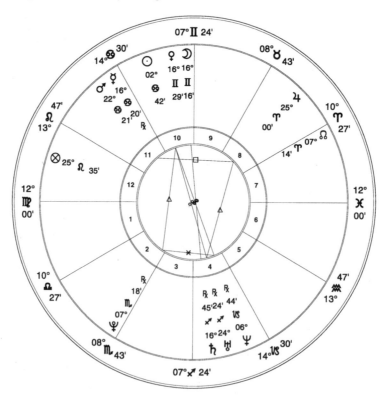

Chart 22: "Will I get the job with Llewellyn?"
June 24, 1987, 10:00 A.M. PST, 116W46, 47N41   Koch Houses

10th houses, suggesting the querent (1st) is asking about a job (10th) about writing, books, or communication (Mercury). The sun and Moon in the 10th house also imply a question about career. Cancer on the cusp of the 11th and Mercury (questions) in the 11th house highlight income from career. Leo on the cusp of the 12th points to work done in solitude, such as writing and editing. The chart appears radical and fit to judge.

In the context of the question, the chart tells me that the "job with Llewellyn" most likely involves writing or editing (Mercury) for the publisher in the solitude of her home (12th). With Virgo rising, Mercury—McEvers' ruler—is retrograde at 16° 20' Cancer in the 11th house. The retrograde significator suggests she might change her mind about the job, or it might involve going back over something as in editing a book (Mercury).

The 6th house rules routine tedious work and the 10th governs career and profession. Since the chart emphasizes the 10th house, I took Gemini on the cusp of the 10th to rule the job. I couldn't imagine McEvers doing 6th house drudge work for Llewellyn. They get people like my editor to do that. Mercury, ruler of Gemini, already rules McEvers so we need to use the planets in the 10th to symbolize the job. There are three planets in the 10th: the Moon, Venus, and the sun—all considered benefics by Bonatus, suggesting a positive answer to the question.

There are no major Ptolemaic aspects between McEvers' ruler Mercury and the three planets representing the job. I think this is why McEvers found the chart puzzling. But, *mirabile dictu,* the Moon and Mercury are in mutual reception and are also mutually applying to an exact semi-sextile in only three minutes of arc. The semi-sextile is favorable for financial matters. The combined mutual application and mutual reception (Moon in Gemini ruled by Mercury, Mercury in Cancer ruled by the Moon) are compelling indications that she will get the job.

Furthermore, consider the following. The fastest body, the Moon at 16° 17' Gemini, will semi-sextile Mercury retrograde at 16° 20' Cancer and then conjoin Venus at 16° 28' Gemini, thus translating the light of Mercury (McEvers) to Venus (the job). This confirms she will get the job.

We see yet another confirmation in the application of the Moon (which always co-rules the querent) to a conjunction with Venus (the job). Venus in this chart also rules the 9th house of publishers (Llewellyn) and the 2nd house (6th of the 9th) of the publisher's employees. The Moon (McEvers) conjoins (comes together with) Venus (the publisher and his employees)—yet another sign that Llewellyn will hire her.

The outcome was that McEvers got the job, which involved editing a book for Llewellyn in the solitude of her home office. The retrograde Mercury (documents) correlated with a re-negotiation of the contract.

## HISTORICAL INTERLUDE
### WILLIAM LILLY AND THE FIRE OF LONDON

William Lilly was a British astrologer whose *Christian Astrology* is the classic western textbook on horary astrology. His fame increased when he predicted the great fire of London (September 2, 1666). He disseminated his predictions via a now-famous woodcut depicting the Gemini twins descending into a conflagration, which is shown below. The chart for the driving of the first pile of the new London Bridge has Gemini rising, and in the astrological community Gemini was associated with the city of London.

    This fire had also been predicted by Nostradamus a century earlier when he wrote, "The blood of the just, which has been spilled in London, requires it be burn with fire in sixty-six." Lilly's prediction of the fire was so well-known that the House of Commons summoned him to appear before an investigating committee to explain what he knew about the conflagration.

# CHAPTER SIX

# Essential Dignity, Almutens, and Other Considerations

C ertain questions require the astrologer to consider the relative strength of the two significators. This chapter will review the essential and accidental dignities of the planets and other factors that affect planetary potency (strength, dignity).

## Astrological Anthropomorphism and Peregrine Planets

Western astrology derives mainly from Babylonian, Egyptian, and Greek sources. The Egyptians named the heavenly bodies after their gods, and the Greeks of Egypt identified the Egyptian gods with their own. The ancients regarded the stars and planets as divinities. They considered their royalty and heroes to be gods whose souls ascended to heaven on their deaths to take their rightful place among the stars. Like earthly kings, the celestial star-gods governed particular realms. Our astrological ideas of essential dignity derive from this anthropomorphic theory.

We saw the importance of planetary dignities in the discussion of translation and collection of light. In the classical definition, a faster planet can only translate the light of a significator if it occupies one of the essential dignities of that significator when the chart is cast. In other words, the translating planet can gather the significator's light only if it starts out from a region of the zodiac in which that significator has dignity (strength).

Similarly, with the collection of light, the classical definition requires the slower (collecting) planet to be simultaneously in an essential dignity of each of the two significators. Suppose, for example, that Saturn wanted to collect the light of Mars and Jupiter. Saturn is slower than both Mars and Jupiter and should be able to collect their lights if the two faster planets will each aspect Saturn. To collect the light of Mars, Saturn would have to lie in a part of the zodiac where Mars has dignity. In addition, Saturn would have to be in one of Jupiter's essential dignities to collect his light. The anthropomorphic idea is that to collect something from you, I must go to a place where you are dignified.

The ancients used only the Sun, the Moon, and the five visible planets to govern particular regions of the zodiac. There were many ways to carve the zodiac depending on the calendar used by the culture. The Babylonians gave us the twelve zodiacal signs. They also used ten-degree divisions of the signs—the faces or decans—and five-day intervals, or the seventy-two "pictures," to measure smaller segments of time. The Egyptians and Chaldeans incorporated the seventy-two "sign" divisions into astrology as the "terms" of the planets. Different traditions have assigned different planetary rulers to the thirty-six decans and the seventy-two terms.

The modern rulers of the decans come from Hindu astrology, which grouped the signs according to the four elements (fire, earth, air, and water). Fire signs are Aries, Leo, and Sagittarius. Earth signs are Taurus, Virgo, and Capricorn. Air signs are Gemini, Libra, and Aquarius. Water signs are Cancer, Scorpio, and Pisces. Modern astrologers call these four groups, each containing the three signs of the same element, the four "triplicities," which are not to be confused with the system of triplicities used by Ptolemy.

In the Hindu system of faces (decanates), each sign rules its own first decan (ten-degree segment). The next sign of the element governs the second decan, and the third sign of the element rules the remaining decan. For example, Mercury and Virgo govern the first decan (face) of Virgo. Saturn and Capricorn, the next earth sign, rule the second decan of Virgo. Lastly, Venus and Taurus, the final earth sign, govern the last decan of Virgo.

By contrast, in the Ptolemaic system, the Sun rules the first decan of Virgo; Venus, the second; and Mercury, the third decan. This is the so-called Chaldean order of decanates that follows the Chaldean order of planets: Saturn, Jupiter, Mars, Sun, Venus, Mercury, Moon. The Chaldean order of decans begins with Mars ruling the first decan (face, decanate, ten-degree segment) of his own sign Aries, the Sun ruling the second decan of Aries, and Venus ruling the third decan of Aries. Next is Mercury ruling the first decan of Taurus, the Moon ruling the second decan of Taurus, and so on through the zodiac.

Following the Chaldeans, Ptolemy then assigned rulers to the faces in descending order of the speed of the planets; starting with Saturn, followed by Jupiter, Mars, Sun, Venus, Mercury, and the Moon. This pattern repeats through the thirty-six faces of the zodiac. You can see this clearly if you look at the faces in Table 6 of Ptolemy's Essential Dignities.

In addition to the Chaldean decans, the Ptolemaic system of triplicities may also take some getting used to. Like modern astrologers, Ptolemy assigned three signs to each of the four elements. The rulerships are a little different, however. The Sun rules fire by day, and Jupiter rules fire by night. Venus rules earth by day, and the Moon governs earth by night. Saturn rules air by day, and Mercury governs air by night. Mars rules water by both day and night.

Ptolemy synthesized the various methods of dividing the zodiac and assigning planetary rulers into his famous table of essential dignities. As a king could govern his country and its many territories, a planetary god could rule a sign and other regions of the zodiac. If a king visited a friendly nation, he might be "exalted" or treated royally. Although the king did not rule the place of his exaltation, he felt quite at home there. You can substitute "planet" for "king" in this discussion. A king or planet has "dignity" when it occupies a region that it rules or where it is exalted.

**Table 6: Ptolemy's Essential Dignities and Debilities as Used By Lilly**
D: Day House N: Night House

| Sign | ♈<br>Aries | ♉<br>Taurus | ♊<br>Gemini | ♋<br>Cancer | ♌<br>Leo | ♍<br>Virgo | ♎<br>Libra | ♏<br>Scorpio | ♐<br>Sagittarius | ♑<br>Capricorn | ♒<br>Aquarius | ♓<br>Pisces |
|---|---|---|---|---|---|---|---|---|---|---|---|---|
| **Ruler** | ♂D | ♀N | ☿D | D☽N | D☉N | ☿N | ♀D | ♂N | ♃D | ♄N | ♄D | ♃N |
| **Exaltation**<br>*Exalted Degree* | ☉<br>19th | ☽<br>3rd | ☊<br>3rd | ♃<br>15th | | ☿<br>15th | ♄<br>21st | | ☋<br>3rd | ♂<br>28th | | ♀<br>27th |
| **Triplicity**<br>*Day*<br>*Night* | ☉<br>♃ | ♀<br>☽ | ♄<br>☿ | ♂<br>♂ | ☉<br>♃ | ♀<br>☽ | ♄<br>☿ | ♂<br>♂ | ☉<br>♃ | ♀<br>☽ | ♄<br>☿ | ♂<br>♂ |
| **Terms**<br>*(Five-day divisions)* | 0°<br>♃<br>6°<br>♀<br>14°<br>☿<br>21°<br>♂<br>26°<br>♄<br>30° | 0°<br>♀<br>8°<br>☿<br>15°<br>♃<br>22°<br>♄<br>26°<br>♂<br>30° | 0°<br>☿<br>7°<br>♃<br>14°<br>♀<br>21°<br>♄<br>25°<br>♂<br>30° | 0°<br>♂<br>6°<br>♃<br>13°<br>☿<br>20°<br>♀<br>27°<br>♄<br>30° | 0°<br>♄<br>6°<br>☿<br>13°<br>♀<br>19°<br>♃<br>25°<br>♂<br>30° | 0°<br>☿<br>7°<br>♀<br>13°<br>♃<br>18°<br>♄<br>24°<br>♂<br>14° | 0°<br>♄<br>6°<br>♀<br>11°<br>♃<br>19°<br>☿<br>24°<br>♂<br>30° | 0°<br>♂<br>6°<br>♃<br>14°<br>♀<br>21°<br>☿<br>27°<br>♄<br>30° | 0°<br>♃<br>8°<br>♀<br>14°<br>☿<br>19°<br>♄<br>25°<br>♂<br>30° | 0°<br>♀<br>6°<br>☿<br>12°<br>♃<br>19°<br>♂<br>25°<br>♄<br>30° | 0°<br>♄<br>6°<br>☿<br>12°<br>♀<br>20°<br>♃<br>25°<br>♂<br>30° | 0°<br>♀<br>8°<br>♃<br>14°<br>☿<br>20°<br>♂<br>26°<br>♄<br>30° |
| **Faces**<br>*0–10 Degrees*<br>*10–20 Degrees*<br>*20–30 Degrees* | ♂<br>☉<br>♀ | ☿<br>♀<br>♄ | ♃<br>♂<br>☉ | ♀<br>☿<br>☽ | ♄<br>♃<br>♂ | ☉<br>♀<br>☿ | ☽<br>♄<br>♃ | ♂<br>☉<br>♀ | ☿<br>☽<br>♄ | ♃<br>♂<br>☉ | ♀<br>☿<br>☽ | ♄<br>♃<br>♂ |
| **Detriment** | ♀ | ♂ | ♃ | ♄ | ♄ | ♃ | ♂ | ♀ | ☿ | ☽ | ☉ | ☿ |
| **Fall** | ♄ | | ☋ | ♂ | | ♀ | ☉ | ☽ | ☊ | ♃ | | ☿ |

When a planet has no essential dignity whatsoever, we call it peregrine. The planets all make a peregrination (long journey) around the zodiac. The word *peregrine* derives from a Latin term meaning "beyond the borders of the field," where the field is the home territory. In English, peregrine means foreign, alien, or from abroad. A king was never peregrine if he traveled among territories he ruled or which exalted him. He felt at home and was not a foreigner in any of these places. If a king visited a land he did not rule and in which he had no exaltation, the king was a foreigner there, that is, he was peregrine, wandering aimlessly and not at home in any way.

Diplomats knew that if their king was visiting a foreign county, it was nice to have an exchange visit going on because they could then get their king out of trouble, should it arise. In astrology we call such an exchange visit a "mutual reception." We can compare a mutual reception to a hostage situation. Suppose, for example, that England and France were not friendly toward one another. If the king of England were visiting France while, at the same time, the king of France were visiting England, then both kings could feel safe. Each king is peregrine (alien) in the foreign country, but presumably nothing untoward will happen to either king while each country receives the ruler of the other. The mutual reception gives the kings exchange status and a way out of a jam.

Let me draw a modern analogy to further clarify the five essential dignities. Imagine each sign of the zodiac as a business housed in a commercial building owned by seven partners (planets). The principal member of the partnership is the primary owner of the business and its headquarters. The chief partner corresponds to the planet that rules the sign. Sometimes an important customer of the business visits the headquarters. That customer is treated royally and feels exalted when he steps inside the building. The principal customer does not own the business but he or she loves to visit there.

In addition, some of the partners use the commercial building by day and others use it by night. For example, in my son's elementary school the teachers use the school building during the day, and the cub scouts and civic organizations use it at night. The day and night users correspond to the day and night triplicities.

The business is further divided into three equal components, and a different partner looks after each of the three divisions. These are the three faces or decanates of the signs. Finally, the building itself consists of five separate rooms of slightly unequal size. Different partners take charge of each of the five rooms, one to a room. Each partner has a special place in the room which he or she governs. These are the five terms of the planets.

If a competitor of the business happens by, he or she is not treated very well and feels at a detriment. If an industrial spy gets caught in the building, he or she gets booted out and takes a fall.

## My Daddy Is Stronger than Your Daddy

Little boys like to compare the strength of their fathers. Horary astrologers like to compare the strength of their significators. This comparison is made by the planet's location around the zodiac belt and by other factors affecting the significator. Planetary strength varies in proportion to the dignity of the planet. The most potent dignity is rulership of a sign of the zodiac. Next in power is exaltation, followed in order by triplicity, term, and face—the weakest form of dignity.

Lilly proposed a point system for rating dignities and debilities of the planets. Lilly gave five points to a planet in its own sign or in mutual reception with another planet by sign. A planet in its exaltation or in mutual reception with another planet by exaltation gets four points. Planets in their own triplicity get three points; in their own terms, two points; and in their own face, one point. I have reproduced Lilly's scoring system in Table 7 for planetary dignities and Table 8 for the Part of Fortune.

In the Lilly point system, if a planet does not have dignity by zodiac location, it is either neutral or debilitated. Planets lose five points for being peregrine, that is, wandering aimlessly without any dignity in the chart. Lilly thought that such undignified planets designated shiftless thieves when posited in angular houses, which gave them the energy to do nefarious deeds. Peregrine planets in the 2nd house could also act as thieves because they were wandering through the house of your valuable possessions.

Planets also lose five points if they occupy the sign opposite the one they rule, that is, when in their "detriment." Planets only get a four-point penalty for traveling through the sign opposite their exaltation, that is, when in their "fall."

As you can see from Table 7, zodiac location is not the only way to gain or lose points. The potency of planets also depends on the aspects they make, their speed, their relation to the Sun, their house position, and many other obscure qualities noted in the annals of horary astrology. Just when you thought your daddy was about to go down to defeat, he cleverly pulls out a secret weapon known only to the horary astrologer. This part of horary is an obsessive-compulsive's dream, and to such horary arcana I devote the rest of this chapter.

---

### Table 7: Lilly's Point System for Dignity & Debility

#### ESSENTIAL DIGNITIES

| | |
|---|---|
| +5 | A planet in its own sign, or in mutual reception with another planet by sign. |
| +4 | A planet in its exaltation, or in mutual reception with another planet by exaltation. |
| +3 | A planet in its own day or night triplicity (not to be confused with the modern triplicities). |
| +2 | A planet in its own term. |
| +1 | A planet in its own Chaldean decanate or face. |

#### ACCIDENTAL DIGNITIES

| | |
|---|---|
| +5 | In the 10th or 1st house. |
| +4 | In the 7th, 4th, or 11th (Good Daemon's) house. |
| +3 | In the 2nd or 5th house. |
| +2 | In the 9th house. |
| +1 | In the 3rd house. |
| +4 | Direct in motion (does not apply to Sun and Moon). |
| +2 | Swift in motion (faster than average). |
| +2 | Mars, Jupiter, or Saturn oriental of (rising before) the Sun. |
| +2 | Mercury, or Venus occidental of (rising after) the Sun. |
| +2 | Moon increasing in light, or occidental of the Sun. |

---

### Table 7: Lilly's Point System for Dignity & Debility (continued)

#### ACCIDENTAL DIGNITIES

| | |
|---|---|
| +5 | Free from combustion and the Sun's rays. |
| +5 | Cazimi (within 17 minutes of the Sun). |
| +5 | Partile conjunction with Jupiter or Venus. |
| +4 | Partile conjunction with Dragon's Head (Moon's North Node). |
| +4 | Partile trine Jupiter or Venus. |
| +3 | Partile sextile Jupiter or Venus. |
| +6 | Partile conjunct Cor Leonis (Regulus) at 29° 50' Leo in January 2000. |
| +5 | Partile conjunct Spica at 23° 50' Libra in January 2000. |

#### ESSENTIAL AND ACCIDENTAL DEBILITIES

| | |
|---|---|
| -5 | In Detriment. |
| -4 | In Fall. |
| -5 | Peregrine. |
| -5 | In the 12th house (of the Evil Daemon). |
| -2 | In the 6th or 8th houses. |
| -5 | Retrograde. |
| -2 | Slower than average motion. |
| -2 | Mars, Jupiter, or Saturn occidental to the Sun. |
| -2 | Mercury, or Venus oriental to the Sun. |
| - 2 | Moon decreasing in light. |
| -5 | Combust the Sun (between 17' and 8.5° from Sol). |
| -4 | Under the Sunbeams (between 8.5° and 17° from Sol). |
| -5 | Partile conjunction with Mars or Saturn. |
| -4 | Partile conjunction with Dragon's Tail (Moon's South Node). |
| -5 | Besieged between Mars and Saturn. |
| -4 | Partile opposite Mars or Saturn. |
| -3 | Partile square Mars or Saturn. |
| -5 | Within 5° of Caput Algol at 26° 10' Taurus in January 2000. |

---

### Table 8: Lilly's Point System for Dignity & Debility of Pars Fortuna

#### PARS FORTUNA STRONG AND FORTUNATE IN THE SIGNS:

| | |
|---|---|
| +5 | Taurus, Pisces. |
| +4 | Libra, Sagittarius, Leo, Cancer. |
| +3 | Gemini. |
| +2 | In the terms of Venus and Jupiter when in Virgo. |

#### PARS FORTUNA IS STRONG WHEN:

| | |
|---|---|
| +5 | Partile conjunct Jupiter or Venus. |
| +4 | Partile trine Jupiter or Venus. |
| +3 | Partile sextile Jupiter or Venus. |

| Table 8: Lilly's Point System for Dignity & Debility of Pars Fortuna (continued) |
|---|

### PARS FORTUNA IS STRONG WHEN:

| | |
|---|---|
| +5 | Partile conjunct Jupiter or Venus. |
| +4 | Partile trine Jupiter or Venus. |
| +3 | Partile sextile Jupiter or Venus. |
| +3 | Partile conjunct the Moon's North Node. |
| +5 | In the 1st or 10th House. |
| +4 | In the 7th, 4th, or 11th House. |
| +3 | In the 2nd or 5th House. |
| +2 | In the 9th House. |
| +1 | In the 3rd House. |
| +6 | Conjunct Regulus. |
| +5 | Conjunct Spica. |
| +5 | Not Combust or Under the Sunbeams. |

### PARS FORTUNA WEAK IN THE SIGNS:

| | |
|---|---|
| -5 | Scorpio, Capricorn, and Aquarius (the signs of the malefics). |
| -0 | Aries ("In Aries he neither gets nor loses"). |

### PARS FORTUNA IS WEAK WHEN:

| | |
|---|---|
| -5 | Partile conjunct Saturn or Mars. |
| -4 | Partile opposite Saturn or Mars. |
| -3 | Partile conjunct the Moon's South Node. |
| -3 | Partile square Saturn or Mars. |
| -2 | In the Terms of Saturn or Mars. |
| -5 | In the 12th House. |
| -4 | In the 8th or 6th House (Houses 8, 6, and 12 are the traditional "bad" houses). |
| -5 | Combust the Sun. |
| -4 | Conjunct Caput Algol. |

## ACCIDENTAL DIGNITY

In addition to dignity by zodiac location, planets can achieve dignity by their house placement. Placement in an angle—houses 1, 4, 7, or 10—gives power to a planet and turns peregrine planets into thieves. Modern astrologers feel the 10th is the strongest house, followed in order by the 1st, 7th, and 4th. In contrast, placement in a cadent house—3, 6, 9, or 12—weakens the significator.

The first-century astrologer Dorotheus used a different point system. To quote him, "The best of the places is the ascendant, then the midheaven, then what follows the midheaven which is the 11th from the ascendant, then the opposite to this 11th place from the ascendant, which is the 5th from the ascendant which is called the house of the child, then the opposite to the ascendant, which is the sign of marriage, then the cardine of the earth, then the 9th place from the ascendant." These are the seven preferred houses of the horoscope. To repeat Dorotheus, the seven good houses are, in order of decreasing potency: 1 10 11 5 7 4 9. Dorotheus also gives his list of the bad places. These evil locations are "the 3rd from the ascendant because it is said that it is the place of joy of the Moon, and the 2nd from the ascendant, then the 8th from the ascendant, which is the sign of death. Of these places which I told you, the first [ascendant] is the strongest. There remain equal to this [ascendant] two places which are the worst of the worst, and they are the 6th and the 12th." To summarize Dorotheus, the evil or bad houses in order of increasing maleficity are: 3, 2, 8, 6, 12.

Lilly took the list of Dorotheus and modified it as follows. Quoting Lilly, "The Angles are most powerful, the Succedants are next in virtue, the Cadents poor and of little efficacy: the Succedant houses follow the Angles, the Cadents come next [after] the Succedants; in force and virtue they stand so in order: 1, 10, 7, 4, 11, 5, 9, 3, 2, 8, 6, 12. The meaning whereof is this, that two Planets equally dignified, the one in the Ascendant, the other in the tenth house, you shall judge the Planet in the Ascendant somewhat of more power to effect what he is Significator of, than he that is in the tenth: do so in the rest as they stand in order, remembering that Planets in Angles do more forcibly show their effects."

Other accidental dignities include favorable aspects to the benefics or the Part of Fortune, freedom from combustion, swiftness of motion, increasing in light, highest elevation (nearest the M.C. in the 9th or 10th houses), closest to the horizon from the 1st or 2nd houses, oriental (eastern) in the chart, wideness of declination (more than seventeen degrees), directness of motion, and conjunction with benefic fixed stars or the Dragon's Head. The Moon or a planet is increasing in light when it is leaving a conjunction with the Sun. It decreases in light when it leaves an opposition with the Sun.

Mars, Jupiter and Saturn have dignity when oriental (east) of the Sun, that is, when they rise before the Sun. According to Lilly, "Saturn, Jupiter, and Mars are Oriental of the Sun from the time of their conjunction with him until they come to his Opposition." The Moon, Mercury and Venus are dignified when occidental (west) of the Sun, that is, when they set after the Sun. Lilly says, "To be Occidental is to be seen above the Horizon, or to set after the Sun is down: Mercury and Venus can make no Sextile, Trine, or Opposition to the Sun: their Orientality is when they are in fewer degrees of the Sign the Sun is in, or in the sign preceding; their Occidentality, when they are in more degrees of the sign the Sun is in, or next subsequent. ... The Moon is Oriental of the Sun from the time of her opposition to her conjunction." To judge whether a planet is oriental or occidental of the Sun, you can mentally rotate the chart so the Sun falls on the Ascendant. Any planets above the horizon are oriental (east of the Sun, rising before the Sun), and any below the horizon are occidental (west of the Sun, rising and setting after the Sun).

## ALMUTENS

In addition to taking as significators the planet(s) that rule or occupy a house, traditional astrologers also considered the Almuten(s) of a house. The Almuten is the planet that has the most essential dignities at the degree of the sign on the cusp of the house. Because the triplicities have different rulers by day and by night, the Almutens will also vary by day and by night, that is, by whether the Sun is above or below the horizon. The same degree of a sign always has the same Almuten, depending on whether it is a day or a night chart.

Table 9 summarizes the Almutens of each degree of the zodiac for both day and night charts. Almutens are calculated by giving five points for sign rulership, four for exaltation, three for triplicity, two for term, and one for face. The planet with the most essential dignities by location is Almuten for that degree. For example, in a day chart Saturn is the Almuten of Libra because Saturn is exalted (four points) and, by day, rules the air triplicity (three points), for a total of seven points. Because planets can tie for total dignities, some degrees have more than

| Table 9: Almutens of Signs by Day and by Night | | |
|---|---|---|
| SIGN | BY DAY | BY NIGHT |
| ARIES | 0–21, Sun<br>21–26, Sun and Mars<br>26–30, Sun | 0–10, Mars<br>10–20, Sun and Mars<br>20–30, Mars |
| TAURUS | 0–30, Venus | 0–8, Moon and Venus<br>8–30, Moon |
| GEMINI | 0–21, Mercury<br>21–25, Mercury, Saturn<br>25–30, Mercury | 0–30, Mercury |
| CANCER | 0–6, Moon, Mars<br>6–13, Jupiter<br>13–30, Moon | 0–6, Moon, Jupiter<br>6–13, Jupiter<br>13–30, Moon |
| LEO | 0–30, Sun | 0–19, Sun<br>19–20, Jupiter<br>20–25, Sun, Jupiter<br>25–30, Sun |
| VIRGO | 0–30, Mercury | 0–30, Mercury |
| LIBRA | 0–6, Saturn<br>6–10, Venus, Saturn<br>10–30, Saturn | 0–6, Saturn<br>6–11, Venus<br>11–19, Venus, Saturn<br>19–20, Mercury, Venus, Saturn<br>20–24, Mercury, Venus<br>24–30, Venus |
| SCORPIO | 0–30, Mars | 0–30, Mars |
| SAGITTARIUS | 0–30, Jupiter | 0–30, Jupiter |
| CAPRICORN | 0–6, Venus, Saturn<br>6–10, Saturn<br>10–19, Mars, Saturn | 0–10, Saturn<br>10–19, Mars, Saturn<br>19–30, Saturn<br>19–25, Mars<br>25–30, Saturn |
| AQUARIUS | 0–30, Saturn | 0–30, Saturn |
| PISCES | 0–8, Venus<br>8–20, Jupiter<br>20–26, Mars<br>26–30, Jupiter | 0–8, Venus<br>8–20, Jupiter<br>20–26, Mars<br>26–30, Jupiter |

one Almuten. In a night chart, or instance, Venus and Saturn are both Almuten for the area from six to eleven degrees of Libra because Venus rules Libra (five points) and also has terms (two points) from six to eleven degrees degrees of Libra, for a total of seven points in that area.

According to Lilly, the Almuten is "that planet who has most dignities in the sign ascending or descending upon the cusp of any house, whereon, or from whence, you require judgment." The Almuten of a house will sometimes vary depending on which house system one uses because the cusps of the various house systems will often be different. The Almuten of the whole chart (or figure) is the planet with the most essential dignities in the horoscope. Lilly used Almutens to find lost or stolen items and advised, "Look to the Lord of the 2nd and his Almuten (viz. he that has most dignities there) there are the goods."

## COMBUST, CAZIMI, AND UNDER THE SUNBEAMS

I think the Arabs favored these rules because they tried to do astrology in the heat of the midday Sun. Bonatus said: "A corporal conjunction with the Sun is the greatest misfortune that can befall a planet." Dorotheus taught that the Sun's rays are so powerful they obscure or burn any planet that gets too close (combust). If the planet is not too close to the Sun but not yet far enough away, it simply gets a bad Sunburn (under the Sunbeams).

Combustion is the astrological version of the myth of Icarus who flew so near the Sun that the wax holding his wings together melted and he fell to his death. According to Lilly,

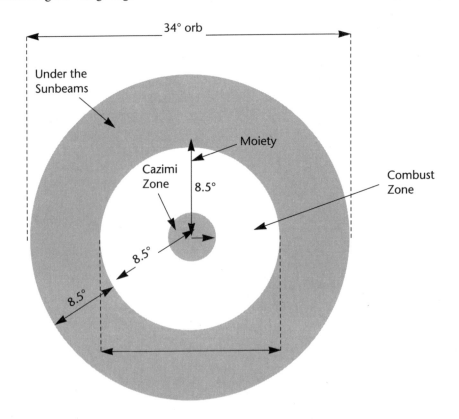

Figure 6: Parameters of Sol's Influence

"A Planet is said to be Combust of the Sun, when in the same Sign where the Sun is in, he is not distant from the Sun eight degrees and thirty minutes, either before or after the Sun. ... the Significator of the Querent Combust, shows him or her in great fear, and over powered by some great person."

The problem with this rule is that the Sun is also the giver of life. To reconcile these conflicting traditions, astrologers developed the notion of "Cazimi" or being in the heart of the Sun. According to Lilly, "All Authors do hold a Planet in Cazimi to be fortified thereby." The Sun has a heart of gold and strengthens a planet so situated. If you believe that one, I'd like to sell you the Brooklyn Bridge.

What would horary astrology be without specific rules to tell you when a planet is combust, Cazimi, or under the beams? Combustion relates to the heliacal (related to the Sun) risings of the planets. The heliacal rising occurs when the planet that was hidden by the Sun's rays becomes visible, either east or west of the Sun. The heliacal setting is the planet's disappearance behind the Sun's rays as it approaches the Sun. The Moon rises or sets heliacally when it is seventeen degrees away from the Sun. This fact gave rise to the following parameters (see also Figure 6):

- Cazimi: Between zero and seventeen minutes from the Sun. "In the heart of the Sun." Corporally joined with the Sun and therefore greatly strengthened.

- Combust: Burned by the Sun's rays when between seventeen minutes and eight and a half degrees from the Sun and in the same sign as the Sun. Outside the body of the Sun but within the moiety of its traditional orb. Burned and weakened by the Sun. Like a third-degree burn. The Moon is especially weak here. The querent is afraid and overpowered by a great person.

- Under the Sunbeams: More than eight and a half and less than seventeen degrees from the Sun; that is, at a distance greater than the moiety but less than the orb of the Sun. Slightly weakened. A bad case of Sunburn.

## THE NEW MOON

The New Moon, especially when applying, is a classically malefic influence in a horary chart. The New Moon occurs when the Moon conjoins the Sun, that is, goes from being combust to Cazimi. Why the Cazimi position of the Moon is so malefic when it greatly benefits the other planets is beyond me. I take this rule with a grain of salt because I have seen New Moon charts in which everything worked out fine. On the other hand, an approaching New Moon in an otherwise negative chart confirms a bad outcome.

## THE FULL MOON

Bonatus advised that if the ruler of the most recent Full Moon before the question fell "in any of the angles of the thing enquired after ... it denotes that the matter will be accomplished." I assume Bonatus means that if the planet ruling the sign of the most recent Full Moon lies in the house of the quesited, or in the derivative 4th, 7th, or 10th of the quesited, the thing will be accomplished. I have not tested this rule, nor do I know of others who have. It would be a fruitful area of horary research.

## TRINES OR SEXTILES BETWEEN THE LIGHTS

If the Moon applies to the Sun by sextile or trine, and no malefic aspect intervenes before the aspect becomes perfect, the astrologer has a strong confirmation of success if other aspects in the chart show a positive outcome.

## BEING BESIEGED

In days of old when knights were bold and attacked each other's castles, the idea of besiegement was in vogue. If you could trap your enemy between two opposing hostile forces, he had no route of escape. Medieval astrologers saw Mars and Saturn as the two evil forces in the universe. Any planet caught between them in the zodiac was "besieged" and in no condition to help the querent. According to Lilly, "Besieging is, when any Planet is placed betwixt the bodies of the two Malevolent Planets Saturn and Mars." Whether the besieged planet is traveling direct or retrograde, its next conjunction would be to a malefic and it would fall into the hands of the enemy.

Modern astrologers include Uranus, Neptune, and Pluto among the malefics. In today's world there is evil at every turn. Some astrologers use major aspects other than the conjunction to determine besiegement. For example, if Venus signifies the querent and she lies between a square to Saturn on forward motion and an opposition to Mars on retrograde motion, she is besieged between the malefics. No matter which way she turns she gets zapped.

Bleeding heart, humanistic astrologer types have also added the idea of positive besiegement. It didn't seem fair that only Mars and Saturn could get into the act. Why couldn't we surround a significator with good? Thus, if the querent's ruler lies between Jupiter and Venus, the querent receives candy, sex, love, kisses, riches, favors and abundance no matter which way he or she turns. It's like being in heaven.

## FAST OR SLOW IN MOTION

In the previous chapter, I listed the average daily geocentric motions of the planets. When a significator moves faster than average, it hastens the outcome of the question. When a significator moves slower than average, things proceed slowly. Dorotheus felt that slow planetary motion was of the nature of Saturn. Noting the speed of the significators can be helpful in assessing timing in a horary chart.

## HAYZ

This is one of the more obscure dignities that Lilly and some other astrologers pull out of their bag of horary tricks. According to Lilly, "HAYZ is when a Masculine and Diurnal Planet is in the day time above the earth, and in a Masculine Sign, and so when a Feminine,

Nocturnal Planet in the night is in a Feminine Sign and under the earth: in questions it usually shows the content of the Question at the time of the Question, when his significator is so found." The feminine, nocturnal planets are the Moon and Venus. The masculine, diurnal planets are the Sun, Jupiter, and Saturn.

## NODAL DEGREES

Ebertin describes the Moon's North Node as a principle of association or alliance, showing contact between people. The Moon's North Node (ascending node, Dragon's Head, or *Caput Draconis*) is a benefic in horary of the nature of Venus and Jupiter. Jones regarded the North Node as "a point of definite assistance," showing a "special cooperativeness from individuals or affairs ruled by the house which holds it." By contrast, the Moon's South Node (descending node, Dragon's Tail, or *Cauda Draconis*) is malefic like Mars and Saturn. Jones said the South Node is a "definite impediment in horary art, principally showing the promise or consequence of self-undoing, indiscretion and lack of common sense."

The Moon's Nodes are the points where the Moon's orbit crosses the ecliptic. It is on the Nodes that eclipses occur. From ancient times astrologers have associated eclipses with fatalities, tragedies, and catastrophes such as the deaths of kings. The exact degree at which a total eclipse occurs is so powerful that it resonates in each sign of the chart. In horary astrology, a planet in the same numerical degree as the Moon's nodes, regardless of sign, symbolizes a fateful event. It is often, though not necessarily, unfortunate and may even represent a catastrophe in the matter. For example, if the Moon's node were at 17° 28' Virgo, then a planet at seventeen degrees, any number of minutes, of any sign, would be in a Nodal degree.

## FRUSTRATION, PROHIBITION, INTERFERENCE

Although these three terms have precise definitions, they are used loosely as synonyms in modern horary astrology. A teenage boy is about to kiss his first date good-night, standing on the front steps of her house. Just then the girl's doting mother opens the door to see what's happening. That's frustration.

There are many definitions of frustration in the horary literature. Lilly used the term *frustration* to refer specifically to the conjunction: "When a swift Planet would corporally join with a more ponderous, but before they can come to a Conjunction, the more weighty Planet is joined to another, and so the Conjunction of the first is frustrated, as Mercury is in 10° of Aries, Mars 12°, Jupiter in 13° of Aries; here Mercury strives to come to Conjunction with Mars, but Mars first gets to Conjunction with Jupiter; whereby Mercury is frustrated of the Conjunction of Mars: in Questions it signifies as much as our common Proverb, The Dogs quarrel, a third gets the Bone."

Related to the idea of frustration is that of prohibition. According to Lilly, "Prohibition is when two Planets that signify the effecting or bringing to conclusion of anything demanded, are applying to an Aspect; and before they can come to a true Aspect, another Planet interposes either his body or aspect, so that thereby the matter propounded is hindered and retarded." In prohibition, one significator is applying to a major aspect with another, symbolizing perfection in the matter, but a third planet in the chart aspects one of the two primary significators before they can aspect each other. The third planet causes an "abscission of light," that is, it cuts off the light of one of the significators and prohibits its functioning. The house governed by the third planet shows the nature of the prohibition.

Simmonite uses the terms *frustration* and *prohibition* synonymously (which frustrates the reader and prohibits understanding). He gives the following example of prohibition and abscission of light: "If Venus, Lady of the Ascendant were hastening to the trine of Mars, Lord of the Seventh, in a question of marriage, it might denote that the match would take place; but if Mercury [faster than either Venus or Mars] were to form an opposition to Mars before Venus reached her trine of that planet, it would be a frustration [prohibition] and would show that the hopes of the querent would be cut off, and if he were Lord of the Twelfth, it might denote that it would be done by a private enemy; if Lord of the 3rd, by means of relations, and so on."

Some authors use the term "interference" to refer to frustration and prohibition. Jones, for example, includes two situations under the heading of interference. The first occurs when the two significators are about to consummate an aspect but one of them "makes another aspect first instead."

Jones' other case involves a third planet completing an aspect to the slower significator before the aspect between the two significators can happen, and so interfering with the process in a different way. Either of these conditions "is a positive indication of interruption or distraction. ... It does not necessarily deny the desired outcome, but shows much trouble."

If the above explanations sound too abstract, think of the significators as two people, Andy and Bob, who are planning to meet to do something together. The applying aspect between them shows what they plan to accomplish. If Andy meets someone else on the way (an intervening aspect), Andy will experience a delay, distraction, or interference in his plans with Bob. If Andy plans to meet with Bob (conjunction) but Bob first meets with Carl before Andy reaches him, that's frustration. If Andy plans to help (trine) Bob but Carl opposes the plan (opposition) before Andy can help Bob, that's prohibition.

## HINDRANCE AND IMPEDITION

Impedition refers to any condition that hinders or impedes the functioning of a significator. Such factors include aspects between significators and malefics, retrogradation, combustion, being cadent, being slow in motion, being in an intercepted sign, besiegement, and so on. Hindrance and impedition are general terms for things that obstruct the significators in a horary chart.

Lilly used "impedition" to refer to any factor that weakened or afflicted a significator. For example, he refers to Jupiter as impedited if conjunct with Mars, and to Saturn as impedited when retrograde. He discusses planets "which hinder or impedite the thing demanded in any question," and includes planets that are "ill-disposed" by being peregrine, retrograde, combust, cadent without aspecting the ruler or cusp of the house, or conjoined to a malefic without reception. Bonatus uses "impedition" synonymously with hindrance and affliction as a general term for the ill-disposition of a planet.

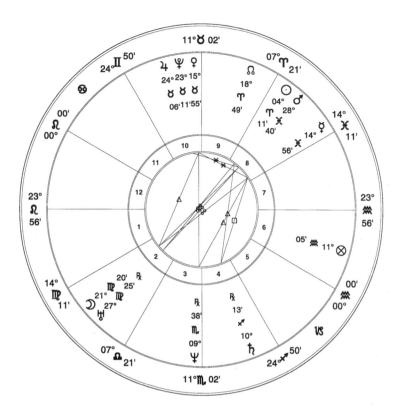

Chart 23: "What has already happened?"
March 24, 1633, 2.26 P.M. GMT 0W10/51N30 Regiomontanus Houses

The following example illustrates Lilly's use of impedition. On March 24, 1633, at 2:26 P.M., a man asked Lilly what had happened to him in the recent past (CA, p. 135). See Chart 23.

Lilly reasoned as follows. With Leo rising, the Sun represents the querent and past events would be shown by its past aspects. During the month or so before the question the Sun (querent) had conjoined Mars, squared Saturn, and sextiled Jupiter. Sun conjunct 4th ruler Mars in the 8th suggested concerns about real estate (4th) and his wife's finances (8th). The Moon in the querent's 2nd house of substance applies to a square of Mars in the 8th, indicating a quarrel with his wife about money.

Saturn is the dispositor of the querent's Part of Fortune and represents his financial resources. Sun having recently squared 7th ruler Saturn shows that he and his wife "had lately been at great variance" and that "she had no mind that he should have any of her estate." His wife wanted to manage her own affairs and keep her estate for her own use "for Saturn is retrograde, a superior planet, and in a fiery sign, and the sign of the 7th is fixed; these show her a virago, or a gallant spirited woman, and not willing to be curbed, or else to submit."

Finally, because the Sun had recently been sextile to Jupiter in the 10th, Lilly said that some prominent attorney had tried to reconcile the difference between the querent and his wife. Reconciliation was possible because the Sun (querent) was applying to a trine with 7th ruler Saturn (the wife). The only problem appeared to be that "Mercury, who is in square aspect with Saturn, did impedite it."

What was the nature of Mercury's impedition of the proposed reconciliation between the querent and his wife? Lilly listed four possible sources of hindrance or impedition:

- Mercury might signify an attorney, lawyer, or document that obstructs the matter.
- As ruler of the 2nd, Mercury could signify disagreements about money.
- As ruler of the 11th, Mercury might represent a pretended friend who stirs up trouble.
- "As the 11th is the fifth from the 7th, a child of the querent's wife might be occasion of continuing the breach."

## REFRANATION

If two significators are applying to an aspect but one of them turns retrograde before the aspect can become exact, the aspect is refrained from perfection. This condition is called "refranation" and symbolizes the failure of the event designated by the aspect to material-ize. Lilly gave the example of Mars at 7° Aries approaching a conjunction with Saturn at 12° Aries. If Mars turns retrograde and "by that means refrains to come to a Conjunction of Saturn, who still moves forward in the Sign, nothing signified by the former Conjunction will ever be effected."

According to Jones, "When a planet is about to approach a desired aspect but, rather than completing it, turns retrograde and does not do so ... it reveals the complete collapse of some project, or the failure of a given effort, due primarily to a lack of adequate preparation." Turn-ing retrograde is no small matter in horary, as you will see in the next two sections.

## RETROGRADE MOTION

When one of the significators is retrograde, it is moving with apparent backward motion in relation to the earth. Backward motion symbolizes going back or returning to a previous condition. The querent or some key person may back out or change his or her mind. The person signified by the retrograde planet may be debilitated, or may be returning to some-thing, or may be reuniting with someone. In McEvers' question about the job with Llewellyn, retrograde Mercury meant she had to re-negotiate the contract. The editing job also involved going back over written material submitted by other authors.

A retrograde significator is in a passive, receptive state. The person represented by the retrograde planet does well to imitate the motion of the planet. It is a good time to review, return, rewrite, re-edit, re-negotiate, reconcile, reunite, or do things that generally involve a turning to the past. Jacobson says retrogrades allow the person to "go back and try again." According to DeLong, if the significator of the quesited is "retrograde or debilitated, the objective, if gained, will likely fall short of expectations and should be reconsidered."

Retrograde Saturn in the 1st house often signifies some misfortune that denies a favor-able outcome. A retrograde 7th house ruler may mean the astrologer will not be able to deliver his or her judgment to the querent. If the question is about a relationship, a retro-grade 7th ruler may mean the other person is reluctant to make a commitment. In real estate questions, a retrograde 4th house ruler implies something about the property is unsatisfactory. If the 6th or 10th house ruler is retrograde, the querent may be returning to former employment. When the significator of a lost object or person is retrograde, the lost object or person will usually come back or return.

## RETROGRADE MERCURY

Mercury is the natural ruler of thought, communication, and questions. Even when it is not a significator, a retrograde Mercury often affects the outcome of the inquiry. According to Llewellyn's *1990 Daily Planetary Guide*, "Whenever Mercury goes retrograde, astrologers find that personal communications get fouled up or misunderstood more often." Mercury represents thinking, thus someone involved in the horary matter may change their mind or desires when Mercury is retrograde. Barbara Watters comments that "ideas which seem brilliant while Mercury is retrograde show serious flaws when it turns direct." In practice, retrograde Mercury is not so ominous as these quotes may make it sound. The basic meaning of a retrograde Mercury is a change or alteration in thought, wish, or communication. Chart 24 shows the effect of retrograde significators.

In May of 1989 a friend called me to ask if I would like to look at a new office suite. The lease on my current office would expire at the end of the year so moving to a new space was a possibility. On May 26, 1989, at 11:56 A.M. EST, I asked, "Should I move to the new

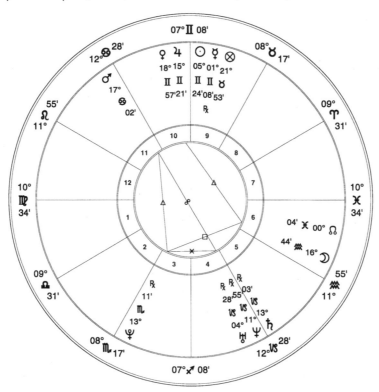

Chart 24: Should I move to the new office?"
May 26, 1989, 11:56 A.M. EST 72W55/41N18  Koch Houses

office?" This is a question about a removal, which is ruled by the 7th house. I am in the 1st house, my current office is the 4th, and the place I would "remove" to is traditionally shown by the 7th.

The Ascendant is at 10° 34' Virgo, which is almost exactly conjunct my natal Sun. The chart is radical and fit to judge. My natal Sun on the Ascendant suggests I may be better off staying where I am. Mutable signs rule the angles so the situation is unstable. My significator, Mercury at 01° 09' Gemini, is retrograde, combust, and void of course. Chances are I will either change my mind or have little power to affect the matter. Retrograde Mercury might also mean that some other key person will have a change of thinking.

Pisces is on the cusp of the 7th house of removals. Jupiter and Neptune rule the new office. Sagittarius on the 4th cusp makes Jupiter the primary ruler of my current office. Since Jupiter rules my present office, I will use the modern ruler Neptune as the primary significator of the place of removal. Mercury (me) makes no aspect to either Jupiter or Neptune, the rulers of the new office. My co-ruler, the Moon, also makes no aspect to the place of removal. No aspects, no action. I am not likely to move. There is also no aspect between me and my present office. What could that mean?

I need to compare the relative strengths of the significators to see which place is better for me. Jupiter rules my current office and is strong in the 10th house near the MC, an argument for me to stay where I am. Neptune is retrograde and besieged between the malefics Uranus and Saturn, a good reason not to go to the place of removal. Because the 7th ruler Neptune is retrograde, the new office may back out of the situation. How can an office do that?

Now for the outcome. My friend and I looked at the office suite and liked it. The location was good and the offices were larger and more attractive than those of my present space. The landlord, however, was unwilling to make some necessary changes such as painting and soundproofing. We tried negotiating with the landlord, but he changed his mind, took the offices off the market, and decided to use them in his own business. In the course of negotiating, I also became less interested in the new office and was planning to back out of the deal but the landlord beat me to it. Retrograde Mercury strikes again.

# CHAPTER SEVEN

# More Arcana, the Method of Lilly, and the Houses of Mr. B

T he earth is tilted on its axis in relation to the Sun. The earth's equator makes a 23.5° angle with the Sun's path, the ecliptic. Astronomers call this tilt the "obliquity of the ecliptic" because the equator and the ecliptic form an oblique angle with one another. The effect of having an oblique ecliptic is that, depending on the time of year, some signs rise more quickly than others over the horizon.

In the northern hemisphere, the signs of short ascension begin at the winter solstice and continue through the winter and spring months. These are Capricorn, Aquarius, Pisces, Aries, Taurus, and Gemini. In horoscopes of the northern hemisphere, the signs of short ascension are often intercepted, that is, contained wholly within a house so that they do not rule house cusps. The situation is the reverse in the southern hemisphere.

The signs of long ascension (northern hemisphere) begin at the summer solstice (0° Cancer) and continue through the summer and autumn. These are Cancer, Leo, Virgo, Libra, Scorpio, and Sagittarius. They take longer to rise over the horizon and may occupy two house cusps in the northern hemisphere. The opposite holds true south of the equator. The ancients called the signs that took longer to rise the "straight signs," and the signs that rose more quickly than average the "crooked signs." The idea behind these designations is that straight signs have been stretched out as you might stretch fabric to get out the wrinkles. Crooked signs have been squeezed together, crumpled, or "scrunched" (as my kids would say) to make them fit into a smaller space.

One might call this ancient theory of straight and crooked (or stretched and crumpled) signs the "rubber band" theory of the ecliptic. Using their rubbery ecliptic, these early astrologers argued that, during long ascension, squares (90°) got stretched into trines (120°), and conversely, during short ascension, trines got squeezed into squares. Ptolemy repeated this idea in the Tetrabiblos when he wrote, "And sometimes, also, among the signs that ascend slowly the sextile aspect destroys, when it is afflicted, and again among the signs that ascend rapidly the trine." Ptolemy is saying that sextiles can be stretched into squares, and trines can be compressed into squares.

The first century horary astrologer Dorotheus used the concepts of straight and crooked to interpret his charts. He said that if the Ascendant sign is "…one of the straight in rising, then this action will be difficult and slow, in which there will be misery and misfortune and trouble," but "… if the ascendant is one of the crooked signs and any one of the benefics is in it or any of them aspects the ascendant, it will remove the burden and help bring this action to a successful conclusion." It takes longer to get through a sign that's been stretched out than a sign that's been scrunched into a small space. William Lilly accepted this theory of the rubbery ecliptic with its stretchable aspects and used it in his horary analyses.

## The Method of William Lilly

The essence of Lilly's method is the effort to answer the question "Whether the thing demanded will come to pass, yea or nea." Lilly devotes a chapter of his *Christian Astrology* to the techniques that allow the astrologer "to know whether a thing demanded will be brought to perfection, yea or nea." First, Lilly assigns planets as significators of the querent and the quesited. "The querent is he or she that propounds the question and desires resolution; the quesited is he or she, or the thing sought and inquired after. The significator is no more than the planet which rules the house that signifies the person or thing demanded." All of this should sound familiar by now.

The ascending sign and its ruler always signify the person who asks the question. The Moon and any planets in the 1st house are always co-rulers of the querent. Regarding the querent, Lilly says, "the sign ascending shall in part signify his corporature, body, or stature: the lord of the ascendant, according to the sign he is in, the Moon and planet in the ascendant, equally mixed together, shall show his quality or conditions."

I cannot improve Lilly's words for his next step so I will quote them verbatim: "Secondly: You must then consider the matter propounded, and see to which of the twelve houses it does properly belong: when you have found the house, consider the sign and lord of that sign, how, and in what sign and what part of heaven he is placed, how dignified, what aspects he has to the lord of the ascendant, who impedites your significator, who is a friend unto him, viz. what planet it is, and what house he is lord of, or in what house posited; from such a man or woman signified by that planet shall you be aided or hindered, or by one of such relation unto you as that planet signifies; if lord of such a house, such an enemy; if lord of a house that signifies enemies, then an enemy verily; if of a friendly house, a friend. The whole natural key of astrology rests in the words preceding, rightly understood." Lilly next lists six ways in which aspects can bring the thing demanded to perfection.

### By Conjunction

When the rulers of the querent and the quesited are, to quote Lilly, "hastening to a conjunction, and in the first house, or in any angle, and the significators meet with no prohibition or refranation before they come to perfect conjunction, you may then judge that the thing sought after shall be brought to pass without any manner of let or impediment." Perfection will occur sooner if the rulers are swift in motion and essentially or accidentally dignified, not so soon if in succedent houses, and "with infinite loss of time, some difficulty, and much struggling" in cadent houses. Notice that Lilly does not mention straight or crooked signs ascending as indicators of the speed of bringing the matter to perfection. He was aware of this ancient rule and chose not to include it in his text.

## By Sextile or Trine

Quoting Lilly again, "Things are also effected, when the principal signifiers apply by sextile or trine aspect out of good houses and places where they are essentially well dignified, and meet with no malevolent aspect to intervene ere they come to be in perfect sextile or trine."

## By Square or Opposition

Lilly writes: "Things are also produced to perfection when the significators apply by square aspect, provided each planet have dignity in the degrees wherein they are, and apply out of proper and good houses; otherwise not." Lilly regarded the 6th, 8th, and 12th houses as bad or malefic. Significators making aspects from bad houses have a hard time bringing matters to perfection.

Here is an example of no perfection by square: see Chart 25, "Can I find the data?" This inquiry was made on March 22, 1990, at 10:08 A.M. CST, 93W06/44N57. The chart has Gemini rising and Jupiter in the first house. The querent's rulers are Mercury at 5° 21'

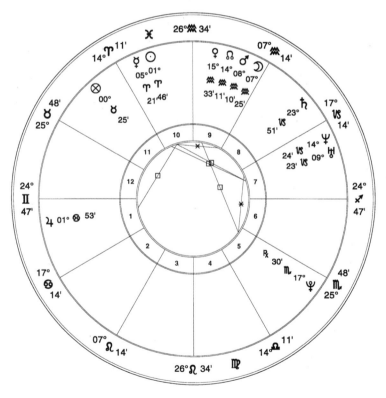

Chart 25: "Can I find the data?"
March 22, 1990, 10:08 A.M. CST, 93W06, 44N57   Koch Houses

Aries, Jupiter at 1° 53' Cancer, and the Moon at 7° 25' Aquarius. Leo is on the 3rd house cusp, making the Sun at 1° 16' Aries the significator of the data. The Sun, exalted in Aries and accidentally dignified in the tenth house, will complete a square to Jupiter in 7' of arc. Jupiter is exalted in Cancer and accidentally dignified in the first house. According to Lilly's rule, the querent should be able to find the data, but when I checked six years later it still had not been found.

Concerning perfection by opposition, Lilly says "Sometimes it happens that a matter is effected when the significators apply by opposition, but it is when there is a mutual reception by house [author's note: here, "house" means the sign the planet rules, not the mundane house], and out of friendly houses, and the Moon separating from the thing demanded, and applying presently to the lord of the ascendant. I have seldom seen any thing brought to perfection by this way of opposition, but the querent had been better the thing had been undone."

## By Translation of Light

We discussed translation of light in the previous chapter. Here is Lilly's definition:

"When the significators both of the querent and quesited are separating from conjunction, or sextile, or trine aspects of each other, and some other planet separates himself from one of the significators, of whom he is received, either by house, triplicity, or term [dignities of the significator], and then this planet applies to the other significator by conjunction or aspect, before he meets with the conjunction or aspect of any other planets; he thus translates the force, influence, and virtue of the first significator to the other, and then this intervening planet (or such a man or woman as is signified by that planet), shall bring the matter in hand to perfection."

Notice that Lilly requires the translating planet to be in one of the essential dignities of the first significator in order to pick up its light properly.

## By Collection of Light

We discussed collection of light in the previous chapter. This is what Lilly has to say about it:

"When the two principal significators do not behold one another, but both cast their several aspects to a more weighty planet than themselves, and they both receive him in some of their essential dignities; then shall that planet, who thus collects both their lights, bring the thing demanded to perfection; which signifies that a person somewhat interested in both parties, and described and signified by that planet, shall perform the thing which otherwise could not be perfected."

Note again that Lilly follows the classical definition in requiring the collecting planet to lie in one of the dignities of each of the primary significators in order to properly collect their light.

## By Dwelling in Houses Plus Translation of Light by the Moon

To quote Lilly, "Lastly, things are sometimes perfected by the dwelling of Planets in houses, viz., when the Significator of the thing demanded is casually posited in the Ascendant; as if one demand if he shall obtain such a Place or Dignity, if then the Lord of the tenth be placed in the Ascendant, he shall obtain the Benefit, Office, Place or Honor desired." Lilly added that this rule holds true only "when the Moon, besides this dwelling in houses, doth transfer the light of the Significator of the thing desired, to the Lord of the Ascendant."

To see an example of Lilly's sixth method of achieving perfection, look back to the chart for Don's secretary in Chapter Three (p. 45). Don wants a female secretary. Sagittarius rules the 6th house of secretaries, so Jupiter is the secretary's ruler. Jupiter is in the first house, that is, "The Significator of the thing demanded is casually posited in the Ascendant." With Cancer rising, the Moon rules Don in this chart. However, the Moon does translate the light from the co-rulers of the secretary, Uranus and Saturn, in the 6th to Don's co-ruler, Jupiter, in the first. Both parts of Lilly's sixth method apply and show the matter will come to perfection. William was a clever man. Now let's see how Lilly applies these principles to an actual horary question.

## THE HOUSES OF MR. B

For a long time William Lilly admired the houses of Mr. B and in 1634 he had a chance to buy them. Unfortunately, Lilly had tied his money up in investments, and he would not have access to it for at least six months. On April 10, 1634, at 6:03 P.M. in London, Lilly asked, "Shall I purchase Mr. B's houses?" See Charts 26A and 26B.

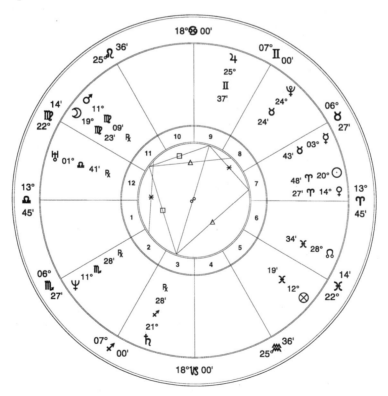

Chart 26A: "Shall I purchase Mr. B's houses?"
April 10, 1634, 6:03 P.M. GMT, 00W06, 51N31 Regiomontanus Houses

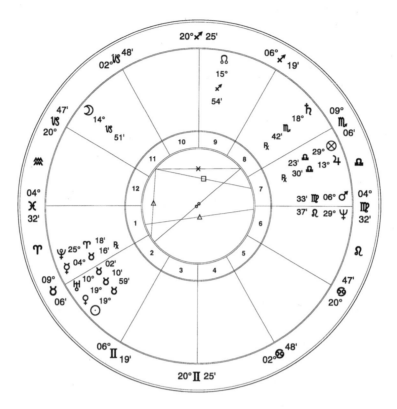

Chart 26B: Natal Chart of William Lilly from John Gadbury
May 11, 1602, 2:09 A.M. GMT, 01W16, 53N38 Regiomontanus Houses

Lilly explained, "I then wanted to know whether I would negotiate with Mr. B and be able to procure the necessary money in time to pay for its purchase ... so I asked this horary question myself, when I was most perplexed and concerned about it." Good timing.

Lilly's natal Jupiter occupies the same degree of Libra that is ascending in the horary chart. Natal Jupiter exactly conjunct the horary Ascendant will confirm a favorable answer. Libra rising makes Venus Lilly's significator. Lilly next uses the rules of Dorotheus to assign rulerships to questions of buying and selling. According to Dorotheus' first-century text, "The ascendant indicates him who buys, the seventh him who sells, and the tenth indicates the price, and the house of the fathers [the 4th] indicates the commodity which is bought or sold." Some modern astrologers would assign the houses differently, but here I will stick to the method of Dorotheus as used by William Lilly.

Aries rules the 7th cusp, making Mars a ruler of the seller. Lilly, however, uses the Sun as the primary significator of Mr. B. Because the Sun is Almuten of the 7th cusp and far stronger than the undignified peregrine Mars, Lilly must have reasoned that the Sun better signified Mr B., the wealthy male homeowner. Lilly notes that Venus (his ruler) will conjoin the Sun which rules Mr. B and also the 11th ruler of Lilly's hopes and wishes. Lilly is coming together with the seller and with his hopes of buying the house. These are good omens.

What about the real estate? In the Dorotheus system, Capricorn on the 4th cusp rules Mr. B's property. The significator of Mr. B's houses is Saturn, which suffers debility by being retrograde and cadent in the 3rd from the Ascendant and in the derivative 12th of the property 4th. Most astrologers would interpret Saturn in this chart to mean the houses were in poor condition.

Lilly wants the houses so badly that he minimizes these impediments by referring to Saturn as having "no material debilities except for being retrograde and cadent." Lilly adds, "The houses were really old [Saturn] but strong and able to stand many years." The symbolism of a retrograde, cadent Saturn does not fit the condition of the houses as Lilly describes it.

Should Lilly buy the houses? Yes. Venus (Lilly) will conjoin the Sun (Mr. B and Lilly's hopes and wishes) and then will trine Saturn (the real estate). Furthermore, Saturn is retrograde so the trine with Venus is by mutual application—a cogent indicator of a positive outcome. Lilly tells us, "This was the main strong argument for my buying the houses."

Before proceeding with such a major investment, we would want other confirmation in the chart. The logical place to look is at the Moon, universal co-ruler of the querent. What aspect will the Moon make to Saturn (the houses)? The Moon is mutually applying within two degrees to a square with Saturn—a compelling negative indication and a warning not to proceed unless there are strong positive green lights in the chart. But Lilly really wants to buy these houses. How will he get around this square? By appealing to the rubber band theory of the ecliptic. If you look carefully, you will see that the Moon in Virgo and Saturn in Sagittarius are both in "straight" signs of long ascension. According to the ancients, long ascension allows us to stretch the square into a trine.

Lilly tells us that the Moon/Saturn "square aspect (but out of signs of long ascension) did much to facilitate the matter and encouraged my going on, suggesting the probability of a contract developing after much time, because of the square." He is trying to have it both ways. On the one hand, Lilly says the stretched-out square facilitates matters, and, on the other, it hinders and delays the signing of the contract. He can't seem to make up his mind whether it's acting like a trine or a square because, in my opinion, he is fudging the negative indications so he can get what he wants. It's hard to be objective when you are your own astrologer.

What was the outcome? Lilly bought the houses and honestly reports the difficulties he encountered. He writes, "The truth of it is, I had a hard bargain, as the chart in every way made clear, and I shall never live to see many of the leases I purchased expire; and as Venus is in Aries, opposite her own sign, so did I do myself harm in the bargain with regard to money. But the love I have for the house I live in, where I lived happily with a good master for a full seven years, and in which I obtained my first wife and was bountifully blessed by God with worldly goods, has made it easy to forget the small hindrances I suffered, nor do I regret it in any way."

If Lilly had brought me the chart, I would have interpreted it, using his system without the rubbery ecliptic, as follows:

Me: "Well, Mr. Lilly, there is some good news and some bad news here. Which do you want to hear first?"

Lilly: "The good news."

Me: "The good news is the mutually applying trine between your ruler Venus and the ruler of the real estate Saturn. This trine is a strong argument in favor of your buying the house."

Lilly: "What's the bad news?"

Me: "There are actually two bits of bad news. The first is that the property ruler Saturn is retrograde and cadent. This means there may be some problems with the property.

"The second piece of bad news is that your co-ruler the Moon will square Saturn, the property. Squares mean obstacles and delays. Chances are the property will cost more than you want to pay and you may experience other frustrations in buying it. Since the Moon is your co-ruler in this chart and carries less weight than your primary ruler Venus, I think the Venus/Saturn trine means you should go ahead and buy the houses, provided you're aware of the problems you will be getting into."

Lilly: "Anything else?"

Me: "Yes, there's the matter of my fee."

# CHAPTER EIGHT

# The Houses in Horary: General Considerations

By now you should realize that the foundation of horary interpretation is the twelve houses of the horoscope. Planets assume importance primarily as rulers of the mundane houses and as significators of the querent and quesited. Planets also serve as natural significators of the matter asked about. Signs are of secondary importance; they identify the house cusps and help to place the planets around the wheel. The crucial step in horary astrology is placing of the question in the appropriate house. For this reason the horary astrologer must have a thorough grasp of the meaning of the twelve houses.

## LILLY'S OVERVIEW OF THE HOUSES

Lilly summarized the house rulerships as follows: "The Ascendant represents the person of the Querent, and the second his Estate, the third his Kindred, the fourth his Father, the fifth his Children, the sixth his Servant or Sickness, the seventh his Wife, the eighth the manner of his Death, the ninth his Religion or journeys, the tenth his Estimation or honor, the eleventh his Friends, the twelfth his secret Enemies." Lilly added that if the question is about the querent's wife, the astrologer takes the 7th house as the new first house and counts derivative houses from there. In other words, "In all manner of Questions the House signifying the party shall be his Ascendant or first house, the next his second house, and so continuing round about the whole Heavens or twelve houses."

## WHICH HOUSE SYSTEM TO USE

Traditional horary astrologers use the Regiomontanus system of houses because William Lilly used it. I used Placidus early in my study of natal astrology but eventually switched to the Koch system. I frequently use Koch in horary work and get good results. Things go better with Koch. The horary chart reflects how our minds grapple with the problem, and no two people think alike. My advice to the beginning horary astrologer is to use the house system he or she is most comfortable with. Each astrologer must try different techniques to develop a method of interpretation that is reliable in his or her own hands.

If you decide to follow Lilly and use Regiomontanus houses, note that Lilly observed Ptolemy's practice of beginning the house five degrees before its cusp. Thus, if the 8th house cusp were at 11° Libra, the 8th house would start at eleven degrees minus five degrees, which is 6° Libra. Planets approaching the cusp of a house from the previous house dwell in the next house when they get within five degrees of the cusp.

To illustrate some of the differences between Koch and Regiomontanus, I will review an example from Simmonite. In his 1850s text, Simmonite recommended that the reader erect a chart for the question, "My absconded mother, is she dead or alive?" The date and time of the question is February 11, 1850, at 6:36 in the evening. Simmonite does not give the location but he resided in Sheffield, England. I cast the chart for his location at 6:36 P.M. in both the Koch and Regiomontanus systems. See Charts 27A and 27B.

There are no classical considerations before judgment. Following the tradition of the ancients, Simmonite placed the mother in the 10th house. Because the question is about the querent's mother, we need to use derivative houses. The 10th is the mother's Ascendant. An early degree (01° 06' Gemini) on the MC indicates she has recently undergone a change of state. Mars occupies the 10th house at 19° Gemini, showing the possibility of an accident or violence. Mars is both a natural ruler of the 8th sign Scorpio and an actual ruler of the querent's 8th house in this chart.

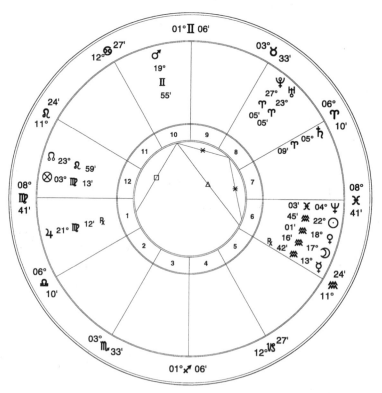

Chart 27A: "My absconded mother, is she dead or alive?"
February 11, 1850, 6:36 P.M. GMT, 01W30, 53N23  Koch Houses

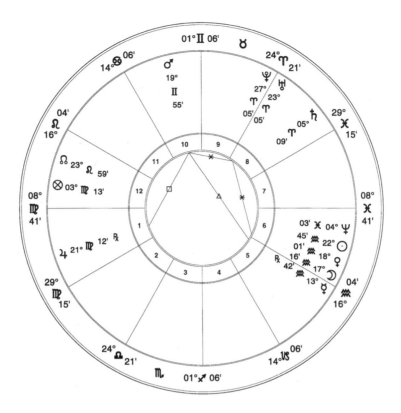

chart 27A: "My absconded mother, is she dead or alive?"
February 11, 1850, 6:36 P.M. GMT, 01W30, 53N23 Regiomontanus Houses

The mother's ruler Mercury (Gemini on 10th cusp) is retrograde, cadent, and under the Sunbeams, all indicating the mother's debility. The natural significators of mothers are Venus and the Moon. Both the Moon and Venus are combust and applying to the Sun. New Moons, especially when approaching the Sun, are classical malefics in horary. Things look bad for the querent's mother.

The New Moon is occurring in Aquarius. Let me digress for a moment about a facet of the signs which is lost to most modern astrologers. Manilius, in summing up astrological lore at the time of Christ, divided the signs by habitat. He describes Cancer and Pisces as aquatic signs because crabs and fishes inhabit the water. Aries, Taurus, Leo, and Scorpio are terrestrial or terrene because the creatures of these signs (rams, bulls, lions, and scorpions) walk the earth. Manilius did not include Gemini, Virgo, Libra, or Sagittarius among the terrene signs, even though they are associated with terrestrial beings, because of their human connection. Finally, Manilius labeled Capricorn and Aquarius "amphibious" signs, at home both on earth and in water. To quote Manilius' poem, "Some signs there are betwixt and between, of a middle dispensation, since Capricorn's nature is compromised by its tail, the Waterman's by his stream: they are signs in which watery and earthly elements are mixed in even compact." (Capricorn had the tail of a fish).

Simmonite concluded the mother had drowned because the natural rulers of the mother, the Moon and Venus, lie in amphibious Aquarius and are both combust the Sun.

The mother's significators—the Moon, Venus, and Mercury—all lie in Aquarius in the natural 6th house of illness and distress. The ancient symbolism of Aquarius shows the mother as amphibious, inhabiting both the earth and a body of water.

The mother's 8th house of death is the 8th of the 10th or the natural 5th of the chart. Capricorn rules the natural 5th cusp. Thus, Saturn rules the mother's death. Where is Saturn in the chart? In the Koch chart, Saturn conjoins the querent's 8th cusp of death, a strong confirmation that the mother is dead. In the Regiomontanus chart, Saturn is six degrees inside the 8th house and has the same significance. I think the Koch house cusp gives a sharper reading.

Mars governs the natural 3rd cusp which is the mother's 6th house (6th of the 10th) of sickness and distress. Mars in the natural 10th occupies the mother's 1st house, showing violence, illness, or distress coming her way. Mars in Gemini shows the affliction to her lungs when she drowned. The end of the matter 4th of the mother 10th is the natural 1st house ruled by Mercury retrograde in Aquarius in the 6th and occupied by Jupiter retrograde in Virgo, the sign of his detriment. The retrograde, debilitated end of the matter significators show that the querent's mother will return in a damaged condition. Retrograde Mercury (primary ruler of the mother and of her end, and natural ruler of lungs) in Aquarius suggests a drowning, perhaps due to backward thinking (Mercury retrograde).

Looking for further confirmation of death, I calculated the Part of Death (Ascendant + 8th cusp - Moon). In the Koch chart this falls at 27° 35' Libra (8° 41' Virgo + 6° 10' Aries - 17° 16' Aquarius). The Part of Death almost exactly opposes Pluto, a natural ruler of death in the querent's 8th. This opposition and the presence of three malefics in the 8th also confirm the death of the mother.

Because the Regiomontanus system has a different 8th cusp, the Part of Death will also be different. In the Regiomontanus chart, the Part of Death is at 20° 40' Libra. This Part of Death makes no close aspects to any planet or point and yields little information in the Regiomontanus chart. Notice also in the Regiomontanus chart how the malefic Uranus moves to the 9th cusp and Pluto enters the natural 9th house which is the mother's derivative 12th house of suicide and self-undoing. If Lilly were reading this chart and if he were aware of the existence of Uranus and Pluto, he might have read these malefics in the mother's 12th as her sudden, intense self-destruction.

This comparison of the Koch and Regiomontanus houses again shows that a consistent use of a system of horary analysis will produce the same answer provided by another consistent system but from an alternate point of view.

What was the outcome? Simmonite tells us, "The querent's mother was found drowned; her mind at times was insane." The insanity is revealed by the two mental planets Mercury and Jupiter retrograde and debilitated and by Neptune (mental illness) applying to the 7th cusp. The prominence of Jupiter (expansion) suggests she might have suffered from manic-depressive illness, which has a high incidence of suicide.

## LET THE CHART BE YOUR GUIDE

To avoid being influenced, even unconsciously, by aspects you see forming in the chart, I suggest trying to assign house rulership to the quesited before casting the chart. Once you erect the figure, the symbolism in the chart will help you fine-tune your rulership assignments. Like Jiminy Cricket, the chart will be your guide.

## THINK BEFORE YOU ACT

Different houses have dominion over the various facets of human existence. Always assign house rulerships on the basis of the meaning or function of the matter in the querent's life. Do not place a matter in a house simply because of the name it bears. For example, contracts as written documents belong in the 3rd house under the rulership of Mercury (communications). The same contract as an agreement between partners belongs in the 7th house under the rulership of Venus (relationships). Is the question about the written document or about the contractual agreement described in the document? The functional meaning tells you which house to use. Think before you act.

Another potentially confusing point about houses is that the same house can represent a thing and its opposite. For instance, the 2nd house can mean both the gain and loss of income, the 5th both pregnancy and abortion, the 7th both marriage and divorce, the 10th both fame and public disgrace, and the 12th both bondage and reprieve. The horary question determines which meaning to use.

## SOME GENERAL CONSIDERATIONS ABOUT THE HOUSES

To assign horary rulers accurately, it helps to have a theoretical understanding of the houses. The twelve houses owe their order to the corresponding signs of the zodiac. The system of house division is an attempt to individualize the zodiac for each nativity. The natural zodiac begins at 0° Aries, the vernal equinox. The 1st house starts at the Ascendant— the Greek *horoscopos*—the point of the ecliptic rising on the celestial horizon at the time and place of birth.

Each house derives its symbolism from its corresponding zodiac sign, its planetary rulers, its associated element, and its relationship to the other houses around the wheel. To understand the deeper connections among the houses, we can view them as six pairs of polar opposites, and also as four groupings of three houses of the same element in trine with one another.

The house position of the Sun in any chart tells the time of day. The Sun rises at the Ascendant, enters the 12th house, and proceeds through the 11th and 10th to reach the MC at noon. Sol then descends through the 9th, 8th and 7th houses to set at the Descendant. The Sun progresses through houses 6, 5, and 4, reaching midnight at the IC, and then through 3, 2, and 1, to rise again at the Ascendant.

The houses below the horizon relate to individual, personal, hidden, subjective, private, and family oriented experience. The 6th through the 1st houses correspond to the period of darkness from sunset to sunrise when the Moon reigns supreme. In contrast, the houses above the horizon correlate with other people, objective situations, and the public view. Carter says, "The last six houses tend to operate on a wider and more general scale than the first six." The 12th through the 7th houses cover the period from sunrise to sunset when Sol illuminates what we do for all to see. The following list pairs the polar meanings of the day and night houses.

| Night Houses | Day Houses |
|---|---|
| *(6, 5, 4, 3, 2, 1)* | *(12, 11, 10, 9, 8, 7)* |
| Night | Day |
| Self | Others |
| Private | Public |
| Subjective | Objective |
| Individual | Group oriented |
| Local environment | World at large |
| Mine | Yours |

To understand the function of the various houses, it helps to think of them as six pairs of polar opposites, each representing a day and a night mode of manifesting experience. Read over the following tabulation to get a sense of the polarity between each house and its opposite across the wheel. In the next chapter we will look more deeply into the houses from the viewpoint of the elements—fire, earth, air, and water.

| Night Houses | Day Houses |
|---|---|
| *1st House* | *7th House* |
| I | You |
| Self | Other |
| Me | My partner; my opponents |
| My body | Your body |
| My physical presence | Where I remove to |
| Initiator | Antagonist |
| New beginning | Immediate outcome (Jones) |
| What I decide | Agreements with others |
| Individuality | Bonding with others |
| | |
| *2nd House* | *8th House* |
| My resources | Your resources |
| My values | Your values |
| My talents | Your talents |
| My possessions | Your possessions |
| My income | Partner's income |
| My money | Money that I borrow |
| | |
| *3rd House* | *9th House* |
| Short trips, visits | Long trips, travels |
| Kin, neighbors | Foreigners, strangers |
| Concrete knowledge | Abstract thought; world view |
| Gossip, rumors | Wisdom, prophecy |
| Early education | College |

**Night Houses (continued)**

*3rd House*
Classroom teaching
Mundane communication
Neighborhood
Writing, reporting

*4th House*
Family
Familial authority
Father
Patriarch
Father
Home
Foundation, roots
Domestic matters
Heredity, ancestry
Personal base of operation
Real estate, land
Natural disaster

*5th House*
Personal enjoyment
Recreational sex
Children
Offspring
One's own children
Inventions
Pregnancy
Speculation, gambling
Self-gratification

*6th House*
Service to others
Sickness
Physical Illness
Servitude / Servants
Self-regulation
Distress
Work, labor
Attention to detail
Small animals, pets
Adjustment
Those who serve
Tenants, lodgers
Craftsmanship
Daily work

**Day Houses (continued)**

*9th House*
Public lecturing
Religion, philosophy
Distant lands
Publishing, disseminating

*10th House*
Career
Government
Judge, administrator
Executive / president / ruler
Mother
Business
Pinnacle of success
Relations with the outer world
Status in the community
Place in the community
Structure of society
Fall from power

*11th House*
Friendship, socializing
Humanitarian concerns
Group associations
Acquaintances, peers
Stepchildren
Modern technology
Hopes and wishes
Counsel, advice
Altruism

*12th House*
Spirituality
Hospitalization
Mental Illness
Confinement / Slaves
Regulation by others
Sorrow, grief
Charity, Welfare
Escapism, undoing
Large or wild animals
Resignation
Secret enemies
Prisoners
Sorcery
Spiritual experience

## HISTORICAL INTERLUDE
## GUIDO BONATUS (BONATTI)

Guido Bonatus (Bonatti) was a thirteenth-century Italian astrologer who achieved fame for his skills at horary and electional astrology. Bonatus was familiar with the work of Ptolemy and with the Arabian astrological writings. His text *The Astrologer's Guide* was a primary source book for William Lilly.

One report has Guido Bonatus, in the employ of Count de Montefeltro, striking a bell to signal when the count's men should don their armor to begin a military campaign. Bonatus was so well-known that Dante includes him in the Inferno as one of the soothsayers whose punishment for divining the future, a task proper to God alone, was to have his head twisted backward so that he cannot see the future for the rest of eternity.

# Elemental Triplicities and Skipping Houses

The polarities between opposite houses allow us to appreciate the houses' deeper connections. The twelve houses consist of four groups, each group made up of three houses (an angular, a succedent, and a cadent house linked to each element). Within each such group, the three houses are in trine aspect with one another. Each set of trines corresponds to one of the classical elements: fire, earth, air, and water. Houses in trine relate harmoniously.

The fire (life) houses are 1, 5, and 9.

The earth (substance) houses are 2, 6, and 10.

The air (relationship) houses are 3, 7, and 11.

The water (terminal, emotional) houses are 4, 8, and 12.

The Sun is the key symbol of the element fire. Sol's fiery nature constitutes the life force of the solar system. The element fire represents the enthusiasm, vitality, confidence, and optimism of the self projecting into the world. The fire houses (1, 5, and 9) show how these factors play out in the life of the individual. The 1st house represents the self, the 5th the self's creative activity, and the 9th the self's expansion through contact with others.

Next let us consider earth. Saturn, the earthiest of planets, is most representative of the earth houses (2, 6, and 10). Saturn stands for structure, building, substance, gravity, and the practical use of matter for tangible, concrete results. The element earth is solid, dependable, careful, and hard-working. The 2nd house represents the native's talents, the 6th his or her practical use of those talents in work, and the 10th the structure that is built from the labor and toil of the 6th.

The next element is air, and Mercury is the quintessential air planet. The winged messenger of the gods, Mercury constantly communicates and creates relationships among people or things. He is an intellectual planet and reflects the preference of the air houses (3, 7, and 11) for ideas and relationships as opposed to concrete reality. The 3rd house signifies relationships in the immediate family, the 7th relationships with a significant other, and the 11th relationships with humanity.

Finally, the Moon is the most watery of the planets. She is sensitive, receptive, passive, protective, motherly, intuitive, and emotional. The Moon reflects the light of the fiery Sun. The Moon and water represent the mother principle (yin) just as the Sun and fire represent the father principle (yang). Water is a symbol for the *Tao* of Chinese philosophy. The Moon symbolizes the predilection of water houses (4, 8, and 12) for merging, fusing, receiving, transforming, nurturing, and connecting emotionally with others.

Water has its hidden undercurrents and signifies all that is hidden, secret, occult, and psychic. The 4th shows our merging with mother in her womb and with our mother earth in the grave. The 8th shows our fusion with a significant other in sexual intercourse and a sharing of our substance with the other for the procreation of children. The 12th reveals our mystical fusion with God and the universe.

Much of what is true for the houses is true of their corresponding signs of the zodiac, their so-called "con-significators." The ancient idea is that each house also has a planetary con-significator, which is the planet corresponding to the house in order of the seven visible Chaldean planets: Saturn, the first planet, con-signifies the 1st and 8th houses. Jupiter, the second planet, con-signifies the 2nd and 9th houses. Mars, the third Chaldean planet, con-signifies the 3rd and 10th houses. The Sun, the fourth "planet," con-signifies the 4th and 11th houses. Venus, the fifth Chaldean planet, con-signifies the 5th and 12th houses. Mercury, the sixth visible planet, con-signifies the 6th house. And finally, the Moon, the seventh Chaldean "planet," con-signifies the 7th house.

Odd-numbered houses are considered masculine" (yang) and even-numbered houses "feminine" (yin). Silly as it may seem, parts of the body correspond to the houses in order from head to toe, starting with the head as the 1st house and ending with the feet as the final 12th house. Finally, in classical astrology the houses begin five degrees before the cusp and end twenty-five degrees after.

## THE MASCULINE FIRE HOUSES: 1, 5, AND 9

### 1st House (Angular/Fire/Masculine)

*Con-significators:* Aries (the 1st sign) and Saturn (the 1st Chaldean planet).
*Color:* White.
*Joy:* Mercury (Mercury, the tongue, does well in the house of the head).
*Body Parts:* Head, face.
*Correspondences:* The querent, querent's physical body and description, temperament, vitality, health or sickness of the querent, corporature, stature, the life, an absent person with whom the querent has no relation; a ship at sea and its safety; anyone with whom the querent identifies or represents in the matter.

The 1st house corresponds to the pioneering first sign Aries. Starting at the Ascendant, it symbolizes the rising Sun. The degree of the zodiac just coming over the horizon represents the spark of life, the new beginning, of a person or question. In the 4th century, Maternus said that the 1st house shows "the life and vital spirit of men." Mars, ruler of the

1st house con-significator Aries, stands for the native's individuality, leadership, purposeful initiation, self-assertion, and important personal interests.

The 1st house represents the querent, his or her appearance and state of mind, and the situation responsible for the question. It describes the querent's self, body, personality, health, and well-being. In transportation questions, it represents the body of the vehicle. Lilly paid close attention to the description of the querent given by the 1st house to determine whether the chart was radical. Here is what Lilly wrote about the 1st house:

"...it represents the head and face of man, so that if either Saturn, Mars, or the South node be in this house, either at the time of the question, or at the time of birth, you shall observe some blemish in the face, or in that member appropriate to the sign that then is upon the cups of the house; as if Aries be in the Ascendant, the mark, mole, or scar is without fail in the head or face; and if few degrees of the sign ascend, the mark is in the upper part of the head; if the middle of the sign be on the cusp, the mole, mark or scar is in the middle of the face, or near it; if the latter degrees ascend, the face is blemished near the chin, towards the neck" (CA, p. 51).

In traditional horary the 1st house has a special significance as the symbol of an absent person with whom the querent has no other relation around the wheel, especially in questions about "whether one absent be dead or alive." Lilly wrote, "If a question be demanded of one absent in a general way, and the querent has no relation to the party; then the first house, the lord of that house and the Moon shall signify the absent party" (CA, p. 151). However, if the question is about whether "one shall find the party at home he would speak with" and the querent is "much conversant" or "familiarly deals" with that person (who is not a family member), then the 7th house represents the other person (CA, p. 147 and p. 154).

Lilly used a rule from Bonatus to employ the 1st house in questions about an ill client or the state of a ship at sea (an ill ship). According to Bonatus, when the astrologer asks about a sick person with the patient's permission, then both the astrologer and the ill party belong to the 1st house. If the astrologer asks without the knowledge or consent of the patient, then the 1st house represents the astrologer and the 7th represents the astrologer's client—unless the client bears a different special relation to the astrologer such as father (4th), mother (10th), child (5th), and so on. (See Bonatti, *Liber Astronomiae, Part IV: On Horary. Project Hindsight Latin Track XIII*: p. 69.)

The 1st house is in trine with the 5th and 9th. It is the end of the matter 4th house of the 10th house of career and the mother.

## Planets Rising in the 1st House

Planets rising in the 1st often describe the querent and show what lies ahead as those planets rise to cross the Ascendant. Benefics in the 1st reveal good fortune on the way. Malefics in the 1st imply oncoming misfortune or disappointment.

Mars in the 1st often means the matter will not work out as planned, feared, or anticipated. Mars here can bring disagreement, strife, dissatisfaction, or a change of plans to the querent. Mars naturally signifies accidents, surgery, inflammations, heat, arguments, and the use of force.

A 1st house Saturn often delays, hinders, frustrates, or disappoints. Saturn freezes or slows action and, like Mars, may stop the progress of something that is wished for or feared. Unless the chart is otherwise strongly positive, retrograde Saturn in the 1st usually dashes the hopes of the querent. If the question is about something lost, it may return in a damaged condition. Saturn rising can also indicate problems with bones or teeth, or a health problem like a cold.

Uranus rising brings sudden, unexpected, shocking events into the life of the querent. Uranus is the natural ruler of uneasiness, agitation, separation, and divorce. His presence in the 1st may reveal an unpredictable situation, or a querent who may change his or her mind.

Neptune in the 1st may indicate confusion, absentmindedness, wishful thinking, or deception. The querent may be vague, tearful, emotional, mysterious, roundabout, impractical, starry-eyed, or self-deceived. With Neptune in the first, the querent may view the situation "through a glass darkly." Such is also the case if Neptune squares or opposes the 1st house ruler.

## 5th House (Succedent/Fire/Masculine)

*Con-significators:* Leo (the 5th sign) and Venus (the 5th Chaldean planet).

*Colors:* Black and White, or Honey color.

*Joy:* Venus (because she delights in the house of pleasure and romance).

*Body Parts:* Stomach, liver, heart, sides, back.

*Correspondences:* Pregnancy, children, the state of the woman with child, the health or sickness of a child, fun, pleasure, romance ("les amours"—Claude Dariot), recreational sex, creative self-expression, self-indulgence, enjoyment, sport, hobbies, gambling, speculation; personal agents or messengers, ambassadors, banquets, ale houses, taverns, plays; the wealth or movable goods of the father.

The Self of the 1st house pours itself out creatively and proudly in the 5th. This is the house of con-significator Leo the boastful Lion, the sign ruled by the fiery Sun, King of the universe. It is the house of fun, joys, holidays, vacations, narcissism, self-expression, excess, grandiosity, self-aggrandizement, self-gratification, all extensions of the self, and the search for admiration and applause. Anything done mainly for show or ostentation belongs in the 5th. It is the house of the self-absorbed, self-gratifying narcissist who feels entitled to everything and views others as extensions of him or herself.

Maternus said the 5th house governs the number of children and their sex. He added, "It is called Bona Fortuna because it is the house of Venus" and it relates powerfully to the Ascendant by trine. He connects Venus with the 5th because this planet is a natural ruler of sensual pleasure.

Because the 5th is a night house, it rules the personal, individual, or private outpourings of the self. The 5th rules one's creativity, pursuit of pleasure, and the means and products of these activities. It rules pregnancy and how it will go, the children so produced, and offspring of any sort. We locate the conception of offspring with the womb in the 4th, and the immediate future of that conception in the 5th house of children and pregnancy. Lilly regarded the 5th house as "wholly unfortunate by Mars and Saturn, and they therein show disobedient children and untoward" (CA, p. 53). In questions about children, Lilly also looked at the Part of Children (CA, p. 232): Ascendant + Jupiter—Mars.

The 5th has dominion over our hobbies, creative activities, brain children, amusements, fun and the places where one experiences fun, pleasure, sporting events, dissipation, courtship, romances, love affairs, flings, sexual activity for pleasure, creative writing or other productions, plays and performers, festivities, and celebrations done for enjoyment. Writing this book was a 5th house activity for me. The 5th rules recreational drug use done for the "high" or pleasure it produces. When drug use becomes an addiction, we place it under Pluto in the 8th of obsession or Neptune in the 12th of self-undoing.

The 5th governs the operations of the law of chance. In financial matters the 5th house rules betting, gambling, and speculation, including stocks. It governs risk taking in general. In the 5th the person is so taken with the self that his or her opinions assume a grand importance, and he or she misperceives personal speculation as the expectable course of the universe. Such is the grandiosity of the 5th. It also rules extensions of the self such as ambassadors, proxies, personal agents, and power of attorney

The 5th house holds sway over love relationships that do not involve commitment such as dates, boyfriends, and mistresses. Dariot called it the house of "les amours." Here we locate recreational sex, including masturbation done for enjoyment. When sexual activity becomes compulsive, we place it in the 8th.

As the 2nd of the 4th, the 5th house rules the father's resources and money. As the 8th of the 10th, the 5th house shows the death of the mother.

The 5th is the end of the matter 4th house of the 2nd house of one's substance and movable goods. Because of the trine aspect, the 5th works harmoniously with the next fire house, the 9th.

## 9th House (Cadent/Fire/Masculine)

*Con-significators:* Sagittarius (the 9th sign) and Jupiter (the 2nd Chaldean planet: $2 + 7 = 9$).
*Colors:* Green and White.
*Joy:* Sun (this is the House of the ancient Sun god).
*Body Parts:* The fundament (buttock and anus), hips, and thighs.
*Correspondences:* Foreign interests and contacts, foreign countries, overseas voyages, long journeys, pilgrimage, profound mental pursuits, expansion of the mind, philosophy, religion, the clergy, attorneys, lawyers, dreams and visions, knowledge, science, learning, the kindred of one's spouse.

The 9th house is associated with the adventurous, traveling, freedom-loving centaur-archer of its con-significator Sagittarius. The first two fire houses, 1 and 5, are below the horizon and relate to more personal matters. As the only fire house above the horizon, the 9th house extends the fire principle of energy and expansion into the realm of the other. It relates to explorations both physical and mental.

Of the 9th house, Maternus said, "In this house we find the social class of men. It also has to do with religion and foreign travel. This house is importantly aspected to the ascendant in trine aspect."

Anything that broadens the mind is located in the 9th house. Commonly this includes college and higher education, religion, philosophy, profound studies, and travel that is more than routine and taken for granted. The 9th governs foreign travel, people at a distance, international finance and trade, foreign communications, and foreigners in general.

The creative manipulation and organization of ideas falls in the 9th house. This includes science, knowledge, the Law, astrology as a system of knowledge, codes of ethics, and the world view of the querent. The clergy and the Church are found here along with lawyers, judges, and other professional classes. The judge as the authority in a lawsuit belongs in the 10th.

The 9th is the house of formalizing and legalizing matters. Here belong orthodox observances, legal procedures, and rituals that legalize like wedding ceremonies, probate hearings, legalizing and adoption, christening a child, appointing a bishop. Publishers and publishing are 9th house matters. Disciplined insight, faith, and prophecy are also located in the 9th. The querent's personal speculations in the 5th correspond to the forecasts of the 9th. Modern astrologers say that the 9th house rules corporations and insurance companies.

Things that are high up or actually in the sky are located in the 9th house. This includes attics and high places, airplanes, space ships, flying saucers if they exist, comets, meteorites, birds, and space shuttles. The 9th house also rules locations and persons closely connected with flight such as flight attendants, airports, and space stations.

The 9th expands those activities that are found in the 3rd house of communication, neighborhood, and siblings. The local meeting of the 3rd becomes the large convention of the 9th. The close kin of the 3rd correspond to the in-laws in the 9th. The trivial publications of the 3rd become the serious books of the 9th. The 3rd house teacher correlates with the 9th house professor or public lecturer. The elementary school of the 3rd contrasts with the university of the 9th.

As the 5th of the 5th, the 9th house represents the children's children or the grandchildren of the querent. Since it rules belief systems, the 9th shows what the querent believes about the question.

The 9th house is the end of the matter 4th house of the 6th house of service, sickness, and co-workers.

## THE FEMININE EARTH HOUSES: 2, 6, AND 10

### 2nd House (Succedent/Earth/Feminine)

*Con-significators:* Taurus (2nd sign) and Jupiter (2nd Chaldean planet).

*Color:* Green.

*Lot:* Pars Fortuna.

*Body Parts:* The neck and hinder part of it toward the shoulders.

*Correspondences:* Estate or fortune, resources, substance, money, income, wealth or poverty, money lent, profit or gain, loss or damage, movable goods, valuables, values, immediate future (according to Jones), querent's second in a duel; "the goods or thing that is lost, stolen or missed" (CA, p. 332).

The possessive, materialistic, stubborn bull of Taurus is the con-significator of the 2nd house. The planet Jupiter and the Part of Fortune are also closely connected with this house. Although it is a point and not a planet, Pars Fortuna and its dispositor naturally signify one's money, valuables, possessions, and lost items.

Maternus wrote about the 2nd house: "This house shows increase in personal hopes and in material possessions. But it is a passive house and not aspected to the ascendant. Therefore it is called the Gate of Hell, because it is not in any way aspected to the ascendant." Maybe this is the origin of the saying, "Money is the root of all evil." Lilly wrote that "the Sun and Mars are never well placed in this house, either of them show dispersion of substance" (CA, p. 52).

Any derivative second house represents the fluid resources of the preceding house. Included here are the movable goods and personal possessions of the querent, his or her money, valuables, wealth, investments as opposed to speculations, anything he or she owns that is not land or real estate. Since they are movable goods, lost or misplaced items are ruled by the 2nd house. So too are intangible resources such as rights of ownership, copyrights, royalties, and income derived from the querent's initiative exercised in the 1st house. As the eighth of the 7th, the 2nd house represents the death of a partner.

According to Marc Edmund Jones, the 2nd house is one of several houses in horary astrology that reveal the future of an event. Jones taught that any second house represents the immediate future of the house preceding it, and any seventh house shows the immediate outcome of an action in its opposite house. In traditional hoary any fourth house indicates the final outcome of its first house matter, the dismissal to certainty, the grave or final resting place when all is said and done. Jones believed that there are subtle but important differences among the various facets of the future shown by these different house relationships.

In searching for lost or stolen items, Lilly recommended looking "to the Lord of the 2nd and his Almuten...there are the goods" (CA, p. 352).

The 2nd house is the end of the matter 4th house of the 11th house of friends, groups, hopes and wishes.

The querent takes his or her resources in the 2nd and puts them to work in the next earth house, the 6th.

## 6th House (Cadent/Earth/Feminine)

*Con-significators:* Virgo (6th sign) and Mercury (6th Chaldean planet).
*Color:* Black.
*Joy:* Mars.
*Body Parts:* Inferior part of the belly, the intestines.
*Correspondences:* Service, sickness, servants, employees, serf-lord relationships, toil, labor, servitude; small animals, small cattle (up to the size of a goat); day laborers, tenants, farmers, shepherds; uncles, father's brothers and sisters.

We associate the sixth house with the unsullied, critical, discriminating, meticulous, hypochondriac virgin of Virgo. The Virgo native loves purity and cleanliness, is dedicated to service and efficient functioning, and has an interest in health and hygiene. Earth signs are known for being practical. In the 6th house the querent puts his or her talents and resources of the 2nd to practical use in routine work. Lilly wrote that "Mars and Venus in conjunction in this house are arguments of a good physician" (CA, p. 54).

Of the 6th Maternus wrote: "In this house we find the cause of physical infirmities and sickness. This house is called Mala Fortuna because it is the house of Mars. This is also a passive house because it is not aspected to the ascendant." Maternus associated Mars with the 6th of illness because Mars is the natural ruler of infections, accidents, injuries, and epidemics and enjoys his stay in the unfortunate 6th house.

Historically the 6th house has ruled servants and any drudgery or service performed by a serf for the lord of the manor. It ruled all relationships in which deference had to be paid to others because of their higher status in the world. The 6th house person performing the service was in a dependent, servile, or inferior relationship in society. For example, the 6th house governs tenants who pay rent to the "land lord."

In the modern world this serf/lord distinction is no longer as meaningful. Nonetheless, we still regard the 6th house as the house of service. It rules service as attendant effort, employees whom we pay to serve us in some capacity, the work they do, employment in general, organized labor, laborers, co-workers, tradesmen, craftsmen, repair men, maids, baby-sitters, and anyone hired as a servant or domestic.

The 6th holds sway over those who serve the community such as the Armed Forces, the police, and fire fighters in their capacity of rendering service. Police as authorities who enforce the law are ruled by the 10th house. Military service is ruled by the 6th, military police power by the 10th.

A person is considered lord of the organ systems of his or her body. The 6th house governs the dependent relationship of the parts of the body to the whole and thus the health of the organism and its malfunction in illness. The 6th also rules therapeutic activity and healing measures including medications and medical regimens. In matters of health, the general well-being of the organism is ruled by the 1st, the sickness or illness by the 6th, any surgery by the 8th, and the hospital by the 12th. Personal habits that perform a service for the individual are also ruled by the 6th house.

As the 3rd of the 4th, the 6th house rules the siblings of the 4th house parent, i.e., the aunts and uncles related to the querent through the father.

The 6th rules small domesticated animals that serve us. Animals in zoos, serving the larger community, are found in the 12th. It rules food and clothing in their useful aspect, food stores and storage, containers, and appliances that serve us. Climate in general is shown by the 6th whereas weather is ruled by the 4th.

Because the 6th is quincunx the 1st house, it is a house of adjustment. The 6th house dominion over sickness and distress derives from the quincunx aspect. The body parts and functions undergo adjusting and realignment in illness.

The 6th is the end of the matter 4th house of the 3rd house of siblings, neighborhood, communications, and short trips.

As the 6th represents the governance of the body parts in health, the earth house above the horizon, the 10th, signifies the governing of the larger world.

## 10th House (Angular/Earth/Feminine)

*Con-significators:* Capricorn (10th sign) and Mars (3rd Chaldean planet).

*Colors:* Red and White.

*Body Parts:* Knees and hams (thighs).

*Correspondences:* Government, vocation, career, status, official office, any position of command or trust, authority, the mother; kings, princes, commanders-in-chief; the judge in a lawsuit (the jurors are signified by the Moon, CA, p. 403); officers in authority; honor, preferment, dignity; kingdoms and empires; the physician's medicine (CA, p. 282); the price of real estate; the querent's boss, anyone in authority over the querent.

The climbing, sure-footed, practical, ambitious goat of Capricorn is associated with the 10th house. As its opposite sign Cancer seeks security in the home, the 10th house con-significator Capricorn seeks security in its position in the outer world. The 10th signifies the querent's position in life, social status, and standing before the world. It represents the authority granted to the querent by his or her place in society. The 10th signifies the business, career, profession, or vocation of the querent, the work done because the querent wants to and not simply for wages. It shows public success, awards and honors as well as public disgrace and shame.

Of the 10th house, Lilly writes that "either Jupiter or the Sun do much fortunate this house when they are posited therein, Saturn and the Moon's South Node usually deny honor..." (CA, p. 55). The Sun is a natural ruler of monarchs, rulers, authority, honor, promotion, preferment, status, recognition, and fame. As such, the Sun bears a close relationship to 10th house matters and feels at home in this house.

Maternus, aware of this Sun/10th house connection, wrote: "This place is the first in importance and has the greatest influence of all the angles. This house we call the Medium Caelum, and the Greeks the Mesuranima, for it is located in the middle part of the universe. In this house we find life and vital spirit, all our actions, country, home, all our dealings with others, professional careers, and whatever our choice of career brings us. From this house we easily see the infirmities of the mind." The 10th aspects the Ascendant powerfully by square.

The 10th represents one of the parents, traditionally the mother. In the 1st century, Dorotheus referred to the 1st cardine (the Ascendant) as representing the native, the 10th (M.C.) as the cardine of the native's "children and of work" and also as the cardine of the "government," the 7th (Descendant) as the cardine of "marriage," and the 4th (IC) as the cardine of the "parents," the "house of the fathers" and the "outcome of the matter." Except for placing children in the 10th, these rulerships correspond to what we use today. Thousands of years of tradition have treated the 4th house as the "house of fathers." The father's spouse belongs opposite him in the 10th house.

The ancients answered general questions about parents from the 4th house. When the question specified the mother, they looked to the 10th for the spouse of the 4th house father. No doubt this rulership developed in a patriarchal society which regarded the father as the primary parent and assigned him to the 4th because he was the parent of primary significance. According to Hone, "a woman was not considered worth a horoscope unless she was of great importance, since we only find them for such as a queen."

Because the 10th is the house of "government," we locate bosses, mayors, presidents, superiors, employers, school principals, college deans, and administrators here along with the administration of any matter. The querent's reputation, success, public office, public image, power in society and fall from power are located in the 10th. Credit as a matter of public reputation is found here.

This house represents all those in power or authority, any superior with a right to give orders, any officer of higher rank in the military or in an organization, and any governing body. Government in any aspect to which the querent is subject is located in the 10th. Advisory bodies in government are found in the 11th as resources of the government. The judge presiding in a court of law is placed here. The jury as the judge's resource is in the 11th. Police power and any person or agency that enforces discipline are symbolized by the 10th.

As the 2nd of the 9th, the 10th house shows profit from 9th house matters such as publications, imports and exports, and foreign or long-distance matters.

The 10th is the end of the matter 4th house of the 7th house of marriage and partnership. As such, it shows how a marriage will end.

## THE MASCULINE AIR HOUSES: 3, 7, AND 11

### 3rd House (Cadent/Air/Masculine)

*Con-significators:* Gemini (3rd sign) and Mars (3rd Chaldean planet).

*Colors:* Red and Yellow, or "Croceall," or Sorrel.

*Joy:* Moon.

*Body Parts:* Shoulders, arms, hands, fingers.

*Correspondences:* Siblings, cousins, kindred, neighbors, movement, communication, immediate environment, local travel, short or inland journeys, letters, rumors, reports, news, intelligence, messengers in general (but messengers as ambassadors of the querent belong to the 5th house).

The chattering busybody twins of Gemini are con-significators of the 3rd house of siblings and local travel. Maternus said that from the 3rd house we predict "everything that concerns brothers and friends. Dea is the name of this house; but is it also the house of travelers." The Moon rejoices in the 3rd because Luna enjoys "travel, trotting, and trudging" and "being seldom quiet," CA, p. 52)

The 3rd house rules the immediate taken-for-granted environment of the querent, including his siblings, near relatives (kindred other than parents and children), neighbors and neighborhood. It is the general house of cousins and close relatives when the maternal or paternal connection is not known. Lilly warns that Mars, Saturn, or the Moon's South Node in the 3rd suggest problems with siblings or neighbors (CA, p. 188).

The 3rd house association with Gemini reveals its dominion over communication, mental activity, and transport of any kind. The 3rd rules transportation and the gathering of facts and information. It governs cars and garages, buses, walking, bicycling, motoring, talking, visiting, newspapers and magazines, computers and software, telephones and tape recorders, tools and gadgets, brothers and sisters, messages and messengers, streets and sidewalks, periodical literature, books as objects, files and filing systems, radios, TVs, typewriters, teachers at any level, news and gossip, elementary education, local meetings, editorial work, and short trips of a routine nature. The 3rd house, Mercury and Gemini rule papers and documents as well as quick trips and commuting. As the 11th of the 5th, the 3rd house rules the friends of children.

According to Jones, third house relationships have special significance for derivative houses. Any group of items belonging to the querent, or any group of persons related to the querent, who are members of a "family" and share a sibling-type relationship to each other, has 3rd house spacing around the wheel. Every other house (skipping one in between) bears a 3rd house relationship to the previous house in the sequence.

For example, in modern horary, if the querent has three brothers, the 1st brother belongs in the 3rd house, the next brother in the 5th house (skipping a house), and the last brother in the 7th house (skipping a house again). If the querent asks about two friends, the first friend is in the 11th house, the second friend is in the 1st house. Or, if the querent has five pets, they are assigned houses in the sequence: 6th house for the first pet, 8th for the second, 10th for the third, 12th for the fourth, and 2nd for the last little animal. As long as the objects belong to the same class and therefore have an abstract sibling type relationship with each other, you can space them out in every other house around the wheel.

The 3rd house is the end-of-the-matter 4th house of the 12th and shows the outcome of confinement, hospitalization, escapism, and hostage situations.

## 7th House (Angular/Air/Masculine)

*Con-significators:* Libra (7th sign) and the Moon (7th Chaldean planet).
*Color:* Dark Black.
*Body Parts:* The hips (haunches), and the area from the navel to the buttocks.
*Correspondences:* Marriage, partnership, open enemies, yokemate, wife, girlfriend, boyfriend, sweetheart, lover, significant other, unrelated person with whom you have dealings, place of removals where one would go (CA, p. 370), adversary in a lawsuit, opposing party in a war; quarrels, duels, wars, contentions, controversies, legal battles, lawsuits; the querent's astrologer or physician, the thief; fugitives, runaways, outlaws; one to whom a message is sent. (Note that the natural signifier of fugitives is the Moon, CA, p. 328.)

Libra, the con-significator of the 7th house, was originally the sign of the claws of the scorpion. The Greeks renamed Libra the yoke because the constellation resembled the yoke worn over the shoulders to balance two buckets or the yoke of the ox that plows the field. Libra as the yoke and its ruler, Venus, goddess of love and money, became the symbols of marriage. Saturn has its exaltation in the sign Libra (the balance and the yoke) because he represents the commitment and restraint symbolized by the yoke of Libra. The essential meaning of the 7th house is a balanced relationship between equals. Lilly wrote of the 7th house that "Saturn and Mars unfortunate herein, show ill in marriage" (CA, p.54).

In the fourth century, Maternus wrote: "From this house we shall inquire as to the nature and number of marriages. But this house is aspected most detrimentally to the ascendant for it is in opposition." Planets opposing the Ascendant can indicate problems with the querent's body or health.

Isaac Newton gave us a fundamental law of physics: for every action there is an equal and opposite reaction. The corresponding principle in astrology is found in the balancing scales of the sign Libra and in the associated 7th house. Marc Edmund Jones used the Newton's symbolism to establish his house-and-its-opposite method of horary analysis. Jones believed that one could read the immediate outcome (opposite reaction) of a question through its opposite or 7th house. In practice, I have not found the Jones method reliable.

Lilly made special use of the 7th as the house of "him you would speak with" (CA, p. 147) and with whom you "familiarly deal with" but have no other relation (e.g., parent, child, etc.) around the wheel. Lilly wrote, "if the Lord of the 7th house be in any of the four Angles, you may conclude the party is at home with whom you would speak with." If the querent (1st house) sends a messenger (5th house), then the 7th represents "him to whom the messenger is sent" (CA, p. 236). However, if you ask "in a general way" whether "one absent be dead or alive" and the "querent hath no relation to he party; then the first house, the Lord of that house and the Moon shall signify the absent party" (CA, p. 151).

The 7th house as the opposite of the 1st shows other people who are on equal footing with the querent. It rules all kinds of partnerships and unions, the marriage partner, committed (yoked) relationships, marriage as well as divorce, open enemies and opponents, and significant others. It has general dominion over any other person with whom one has dealings. If the querent refers to another person by name, that person may have specific location in another house, (e.g., a child in the 5th) but he or she also has placement in the 7th. The aspects made by 7th ruler to the querent's significator should confirm the aspects between the specific ruler of the person and the ruler of the querent.

Lilly also used the 7th to answer questions about whether to "remove from one house or place to another, or to stay or abide in any place or not" (CA, p. 212). Here the 4th represents the current residence and the 7th, as 4th of the 4th, signifies the place (or dwelling) to which one would remove.

The 7th represents the other party in any contest, dispute, lawsuit, or agreement. It rules personal counselors and consultants such as doctors, therapists, lawyers, or astrologers whose professional help we seek. All contacts with equals, joint activities, sharing of experience, and cooperation or competition with others are found in the 7th. All contracts, agreements and contractual relationships between equal partners are ruled by the 7th. A contract as a written document per se is ruled by the 3rd but as a legal agreement by the 7th.

In questions of theft, the 7th rules the thief (as do peregrine planets in an angle or in the 2nd house). The 7th also rules runaways, criminals at large, and fugitives from justice.

As the 4th of the 4th, the 7th rules the father of the father, i.e., the paternal grandfather of the querent. As the 4th of the 10th, the 1st house rules the maternal grandfather. As the 4th of the 4th, the 7th is the end of the matter house of the querent's parents, especially the father.

## 11th House (Succedent/Air/Masculine)

*Con-significators:* Aquarius (11th sign) and the Sun (4th Chaldean planet: $7 + 4 = 11$).
*Colors:* Saffron or Yellow.
*Joy:* Jupiter (which rejoices in the trust and confidence of the 11th house).
*Body Parts:* The legs to the ankles.

*Correspondences:* Friends and friendship, fidelity or falseness of friends; hopes, wishes, trust, confidence, praise and dispraise, counsel; the thing at present hoped for, the love and concord of friends and acquaintances; the wealth, resources, and goods of the person in command.

The detached, intelligent, eccentric, new age water bearer and the wavy electrical lines of Aquarius are associated with the 11th house. Having learned to relate to a significant other in the 7th, the native learns to make connections with humankind in the final air sign Aquarius, con-significator of the 11th house.

Maternus described the 11th as follows: "It is called the Bonus Daemon or Bonus Genius, by the Greeks Agathos Daemon. The Medium Caelum is often found in exact conjunction with this house [using equal houses from the Ascendant]. It is, furthermore, the house of Jupiter, and not indifferently aspected to the ascendant; it can be seen to be in sextile aspect." The ancients associated the 11th with Jupiter because they felt it was an especially fortunate house that the greater benefic would rejoice in.

The 11th rules the hopes, wishes, goals, objectives, and desires of the querent. It rules friends, colleagues, social life, casual ties, clubs, societies, and group associations. Acts of friendship and friendly advice are found here along with counsel and counselors in general. Bruce Scofield argues that one's professional clients also belong to the 11th house (perhaps as the income 2nd of the career 10th).

In questions about governments, the 11th rules counseling bodies such as legislatures, city councils, and boards of directors. In a court of law the jury as a counseling body to the 10th house judge is found in the 11th. A blind question such as "Will I get my wish?" belongs in the 11th house.

As the 2nd of the 10th, the 11th house shows profit from the querent's career or business. As the 8th of the 4th, the 11th shows the death of the 4th house parent. As the 5th of the 7th, the 11th reveals the romantic aspects of the marriage partnership. The 11th also rules the querent's group and club activities, his socializing with friends, and his involvement in humanitarian causes.

The 11th is the 4th of the 8th and rules the end of the matter of joint finances and goods of the dead.

## THE FEMININE WATER HOUSES: 4, 8, AND 12

The element water governs protection, intuition, fusion, mysticism, secrecy, and endings. The water houses are often called the hidden and terminal houses of the chart.

### 4th House (Angular/Water/Feminine)

*Con-significators:* Cancer (4th sign) and the Sun (4th Chaldean planet).
*Color:* Red.
*Body Parts:* Breast, lungs.
*Correspondences:* Father, home, earth, foundations, base of operation, lands, mining, agriculture, real estate, houses, tenements, inheritances, tillage of the earth, treasure lying hid

in the ground; the end of a sickness, the end of anything, the grave; towns and cities, ancient dwellings, gardens, fields, pastures, orchards, the quality of the grounds one buys; regarding something lost, missing, or stolen, "the place where it is laid" (CA, p. 332).

The 4th house is associated with the protective, security seeking, retentive crab of the sign Cancer. The ancients called the 4th the house of the fathers. According to Maternus, the 4th house shows us "family property, substance, possessions, house-hold goods, anything that pertains to hidden and recovered wealth." We saw the importance of the symbolism of hidden and recovered wealth in Sara's second question (see p. 24).

Any 4th house is the base of operations, the foundation, and the point of final recourse of its 1st house. The 4th house represents land, real estate, the home, the womb, the grave, and the parent of final appeal, usually the father.

The 4th house has special significance in horary as the end of the matter of the 1st house question posed by the querent, its ultimate outcome, its final resting place, its dismissal to certainty. Aspects to the ruler of the 4th, to planets in the 4th, and sometimes to the cusp of the 4th reveal how the matter will end for the querent when all is said and done. As the house of the "cardine under the earth," it rules buried treasure and things hidden underground. The IC is the darkest, most secret place in the chart.

The 4th has dominion over parks and gardens, the weather, monuments and memorials, natural resources on or beneath the earth, groups of homes such as towns and cities, and the manifestation of natural forces such as earthquakes, floods, and storms. The 4th house rules the womb and the feeling of security outside the womb. As the final resting place or end of the matter, it rules old age, the grave, museums, history, and anything that has been preserved.

Questions about real estate, about buying a home or the quality of the home are located here. As the 10th of the 7th, the 4th house stands for the career or business of the partner. As the 6th of the 11th, it represents the health of friends.

Ashes to ashes, dust to dust. In the 4th house our physical body returns to the earth from which it came. The watery quality of the 4th house symbolizes our final merging with mother earth.

## 8th House (Succedent/Water/Feminine)

*Con-significators:* Scorpio (8th sign) and Saturn (1st Chaldean planet: $1 + 7 = 8$).

*Colors:* Green and Black.

*Body Parts:* Bladder and sex organs.

*Correspondences:* Death, transformation, joint finances, the estate of the dead, wills, legacies, fear and anguish of mind, danger, penetration, rape, orgasmic sex, rebirth; money owed to the querent, loans, money of others; garbage, elimination, butchers and surgeons, hemorrhoids, kidney stones, strangury (painful strained urination), poisons; the partner's wealth or movable goods.

The 8th house is associated with the deadly penetrating sting of the scorpion. Its rulers Mars and Pluto give the eighth house its injurious, cutting, piercing quality. As we fuse with the earth in our final resting place in the 4th, we merge with a significant other in the sexual intercourse of the 8th. The modern ruler of Scorpio, Pluto symbolizes the seed that must die in order to grow.

Maternus called the 8th a passive house and said, "From this house is discovered the kind of death. But it is necessary for us to know that no planet rejoices in this house, except the Moon, and then only in nocturnal charts. If the waxing Moon is found in this house in a nocturnal chart, and if she is not in aspect to any unfavorable planets, and if Jupiter is in trine or sextile aspect to her in her own sign or in the sign of Venus or Mercury or Jupiter, or in the terms of any of these planets, this portends the greatest good fortune and riches beyond measure, great glory of material power and outstanding recognition in worldly position." The 8th house doesn't sound that bad under the right circumstances.

The 8th house represents death and rebirth, matters of the dead such as wills and legacies, orgasmic sex which regenerates the species, obsessions and compulsions, and matters that are occult or hidden. Like the 6th house, it lies five houses away in quincunx with the Ascendant. The quincunx implies a need for adjustment and restructuring.

The 8th governs occupations connected with elimination, injury and death. This includes undertakers, coroners, surgeons, butchers, sanitation workers, and garbage men and women. The dominion of Mars and Pluto over probing and penetration connect the 8th house, through its con-significator Scorpio, to research, depth psychology, psychoanalysis, and the occult. Negatively, penetration relates to rape, murder, sadism, sodomy, and other ways people pierce one another. The sex of the 8th is vastly different from the recreational sex of the 5th house where Venus rejoices.

Questions about joint finances, pensions, income tax returns, retirement money, insurance, and inheritance are located here. If the 7th is used as the place the querent wishes to move to, then the 8th is the future or profit of that move. The 8th rules regeneration both literally and symbolically as in the restructuring of a corporation.

The 8th house rules garbage, refuse, waste, elimination, injury, sexually transmitted disease, surgery, deep emotions, envy, malice, jealousy, peril, danger, and destruction. The significator of a lost object in the 8th may mean the item is out in the garbage.

In financial matters, the 8th rules the money of the partner, wills, legacies, goods of the dead, taxes, fees, bankruptcy, alimony, pensions, retirement premiums, public funds, recovery of debts, escrow, mortgages, loans, joint resources, mutual profits, insurance payments as a beneficiary, the money of a defendant in a lawsuit, the funds of the 7th house seller of goods, and the profit of a partnership or of a removal.

As the 2nd from the 7th it reveals the state of the other person's money. The borrowing or loaning of money is a form of partnership or legal agreement which is located in the 7th, and the money loaned per this agreement is ruled by the 2nd from the 7th or 8th house of the radical chart.

The 8th is the 4th of the 5th and represents the end of 5th house matters related to children, pleasures, and creative activities.

## 12th House (Cadent/Water/Feminine)

*Con-significators:* Pisces (12th sign) and Venus (5th Chaldean planet: 5 + 7 = 12)
*Color:* Green

*Joy:* Saturn (because Saturn delights in misery, obstruction, and undoing.)

*Body Parts:* The feet.

*Correspondences:* Sorrow, fear, tribulation, mischief, despair, confinement, imprisonment, self-undoing, all manner of affliction; karma, the past, reprieve, witches, large animals, great cattle (larger than a goat), secret informers, those who maliciously undermine their neighbors, banished men; secret enemies not named, anyone committed to prison, captives, slaves, hostages; institutions of confinement, monasteries, hospitals, prisons, infirmaries, places of retreat.

The dreamy, mystical, hidden, emotional, poetic, psychic, sacrificial Christ-like fishes of Pisces are associated with the 12th house. Maternus was not a fan of the 12th house. He wrote, "This house the Greeks call *Cacos Daemon*; we call it *Malus Daemon*. From this house is easily determined the nature of enemies and the character of slaves. Also we find defects and illnesses in this house. But it is a passive house because it is not aspected to the ascendant. It is, moreover, the house of Saturn."

Maternus connected the 12th to Saturn because Saturn is the greater malefic that naturally rules the misfortunes of the 12th where Saturn rejoices. The 12th is the house of our mistaken ways, our deepest secrets, our sorrows, whatever we keep hidden from others and often from ourselves, our hang-ups, our unconscious, our hardest sacrifices, our mistakes, our trial and tribulations, and our own undoing.

The 12th house rules incarceration, confinement, and release from confinement. Any type of involuntary limitation of the freedom of the querent is located here. In the 12th house are found hospitals, prisons, jails, zoos, reform schools, nursing homes, involuntary stays, protective custody, concentration camps, and insane asylums. Because mental and emotional problems also involuntarily limit the individual, the 12th house rules alcoholism, psychosis, delusions, hallucinations, pipe dreams, neurosis, and psychological maladjustment. It represents self-harm, suicide, sacrifice, and basic inadequacies or limitations of the self. The law of karma as it limits the individual is placed in the 12th.

On the other hand, the possibility of release from confinement is also ruled by the 12th. The literal escape from bondage through parole, reprieve, rescue, liberation, pardon, or getting out on bail is shown here. Release from mental or emotional bondage through psychotherapy, meditation, suicide, charitable work or other circumstances is also shown by the 12th. Widowhood as grief and as release from the marriage bond belongs in the 12th. Reincarnation as a type of bondage or release from karma is often assigned to the 12th house.

The 12th has dominion over those who are confined or who escape from confinement such as hospital patients, prisoners, hostages, mental patients, and escaped convicts. It rules hidden enemies who work behind the scenes to limit or hinder us. It also rules feelings and attitudes that hinder the personality such as envy, malice, enmity, worry, fear, and self-destructive thoughts. The 12th rules unexpected misfortune and help with misfortune through kindness or charitable work.

The 12th governs work done in seclusion or behind the scenes such as work done in a home office. In the 12th we find retreats and places of retreat, recluses, confidential matters, secret societies, private activities, remote out of the way places, mysterious locations and conditions, undisclosed matters, and secrets. It also rules bondage, persecution, plots, kidnapping, assassination, ambushes, treason, secret enemies, subversions, clandestine acts, and the state of being hidden or invisible.

As the 6th of the 7th, the 12th house rules the sickness of the partner. As the 3rd of the 10th, the 12th rules the siblings of a parent, that is, the aunts and uncle of the querent on the mother's side. The 6th house rules the querent's aunts and uncles on the father's side.

The 12th is the 4th of the 9th and shows the end of the matter of publications, college education, foreign travels, and so on.

## A HOP, SKIP, AND A JUMP—SOME MODERN NOTIONS ABOUT THE HOUSES

It is hard enough to assign rulerships when only one matter concerns the astrologer. To complicate matters, some questions ask about a group or family of related issues. In horary analysis it is best to keep things as simple as possible. You should only resort to the schemes described below when the question forces you to. Otherwise, stick to the basic twelve houses for best results and don't get bogged down in horary trivia. The techniques outlined in the remainder of this chapter are used, by and large, by modern horary astrologers.

### Sibling or Third House Spacing of Similar, Owned Objects

Families consist of parents whose children are called siblings. Modern horary astrologers often extend the idea of a sibling to any group of objects or persons of similar kind belonging to a family. In this analogy the querent as owner becomes the symbolic parent of the group of sibling-like objects. For example, in the mental health field the current patients of a psychoanalyst are referred to as analytic siblings.

If the querent owns three homes, these homes are of like kind and bear a sibling-type relationship to one another. We place the first home in the natural real estate 4th house of the chart. The second home goes in the 6th house, that is, the 3rd of the 4th. The third home gets the 8th house, or the 3rd of the 6th. If the querent owns more than three properties, we keep skipping houses around the wheel to locate each of the homes. Such spacing would be important in a question such as, "Should I place my second or my third home on the market?"

The principle is to locate objects related abstractly as siblings to every other house around the wheel. To qualify for sibling status, the objects must all belong to the querent and be of similar kind. The querent must be able to refer to them as my children, my homes, my pets, my lovers, and so on.. A first sibling belongs in the natural 3rd house, a second sibling in the 5th, a third sibling in the 7th, a fourth sibling in the 9th, and so on. If the querent asks, "Will my brother be safe?" you would use the 3rd house as the generic house of siblings. If the querent specifies, "Will my fourth brother come home?" you can still use the 3rd house for any sibling, but you may also want to check the 9th house of fourth siblings to confirm the answer.

Modern horary astrologers apply the same principle to the schools attended by the querent. The list below illustrates third house spacing of one's schools:

Elementary School: 3rd house

Junior High School: 5th house

High School: 7th house

College: 9th house.

What if the querent asks a question about higher education and has attended college, graduate school, and a professional school? You could keep skipping houses around the chart to find the present level of education, but the simplest solution is to use the 9th as the ruler of all higher education. Again, only skip if you have to. Now we must turn to the tricky matter of a group of objects or persons that does not yet belong or relate to the querent.

## Non-Sibling Relationships—Spacing Similar Non-owned Objects

General Principle: Stand in the house of the thing you own. For a moment, consider the house of the thing you own a new first house and, from there, look to the house of the thing you want.

When the querent asks about more than one object of the same kind but one of them does not belong to the querent, the sibling relationship does not apply. If the querent owns one home and wants to buy a new one, you cannot regard the new home as a sibling of the first residence because the querent does not yet own it. The new home is not yet a member of the querent's family. The new home does not become a sibling of the old home until the querent buys it. There is not yet a symbolic parent-child bond.

In this case, the astrologer cannot place the new home in the 3rd of the 4th house. Only a second home already owned by the querent goes in the 6th. Parenthetically, the 6th house rules the lodgers or tenants who occupy a property owned by the querent.

To place an object not owned by the querent if he or she already owns one such object requires some mental gymnastics. You assign the object already owned to its natural house. The new object bears the same relationship to the old object as the old object does to the querent. In other words, the astrologer momentarily regards the natural house of the old object as a new first house and counts around the wheel from that house to find the house of the new object. I wish I could think of a simpler way to say all that.

To continue with our example, a home already owned by the querent belongs in the fourth mundane house. A home the querent wishes to buy bears a fourth house relationship to the natural 4th house and lies in the 7th house of the chart. This principle explains why the 7th is the house of removals. The querent's current residence is in the 4th house. The place where he or she wants to go (remove to) is in the 4th of the 4th, or the 7th. Nonetheless, the ancients used the 4th house for the home the querent wanted to buy, regardless of any other property owned by the querent.

In a similar way, some drudge work the querent is now doing belongs in the 6th house. A tedious job he is seeking when he already has a routine task is located in the 6th of the 6th, or the 11th house. It is as if the querent stands in the current work place and looks to the next place of employment, which is six houses away. Again, the house of the new task is as far away from the old one as the old task is from the querent. In practice, the astrologer rarely needs to go into such detail. Most questions about jobs can be answered from the natural 10th and 6th house rulerships.

On the other hand, suppose a person asks, "Should I leave the job with IBM and take the job with Wang?" The first career mentioned goes in the 10th house. The second career move goes in the 10th of the 10th, or the 7th house of the chart. The status of the rulers of the 7th and the 10th and their aspects to the ruler of the 1st would tell what career move is the better choice.

## Sequential Legal Personal Relationships—Seventh House Spacing

According to Mark Edmund Jones, the laws of society demand that certain relationships come into the life of the querent only in a sequence in which a newcomer replaces a predecessor. Marriage is such a relationship. Jones gives a method to space sequential legal relationships. Not all astrologers agree with him.

In the United States the querent may take a second spouse only after the death or divorce of the first spouse. Jones spaces such relationships by moving from the house of the quesited to its opposite. The 7th house governs the first spouse, the opposite 1st house rules the second spouse, the 7th house rules the third spouse, and so on, back and forth across the wheel. The astrologer only resorts to this spacing when the question demands it. Otherwise, any question about a spouse belongs to the 7th house. Keep it simple.

In societies that allow bigamy, a sibling relationship exists among the wives in the harem. The sultan's first wife goes in the 7th, the second wife in the 9th, the third wife in the 11th, the fourth wife in the 1st, and so on. A new woman whom the sultan eyes that is not already a member of his harem would fall in the 5th house of paramours—until he marries her and she takes her place in the every-other-house spacing of her siblings in the harem around the wheel.

If we apply the Jones' rule for sequential legal relationships to stepmothers, we locate the biological mother in the tenth, the first stepmother opposite her in the fourth, and a second stepmother back in the tenth. If the querent regards the stepmother as a mother, it is simplest to use the 10th for both mother and stepmother.

## SPECIAL CASES OF LOCATING THE QUESTION

Entire books have been written about special cases of horary questions. Different astrologers may approach the same problem differently. To give a flavor of the range of possibilities, I will briefly review the controversy over the appointment of mothers and fathers in the horary chart.

### Mother/Father

As explained previously, the ancients called the 4th house the "house of fathers" and always located the father there. They gave the mother the 10th house because it is the 7th house of the 4th and signifies the father's spouse. Traditional horary astrologers have always stuck to this assignment with good results. In the modern world, with changes away from a patriarchal society, these house rulerships appear to be shifting. The reader will have to experiment to see which works best. Jones thought that if you consistently reversed the traditional mother/father rulerships, the universe would bring you questions that worked in your system. I adhere to the traditional rulerships and assign the father to the 4th house.

## HISTORICAL INTERLUDE
## DOROTHEUS OF SIDON

Dorotheus of Sidon was an influential astrological poet whose work spanned the third quarter of the first century. He wrote an important text on horary and electional astrology (in Greek *katarchai* for "beginnings") in which he summarized what was known up to that time. He taught that favorable days occurred when the Moon transited through your natal Sun sign or through a sign in trine with it, and unfavorable days are ones when the Moon travels through a sign square or opposite to your natal sun sign.

Among many other things, Dorotheus discussed the considerations before judgment and summarized the rules for finding lost objects. He also mentioned the "terms"—unequal fivefold divisions of the zodiac signs—that came to Greece from Egyptian astrologers.

# Notes on the Planets and Signs in Horary

Western astrology is an amalgam of diverse and often conflicting traditions. We saw in a previous chapter, for example, how the decanates of the zodiac signs received one set of rulerships from the Chaldeans and another from the Hindus. Traditional horary stuck with the Chaldean system, but modern natal astrologers prefer the wisdom of India.

## THE JOYS OF THE PLANETS

The joys of the planets are yet another set of planetary assignments to houses and signs that was assimilated into Western astrology. One tradition appointed the same planet to govern both a mundane house and its corresponding sign of the zodiac. Another tradition assigned each of the seven classical planets to the mundane house where it especially rejoiced. In addition, the classical planets rejoice in certain signs. According to Lilly, "Aquarius is the joy of Saturn, Sagittarius of Jupiter, Scorpio of Mars, Libra of Venus, Virgo of Mercury" (CA, p. 176).

Below is a list of planetary joys derived from the fourth century text of Firmicus Maternus and the work of William Lilly.

| Table 10: The Joys of the Planets | | |
|---|---|---|
| House of Joy | Planet | Sign of Its Joy |
| 1st House | Mercury | Virgo |
| 3rd House | Moon | Cancer |
| 5th House | Venus | Libra |
| 6th House | Mars | Scorpio |
| 9th House | Sun | Leo |
| 11th House | Jupiter | Sagittarius |
| 12th House | Saturn | Aquarius |

Mercury is the natural ruler of communication and concretely of the tongue. The 1st house governs the physical body and specifically the head because of its association with Aries and Mars. Mercury rejoices in the 1st house because the tongue enjoys being in the head. If you know anyone with a 1st house Mercury, check to see how they love to talk.

The Moon governs the trivial happenings of everyday life. The 3rd house also rules taken-for-granted daily trotting and trudging. The Moon joys in the 3rd because it shares with the 3rd house dominion over local travel and humdrum happenstance.

Moderns like to think of Venus as a goddess of pure love. To the ancient Greeks and Romans she was rather a floozy, given to self-indulgence and the pleasures of the flesh. Because of her party-going and artistic nature, Venus rejoices in the 5th house of fun, enjoyment, sensuality, and creativity.

Mars, the lesser malefic, likes to make people suffer. He does this partly through sickness, fevers, inflammations, cuts, injuries, accidents, and epidemics. Because he enjoys inflicting bodily suffering, Mars grows ecstatic in the 6th house of illness, upset, and distress. Mars also symbolizes the human energy needed to do the laborious drudgery of the 6th house.

Maternus called the 9th the house of the "Sun god." The Sun does well here because the 9th house, like the Sun, has the nature of fire. The 9th is also in trine aspect with the other two fire houses, the 1st, where the Sun is exalted, and the 5th which the Sun rules.

Some authors also feel the Sun rejoices in the 10th house, or at least is especially fortunate there. Here Maternus locates "life and vital spirit," both naturally signified by the Sun. Sol governs kings, presidents, honor, preferment, promotion, and success—all 10th house matters. As king of the universe, it is only fair that the Sun should rejoice in two houses, the 9th and the 10th. Jupiter also does well in the 10th.

The ancients, including Ptolemy, called the 11th the house of the Good Daemon and regarded it as especially fortunate. It was only natural to assign Jupiter, the greater benefic, to this house because Jupiter signifies prosperity, expansion, and good luck.

Finally, the ancients regarded the 12th as the house of the Evil Daemon. The 12th and the 6th houses were the two most unfortunate places around the wheel. Which planet most loves misery? Saturn, of course. Saturn delights in the suffering, self-undoing, sacrifice, suicide, assassinations, secret enemies, karma, widowhood, grief, sorrow, hospitalization, limitations, and confinement of the12th. He couldn't be happier anywhere else in the chart.

## SOME NOTES ABOUT THE SIGNS

Astrologers usually divide the twelve signs into groups according to the four elements (fire, earth, air, and water) and the three qualities (cardinal, fixed, and mutable). The fire signs (Aries, Leo, Sagittarius) are outgoing, energetic, self-assertive, forceful, positive, adventurous, and active. The earth signs (Taurus, Virgo, Capricorn) are conservative, methodical, down to earth, stable, concrete, practical, and solid. The air signs (Gemini, Libra, Aquarius) are intellectual, like to make connections, sociable yet detached, indecisive, fond of abstractions, and like to communicate. The water signs (Cancer, Scorpio, Pisces) are intuitive, receptive, sensitive, moody, quiet, reticent, sympathetic, protective, secret, occult, and deep.

In addition to their elemental qualities, the signs can act in one of three modes: Cardinal, Fixed, or Mutable. These are often called the three Qualities of the signs and derive from the *Gunas* of Hindu philosophy. Each quality (or quadrature) consists of four signs, one for each element.

The Cardinal or Movable signs (Aries, Cancer, Libra, Capricorn) are the signs of the solstices and equinoxes that initiate the four seasons of the year. Cardinal signs are initiatory, directly involved, quick to act, decisive, powerful, energetic, and enterprising. They take the lead and like to manifest in the world. A prominence of cardinality in a horary chart shows a quick resolution of the matter.

The Fixed signs (Taurus, Leo, Scorpio, Aquarius), as the middle signs of the four seasons, are "middle-of-the-road," stable, stubborn, deliberate, determined, persistent, organized, goal-oriented, conservative, and set in their ways. They are slow to change but, when they do, the change is often drastic. Much fixity in a horary chart shows conditions that are entrenched and hard to alter.

The Mutable or Common signs (Gemini, Virgo, Sagittarius, Pisces), as the ending signs of the four seasons—getting ready to make the change—are adaptable, flexible, pliant, impartial, clever, mentally alert, mercurial, and interested in people and relationships. They prefer to write or study about action rather than engage in it. Prominent mutability in a horary chart suggests changeable or unstable conditions in which the querent will need to follow the lead or bend to the needs of others. Table 11 shows the relationship between Modes or Qualities and the Elements among the signs.

| Table 11: Relationship Between Modes (Qualities) Among Elements and Signs | | | |
|---|---|---|---|
| Element | Cardinal | Fixed | Mutable |
| Fire | Aries | Leo | Sagittarius |
| Earth | Capricorn | Taurus | Virgo |
| Air | Libra | Aquarius | Gemini |
| Water | Cancer | Scorpio | Pisces |

In the next section we will review the principal characteristics of each of the zodiac signs that are relevant to horary astrology. The student of traditional horary may also wish to review *Christian Astrology,* pages 93 to 101, for Lilly's attributions.

## Key Horary Attributes of the Twelve Signs of the Zodiac

### Aries

*Ruler:* Mars.

*Exaltation:* Sun (especially the nineteenth degree of Aries).

*Detriment:* Venus.

*Fall:* Saturn.

*Manifestations:* The Ram. The first sign. New beginnings, self-assertion, pioneering spirit, leadership, power of the offense, initiative, implementation of the will, "me first," the self, the head of the body, the brain. Positive, diurnal, Cardinal, hot, dry, fiery, choleric, violent, bestial, four-footed.

*Occupations:* Engineering, the Armed Forces, work requiring initiative and action.

*Places:* Sandy or hilly grounds. Unfrequented places. Where tools or instruments are used. Places that use iron and heat, furnaces, glass making businesses, and bakeries. Near heat or warmth. Roofs, ceilings, plastering, coverings of roofs. Near blood. Places of the nature of Mars: fiery, aggressive, given to use of instruments and force. EAST.

*Color:* White mixed with red.

## Taurus

*Ruler:* Venus.

*Exaltation:* Moon (especially the 3rd degree of Taurus).

*Detriment:* Mars.

*Manifestations:* The Bull. The second sign. Determination, sustenance, practicality, persistence, the Earth Mother, sensuality, safety, firmness. The neck and throat, the sign of the voice. Negative, nocturnal, cold, dry, melancholy, bestial, four-footed.

*Occupations:* Singing, agricultural pursuits, building, architecture, finance, banking, work with a set routine.

*Places:* Cellars, low rooms, pastures, feeding grounds, gardens, banks, where valuables are kept, dark closets, lawn shrubs. Farm buildings, low rooms, on the ground, rooms with low ceilings, tiled floors, dark closets, ground floor storerooms. SOUTH by EAST.

*Color:* Yellowish white.

## Gemini

*Ruler:* Mercury.

*Exaltation:* Moon's North Node (especially the 3rd degree of Gemini).

*Detriment:* Jupiter.

*Fall:* Moon's South Node.

*Manifestations:* The Twins. A double sign. The third sign. Flexibility, adaptability, speech, communication, commerce, the taken-for-granted environment, sociability, changes, movement, travel, visiting, the media, transport, vehicles, computers, software. The lungs, shoulders, and upper arms. Positive, dual, mental, barren, human, double-bodied or bicorporeal.

*Occupations:* Mental occupations, writing, teaching, learning, studying, journalism, advertising, sales, work involving travel, the collection or dissemination of information.

*Places:* Studies, libraries, cars, trains, buses, where books are kept, desks, places for learning, schools, containers, storehouses. An upstairs room, in a drawer, the upper part of a room or piece of furniture. Trunks, chests of drawers, filing cabinets, storage receptacles, small appliances, thermometers, measuring tools. In an automobile or in the garage.

Among papers or books. Hills, airy locations, high places, mountains. Places of the nature of Mercury: mental, intellectual, communicative, given to comings and goings, sorting, filing, and detailed work. WEST by SOUTH.

*Color:* White mixed with red.

## Cancer

*Ruler:* Moon

*Exaltation:* Jupiter (especially the 15th degree of Cancer); Neptune.

*Detriment:* Saturn.

*Fall:* Mars.

*Manifestations:* The Crab. The fourth sign. Self-protection, nurturing, mothering, security, the home, domesticity, counseling, feeding, comforting, moods, emotions, memory, history, the "homebody," the chest and elbows, the breasts and stomach. Negative, cold, moist, nocturnal, fruitful, mute, reticent.

*Occupations:* Catering, the hotel business, laundry work, nursing, social work, occupations involved with liquids, careers related to serving the needs of women or of the public, supplying domestic needs.

*Places:* Oceans, navigable waters, bodies of running water, rivers, lakes, springs, wells, moist areas, sinks, trenches, pumps, cellars, damp basements, laundry rooms. Near water or food. Near liquids or water fixtures. The womb, the grave, cemeteries, the final resting place. Low in a room. Places of the nature of the Moon: mothering, nurturing, feeding, protecting, making secure, nursing, helping. NORTH.

*Colors:* Green; light brown, reddish brown, or russet.

## Leo

*Ruler:* Sun.

*Detriment:* Saturn and Uranus (modern ruler of Aquarius).

*Manifestations:* The Lion. The fifth sign. Cosmic splendor, kings, royalty, pride, individuality, the ego, generosity, self-importance, acting, drama, warm-heartedness, loyalty, the desire to rule others, exhibitionism and the wish for admiration. The upper back, the spine, the heart, the forearms and the wrists. Positive, bestial, four-footed, barren.

*Occupations:* Entertainment, theater, stockbrokers, jewelry, cosmetics, ostentation, ornamentation, showiness, promotion, occupations that allow for creative expression of the self.

*Places:* Parks, woods, forests, "where the wild things are," haunts of animals, jungles, amusement parks, playgrounds, places for fun or entertainment, children's rooms, playrooms, recreation rooms, theaters, forts, palaces, ostentatious buildings, high visible places. Rocky or high areas. Fireplaces, furnaces, chimneys, ovens, stoves, near heat. Places of the nature of the Sun: showy, gaudy, pompous, prominent, hot, authoritative, self-involved, fun loving. EAST by NORTH.

*Colors:* Red or green.

## Virgo

*Ruler:* Mercury.

*Exaltation:* Mercury (especially the 15th degree of Virgo).

*Detriment:* Jupiter, Neptune (modern ruler of Pisces).

*Fall:* Venus.

*Manifestations:* The Virgin Holding Grain. The sixth sign. Hypochondriac, health conscious, pure, perfectionist, interested in details, critical, worried, meticulous, analytical, helpful, devoted to serving others, kow-towing, discriminating, practical, the Immaculate Conception. The hands, abdomen, and intestines. Negative, cold, dry, sterile, barren, human.

*Occupations:* Secretaries, editors, teachers, nurses, doctors, clerical workers, assistants, therapists, medical technicians, work requiring technical or analytic ability, service occupations.

*Places:* Inside something like a pocket or container, storehouses for dairy products, refrigerators, pantries, places where grains are kept, closets, desks, cabinets, where things are filed and stored, home offices, studies. Sick rooms, medicine cabinets. Doctors' offices. Rooms where work is done. Unostentatious, utilitarian places. SOUTH by WEST.

*Colors:* Black or speckled.

## Libra

*Ruler:* Venus.

*Exaltation:* Saturn (especially the 21st degree of Libra).

*Detriment:* Mars.

*Fall:* Sun.

*Manifestations:* The Scales, Balance, Yoke, or Claws. The seventh sign. Because Libra is the sign of yoking with another, Saturn exalts in the responsibility of bonding, whereas the Sun, representing the individual ego, is in his fall. Justice, balance, cosmic reciprocity, indecision, harmony, marriage, partnerships, union, diplomacy, tact, laziness, agreements, peace, significant others. The lower back and kidneys.

*Occupations:* Careers involving partnerships and the adjustment of relationships. The arts, politics, the Law, counseling, consulting.

*Places:* Attics, mountain tops, sides of hills, stony or sandy ground, places with clean air, closets (according to some sources), wardrobes, china closets, among items of adornment, women's pocketbooks, upper rooms, high places, tops of furniture, the top drawer, bookshelves, high in a room. Places of the nature of Venus. WEST.

*Colors:* black; dark crimson; tawny; pastels.

## Scorpio

*Rulers:* Mars, Pluto (modern ruler).

*Exaltation:* Uranus

*Detriment:* Venus.

*Fall:* Moon.

*Manifestations:* The Scorpion. The eighth sign. Death and rebirth, regeneration, transformation, deep devotion, magnetism, self-containment, healing power, probing, penetration, resourcefulness, research, refuse, elimination, the underworld, emotional intensity, secretiveness, stinging. The pelvis and the sexual organs. Negative, nocturnal, cold, moist, watery, fruitful, bestial, mute, reticent.

*Occupations:* Police, surgeons, bankers, miners, the Armed Forces, undertakers, garbage men, criminals, the Mafia, the underworld, occupations involving death, work requiring research or intense concentration.

*Places:* In the garbage, lost, gone forever, near water, near refuse, where vermin and reptiles breed, the habitat of creeping beasts, marshes, swamps, cockroach infested locations, near plumbing, kitchens, washrooms, toilets, bathrooms, cemeteries, places connected with death, with other people's money or valuables. Near foul-smelling, stagnant water. Locations subject to flooding. Damp, moldy places. Underground tunnels, secret drawers, hidden doors, haunted houses if you believe in ghosts. Places of the nature of Mars and Pluto: penetrating, cutting, intense, deep, hidden, connected with death and regeneration. NORTH by EAST.

*Colors:* Black; dark brown.

## Sagittarius

*Ruler:* Jupiter.

*Exaltation:* Moon's South Node (especially the 3rd degree of Sagittarius).

*Detriment:* Mercury.

*Fall:* Moon's North Node.

*Manifestations:* The Centaur-Archer, Aiming at the Stars. The 9th sign. Explorers, philosophers, travelers, adventurers, *Star Trek,* enthusiasm, cosmic progress, abundance, cosmic consciousness, higher education, mental journeys, the Law, the Church, ceremonies, weddings, horses, the out of doors, interest in athletics, hunting. The hips, thighs, and sacral region. Positive, hot, dry, mutable, double-bodied. The first half of Sagittarius is human, the second half bestial.

*Occupations:* The legal profession, the clergy, publicity, travel, import and export business, foreign involvement, prophecy, forecasting, exploration, occupations that require foresight and adventurousness.

*Places:* Mountains, hills with trees, highlands, rising places. Large upper rooms, fireplaces, near heat. Churches, places of worship, colleges, places where sports are played. Near hunting equipment, horse stables. The highest place, upper rooms near the fireplace or radiator, balconies, areas close to the ceiling. Places of the nature of Jupiter: expansive, wide-ranging, intellectual, scientific, prophetic, gregarious. EAST by SOUTH.

*Colors:* Yellow or reddish green.

## Capricorn

*Ruler:* Saturn.

*Exaltation:* Mars (especially the 28th degree of Capricorn).

*Detriment:* Moon.

*Fall:* Jupiter.

*Manifestations:* The Goat with the Tail of a Fish. The tenth sign. Ambition, patience, conservatism, career-mindedness, executive ability, responsibility, discipline, relentless climbing, cosmic order and justice, organization. The knees, skin, bones, skeletal system, and teeth. Negative, nocturnal, cold, dry, bestial, amphibious (mixed water and earth).

*Occupations:* Public administration, government work, politics, occupations requiring persistence and organizational ability.

*Places:* Dark places, barren fields, bushy or thorny land, dunghills, lumber yards, tool houses, low places, depressed places, dark corners near the ground or floor. Business districts. Places where lumber, farm tools, or leather are used. Locations of the nature of Saturn: dark, sparse, barren, uncomfortable, gloomy. SOUTH.

*Colors:* Black, dark brown, russet.

## Aquarius

*Rulers:* Saturn, Uranus (modern ruler).

*Detriment:* Sun.

*Manifestations:* The Water Bearer. The eleventh sign. Detached, scientific, humanitarian, progressive, nonconformist, freedom-loving, modern, independent. The lower legs, ankles, and blood circulation. Positive, hot, moist, rational, human, amphibious (the water bearer is a mixed symbol of a terrene and an aquatic theme).

*Occupations:* Work in public corporations, or involving electricity, inventiveness, lecturing, counseling, advising, water distribution, modern technology, or astrology.

*Places:* Hilly uneven grounds, places recently dug up, stone quarries, vineyards, sources of springs, places off the floor, roofs, eaves of houses, near windows, places for machinery, lecture rooms, where computers are, modern buildings, aircraft, places where modern technology is used. In a body of water but near the shore. Near the Jacuzzi or hot tub. Rooms in turrets, high balconies, near air conditioning units, drafty areas near windows. Upstairs rooms, high in a room. Places of the nature of Uranus: modern, innovative, windy, unusual, technological, electronic. WEST by NORTH.

*Colors:* Sky blue; technological tones.

## Pisces

*Rulers:* Jupiter, Neptune (modern ruler).

*Exaltation:* Venus (especially the 27th degree of Pisces).

*Detriment:* Mercury.

*Fall:* Mercury.

*Manifestations:* The Two Fishes Joined Together and Swimming in Opposite Directions. The sign of Christianity. The twelfth sign. Sacrifice, charity, welfare, prayer, spirituality, mysticism, poetry, creativity, illusion, compassion, empathy, saintliness, confusion, bondage, delusion, deceit misinformation, suffering, captivity, confinement, victimization, hospitalization, suffering, salvation, life after death, inhibition of the self, karma, the Past, the end of a cycle. The feet, the liver, and the lymphatic system. Negative, cold, moist, fruitful, double-bodied, mute, reticent, sickly, unfortunate.

*Occupations:* Religious life, nuns, priests, ministers, monasteries, nurses, work in hospitals, medical occupations, work in prisons or asylums, those who care for the mentally ill or the detained, photographers, musicians, poets, film makers. Work connected with oils, chemicals, alcohol, drugs, or the sea. Footwear.

*Places:* Along the coast, marshy grounds, rivers and ponds, swimming sites, fishing areas, aquariums, places near water, pumps, wells, religious sites, secluded regions. Places connected with liquids, chemicals, oils, medicines, healing techniques. Hospitals, clinics, infirmaries, places of confinement, jails. Dark rooms used in photography, movie theaters. Cold damp floors, rooms with low ceilings. Floors, floor coverings, where shoes are kept. Ground that is low, secluded, or susceptible to flooding. Places of the nature of Neptune: damp, secret, spiritual, sacrificial, long-suffering, sympathetic, poetic, inspirational. NORTH by WEST.

*Color:* Glistening white.

This chapter closes with Figure 7, Ptolemy's wheel of planet/sign attributions, and Table 12, a catalog of some of the common properties ascribed to the zodiac signs.

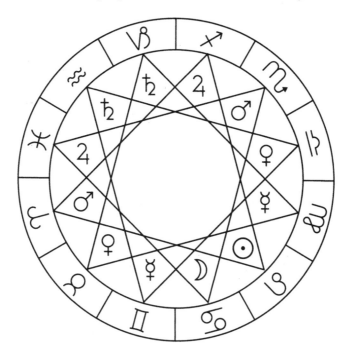

Figure 7: Ptolemy's Attributions of Planets to Signs

| Table 12: Some Commonly Used Properties of the Signs | |
|---|---|
| Barren (Sterile) | Gemini, Leo, Virgo. |
| Semi-Barren: Aries | Sagittarius, Aquarius. |
| Fruitful | The water signs: Cancer, Scorpio, Pisces. |
| Semi-Fruitful | Taurus, Libra, Capricorn. |
| Bestial | Aries, Taurus, Leo, Capricorn, last half of Sagittarius. |
| Human | Gemini, Virgo, Aquarius, the first half of Sagittarius. |
| Four-footed signs | Aries, Taurus, Leo, Sagittarius, Capricorn. |
| Amphibious signs | Aquarius and Capricorn (both have aquatic and terrene elements). |
| Mute or Reticent | The water signs Cancer, Scorpio, Pisces (these animals have no voice). |
| Equinoctial signs | Aries and Libra. |
| Tropical (solstitial) signs | Cancer and Capricorn. |
| Northern or Commanding Signs | Aries, Taurus, Gemini, Cancer, Leo, Virgo (when the Sun has north declination). |
| Southern or Obeying Signs | Libra, Scorpio, Sagittarius, Capricorn, Aquarius, Pisces (when the Sun has south declination). |
| Signs of Short Ascension ("crooked" or "scrunched") | Capricorn, Aquarius, Pisces, Aries, Taurus, Gemini (in the northern hemisphere). |
| Signs of Long Ascension ("straight" or "stretched") | Cancer, Leo, Virgo, Libra, Scorpio, Sagittarius (in the northern hemisphere). |
| Dual or Double-bodied signs | Gemini, Pisces, and Sagittarius (Ptolemy included Virgo). |
| Positive (masculine) signs | Aries, Gemini, Leo, Libra, Sagittarius, Aquarius. |
| Negative (feminine) signs | Taurus, Cancer, Virgo, Scorpio, Capricorn, Pisces. The even numbered earth and water signs were traditionally considered unfortunate when rising. They are also called the Feminine or Nocturnal signs. |
| Day House | The positive, masculine signs are the "Day Houses" of the planets that rule them. For example, the Day House of Saturn is Aquarius and the Day House of Mars is Aries. The Day House of the Sun is Leo, but the Day House of the Moon is Cancer. |
| Night House | The negative, feminine signs are the "Night Houses" of the planets that rule them. For example, the Night House of Saturn is Capricorn, and the Night House of Mars is Scorpio. The Night House of the Moon is Cancer, but the Night House of the Sun is Leo. |

# CHAPTER ELEVEN

# Critical Degrees, Fixed Stars, Arabic Parts, and Solstice Points

This chapter deals with additional factors that are useful in horary interpretation. Critical degrees, which come to us by way of India, are the cusps of the Hindu lunar mansions. Fixed stars are the points of light in the heavens that do not wander (the planets are the wanderers). Arabic parts are points around the zodiac wheel that are mathematically derived from the positions of the planets and house cusps. Solstice points are reflections of the positions of planets and points in the solstitial axes of the horoscope. These techniques are often helpful as adjuncts or confirmations of the interpretation suggested by the primary significators.

## CRITICAL DEGREES: TENSION AT THE BORDERS

Horary astrologers regard certain degrees of the zodiac as "critical" and pay attention when a significator falls in such a degree. The modern critical degrees lie at the boundaries between adjacent signs, and the traditional critical degrees separate the lunar Mansions. A planet in a critical degree is like a person wandering through the demilitarized zone between North and South Korea, or hanging out near the Berlin Wall during the Cold War. It's a risky place to be.

A cusp between two zodiacal segments is a pivotal, destabilizing zone. A significator at a critical degree is teeter-tottering between two realms of experience, and must make a choice about which way to go. Hence, critical degrees signify a crisis that requires resolution. Natal astrologers often say that people born on the cusp between zodiac signs are constantly buffeted by conflicting trends in their personalities.

The beginning and ending degrees of any sign imply a change of state. At 0° the planet has just entered a new sign, symbolically a new set of circumstances. Planets at early degrees continue to feel the tug of the previous sign. Planets at early degrees will also be quite active in their new location because they will form a major or minor aspect to all the other planets in the chart before they again change sign.

At 29° the significator is about to leave its sign and undergo a change of state. We can liken this process to ice becoming water, or water becoming steam. A planet at 29° is "impatient," can hardly wait to enter the next sign. As Ivy Jacobson puts it, such a planet is "at the end of its rope." Furthermore, a planet in the last degree is in the terms (an essential dignity) of Mars or Saturn and thus under a malefic influence.

## THE LUNAR MANSIONS: A LITTLE MOON MAGIC

In addition to the first and last degrees of any zodiac sign, certain degrees were traditionally considered critical by virtue of lying on the boundaries between the Mansions of the Moon. In societies that used a lunar calendar, the lunar month of twenty-eight days was the key unit of time measurement. The Moon's actual "sidereal" revolution around the earth as viewed from the Sun is twenty-seven days, seven hours, forty-three minutes, and eleven seconds. Because the earth is also moving around the Sun as the Moon travels around the earth, it takes a little longer for the Moon to go from one Full Moon to the next. This full cycle of the Moon as viewed from the earth (the Moon's "synodic" revolution) takes 29.53 days.

The twenty-eight-day lunar month closely approximates the actual lunar revolution. For reasons based on magic rather than science, the ancients used twenty-eight days for the Moon's revolution. Each lunar day is considered a "mansion" of the moon. The cusps between the lunar mansions signify the end of one phase of activity and the beginning of another. Critical times occur when a planet moves from one lunar mansion to the next. A planet in a critical degree has just entered a new lunar mansion and is in a tense, unresolved stated.

Dividing the 360 degrees of the zodiac into twenty-eight lunar mansions means that each lunar mansion contains 12.85° of ecliptic longitude, which in degree notation is 12° 51' 26". The reader will note that the width of a lunar mansion is approximately the average daily motion of the Moon.

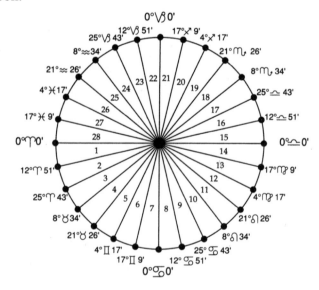

Figure 8: The Mansions of the Moon

We start measuring the lunar Mansions at the vernal equinox or 0° Aries, which is the first critical degree. Because there are 12° 51' 26" in each lunar Mansion, the next one starts at 12° 51' 26"Aries. Astrologers often round this off to 13° Aries, but inspection of the following table shows that 12° Aries is just as critical as 13° Aries. This table will make clear the derivation of the remaining critical degrees as they repeat around the zodiac in the cardinal, fixed, and mutable signs.

| Table 13: Critical Degrees | | | |
|---|---|---|---|
| Triplicity | Degrees | Minutes | Rounded Off |
| Cardinal | 0 | 0 | 0 |
| | 12 | 51 | 13 |
| | 25 | 42 | 26 |
| Fixed | 8 | 34 | 9 |
| | 21 | 25 | 21 |
| Mutable | 4 | 17 | 4 |
| | 17 | 8 | 17 |

## FIXED STARS AND MALEFIC DEGREES

The ancients discovered the existence of planets when they noticed that certain "stars" wandered, that is, did not remain fixed to the canopy of the heavens. The planets get the most astrological fanfare these days, but in the past the astrologers also paid close attention to the fixed stars. The number of fixed stars is countless; and, fortunately, only a few are regarded as significant in Western horary astrology. Such potent fixed stars generally have a northern latitude, or if southern, have a declination near the ecliptic. Astrologers tend to use the brighter, more prominent stars.

Most horary astrologers consider fixed stars only when they conjoin a significator, the Ascendant, or other angle, within an orb of one degree. Some astrologers also regard a close opposition to a fixed star as important. There is no question that a horary significator in close conjunction to a fixed star will be affected for better or worse depending on the nature of the star.

Below is a list of some important fixed stars with their positions for January of the year 2000 and their meanings in horary astrology. To find the past or future position of a fixed star, note that the fixed stars appear to "move forward" in the zodiac at a rate of one degree (one degree) every seventy-two years. In other words, because we choose to move the vernal equinox (0° Aries) backward each year with respect to the constellations of the zodiac (precession), all the fixed stars appear to move forward by the same amount (the actual annual movement of the stars is so slight that we can ignore it). The equinox itself takes about 25,868 years to complete its 360-degree precession backward through the twelve constellations of the zodiac.

Here is the arithmetic: 360° divided by 25,868 years equals 0.01392° per year. Converting degrees to decimals, we see that the fixed stars appear to move forward in the zodiac at about 0° 0' 50" per year. That's very slow. Thus, for each year in the future you need to add fifty seconds of arc, and for each decade into the future you must add about eight minutes of arc, to get the new position. To find a past position, you subtract the same amount for each year or decade going back.

Now for the list of the handful of fixed stars I pay attention to in horary analysis. I only consider them when they conjoin a significator within one degree. They are listed here in order of ecliptic longitude, according to their January 2000 positions.

## Caput Algol: 26° 10' Taurus

Caput Algol is the head of the Medusa, which Perseus chopped off while looking at its reflection in his shield. If you look at it directly, the evil countenance with its snakes for locks turns you into stone. Caput Algol is a most malefic influence. At its worst, it signifies decapitation (beheading), disaster, and death. See the chart for ValuJet Flight 592 on page 30 in Chapter Two. More commonly, a significator conjoining this malefic represents a person who will lose his head over the matter.

## Alcyone: 00° 00' Gemini

Not far beyond the Medusa's head is Alcyone of the Pleiades or the Weeping Sisters. Maybe she is crying because Medusa got her head chopped off.. Whatever the reason, your signification's conjunction with Alcyone will give you something to cry about.

## Being One's Own Worst Enemy: 22° Leo

22° of Leo is apparently a malefic degree, not a fixed star, which signifies putting one's worst foot forward and being unable to work in one's own best interest. Since most of us do this quite well without celestial assistance, I question whether a degree of the zodiac needs to be set aside for this purpose. On the other hand, my natal Mercury is near this degree and my wife tells me I have a tendency to put my foot in my mouth, so maybe there is something to it.

## Regulus: 29° 50' Leo

Lilly gave Regulus six (6) points in his system of accidental dignities. He regarded this heart of the lion, Cor Leonis, as the most benefic fixed star in the universe. The lion has a heart of gold and shares his good fortune with you when you get close enough by conjunction. Because Leo would be king, Regulus is a royal star and favors matters of status and leadership. Lilly said that Regulus gives glory, wealth, and great honors, chiefly by military preferment

## Vindemiatrix: 9° 56' Libra

This is the traditional fixed star of widowhood. If you see this prominent in your spouse's chart, watch out. The location of this star is used to calculate the Part of Widowhood = Ascendant + Vindemiatrix - Neptune.

## Spica: 23° 50' Libra, and Arcturus: 24° 14' Libra

It's hard to discuss Spica without mentioning her tag-along Arcturus. These two benefic stars are the only rays of good fortune in the Via Combusta (mid-Libra to mid-Scorpio). Spica has the nature of Venus, the lesser benefic. If your significator happens to be within a degree of either star, it won't get burned by the heat and stung by the scorpion. Instead, it will receive rewards and prosperity. Spica conjoining Mars in the 10th in the Via Combusta (see p. 68) gave Joan McEvers' son a successful stained glass business. She overlooked Spica in reading this chart, but in Volume II of her series *The Only Way to Learn Astrology* she calls Spica the "Lucky One" and describes it as signifying "wealth, fame, honor, glamour."

## Serpentis: 19° Scorpio (always)

Serpentis is not a fixed star. According to some astrologers, it is a particularly nasty degree of the zodiac. It has a fixed symbolism and does not precess with the equinoxes. Those who use Serpentis call it "the accursed degree of the accursed sign whose malefic influence never weakens." Wow, that's bad! It has the tragic nature of Saturn combined with Mars. Serpentis rarely comes up prominent in my charts. I include it here because Derek Appleby gives several convincing examples of its evil nature in his book on horary. On the other hand, Olivia Barclay, on page 211 of her text, gives an example "Shall I go to Australia?" where the Ascendant ruler is at 19° 08' Scorpio and things work out splendidly for the querent. What's good for the goose may not be good for the gander.

The reader will find a more complete list of fixed stars, including most of the ones Lilly used, with their longitudes and keywords, in Appendix A.

# THE NOT-NECESSARILY-ARABIC POINTS, LOTS, OR PARTS

The Parts are significant points around the horoscope. The term "Arabic Part" is partly a misnomer because the Parts existed long before the Arabs wrote about them. They got the name "Arabic" because eighth and ninth century Arab astrologers went overboard with the Parts they had inherited from the Babylonian, Egyptian, and Greek astrologers. The most prominent Arab astrologer of the ninth century, Abu Ma'shar, reported learning ninety-seven parts from the ancient Babylonians and Egyptians. The first century book by Dorotheus discusses several of these Parts or Lots.

When I said the Arabs went overboard inventing new Parts, I wasn't kidding. Here are some of the Parts the Arabs came up with: the Parts of barley, beans, onions, lentils, rice, sesame, sugar, dates, honey, wine, silk, salted things, pungent foods, sweet medicines, dismissal, resignation, lost animals, lawsuits, torture, decapitation, clouds, floods, sultans, secrets, and urgent wishes, to name a few. I suppose if you lost your bag of groceries, many of these would come in handy.

In practice, I always use the Part of Fortune. Although it is a point on the ecliptic and not a planet, I regard Pars Fortuna as a co-ruler of the 2nd house of money, income, and valuable possessions. I usually ignore the other Parts unless the question is so important or confusing that I need as much information as I can get from the chart.

Pars Fortuna was an invention of Hellenistic Egypt, but it derived from the Babylonian tradition of worshipping the Moon as the great god Sin. Because of the tremendous significance of the Moon, early astrologers gave the Moon a special "lot" in the horoscope. They called Pars Fortuna the "place of the Moon" or the "horoscopos (Ascendant) of the Moon."

The natural symbolism of the Ascendant is of the Sun rising over the horizon at dawn. The Part of Fortune is to the Moon what the Ascendant is to the Sun. In other words, Pars Fortuna is the symbolic "Ascendant" or dawning of the Moon in the chart. The ancients considered the Part of Fortune to be equal in importance to the Ascendant, and they regarded the Ascendant as the most powerful point in the chart.

The meaning of the Part of Fortune allows us to derive a formula for its calculation. The Moon is as far from Pars Fortuna as the Sun is from the Ascendant. In other words, the distance from the Part of Fortune to the Moon is equal to the distance from the Ascendant to the Sun. Algebraically, this becomes the formula:

$$\text{MOON - PARS FORTUNA = SUN - ASCENDANT}$$

If you remember your algebra, and transpose the equation, you get the following:

$$\text{MOON = PARS FORTUNA + SUN - ASCENDANT;}$$

$$\text{MOON - SUN = PARS FORTUNA - ASCENDANT.}$$

In English, this last formula is the same as saying that the distance from the Sun to the Moon is the same as the distance from the Ascendant to the Part of Fortune.

And finally,

$$\text{PARS FORTUNA (by day) = ASCENDANT + MOON - SUN.}$$

I say "by day" because the Arabs used two Parts of Fortune, one for day charts and one for night charts. Because the Sun ruled the day, the diurnal (day) Part of Fortune is the point where the Moon would be if the Sun were on the Ascendant. Because the Moon rules the night, the nocturnal (night) Part of Fortune is the point where the Sun would lie if the Moon were on the Ascendant. The formula for the night Part of Fortune is:

$$\text{PARS FORTUNA (by night) = ASCENDANT + SUN - MOON.}$$

William Lilly regularly used the Part of Fortune in his charts. He used only the daytime Pars Fortuna and did not feel a need to use a different formula for nighttime charts. The only other part that Lilly used in *Christian Astrology* (CA, p.238) is the part of children (Pars Filiorum = Ascendant + Jupiter - Mars) to answer the question, "Will I ever have children?" This example was discussed on pages 43 and 44 in Chapter Three.

As with fixed stars, there are dozens of Parts available to the horary astrologer. Most astrologers, however, use only a handful of Parts; for example, the Part of Death (Ascendant + 8th Cusp - Moon), the Part of Sickness (Ascendant + Mars - Saturn), the Part of Marriage (Ascendant + 7th Cusp - Venus), and the Part of Mother (Ascendant + Moon - Venus).

Notice that the Part of Death depends on the 8th cusp, which will vary depending on which house system you use. Most likely, the Arabs used the equal house system in which the 8th house cusp is exactly quincunx the Ascendant. There is another formula for the Part of Death that includes Saturn, the natural significator of death; this medieval Part of Death is the 8th cusp + Saturn - Moon. There is also a Point of Death described by Charles Emerson that is independent of the 8th cusp. Emerson's Point of Death has the formula Mars + Saturn - MC and is extremely helpful in questions about illness, death, and dying.

There is a logic to the way the parts are derived. Parts generally take the angular distance between two natural significators and project that distance from the Ascendant. Thus, mothers are naturally signified by both the Moon and Venus, the Moon being the more motherly of the two. The angle between the Moon and Venus thus symbolically relates to the querent's mother. Since the querent is at the Ascendant, the astrologer adds the distance between the mother's two significators to the Ascendant to see what relation she has to the querent at the Ascendant. Doing this will locate a point around the wheel that is the Part of the Querent's Mother.

Let's do a similar analysis for the Part of Sickness. The two malefics are Mars and Saturn. Mars rejoices in the 6th house of illness, and Saturn delights in the 12th house of confinement. The angle between Mars and Saturn must symbolize something about the querent's sickness and confinement. By subtracting the longitude of Saturn from the longitude of Mars, you get the angle between them. To see how that angle affects the querent, you start at the Ascendant (representing the querent) and measure that same distance between Saturn and Mars out from the Ascendant. This procedure will locate a point on the wheel that is the Part of the Querent's Sickness.

Modern astrologers calculate the Parts. The Arabs used the astrolabe to rotate the chart and place the significant points around the wheel. For example, if you rotate the chart so that the Sun is on the Ascendant, the Moon will be on the Part of Fortune in a daytime chart. Similarly, with the Sun rotated to the Ascendant, Mercury will be on the Part of Commerce, Venus on the Part of Love, Mars on the Point of Passion and the Sword, Jupiter on the Point of Increase (and Pomegranates), Saturn on the Point of Fatality (and the Hour Glass), Uranus on the Part of Catastrophe (and lightning), Neptune on the Point of Treachery, and Pluto on the Point of Organization. The algebraic formula for all these parts is Ascendant + Planet - Sun. (For the interested reader, I have included an extensive list of Arabic Parts in Appendix B.)

The following chart illustrates the use of Arabic Parts by Ganivet, a fifteenth-century horary astrologer. Robert Zoller reported this chart in his well-researched book *The Arabic Parts in Astrology*. It is the horoscope of a decumbiture from the book *Amicus Medicorum* by Jean Ganivet. See Chart 28.

I calculated this chart by computer and got slightly different values from those reported by Ganivet who used fifteenth-century tables. Ganivet used Campanus houses. A decumbiture is literally a "lying down." A horary chart erected for the time the person took ill is called a decumbiture chart. In such a chart, the 1st house stands for the patient.

About 7:18 in the morning of August 7, 1431 (a Mars day), at 04E53 / 45N31, the physician Dr. Henry Amici asked the astrologer Jean Ganivet to erect a decumbiture chart for the lord Dean of Vienne who had fallen ill. Ganivet told the doctor his patient was going to die. It is a Mars day and Mars rules the 8th house of death in this chart; the chart is radical and fit to judge. Let's see how Ganivet interpreted the chart.

The 1st house represents the ill Dean who has three significators in this chart. With Virgo rising, Mercury is the Dean's primary significator. Mercury also conjoins the Ascendant,

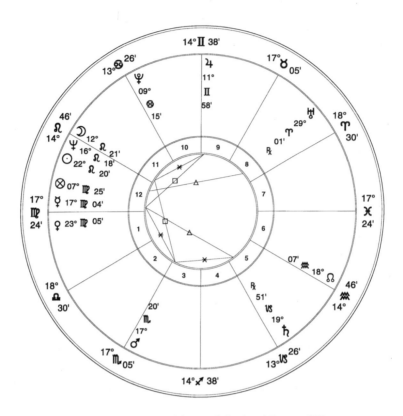

Chart 28: Decumbiture of the Lord Dean of Vienne
August 7, 1431, 7:18 A.M. GMT, 04E53, 45N31  Campanus Houses

making this planet the Dean's significator twice over. The Moon is the universal co-ruler of the Dean, and Venus occupying the 1st house is also a co-ruler. As ruler of the Ascendant, Mercury also signifies the Dean's health and well-being. Ganivet notes that the Moon is under the Sunbeams and applying to a New Moon with the Sun. As you recall, the applying New Moon is a most malefic influence in traditional horary astrology. The approaching New Moon was enough to make Ganivet give a bad prognosis.

But one factor is not enough; the astrologer must have confirmation of such a negative outcome. Ganivet next looked to the condition of Mercury, the Dean's primary ruler. Mercury is strong at the Ascendant and in his own sign. Unfortunately, Mercury is becoming stationary and is about the turn retrograde in the near future. The symbolism was too much for Ganivet. He pronounced that, like Mercury, the Dean's health would come to a standstill and then reverse itself. Because Mercury rules the mind, Ganivet said the Dean would become delirious as Mercury turned backward. Ganivet wanted more confirmation so he turned to the Arabic Parts. Specifically, he used the Part of Life (Ascendant + Saturn - Jupiter), the Part of the Killing Planet (Ascendant + Ascendant Ruler - Moon), and the Part of Death. Ganivet used the older formula for the Part of Death (8th cusp + Saturn - Moon).

I will calculate each from this chart to show you how it is done. It helps to convert each planetary position to ecliptic longitude using Table 14.

**Part of Life = Ascendant + Saturn - Jupiter.**
17° 24' Virgo + 19° 51' Capricorn - 11° 58' Gemini.
167.4 + 289.85 - 71.97 = 385.28
385.28 - 360 = 25.28 or 25° 16' Aries, which can be rounded to 25° Aries.

**Part of the Killing Planet = Ascendant + Moon - Ascendant Ruler.**
(Here, Mercury rules the Ascendant, so the formula is Ascendant + Moon - Mercury.)
17° 24' Virgo + 12° 21' Leo - 17° 04' Virgo
167.4 + 132.35 - 167.07 = 132.68 or 12° 41' Leo, which can be rounded to 13° Leo.

**Part of Death = 8th cusp + Saturn - Moon.**
18° 30' Aries + 19° 51' Capricorn - 12° 21' Leo
18.5 + 289.95 - 132.35 = 176.1
or 26° 06' Virgo, which can be rounded to 26° Virgo.

| Table 14: | |
|---|---|
| **The Ecliptic Longitude of the Signs** | |
| 0° Aries = 0° | 0° Libra = 180° |
| 0° Taurus = 30° | 0° Scorpio = 210° |
| 0° Gemini = 60° | 0° Sagittarius = 240° |
| 0° Cancer = 90° | 0° Capricorn = 270° |
| 0° Leo = 120° | 0° Aquarius = 300° |
| 0° Virgo = 150° | 0° Pisces = 330° |

Ganivet noted that the Part of Life lies in the 8th house of death, the Part of Death lies in the 1st house of life, and these two parts are in opposition. These placements all confirm a death. In addition, the Part of the Killing Planet lies between the Moon and the Sun, and the Moon (co-ruler of the Dean) will conjoin the Part of the Killing Planet in only twenty seconds of arc. The Dean is rapidly approaching death, perhaps in twenty hours, or at most in twenty days. Twenty hours is more likely because the Dean's other co-ruler, Venus, will oppose the Part of Life in only 2° (two days), and will conjoin the Part of Death in the 1st house in 3° (three days). All the evidence suggests that the Dean's days are numbered.

What was the outcome? Ganivet tells us that the Dean "became delirious before one natural day and died before two." Ganivet did not follow the method I am advocating in this book of considering first the aspects between primary significators. In this chart Mars rules the 8th house of death. Mercury is applying to a sextile with Mars which would normally be a good sign, except that Mercury (the Dean's principle ruler) turns retrograde before completing the sextile. Mercury is refrained (refranation) by turning retrograde from a good relationship with the ruler of death. The Dean's co-ruler, the Moon, will form a square with Mars, the death planet in this chart. Both Mercury's refranation and the Moon's square to the 8th house ruler suggest that the Dean will bite the dust.

## Solstice Points or Antiscions

The word "Sol-stice" comes from the Latin and means "the Sun stands still." The solstices occur twice each year: the Summer Solstice begins summer (0° Cancer) when the Sun reaches its most northern point above the Celestial Equator, and the Winter Solstice begins winter (0° Capricorn) when the Sun reaches its most southern declination. The solstice points or Antiscions are reflections of each other along the Ecliptic on either side of the Summer and Winter Solstices.

In other words, the antiscia are the two points on the ecliptic the same distance east or west of the summer or winter solstice. They represent the two days of the year when the Sun has the same declination north or south of the Celestial Equator. Because antiscion points are equidistant from the Solstices, the midpoint of a planet's position and its antiscion is always one of the Solstices, that is, 0° of Cancer or Capricorn. For example, the antiscion of 9° Capricorn is 21° Sagittarius. The signs and their corresponding antiscion signs are: Aries / Virgo, Taurus / Leo, Gemini / Cancer, Libra / Pisces, Scorpio / Aquarius, and Sagittarius / Capricorn.

Some modern astrologers believe that solstice points represent turning points in the life of the native. The following table shows which signs, degrees and minutes are reflected upon one another:

| Table 15: Signs, Degrees, and Minutes of the Solstice Points (Antiscions) | | | |
|---|---|---|---|
| Sign and Its Reflection Across the Solstice Axis | Degree and Its Antiscion | Minute and Its Antiscion | |
| Capricorn / Sagittarius | 1° / 29° | 1' / 59' | 16' / 44' |
| Aquarius / Scorpio | 2° / 28° | 2' / 58' | 17' / 43' |
| Pisces / Libra | 3° / 27° | 3' / 57' | 18' / 42' |
| Aries / Virgo | 4° / 26° | 4' / 56' | 19' / 41' |
| Taurus /Leo | 5° / 25° | 5' / 55' | 20' / 40' |
| Gemini / Cancer | 6° / 24° | 6' / 54' | 21' / 39' |
| Cancer / Gemini | 7° / 23° | 7' / 53' | 22' / 38' |
| Leo / Taurus | 8° / 22° | 8' / 52' | 23' / 37' |
| Virgo / Aries | 9° / 21° | 9' / 51' | 24' / 36' |
| Libra / Pisces | 10° / 20° | 10' / 50' | 25' / 35' |
| Scorpio / Aquarius | 11° / 19° | 11' / 49' | 26' / 34' |
| Sagittarius / Capricorn | 12° / 18° | 12' / 48' | 27' / 33' |
| | 13° / 17° | 13' / 47' | 28' / 32' |
| | 14° / 16° | 14' / 46' | 29' / 31' |
| | 15° / 15° | 15' / 45' | 30' / 30' |

Using Table 15, we see that 10° Capricorn has its solstice point (antiscion) at 29° 60' (another way to say 30°) minus 10°, or 20° Sagittarius. The solstice point of Caput Algol (at 26°01' Taurus in 1990) lies in Leo at 29° 60' minus 26° 01', or 3° 59' Leo. The solstice point (antiscion) of Spica (at 23° 50' Libra in 2000) is in Pisces at 29° 60' minus 23° 50', or at 6° 10' Pisces.

According to Henry Coley, "the learned do hold an Antiscion to be equivalent to a sextile or trine Aspect, especially if they were Fortunate Planets; and a Contrantiscion to be of the nature of a square or opposition." Lilly looked for the antiscions of planets in a horary chart to see if there were conjunctions or oppositions to the antiscion degrees. He stated that the antiscions "of good planets...are equal to a sextile or trine," whereas contrascions are "of the nature of a square or opposition." A contrascion (or contrantiscion) is the point opposite (180° away from) the antiscion degree. In other words, the contrascion of a planet is the antiscion of the point opposite to the planet on the ecliptic. Lilly used the word "contra-antiscion" for contrascion.

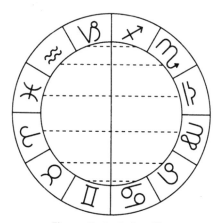

Figure 9: Antiscion Signs

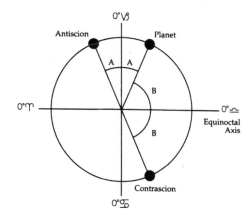

Figure 10: Contrascions (Contrantiscions)

There is a link between antiscions / contrascions and parallels / contraparallels of declination. A conjunction to an antiscion degree means that the two planets occupy the two points on the Ecliptic where the Sun has the same declination. Thus, if the antiscion of a benefic (Venus or Jupiter) conjoins a significator, the relationship is reminiscent of a parallel of declination, and this supports a positive outcome. A conjunction to a contrascion degree means that the two planets occupy the two points on the Ecliptic where the Sun has equal but opposite declinations. If the antiscion of a malefic (Mars, Saturn, Uranus, Neptune, Pluto) falls opposite a significator, the relationship is similar to a contraparallel of declination, and this supports an unfortunate outcome.

Conjunctions and oppositions to solstice points provide useful information in horary judgment. The chart for Sara's baby illustrates their use, as does the chart for ValuJet Flight 592 on page 30 in Chapter Two.

Figure 11 (on the following page) is a graphic representation of the relation of antiscion and contrantiscion signs. The horizontal lines lines connect the antiscion signs, while the vertical lines connect the contrantiscion signs.

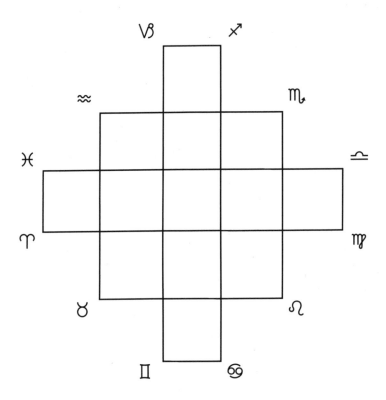

Figure 11: Matrix of Antiscions and Contrantiscions

# CHAPTER TWELVE

# Finding Lost Items

Perhaps the most gratifying aspect of horary astrology is the ability to locate lost or missing objects, animals, and people. This chapter brings together information needed to interpret questions about things that are lost, misplaced, or stolen. Let me illustrate with a case example.

## THE CASE OF THE MISSING KITTEN

On January 13, 1994, at 8:24 P.M., I received a phone call from a woman in New York City. Her kitten had been missing for over twenty-four hours and was nowhere to be found. She couldn't understand how the kitten might have escaped from the apartment. See Chart 29.

Seven degrees of Virgo rise on the Ascendant, fitting for a question about a young kitten (Virgo is associated with the 6th house of pets). The querent is ruled by Ascendant-ruler Mercury and is co-ruled by the Moon, which in this chart lies in the 6th house of pets and shows what is on the querent's mind.

The missing kitten is shown by the 6th house with Aquarius on the cusp. Saturn is the traditional ruler of Aquarius and is Almuten of the 6th. Thus, Saturn signifies the sought-after kitten. Saturn occupies the 6th house (the 1st house of the kitten in the turned chart), suggesting that the kitten is still at home but is concealed and will be hard for the querent to find because it is in the cadent 6th of the querent. The Moon co-rules the querent and is applying to conjoin Saturn (the kitten) in nine degrees, implying that querent and kitten will be reunited, perhaps in nine hours.

Where is the kitten? Saturn lies toward the end of its sign at 28° Aquarius. Lilly wrote that "If your significator be going out of one sign and entering another, the thing is behind something or other, or is carefully fallen down betwixt two rooms, or near the threshold or joining together of two rooms, and is higher or lower in the place according to the nature of the sign, etc." (CA, p. 203). Aquarius often signifies upper rooms and locations near

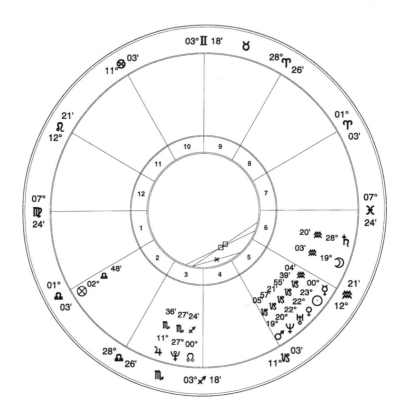

Chart 29: Missing Kitten
January 13, 1994, 8:24 P.M. EST, 73W01, 41N19 Regiomontanus Houses

modern or electronic gadgets. Because Aquarius is the water bearer, it can symbolize places near water. Fixed signs imply places low down or near the floor.

The querent searched the upstairs rooms in her loft, especially the areas near electronic equipment like stereos and computers, but she did not find the kitten. The next evening she called to tell me she found the kitten in the upstairs bathroom. The small animal had entered the small door that is used to service the Jacuzzi and could not get out. The querent's pet had spent two days trapped inside the housing of the Jacuzzi, a modern electronic gadget connected with water!

## WHERE IS IT?

Let us now review the locations indicated by the mundane houses. If an item is lost, the house position of its significator will often show where it can be found. The signs are also helpful in this regard. Locations suggested by the signs were reviewed in the Chapter 10.

### Locations Suggested by the Mundane Houses

Angular houses imply that the lost object is where it ought to be, in the home or office, or where it is usually kept, in a place the querent frequents, nearby, quick and easy to find. Angular houses signify public or visible happenings.

Succedent houses imply the lost item is not in its usual place and will be harder and take longer to find. The item may not be in the house, but it is usually nearby and may be out of doors, perhaps in an outbuilding, a garage, or in the yard.

Finally, cadent houses refer to places either literally far off or, if close by, symbolically distant by being hidden from view and almost impossible to find. Significators in cadent houses show the item may take a long time to locate, and may be found only indirectly, possibly by another person. Cadent houses signify hidden, concealed, or secret locations.

The following information on the individual houses is derived from various horary authors, both modern and classical. Some of the traditional locations may sound archaic. The reader should be creative, using the meanings below as symbols of possible locations. For example, a few years ago a friend was visiting for a weekend from Washington, D.C. She asked me to look at her transits and I noticed a lot of minor aspect activity (Moon, Mercury, Venus) in her twelfth house, all peaking on Monday. With tongue in cheek, I told her she might have an encounter with a large animal, like a cow. The 12th rules large animals. She returned to Washington on Sunday and called me Monday evening, sounding quite amused. My friend was undergoing psychoanalysis at the time. When she entered her analyst's office Monday morning, she noticed that he had placed a new painting over his couch. The painting depicted cows grazing in a field. She burst out laughing and had a lively analytic session.

## Some Horary House Locations

Note that if the significator of the missing object is in an angular (houses 1, 4, 7, 10), it should be easy to find; succedent (houses 2, 5, 8, 11), harder to find; and cadent (houses 3 ,6, 9, 12), concealed and very difficult to find. If the significator of the lost object lies in an intercepted sign, the item is enclosed and not in the open. If near a house cusp, then near a door, window, or passage between rooms. If "going out of one sign and entering another, the thing is behind something or other, or is carefully fallen down betwixt two rooms, or near the threshold..." (Lilly, CA, p. 203). Below are some locations signified by the individual houses. As you do your own charts, feel free to add to this list to indicate where the item was found.

*First House:* Where the querent spends the most time, on the querent's body or person, at home, in the most used room, in the querent's office. Where the querent usually keeps his possessions. The entrance to the house, the front porch, in a personal place of the querent. With a grandparent (4th of 10th). East.

*Second House:* Where the querent keeps money, valuables, or possessions. In a pocketbook, wallet, safe deposit box, vault, file cabinet. In the home of a friend (4th of 11th) East Northeast.

*Third House:* On or in a desk. Among papers, books, or newspapers. In a study, library, a place where one writes. In or near the car. In places connected to travel, letters, education, communication, the media. Near a telephone, radio, or television. In the neighborhood. With a sibling. North Northeast.

*Fourth House:* In the home. In a child's bedroom or under a child's bed (12th of the 5th). In the middle of the house, or the oldest part of the house. In a kitchen, pantry, or basement. With a parent. With the oldest person in the house. In the yard or garden. North.

*Fifth House:* In a recreation room. In a place for play, hobbies, pleasure, or amusement. A child's room. With a sweetheart. In a bar or tavern. In a theater or banquet hall. North Northwest.

*Sixth House:* In a container or pocket, inside something. In a place where one works or does chores. In a cupboard, closet, drawer, or file cabinet. Near a pet or small animal. With a tenant, a coworker, a maid or servant. In or near a sick room, bathroom, or medicine cabinet. In a clinic or doctor's office. West Northwest.

*Seventh House:* Where the partner spends the most time, with the partner, in the spouse's room, at the partner's office, in the living room, with one's personal consultant or attorney, with the astrologer. The father's place of residence, the paternal grandfather (4th of 4th), the maternal grandmother (10th of 10th), with a niece or nephew (5th of 3rd). West.

*Eighth House:* In the garbage. Dead and gone (with other negative indicators in the chart, the item may be unrecoverable). Near water or plumbing, near places of elimination. The bathroom. Where research is done. Places related to sex, death, and legacies. Where other people's money is kept or handled. Among a partner's possessions or valuables. Southwest.

*Ninth House:* Far away, distant, not close to where you are. Places related to voyages, heights, long distance travel, foreign countries, the church, publishing, colleges, or higher learning. With in-laws (3rd of the 7th). With grandchildren (5th of the 5th). South Southwest.

*Tenth House:* In the office. Where one works (e.g., for a teacher: the classroom). In the hallway, parent's room, mother's room, dining room. In a department store or public building. With the boss, where those in authority are. The structural parts of a building. In a public place. South.

*Eleventh House:* With friends. In clubs, lodges, meeting places. In a partner's work area (6th of the 7th). With a stepchild (5th of 7th). Places the querent hopes or wishes to be. Southeast.

*Twelfth House:* In the bedroom, or under the bed. In places of confinement, hospitals, retreats, institutions, secluded places, private spots. In places for prayer, sleep, or meditation. In hidden, out of sight, mysterious places. In the sick room (with the 6th), the infirmary. With a secret enemy. Places connected to large animals. East Southeast.

## Places Designated by the Elements

Each of the four elements suggests a particular place or location where a missing object or person may be found.

*Fire signs* suggest warm places, where heat is, near chimneys, near walls, near fireplaces, near stoves, or where heat might be generated. Fire locations are also upper rooms and near wall or partitions. Since Mars is a fire planet and his metal, iron, is used to contain heat, an object signified by fire may be near something made of iron or steel. Fire signs imply a position midway up in a room. Their direction is east.

Significators of lost objects in the Via Combusta (burning way) may have a similar meaning to planets in fire signs. The missing item may be near heat, near things connected with heat such as thermostats or furnaces, or near combustion as in an automobile with its combustion engine. Because the Via Combusta spans the ancient sign Scorpio, the lost object may be hidden or near liquids of some kind.

*Air signs* refer to places high up or upstairs, upper floors, tops of rooms, roofs, eaves, high shelves. Outdoors air signs refer to tree, hillsides, mountain tops, or even in the air as in an airplane. If the significator of the item is in an air sign, it is probably high up in a room. The lost item may be near a window, in a garret, or in some open place with clean, fresh air. Although Aquarius (the Water Bearer) is an air sign, significators in Aquarius often symbolize amphibious places near water (e.g., a Jacuzzi). The direction of air signs is west.

*Earth signs* show something low or on the floor, at or below the ground level, in the garden, in the yard, possibly in the cellar, or buried in the ground. Outdoors the object may be near a bridge. Earth refers to earthen things, stone, cement, pavement, mud or clay walls, things on the ground, the first floor of a building, the structural elements of things. The direction of earth signs is south.

*Water signs* imply a location low in a room, near water or other liquids, where moisture is, near fountains, plumbing, bathrooms, sinks, tubs, rivers, lakes, oceans, low lands, low places. The ruler of a lost item in a water sign may mean the item is near water as under a sink, but it also might be near an oil tank, near the gearshift with its transmission fluid in a car, near some containers of cleaning fluid, etc. Cancer refers to pure or running water, Scorpio to filthy liquids, oils, and dyes, and Pisces to standing waters, liquors, and wines. The direction of water signs is north.

## Places Designated by Triplicity

*Common or Mutable signs* (Gemini, Virgo, Sagittarius, Pisces) suggest that the missing object is in the house. If outdoors, common signs indicate watery places, ditches, and pits.

*Fixed signs* (Taurus, Leo, Scorpio, Aquarius) indicate a hidden location, a place low or near the floor. If outdoors, fixed signs signify good quality flat land.

*Cardinal signs* (Aries, Cancer, Libra, Capricorn) refer to high places, like roof and ceilings, and to ground that has been recently dug. If outdoors, cardinal signs indicate hills and newly built structures.

## A MODERN EXAMPLE: WHERE ARE RACHEL'S MISSING EYEGLASSES?

On the morning of September 15, 1992, at 7:21 A.M. EDT, I received a message from my friend Rachel that she would like help locating her missing eyeglasses. Rachel, who shares an office suite with my wife, is a total skeptic of astrology. She had misplaced her rather expensive eyeglasses two days earlier and was calling in desperation because she could not find them. She felt she had nothing to lose by asking the question of an astrologer. I was testing Regiomontanus houses at the time. See Chart 30.

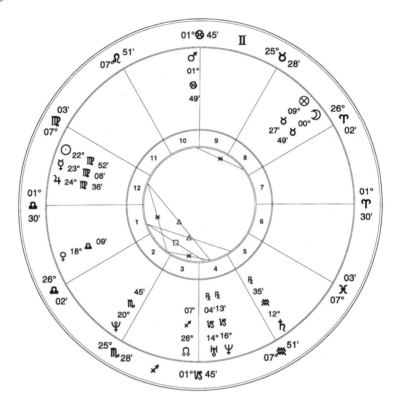

Chart 30: Rachel's Eyeglasses
September 15, 1992, 7:21 A.M. EDT, 73W01, 41N19 Regiomontanus Houses

I assumed that the early Ascendant reflected Rachel's disbelief that I could be of help, and I decided to read the chart nonetheless. Rachel is represented by 1st house ruler Venus and by the Moon. The missing eyeglasses are signified by 2nd house Venus. The fact that Venus rules both the Ascendant and second house suggests that the missing item is still in Rachel's possession. Furthermore, 2nd ruler Venus lies in the 1st house, suggesting that the glasses are in a place where they are usually kept and perhaps on Rachel's person. Because Venus is separating from squares to Uranus and Neptune, I assumed that Rachel had misplaced the glasses during a period of stress and inattention two days earlier.

According to Lilly, if the 2nd ruler lies in the 1st house, "you may judge the thing is in that part of the house which he himself [the querent] most frequents, or wherein he doth most abide, or is conversant, or where himself layeth up his own commodities" (CA p. 202). This interpretation is reinforced by the fact that the Moon (also representing Rachel) lies in Taurus in the 8th (both symbols of places where valuables may be kept) and is approaching a conjunction with the Part of Fortune whose dispositor is Venus in the 1st.

I assured Rachel that she would find her eyeglasses soon, most likely in a place where she normally keeps them. She decided to wait another day before ordering new glasses. The next afternoon she reached for something in her pocketbook and discovered her missing eyeglasses at the bottom of her purse. Although she had looked through her pocketbook previously, she had not seen them. Remaining true to her skepticism of astrology, Rachel asked my wife if she had found the glasses elsewhere in the office and placed them in her pocketbook to make the chart turn out as predicted!

## AN HISTORICAL EXAMPLE: THE THEFT OF THE SLAVE GIRL'S LINEN

In the year A.D. 478, in Syene (Aswan), somebody stole a slave girl's linen. Distraught, the young maiden consulted her local astrologer, Palchus, who promptly told her where to find it. Fortunately for us, Palchus recorded his analysis and made it available for modern eyes. In *Greek Horoscopes* Neugebaur and Van Hoesen reported the date of the theft as August 29, 478, during the fourth hour of the night (around 10:30 P.M.), at Syene (32E57 /24N04). See Chart 31. Palchus does not specify a house system, so I used Porphyry, which was a popular third-century system. The fifth-century ephemerides were not as accurate as modern computer generated ones, and the positions given by Palchus vary somewhat from modern calculations.

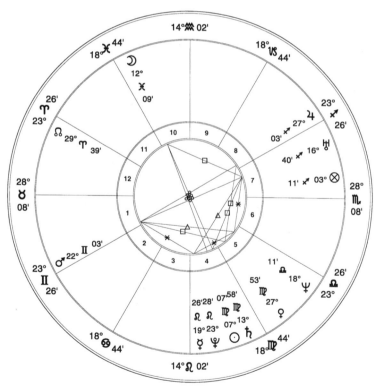

Chart 31: Palchus / The Theft of the Slave Girl's Linen
August 29, 478, 10:30 P.M. LMT, 32E57, 24N04  Porphyry Houses

Because the modern calculations are a degree or two later than Palchus' figures, you might think the date is off by a day or two. The date appears correct, however, because Palchus refers to the theft occurring during the Full Moon. The Moon opposed the Sun shortly before the slave asked the question. Here is a list comparing the modern and older chart positions.

| Chart Component | Palchus' Figure | Modern Figure |
|---|---|---|
| Sun | 4° Virgo | 7° Virgo |
| Moon | 9° Pisces | 12° Pisces |
| Mercury | 18° Leo | 19° Leo |
| Venus | 24° Virgo | 28° Virgo |
| Mars | 20° Gemini | 22° Gemini |
| Jupiter | 26° Sagittarius | 27° Sagittarius |
| Saturn | 11° Virgo | 14° Virgo |
| Ascendant | (10:30 P.M. LMT) | 28° Taurus |
| Midheaven | (10:30 P.M. LMT) | 14° Aquarius |
| Moon's No. Node | Aries | 29° 39' Aries |
| Pars Fortuna | Scorpio | 3° 11' Sagittarius |

There is an apparent discrepancy between the fifth century Part of Fortune and the modern computation. Today's formula for Pars Fortuna (Ascendant + Moon - Sun) was used by the ancients only for daytime charts. It represents the point the Moon would occupy if the Sun were rising. This diurnal Part of Fortune computes to Ascendant (28° 08' Taurus) + Moon (12° 09' Pisces) - Sun (7° 07' Virgo), or 58.13 + 342.15 - 157.12 = 243.16, or 3° 11' Sagittarius.

The ancients calculated two Parts of Fortune, one for daytime and the other for night-time charts. They reasoned that the Sun was lord of the day and the Moon was queen of the night. The formula for the nocturnal Part of Fortune is Ascendant + Sun - Moon. It is the point the Sun would occupy if the Moon were rising on the Ascendant, the most powerful angle in the chart and a fitting place for a ruler to be. At night the ancients placed the Moon on the Ascendant to calculate Pars Fortuna, and during the day they placed the Sun there.

Using the nighttime Part of Fortune, we calculate: (Ascendant) 58.13 + (Sun) 157.12 - (Moon) 342.15 = -126.9. Since we can't have a negative number and are dealing with points on a continuous circle, we must subtract 126.9 from 360 (the number of degrees in a full circle), to get 233.1, or 23° 06' Scorpio. As a good Greek-Egyptian astrologer, Palchus was careful to use the nocturnal Part of Fortune in a 10:30 P.M. chart, four hours after sunset, when the Moon reigned supreme.

Palchus identified the thief and assured the girl that she would soon get her linen back. How did he do this? His reasoning may seem a little odd to the modern horary astrologer, but it shows us how our thinking about finding lost objects evolved. Palchus deduced that the linen was out of sight because the nocturnal Pars Fortuna was in Scorpio, a hidden sign. Recall that the Lot of Fortune is a co-ruler of the 2nd house of money and movable possessions. As ruler of the Ascendant (at 28° Taurus), Venus governs the slave girl who makes the inquiry.

Palchus noted that both the Sun and the Ascendant-ruler, Venus, applied to a trine with the Ascendant. The Moon, furthermore, was approaching a sextile to the Ascendant. He took these favorable aspects to mean that the thief was a member of the household and that the stolen item would be recovered. The Full Moon was "in contact with the diameter of Saturn." This indicated that "the thief was an old man." Mercury is the natural ruler of thieves. Because Saturn was in Mercury's sign of the Virgin (Virgo), the thief must be "an educated person and a rascal and frustrated in intercourse." Palchus did not hold Virgo in high esteem. He made this comment long before the days of that other educated rascal Richard Nixon, who has Virgo rising, showing his personality and state of mind. Was Nixon also "frustrated in intercourse"? I wonder.

Although Palchus seemed unaware of them, two other horary methods identify Saturn as the thief. First, Saturn at 13° 58' Virgo in the 4th house is a peregrine planet in an angle. Lilly used peregrine planets in angles or in the 2nd house to signify the thief. Mars, ruler of the 7th, is peregrine at 22° 03' Gemini in the 1st house and could represent a thief.

A rule of Guido Bonatus also fingers Saturn as the thief. Bonatus used the planet from which the Moon most recently separated as a co-ruler of the querent and the planet which the Moon will next aspect as a co-ruler of the quesited. In this chart the Moon's next aspect is an opposition to Saturn. The method of Bonatus identifies Saturn as the quesited thief.

Palchus was using the Egyptian rather than the Ptolemaic terms of the planets, as evidenced by his statement that the Moon (the stolen goods) was in the terms of Venus, showing that the linen belonged to a woman (Venus). The Moon is in the Egyptian terms of Venus but in the Ptolemaic terms of Jupiter. Maybe the ultimate owner of the linen was her master (Jupiter), most likely a corpulent, well-to-do man.

Venus, ruling the querent, is in her fall in Virgo. Palchus reads this to mean that the querent "was a humble person or slave and that the lost article was old and wretched because it (Venus) was in evening phase." Venus was the evening star that day. He next gives his reasons why the linen (the Moon) would be found. First, he says, the Moon is moving from Pisces into Aries, the sign of Mars, and the Moon's next conjunction will be with Mars, which governs the sign that next receives the Moon. Mars is also the dispositor of the Part of Fortune, which Palchus calculated to be in Scorpio. As the dispositor of Pars Fortuna, Mars bears its "likeness" and conveys that good fortune to the Moon in the upcoming conjunction.

Furthermore, the Sun in Virgo will trine the "horoscopos" (Ascendant) in Taurus and will sextile Pars Fortuna in Scorpio. The Sun is also "in company with the ruler of the horoscopos" (Venus) since both are in Virgo and Venus is separating from a conjunction with the Sun. In addition, the Sun is "diametrical to the Moon" (in Pisces).

These various indications, Palchus reported, "by every scheme made the finding quick." He added that because the Ascendant ruler (Venus) was in her own "triangle" (Virgo, Capricorn, Taurus) and because Jupiter, ruling the Moon's sign Pisces, had dignity in its own sign Sagittarius, "the finding took place."

## A NOTE ABOUT CALENDARS

To calculate the chart for the slave girl's linen, I had to convert the date and time given in an ancient text to the modern calendar. I ran into a similar problem when I wanted to run the chart for the Dean of Vienne through my computer. If you read Lilly's original examples, you will find that the dates used by Lilly do not match today's Gregorian calendar.

The West used the Julian calendar from 45 B.C. to A.D. 1582. The Julian calendar placed the vernal equinox at March 25 and set the length of the year to 365.25 days. It also created a leap year every four years to compensate for the extra quarter day each year. Because 365.25 days is not the exact the length of year, the equinox began to move backward in time. At the beginning of the Julian calendar, the spring equinox fell on March 25. By the year A.D. 325 it occurred on March 21, and by 1570 it fell on March 11.

Pope Sixtus IV summoned Regiomontanus to Rome in 1474 to reconstruct the calendar, but Regiomontanus died before completing the task. If only he had done a horary chart before accepting the assignment! A century later a physician from Verona, Aloysius Lilius, worked out the mathematics of a calendar that would accurately time the seasons. Dr. Lilius died before he could do much with his system. Fortunately, his brother preserved it and gave it to Pope Gregory XII. Pope Gregory convened a committee that spent five years revising the calendar to the modern one that bears his name. This new calendar dropped 10 days by changing October 5 to October 15, 1582. The length of the solar year was also corrected to 365 days, 5 hours, 49 minutes, 12 seconds.

If you work with old sources, you will need to check your dates and calendars systems to be sure you have accurate information. The Gregorian calendar went into effect in 1582 throughout the Roman Catholic empire, but the Protestant world was slow to accept it. Germany, Denmark, and Sweden waited until 1700, and Russia until 1918. Great Britain did not make the change until 1752. By then the British had to drop 11 days by changing September 3 to September 14, 1752. Lilly's charts are for dates prior to 1752 and require a ten-day correction. Also, in Lilly's time, the convention was to begin the new day at noon rather than at midnight as we do today.

In summary, to convert the older Julian dates to the current Gregorian calendar, do the following. For Julian dates from October 15, 1582 through February 28, 1700, you add ten days; from March 1, 1700 through February 28, 1800, you add eleven days; from March 1, 1800 through Feb 28, 1900, you add twelve days; and from March 1, 1900 through February 28, 2000, you add thirteen days.

## WHICH WAY DID HE GO? DIRECTIONS IN HORARY

Tables 16, 17, and 18 (opposite) present the traditional horary wisdom on locating directions in a chart. Where you find the significator by house and by sign is where the lost object or person will be. Usually the astrologer must synthesize multiple indications into a meaningful statement. Various textbooks give different rules which don't always work out in practice. Reviewing the chart with the querent will often jog his or her memory and bring to light forgotten facts that help in locating the object.

| Table 16: Direction by Sign | |
|---|---|
| Aries: EAST<br>Taurus: S by E<br>Gemini: W by S | Libra: WEST<br>Scorpio: N by E<br>Sagittarius: E by S |
| Cancer: NORTH<br>Leo: E by N<br>Virgo: S by W | Capricorn: SOUTH<br>Aquarius: W by N<br>Pisces: N by W |
| Note that signs can also be grouped by element: | |
| FIRE signs are EAST<br>Aries: EAST<br>Leo E by N<br>Sagittarius: E by S | EARTH signs are SOUTH<br>Capricorn: SOUTH<br>Taurus: S by E<br>Virgo: S by W |
| AIR signs are WEST<br>Libra: WEST<br>Aquarius: W by N<br>Gemini: W by S | WATER signs are NORTH<br>Cancer: NORTH<br>Scorpio: N by E<br>Pisces: N by W |

| Table 17: Direction by House | |
|---|---|
| 1st: EAST<br>2nd: ENE<br>3rd: NNE | 7th: WEST<br>8th: WSW<br>9th: SSW |
| 4th: NORTH<br>5th: NNW<br>6th: WNW | 10th: SOUTH<br>11th: SSE<br>12th: ESE |
| Note that the houses follow the points of a compass. | |

| Table 18: Height, Level, or Location by Element | |
|---|---|
| FIRE signs | Middle height, mid-level; near a wall or partition, heat or fire, iron, chimneys, stoves, fixtures. |
| EARTH signs | Low, on or in the ground, at floor level, under the earth, near pavement, near a bridge. |
| AIR signs | High up, highlands, upper level, above ground, upstairs, near windows, near clean air, near hills and trees. |
| WATER signs | Lowlands, lower level, near moisture or liquids, damp places, bathrooms, kitchens, laundry rooms, near plumbing. |

Let's see how William Lilly applied these rules to the case of the missing dog. On September 8, 1646, at 4:05 P.M. LMT, a client asked Lilly about a missing dog, "What part of the city they should search? and, should he be found?" See Chart 32.

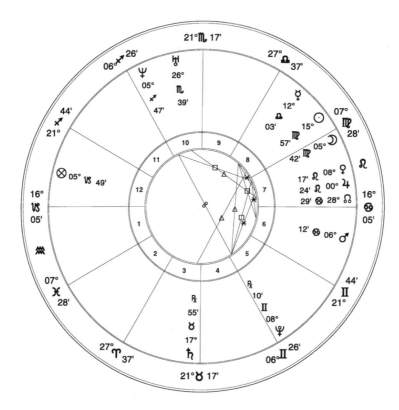

Chart 32   Missing Dog
September 8, 1646, 4:05 P.M. LMT, 00W10, 51N30   Regiomontanus Houses

With Capricorn rising and the Moon's South Node (of the nature of Saturn) near the Ascendant, the querent's ruler is Saturn and the querent was saturnine. Lilly described him as "vitiated both in body and mind; that is, he was a little deformed in body, of small stature, and extremely covetous in disposition."

The 6th house rules pets. Some modern astrologers say that if pets are love objects, they belong in the 5th; but this saturnine, covetous, deformed man would hardly keep a dog as a love object. With Gemini on the 6th, Mercury signifies the dog. Looking at Table 16, we see that Gemini, the sign of the cusp of the dog's house, is West by South. Mercury, the dog's significator, is in the 8th house in Libra. The 8th house is WSW and Libra is a western sign.

The Moon is a general significator of runaways and fugitives. Here Luna is at the end of the 7th or just inside the 8th house (Regiomontanus system) and in Virgo. The 7th house is West, the 8th house WSW, and Virgo is South by West. Let's list the various indicators:

- Ruler of quesited (Mercury) by house: 8th—WSW.

- Ruler of quesited (Mercury) by sign: Libra—West

- Sign on cusp of quesited house: Gemini—W by S

• Sign of the Moon: Virgo—S by W

• House of the Moon (7th—8th) West to WSW.

Lilly ignored the house positions and considered only the sign placements. Mercury is in Libra (West), Gemini (West by South) is on the cusp of the quesited house, and the Moon is in Virgo (South by West). Lilly concluded that "the plurality of testimonies shewed the dog ought to be west from where the owner lived."

Rarely are the indicators of direction so consistent as in Lilly's case of the missing dog. The astrologer usually has to be creative at synthesis to get the right answer. Because the dog's ruler Mercury was in an air sign, Lilly concluded "the dog was in some garret or upper room; and, as the Moon was under the beams of the Sun, and Mercury, the Moon, and the Sun were in the 8th house, that he was kept privately, or in great secrecy." Like Palchus, Lilly regards Scorpio and the 8th house as symbols of hidden or secret places. Being under the rays of the Sun also hides the light of the Moon. Because the Moon rules fugitives, the hidden Moon signifies the state of the missing dog.

Lilly also experimented with finding lost objects in the home and came up with the following system for locating anything mislaid or missing at home, but not stolen. To find the lost item, he synthesized the eight indicators of direction and location shown in Table 19.

---

**Table 19:**
**Lilly's Eight Indicators for Finding Missing Things**

1. The Ascendant sign.
2. The sign of the ruler of the Ascendant.
3. The sign on the 4th house (cardine under the earth).
4. The sign of the ruler of the 4th.
5. The sign of the Moon.
6. The sign on the 2nd cusp (movable possessions).
7. The sign of the ruler of the 2nd.
8. The sign of the Part of Fortune.

---

Different astrologers have different systems for finding lost objects. Joan McEvers looks primarily at the house and sign of the planet ruling the 2nd (movable possessions), and then at the dispositor of the Part of Fortune, if necessary, for further information.

Ivy Jacobson also assigns movable possessions to the 2nd house, but she places the possibility of mislaying objects in the 4th. She has a slightly more elaborate system than McEvers but is less detailed than Lilly. Jacobson considers the following four significators to locate a missing article:

• The ruler of the 2nd (movable possessions)

• The Moon (natural ruler of fugitives)

• Venus (natural ruler of valuables)

• The dispositor of the Part of Fortune.

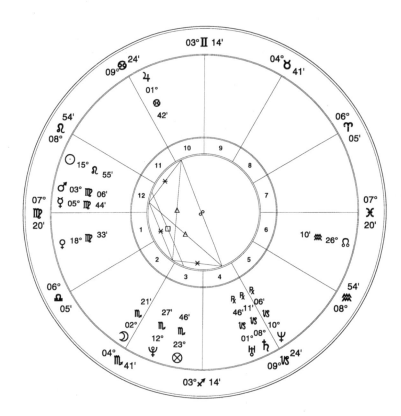

Chart 33: "Where are My Watch and Ring?"
August 8, 1989, 6:49 A.M. EST, 73W01, 41N19  Koch Houses

I will now give an example to compare these three methods. Chart 33 is for a question of my own. Let's see if we can find the lost object. On August 8, 1989, I was about to leave for work when I could not find my watch and ring. I knew they were at home because I remembered taking them off the previous evening. I quickly searched the usual places I might leave them and they were nowhere to be found. I cast the chart for 6:49 A.M. EST on August 8, 1989, the time I was most solicitous abut the matter.

Let's see if the chart can tell me the location of my watch and ring. The Virgo Ascendant conjoins my natal Part of Fortune. This is a good sign. I should get the items back. Venus is in Virgo in the first house, another good sign, because Venus is benefic and is the natural ruler of rings. Libra is on the 2nd cusp so Venus is also the 2nd house ruler of lost items in this chart. The placement of Venus in the first house confirms that the ring is at home in a place I frequently use or where it ought to be.

McEvers would look mainly at the position of Venus, ruler of the 2nd. Venus is EAST by mundane house and SOUTH by WEST according to sign. The missing objects ought to be in the east part of the house, southwest corner; or else, in the southwest part of the house, eastern side of the room. The dispositor of Pars Fortuna is Mars which is in Virgo in the 12th. Virgo is S by W, and the 12th is E by SE. The direction S by W is repeated and ought to be a key in finding the watch and ring.

Ivy Jacobson would add the Moon and Venus to McEvers' list. Venus is already the ruler of the 2nd house. The Moon is in the 2nd house, making it a co-ruler of the lost objects.

The Moon is also a natural ruler of fugitives and lost things. Unfortunately, here the Moon is in the Via Combusta, one of the classical considerations before judgment. Will I have trouble reading the chart or finding the objects? Will the perverse nature of the combust zone play a sadistic trick on me? We shall see.

To review, Jacobson says to look at:

- The ruler of the 2nd—Libra here—Venus.
- Venus (natural ruler of possessions).
- Moon (natural ruler of fugitives).
- Dispositor of the Scorpio Pars Fortuna—Mars.

According to Jacobson, because the ruler of the 2nd cusp is in the 1st house, the lost items are in the home or where the querent usually keeps such things. She says to use the house positions to find the part of the home to go to first, then to use the sign positions to tell where to go once you get there. The sign's element will designate whether it is low, middle, or high in the location. Let me make a little chart to sort this all out:

| Planet | Sign | Direction | House | Direction |
|--------|---------|-----------|-------|-----------|
| Venus | Virgo | S by W | 1st | EAST |
| Venus | Virgo | S by W | 1st | EAST |
| Moon | Scorpio | N by E | 2nd | N by E |
| Mars | Virgo | S by W | 12th | ESE |

I already know the watch and ring are at home. I simply don't remember where I put them the previous evening. To find this out, I follow Jacobson's rules and look at house positions first. The houses suggest I should go EAST. This takes me into the living room. Next I consider the sign positions which are predominantly South by West. I look in the southwest corner of the living room. The earth and water signs suggest the missing items are on the floor. Guess what, they're not there! Ivy Jacobson strikes out.

But wait a minute. I must remain firm in my conviction that the answer is in the chart. Maybe the problem is the Via Combust Moon. Jones said the Via Combusta symbolizes a perverse satisfaction in confusion. Suddenly it occurs to me that the Via Combust Moon may be telling me the chart is deliberately trying to mislead me by representing things backwards and delighting in the resulting chaos.

Let me redo the analysis, this time reversing Jacobson's instructions. Instead of first looking at the house positions, I will read the sign positions. The signs are mainly SOUTH BY WEST so I go to the southwest part of the house which is my bedroom. This makes sense because I usually leave the watch and ring in the bedroom. Venus in the 1st house suggests the objects are at home in a place they normally should be.

Following the perverse symbolism of the Via Combust Moon, I look to the house positions second. These are mainly EAST and then either NORTH or a little SOUTH. I go to the east wall of the bedroom, north corner, and then a little south. Instead of looking on the ground (earth and water signs), I do the opposite. I look up, and there, midway up the wall, is a thermostat, and on the thermostat are my watch and ring. Voila! When I did everything Ivy Jacobson told me to do but exactly backwards, I got the right answer. McEvers would have told me to try either combination of directions, and one of them would have led me to the lost items.

Let me clarify a trick of my own that is sometimes helpful. To decide the sequence in which to follow directions, I rank-order their prominence in the chart. Among the sign positions, S by W occurs three times, and N by E only once. Thus, I would go S by W first, and then N by E. Looking at the house positions, EAST occurs twice, N by E once, and ESE once. Clearly EAST predominates so I would go to the east wall first. Then it's a toss-up between N by E and ESE. I would go northeast first because the Moon suggests northeast by both house and sign. Finally, I would look slightly south (ESE) from the northeast corner of the eastern wall, and there would be the lost items. In retrospect, it occurred to me that Mars, dispositor of Pars Fortuna, in Virgo fits because Mars rules heat and Virgo rules regulation of climate. The location on the thermostat makes sense.

What about the Via Combust Moon? Maybe it wasn't so perverse after all. The Moon, as co-ruler of the lost items, in the burning way showed their position on the thermostat which regulates the heat in the home. How literal can symbolism get?

Now let's see if William Lilly would have found my watch and ring with the eight points he would cover:

1. The Ascendant sign (Virgo): S by W.

2. The sign of the Ascendant ruler Mercury (Virgo): S by W.

3. The sign on the 4th house (Sagittarius): E by S.

4. The sign of the ruler of the 4th (Cancer): NORTH.

5. The sign of the Moon (Scorpio): N by E.

6. The sign on the 2nd cusp (Libra): WEST.

7. The sign of the ruler of the 2nd (Virgo): S by W.

8. The sign of the Part of Fortune (Scorpio): N by E.

Secondly, as grouped by element:

One Fire sign (Sagittarius): EAST by SOUTH x 1

Three Earth signs (Virgo x 3): SOUTH by WEST x 3

One Air sign (Libra): WEST x 1

Three Water signs (Scorpio x 2 and Cancer x 1): NORTH by EAST x 2 + NORTH x 1

Now, rank-ordering the directions given by Lilly's eight points, we get:

SOUTH by WEST: 3

NORTH by EAST: 2

EAST by SOUTH: 1

WEST: 1

NORTH: 1

My goodness, this is confusing! What do I do now, William?

Lilly says if the ruler of the 2nd is in an angle, the item is within the home. Good. I already knew that, but where in the home? Quoth Lilly: "If the Lord of the 2nd be in the Ascendant, or in the sign wherein the Lord of the Ascendant is, or in one of his houses, you may judge the thing is in that part of the house which he himself most frequents, or wherein he doth most abide, or is conversant, or where he layeth his own commodities, or such things as he most delight in." See where Jacobson got her rules? According to Lilly, the misplaced items must be in the bedroom or at my computer desk because these are the places I most frequent and where I usually keep things.

Now to Lilly's compass directions. He takes his eight points, ignores the mundane houses, and uses the quality of the signs to find what part of the house the item is in, "according to the greater number of testimonies." There are three Virgos in the list, more than any other sign, so I should go south and west, back into my bedroom.

Lilly doesn't tell us what to do next so I'll follow my own rule of sequencing directions in order of their prominence in the chart. The second most prominent sign, Scorpio, which tells me to go northeast, and also takes me to the thermostat. Maybe the Moon and Part of Fortune in Scorpio refer to the bathroom on the other side of the wall.

In summary, Lilly took me to the thermostat directly, McEvers gave me the correct location as one of two possibilities, and Jacobson led me astray unless I reversed her directions in accord with the perverse nature of the Via Combust Moon.

Before going on to the next chapter, test yourself with the following horary quiz.

## A QUIZ FOR THE READER

### Question: Where is my missing wallet? (Chart 34)

Study the chart on the next page before reading the answer, which is inverted at the bottom of this page. No cheating!

Hint: Cancer rises so the Moon represents the querent. Leo on the 2nd cusp indicates that the Sun symbolizes the wallet. Moon applies to a trine of the Sun: the wallet will return. Sun in Gemini (transportation) in the 11th suggests a southeast direction. Mars disposes the Part of Fortune and thus also represents the wallet. The Moon (the querent) is separating from an opposition with Mars (the wallet), showing their recent separation. Mars (the wallet) has just completed a trine to the Ascendant (querent), indicating that he found his wallet shortly before asking the question. The late Ascendant often occurs when the querent already knows the answer and is just asking a horary question "to see what the stars will say."

The querent noticed his wallet missing while he was at home in his kitchen. He noted the time and decided to ask a horary question. Before he had time to cast the chart, he found his wallet in his red car, which was southeast of his location. Does the chart indicate where the missing item was? What degree rising would you expect if he cast the chart after he already knew the answer?

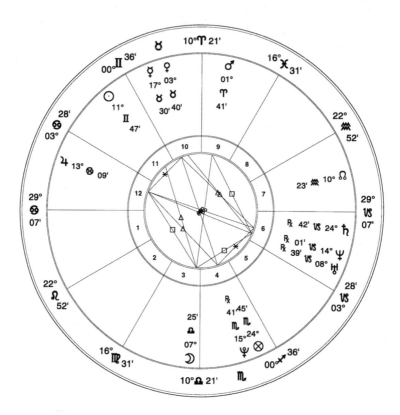

Chart 34:  Missing Wallet
June 2, 1990, 8:08 A.M. CST, 93W016, 44N59 Koch Houses

# CHAPTER THIRTEEN

# Two Cases of Missing Cases, and the Church's Stolen Silver

W hile I was in the midst of writing the first edition of this book, the universe provided me with a jarring opportunity to test the horary hypothesis. I wrote this book in bits and pieces whenever I could find a few minutes of free time. As a true Virgo, I discovered the most efficient way to get writing done was to carry my materials with me in a briefcase. If time opened in my daily schedule, I could research a reference, revise a chapter, or work on a chart.

On Wednesday, November 29, 1989, I was late for a 10:00 A.M. meeting at the hospital. I got to the parking lot a few minutes after 10:00, quickly parked the car, and rushed to the meeting. When I returned to the car an hour later, I found the window smashed and two briefcases missing. Gone were my appointment book and office papers, the entire first draft of this book, several textbooks and journals, and sundry other valuables. Needless to say, I was agitated and depressed about the loss of many hours of work, and annoyed with myself for being so careless. Fortunately most of the text of this book was in the computer. Irreplaceable were the hours of research notes I had not yet had time to enter into the word processor.

The hospital is in an inner city neighborhood, known for its crack addicts, and I assumed the thief was one of the young men who hung out on the street near the hospital. I knew of others who had been robbed and who had found their pocketbooks or briefcases in garbage dumpsters nearby. Hoping the thieves would not care for my notes, I began to search the neighborhood. Suddenly it occurred to me to do a horary chart. At 11:23 A.M., I looked at my watch and asked the question, "Where are my papers, where is the thief, and will I get my things back?"

For the next several days I was busy getting the car window repaired, changing the locks (because they stole my spare car keys), calling the police, contacting the insurance company, and doing myriad other things you need to do after a robbery. I felt incredibly discouraged about the disappearance of my research and despaired of ever seeing it again. Feeling hopeless, I did not erect the horary chart until the weekend.

When I finally turned on the computer, the first thing I checked was Wednesday's transits to my natal chart. On 11/29/89 transiting Mercury in Sagittarius was in my 3rd house of cars and documents exactly opposite Uranus in Gemini (of cars and documents) in my 9th house of books and publications. Transiting Mars in Scorpio in my 2nd house of possessions and money had recently formed an exact quincunx to my natal Uranus in the 9th. If I had noticed these transits before the Wednesday meeting at the hospital, I would have been more careful with my briefcase and automobile. In addition, this was the week that Mars by solar arc direction was conjoining natal Pluto.

Chart 35 for my question has a void of course Moon in Sagittarius. According to Bonatus and Lilly, the Moon can perform when void of course in Sagittarius, but I still felt I should be cautious in reading the chart.

The presence of the Moon's North Node and the Part of Fortune in the 1st house was encouraging. As they approached the Ascendant, these two benefic influences seemed to promise some good was coming my way.

The angles were mixed with fixed Aquarius rising and mutable Sagittarius on the MC. I took this to mean that matters would initially seem entrenched and hopeless but that things would change and develop rapidly after a while. The end of the matter 4th house has mutable Gemini on the cusp, making Mercury ruler of the final outcome. Mercury is in his detriment in Sagittarius, but is strong in the 10th house and is in his own Ptolemaic terms. I interpreted this to mean I might get some things back but not others.

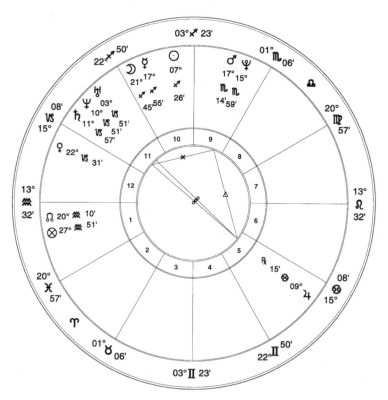

Chart 35: The Theft of This Book
November 29, 1989, 11:23 A.M. EST, 72W55, 41n18  Koch Houses

My usual practice is to use traditional rulerships for Scorpio, Aquarius, and Pisces. In this chart the modern rulerships for the 1st and 2nd houses also seemed to fit the situation. Aquarius on the 1st cusp represents me, the querent. Saturn, the traditional ruler of Aquarius, described how depressed I felt about the theft. Uranus also fit because I was agitated and shaken up by the theft of my astrology (Uranus) notes. Should I use Saturn or Uranus as my primary ruler? The chart would have to guide me. The Moon, as usual, was my co-ruler.

Pisces is on the 2nd cusp of movable goods. Jupiter, the traditional ruler of Pisces, is retrograde in Cancer in the 5th house. Jupiter's retrograde condition implied the missing objects would return. On the other hand, Neptune (dishonesty) might better describe my pilfered notes and books on horary. Neptune is in Capricorn in the 11th, between Uranus and Saturn. In addition, Aries is intercepted in the 2nd house, making Mars a co-ruler of the lost items. In questions of missing or stolen goods, the Moon is often a co-significator of the lost items.

At this point the chart was appearing incredibly complicated. I wasn't sure if I should use the traditional or modern rulerships. I looked to the chart to guide me. Saturn (me) had just left a conjunction to Neptune (the goods). I had carelessly left my briefcase in a parked car in a bad neighborhood. The symbolism fit. retrograde Jupiter (the goods) had also just passed an opposition to Saturn (me). I had recently been separated from my goods. This symbolism was also apt.

At some future time Jupiter would turn direct and again oppose Saturn. The turning direct could mean a return of the goods, but the second opposition to Saturn could signify a final loss or separation. Here was a mixed message and a classic case of good and bad news. Uranus, my co-ruler, would eventually conjoin Neptune (the goods). They were seven degrees apart. Did this mean I would be reunited with my property in seven hours, seven days, seven weeks...?

My primary traditional ruler Saturn was strong in his own sign Capricorn and his own 11th house. My modern co-ruler Uranus was also at home in the 11th. Jupiter (the lost items) was in his dignity in Cancer and well-placed in the 5th, a fire house. These dignities seemed to imply I would get some things back.

What about the thief? The ruler of the 7th and peregrine planets in angles or in the 2nd house designate the thief. With Leo on the 7th cusp, the Sun ruled the thief. Usually the Sun signifies men aged thirty-five to forty-five. This puzzled me because the addicts I'd seen on the street looked like they were in their mid to late twenties, more fitting the planet Mars. Sol was strong in Sagittarius, a fire sign, and in the 10th where he rejoices. I concluded that a Solar man, around forty years old, had broken into my car and would get away with it.

The Moon, a feminine planet, was peregrine at 21° 46' Sagittarius in the angular 10th. A woman was also involved. The Moon (female thief) and Jupiter (the goods) were in mutual reception. The Solar man who broke into my car must have passed some of the goods (Jupiter) to a woman accomplice (the Moon). Mutual receptions may show a change of location.

Because the stolen items had three rulers—Jupiter, Neptune, and Mars—they may have been divided three ways. The complicated indications of the chart were beginning to give a plausible, though not provable, explanation.

The chart confirmed some of the information I already knew about my stolen check-book. I had called the bank about my missing checks and discovered that a woman named Deborah B_____ had forged my name to a check within hours of the robbery and cashed it at a branch of my bank in a neighboring town to the southwest. When I reported the forgery to the police, the detective said, "Oh, Debbie B_____, she does a lot of this stuff."

My reading thus far was that I would get some things back but not others. The male thief would get away with it. The bank's location indicated that the checkbook went southwest, which was the house direction of Mars. I took this to mean that Mars represented the stolen checkbook and appointment book which were together in the same wallet. Because Mars was in Scorpio, I assumed Debbie B_____ had thrown my check register and appointment book into the garbage (Scorpio). I would probably never see those things again.

I wanted to know in what direction the other goods might be so I could search for them. With this in mind, I made the following list:

| Condition | Planet | Sign | Direction | House | Direction |
|---|---|---|---|---|---|
| 2nd Ruler | Jupiter | Cancer | North | 5th | NNW |
| 2nd Ruler | Neptune | Capricorn | South | 11th | SSE |
| Lost Items | Moon | Sagittarius | E by S | 10th | South |
| Possessions | Venus | Capricorn | South | 12th | ESE |
| 3rd Ruler | Saturn | Capricorn | South | 11th | SSE |
| 2nd Co-ruler | Mars | Scorpio | N by E | 9th | SSW |
| Documents | Mercury | Sagittarius | E by S | 10th | South |

I included all the planets ruling the 2nd house, the dispositor of the Part of Fortune, Venus as natural ruler of possessions, the Moon as natural ruler of fugitives, and Mercury and the 3rd house ruler as natural signifiers of books and papers since these were the specific items I was looking for. Because Taurus is on the 3rd cusp of papers, I counted Venus twice. I gave Mars less weight because he rules an intercepted sign. The evidence also suggested that Mars ruled the checkbook but not the missing papers.

The most commonly occurring sign is earthy Capricorn. The thieves most likely threw my briefcases on the ground in a southeast location, possibly near water because of the prominence of the water signs Cancer and Scorpio. They probably first brought the brief-cases to an upstairs room (Sagittarius) to search for valuables.

The preponderance of indicators suggested that I look south and east of the parking lot. The dual rulership of Pisces on the 2nd continued to bother me. Jupiter was north or NNW, and Neptune was south or SSE. Depending on which ruler was primary, I search in exactly opposite directions. The majority of indicators agreed with Neptune, but this contradicted my usual horary practice of using Jupiter as the traditional ruler of Pisces.

I stuck with my hypothesis that the mutual reception meant the crook first went north-west in the direction of Jupiter (primary ruler) and then switched locations (mutual reception with Moon) and ended up southeast in the direction of Neptune. This made sense because the 5th house rules parks and playgrounds, and there is a school playground across the street from the scene of the crime, just northwest of the parking lot. The southeast part of the parking lot has a high fence that would be difficult to scale.

To summarize my hypothesis: the thief or thieves broke into the car, ran to the playground first, and then went south and east to an upstairs room (Sagittarius) where they took what they wanted and threw the rest away on the ground level (Capricorn). On Monday morning I left for work early and drove around the neighborhood southeast of the parking lot. My briefcases and papers were nowhere to be found. I had decided to post a reward for the missing papers on the theory that a drug addict had stolen them and would have no use for astrology notes. I was hoping he would exchange them for cash. I spoke to the owner of a small grocery store who knew the local population. He agreed to post the notice and act as a go-between in paying the reward, no questions asked.

The decision to post a reward on Monday was based partly on reading the chart and partly on common sense and desperation. The chart implied that I would hear something in six or seven days. To explain how I read this, I need to discuss the timing of events in horary.

There are two ways to time events in horary. The first is to see how long an aspect will take to perfect in the ephemeris. This method is the same as using transits to time events from a natal chart. The day the aspect perfects in the ephemeris is the day the event described by the aspect will manifest.

The second method is a symbolic system which equates the number of degrees before the aspect becomes exact to the number of hours, days, weeks, months, years, or other unit of time. Both methods can be used in conjunction, and neither is accurate all of the time. In the symbolic system, the unit of time is determined by the sign and house position of the faster planet that is about to make an aspect.

Tables 20 and 21 list the traditional system. In practice, you can't be too literal about the time units given in the tables. Common sense and the general feel of the chart are the best guides.

| Table 20. Measurement of Time | |
|---|---|
| Angular Houses or Cardinal Signs | FAST (Minutes, Hours, Days) |
| Succedent Houses or Mutable Signs | SLOWER (Days, Weeks, Months) |
| Cadent Houses or Fixed Signs | SLOWEST (Weeks, Months, Years) |

| Table 21. House and Sign Grid for Time Measurement | | | | | | | |
|---|---|---|---|---|---|---|---|
| METHOD ONE | | | | METHOD TWO | | | |
| *Mode* | Angular | Succedent | Cadent | *Mode* | Angular | Succedent | Cadent |
| **Cardinal** | Hours | Days | Weeks | **Cardinal** | Days | Weeks | Months |
| **Mutable** | Days | Weeks | Months | **Mutable** | Weeks | Months | Years |
| **Fixed** | Weeks | Months | Years | **Fixed** | Months | Years | Indefinite |

Back to the theft. I thought something would happen regarding my stolen goods in six or seven days for the following reasons:

- The Ascendant would conjoin the Moon's North Node in six degrees.
- Uranus, co-ruler of the 1st, would conjoin Neptune, co-ruler of the 2nd, in seven degrees.
- Jupiter, although retrograde, would eventually turn direct and oppose Saturn. They were three degrees apart. I would soon learn about being separated (opposition) from some of my belongings.
- The Moon, my co-ruler, was less than a degree from a semi-sextile to Venus, my possessions. Semi-sextiles are 2nd house aspects.
- The Moon would conjoin Venus on Saturday, December 2, ephemeris time.
- The Moon would conjoin the Ascendant on Monday, December 4, ephemeris time and would conjoin the North Node and the Part of Fortune later that day by transit.

Because of these favorable transits of the Moon to the horary chart, I decided to post the reward notice on Monday. I noticed that the transiting Moon would sextile transiting Mercury Monday morning. I elected to post the notice a few minutes before this sextile became exact. My reasoning was that the Moon represented me, Mercury my papers, and the sextile the opportunity for their return.

About an hour later I got a phone call from the manager of the grocery store. A woman who lived in the neighborhood saw my notice and reported seeing the briefcases on the grounds of the public housing project two blocks southeast of the parking lot. She thought the police had picked them up.

I felt elated and immediately called the police who said they did not have the briefcases in their possession. I felt dejected again, but not for long. In the afternoon mail, I received a letter from the police saying they had my briefcases. The officer I spoke to in the morning was mistaken. I got back my astrology notes and books from the police later that day. All the valuables were missing, of course, and so were my checkbook and my appointment book with my entire schedule for 1989.

The public housing project where the police found my stolen goods consists of a set of buildings with garages on the ground level, and three stories of apartments above. As the chart suggested, the thief had most likely taken the briefcases to his upstairs apartment and thrown the unwanted contents on the ground below.

My astrology notes were irreplaceable and I was ecstatic about finding them. I would have to re-purchase the material things that were stolen. My 1989 schedule would be a pain to reconstruct but with due Virgo diligence I could do just that.

About two weeks later my secretary saw another robbery occurring outside the window of her office which is next to the parking lot. A forty to forty-five-year-old man smashed in the window of a car, stole some goods, and quickly ran off in a northwest direction. The *modus operandi* was identical to the theft of my briefcase, and I can only guess that the same man did both thefts and the chart was correct in giving the age of the thief.

And what about the Part of Fortune in the 1st house? Did something good come to the querent as it approached the Ascendant? Perhaps the material for this chapter was the fortunate outcome.

## THE CASE OF THE MISSING EYEGLASS CASE

I would now like to present a case that shows the usefulness of color symbolism in the horary chart. On September 10, 1989, a Sunday, at 9:24 A.M. EST, my wife, though skeptical about astrology, asked me to do a chart to find her missing eyeglass case. She had searched for several days and could not find it. See Chart 36.

The horary question is, "Where is my missing eyeglass case?" The querent is my wife, Linda. The Ascendant at 3° 25' Scorpio is in the Via Combusta and warns that the astrologer might have some difficulty reading the chart. Perhaps the Via Combust Ascendant refers to the perverse satisfaction my wife would take in proving astrology wrong. On the other hand, when the chart is radical, activity in the Via Combusta will somehow describe the situation. Maybe my wife was burned up about losing her eyeglass case, or maybe the lost object burned in a fire or is near something that has to do with combustion.

The 2nd house ruler is Jupiter in Cancer (exalted) in the 9th. There are no other planets ruling the 2nd house. As the primary ruler of the missing item, Jupiter, by house, suggests Linda lost it south and slightly west of her current location. Because Jupiter is in the 9th house, she might have lost it on a trip, possibly related to education. We had recently returned from a long-distance (9th house) summer vacation, but Linda remembered having the eyeglass case after we returned. Not long before Linda's question, I had heard a lecture by Joan McEvers about the use of colors of the planets, signs, and houses to help locate

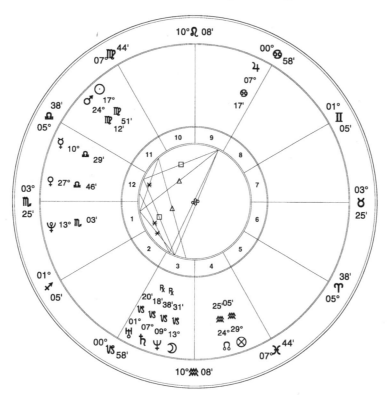

Chart 36 "Where Is My Missing Eyeglass Case?"
September 10, 1989, 9:24 P.M. EST, 73W01, 41N19 Koch Houses

objects. I decided to try this method here. According to Lilly and Simmonite, Jupiter's colors are red mixed with green, also ash; and Cancer's colors are green or russet. The 9th house is green and white.

I asked my wife if she had traveled anywhere south and west and put her eyeglass case near something red, green, white, or ash. She suddenly recalled dropping her pocketbook the week before when she took our son to "get acquainted day" at kindergarten. The school is southwest of our home. From my son's point of view the trip to kindergarten was a 9th house matter.

My wife drives a red car with an ash interior. When she arrived, the parking lot was full so the school guard directed her to park in the field next to the school. As she got out of her red car with its ash interior, she dropped her pocketbook onto the green grass. Some white tissues also fell out. The spilling of the pocketbook fit exactly the color scheme suggested by the chart. Maybe that's where she lost the eyeglass case.

I studied the chart for other clues. Here's the Jacobson list of significators:

| Condition | Planet | Sign | Direction | House | Direction |
|---|---|---|---|---|---|
| 2nd Ruler | Jupiter | Cancer | North | 9th | SSW |
| | Moon | Capricorn | South | 3rd | NNE |
| | Venus | Libra | West | 12th | ESE |
| Dispositors of | Saturn | Capricorn | South | 3rd | NNE |
| Pars Fortuna | Uranus | Capricorn | South | 3rd | NNE |

Jacobson says to follow the houses first and then the signs. The houses are mainly north and east. Going northeast in my home takes me into the living room. The signs are mainly south Capricorn. Going south from the living room takes me into the garage.

The Moon and the dispositors (Saturn and Uranus) of the Part of Fortune, which is at 29° Aquarius in the 4th, are in the 3rd house of local trips, early education, garages, and automobiles. Third house colors are red and yellow. Capricorn's colors are black and dark brown, and Capricorn signifies dark places near the ground. My wife's red car is in the garage. I searched the car, looking carefully under all the seats, but found no eyeglass case.

Several aspects in the chart, however, suggest Linda will get the lost item back. Saturn, dispositor of Pars Fortuna, is retrograde, implying a return of her possession. Saturn is dignified in Capricorn and when he turns direct will be six degrees away from a sextile to Pluto, co-ruler of the querent in the 1st house. Jupiter, exalted at 7° Cancer, is six degrees from a trine to Linda's co-ruler Pluto, which is dignified at 13° Scorpio. Jupiter and Saturn are both cardinal and cadent; Pluto is fixed and angular. It will take six weeks to find the missing object.

The cluster of planets in the 3rd house makes me think she lost it in the car, in the garage, or on a short trip. Because the 3rd house planets are all in Capricorn, the eyeglass case is probably in a dark place near the floor. The Part of Fortune itself at 29° Aquarius suggests she may have dropped it behind something. The Moon, her co-ruler, has recently separated from

Neptune, showing her carelessness in dropping her pocketbook. Saturn (her possessions) is also moving away from a conjunction with Neptune, reinforcing this interpretation.

All the significators of the missing eyeglass case are cadent. The lost item is probably hidden, out of sight, and will be difficult to find. It will be found only indirectly and possibly by another person. The majority of significators are in earth or water signs. The case is low or at ground level, and may be near water or fluids of some kind.

The outcome: Six weeks later my wife left a message on my office answering machine. There was amusement and disbelief in her voice. She had found her eyeglass case in her car with its combustion engine. She dropped a pen down between the gear shift and the side of the front passenger seat. When she reached to pull out the pen, she found her eyeglass case hidden deep in the ash colored fabric between the seat and the gear shift containing fluid). She suspected me of finding the case elsewhere and planting it in her car. To this day she takes perverse satisfaction in teasing me about placing the eyeglass case in her car. I swear I had nothing to do with it.

Next let's consider a classic horary chart from none other than Nostradamus

## Nostradamus and the Case of the Missing Church Silver

In February of 1562 (two centuries before Lilly wrote *Christian Astrology*), the bishop of the Cathedral Church of Orange, France, asked Nostradamus to help find some stolen goods. It seems that a thief or thieves had absconded with the cathedral's silver, which included a precious and irreplaceable antique chalice. A rumor was circulating that the stolen goods were in Avignon, a region to the west of the Cathedral.

Nostradamus cast a horary chart for the time he understood the question: February 3, 1562, at 6:39 P.M., 48N50 / 02E30. See Chart 37. It was a Mars day during a Jupiter hour. Nostradamus was residing in Salon-de-Crau, Provence at that time, but he used the Regiomontanus tables for Paris, France.

Modern calculations give us slightly different planetary positions than those used by Nostradamus. Listed below is a comparison of the current and the 1562 planetary data:

| Planet | Nostradamus | Modern Calculation |
|--------|-------------|--------------------|
| Sun | 24° Aquarius | 24° Aquarius 40' |
| Moon | 3° Pisces | 25° Aquarius 15' |
| Mercury | 17° Capricorn | 29° Capricorn 37' |
| Venus | 29° Capricorn | 29° Capricorn 09' |
| Mars | 3° Taurus | 3° Taurus 11' |
| Jupiter | 23° Taurus | 22° Taurus 27' |
| Saturn | 0° Cancer | 28° Gemini 23' RX |

Nostradamus wrote to the bishop that the thief was a "brother of the church with a warlike nature." The thief had not acted alone but had a partner in crime—another of the church brothers. According to Nostradamus' reading of the horary chart, these thieving church

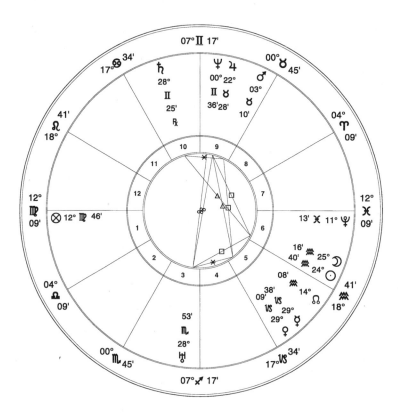

Chart 37: Nostradamus—Stolen Silver
February 3, 1562, 6:39 P.M. GMT, 02E30, 48N50  Regiomontanus Houses

brothers had concealed the stolen silver in their houses and were planning to melt it before selling it. Nostradamus added that the rumor about Avignon was false, and in fact the rumor was being spread by the thieves to deflect suspicion from the fact that it was an inside job.

Nostradamus does not give the astrological details of how he read the chart. He was, however, familiar with the horary literature and used traditional principles to interpret his charts. Let us apply the standard horary rules to see how Nostradamus arrived at his conclusions.

As usual, the Ascendant, its rulers, and any planets in the 1st house signify the querent. In this chart with a Virgo Ascendant, Mercury represents the bishop who is asking the question. In Lilly's point system (CA, p. 115) Mercury receives seventeen points and is the most dignified planet in the chart. A well-fortified Mercury "represents a man of subtle and political mind, and cogitation, an excellent debater or logician, arguing with learning and discretion, and using much eloquence in his speech" (CA, p. 77). This dignified Mercury in celibate Virgo is probably descriptive of the bishop who asked for Nostradamus' assistance.

The Moon in a horary chart is a co-signifier of the querent. Here the Moon lies in the 6th house of distress and worry, symbolizing the state of the bishop. In addition, the Moon is combust the Sun, indicating the bishop's difficulty with finding the hidden treasure. The Moon is also a natural signifier of silver ("the silvery Moon") and its combustion must have led Nostradamus to conclude that the thieves wanted to melt down the silver by subjecting it to combustion.

Moveable goods are shown by the 2nd house, its rulers and planets therein, and by the dispositor of the Part of Fortune. Here Libra rules the 2nd cusp and Saturn is Almuten of the 2nd. Thus, Venus and Saturn may also represent the stolen silver. Furthermore, the possessions of the 9th house cathedral are shown by its second house which is the 10th house of the radical chart. Mercury disposits the Virgo Part of Fortune. In addition, Gemini lies on the cusp of the 10th and Saturn occupies the 10th. Thus, both Mercury and Saturn may represent the stolen goods. In summary, possible rulers of the stolen silver are: the Moon, Mercury, Venus, and Saturn. The planet Saturn is a likely candidate to rule the ancient and priceless silver chalice. Saturn being retrograde suggests that the chalice will return.

Furthermore, because Mercury rules both the bishop (as Ascendant ruler) and the missing silver (as 10th ruler and dispositor of Pars Fortuna), it seems likely that the silver will return to the bishop. This interpretation is strengthened by the mutual reception between Saturn (the ancient chalice) in Gemini and Mercury (the bishop) in Capricorn. In addition, the Part of Fortune conjoins the Ascendant—another argument for the church's fortune returning to the inquiring bishop.

Who is the thief? The traditional rule is that peregrine planets in the angles or in the 2nd house can represent the thief. This chart has no less than six peregrine (totally undignified) planets: Mercury, Venus, Sun, Mars, Jupiter, and Saturn. In the radical chart, only Saturn in the 10th in Gemini lies in an angle.

Nostradamus, however, says there is more than one thief. He undoubtedly used the turned chart with the 9th house of the cathedral as the new 1st house of the turned chart. If we consider the radical 9th to be the new first house, then the peregrine planets in angles of the turned chart are: Mars and Jupiter in the radical 9th (turned 1st), and the Sun in the radical 6th (turned 10th). Based on the turned chart, Nostradamus wrote to the bishop that the stolen silver was "to be divided among canons who are at present acting like soldiers" (peregrine Mars); and of the thieves, "there were only three, and they brothers of the church" (Leoni, p. 769).

To retrieve the stolen silver, Nostradamus advised the bishop to cite his authority as an astrologer of renown and to read the following passage to the congregation:

"...rest assured, my venerable Lords, if that which was stolen is not brought back one way or another, that they [the thieves] will die the most miserable death, more lingering and more violent and of more inconceivable intensity than ever before occurred—unless everything is restored and replaced in its ancient repository..." (Leoni: *Nostradamus and His Prophecies,* Bell Publishing Company, 1982, p. 771).

Unfortunately, we have no record of whether the stolen silver was ever returned to the cathedral. If any reader should visit the Cathedral of Orange, France, please let me know how it turned out.

## DISTANCES IN HORARY ASTROLOGY

One of the less believable claims of horary is the ability to calculate the distance between the querent and a missing object or person. This involves considering the celestial latitude of the significator of the missing item or person and the cardinality of the sign it occupies. Presumably, zero latitude means a short distance, north latitude a bit farther, and south latitude farther still. Significators in angular signs are close to the querent, in succedent signs farther, and in cadent signs the farthest. Both Simmonite and Jacobson give specific measures of distance for computational purposes. I have not found these measures particularly reliable.

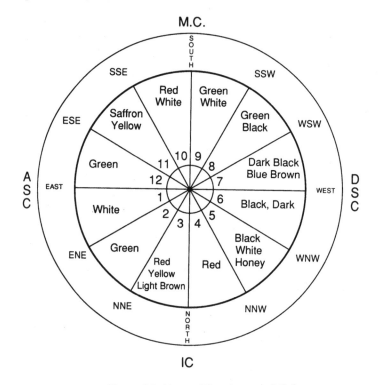

Figure 12: House Directions and Colors

| Table 22: Sign Colors | |
|---|---|
| **Aries** | White mixed with red |
| **Taurus** | White with lemon |
| **Gemini** | White mixed with red or orange |
| **Cancer** | Green, russet |
| **Leo** | Red, green |
| **Virgo** | Black, black speckled with blue |
| **Libra** | Black, dark crimson, tawny, pastels |
| **Scorpio** | Brown, black |
| **Sagittarius** | Yellow, green sanguine |
| **Capricorn** | Dark, black, russet, dark brown |
| **Aquarius** | Sky-color, blue, electrical tones |
| **Pisces** | White and glistening, turquoise |

| Table 23: House Colors | |
|---|---|
| 1st | White |
| 2nd | Green |
| 3rd | Red, Yellow, Sorrel |
| 4th | Red |
| 5th | Black, White, Honey |
| 6th | Black, Dark |
| 7th | Blue-Brown, Jet |
| 8th | Black, Green |
| 9th | Green, White |
| 10th | Red, White |
| 11th | Saffron, Deep Yellow |
| 12th | Green |

| Table 24: Planet Colors | |
|---|---|
| Pluto | Dark hues, scarlet, luminous pigments |
| Neptune | Sea green, turquoise, gray, lavender |
| Uranus | Plaids, checks, mingled colors, electrical tones, multicolored |
| Saturn | Black, green, brown, pales, wan, leaden, ashen, wooden, dark |
| Jupiter | Red mixed with green, ash, sea green, deep blue, purple, violet, a mixture of yellow and green, bright, clear, azure |
| Mars | Fiery red, scarlet, carmine, iron or rust-colored, shining colors, saffron, yellow |
| Sun | Yellow, yellow/purple, gold, scarlet, purple, clear red, orange |
| Venus | Bright shining colors, white, purple, bluish, milky blue mixed with brown or green, sky blue, green, yellow, copper, brass |
| Mercury | Dusky silver, sky color, light blue, azure, dove colored, mixed and new colors, gray with sky-blue, clear |
| Moon | White, opal, light cream, pearl, silvery, spotted with white, other mixed colors, pale yellowish white, pale green, pale blue |

The table below is derived from Simmonite and McEvers. For planets in signs, use the planet with the ruler of the sign.

| Table 25: Colors of Planetary Combinations | |
|---|---|
| MOON/Mercury | Buff, Fawn |
| MOON/Venus | Light Blue, Bluish White |
| MOON/Sun | Light Yellow, Green |
| MOON/Mars | Light Glistening Red |
| MOON/Jupiter | Bright Green |
| MOON/Saturn | Deep Russet, Gray |
| MOON/Uranus | Fine Checked Plaid |
| MOON/Neptune | Aqua |
| MOON/Pluto | Brown |
| MERCURY/Venus | Purple or light mixture |
| MERCURY/Sun | Light Gray |
| MERCURY/Mars | Tawny Red, Brick |
| MERCURY/Jupiter | Spotted Green |
| MERCURY/Saturn | Dark Blue or Gray |
| MERCURY/Uranus | Light Blue Plaid |
| MERCURY/Neptune | Gray Blue, Denim |
| MERCURY/Pluto | Deep Gray, Mauve |

| Table 25 (continued) | |
|---|---|
| VENUS/Sun | Olive |
| VENUS/Mars | Pink, Light Red, Crimson |
| VENUS/Jupiter | Greenish Gray, Lavender |
| VENUS/Saturn | Light Gray, Light Blue-Gray |
| VENUS/Uranus | Blue and White Plaid |
| VENUS/Neptune | Purple and Blue |
| VENUS/Pluto | Soft, Dark Colors |
| SUN/Mars | Olive, Coral |
| SUN/Jupiter | Deep Shining Red |
| SUN/Saturn | Shining Bronze, Blackish Orange |
| SUN/Uranus | Green and Purple Plaid |
| SUN/Neptune | Green and Blue Mixtures |
| SUN/Pluto | Deep Purple |
| MARS/Jupiter | Tawny Light Spotted, Tan, Brown Mixture |
| MARS/Saturn | Dark Reddish Brown, Tawny |
| MARS/Uranus | Red Plaid |
| MARS/Neptune | Deep Purple Mixture |
| MARS/Pluto | Blood Red |
| JUPITER/Saturn | Dark Green with Dark Red Spots, Dark Green with Black and Brown |
| JUPITER/Uranus | Green and Red Plaid |
| JUPITER/Neptune | Turquoise Gray, Green |
| JUPITER/Pluto | Dark Ashen Tones |
| SATURN/Uranus | Green Plaid |
| SATURN/Neptune | Murky Green, Blue |
| SATURN/Pluto | Mixtures of Black |
| URANUS/Neptune | Dark Blue Plaid, Turquoise Plaid |
| URANUS/Pluto | Dark Brown and Black Plaid |
| NEPTUNE/Pluto | Burgundy |

# CHAPTER FOURTEEN

# A Potpourri of Case Examples

I n this chapter I will present several horary examples. My goal throughout has been to teach the reader to think like a horary astrologer. The examples here show the diversity of matters that horary analysis can address. I have included charts where I was wrong as well as those where I got the right answer. The reader may wish to apply other methods of horary interpretation to these examples to test which rules are effective.

## CHART 38: "WHERE ARE MY KEYS?"

People are always misplacing their keys. On December 9, 1989, my wife's parents were visiting from out of state. My mother-in-law discovered that her house keys were missing and at 2:26 P.M. asked me to do a chart to find them. See Chart 38.

There are no classical considerations before judgment. The 7th cusp represents me, the astrologer. Scorpio is on the cusp and both Mars and Pluto, the rulers of Scorpio, are contained within the 7th house in the Via Combusta. Because my ruler is Via Combust and therefore afflicted, I may have some problems reading the chart or satisfying the querent. Jacobson regards Pluto in the 7th as a modern stricture similar in nature to Saturn in the 7th.

Gemini is on the cusp of the 2nd house of movable goods. Mercury signifies the lost keys. Mercury and Uranus are the natural rulers of keys. Both Mercury and Uranus are in Capricorn in the 8th house. I tell my wife's mother that her keys are either at ground level or on the floor (Capricorn), probably in a dark place, near water or plumbing (8th house), possibly near garbage (8th), southwest (8th) and then south (Capricorn). She remembers using the keys to re-enter her upstairs condominium from the ground level garage just before the trip. There are a garbage can and some pipes near the garage entrance to the condo. She thinks she might have left the keys in the door inside the garage which is now dark with its door shut and the lights off. I can't wait till she finds out if the analysis is correct.

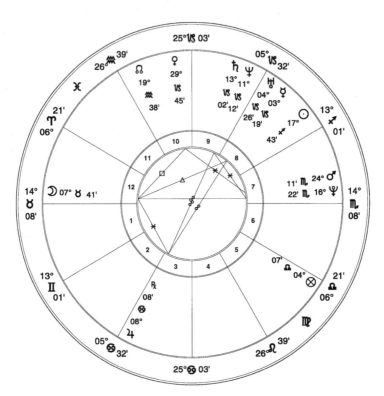

Chart 38: "Where Are My House Keys?"
December 9, 1989, 2:26 P.M. EST 73W01/41N19 Koch Houses

About 9:30 P.M. the same day my father-in-law reached into his pocket and discovered he had the missing keys. My interpretation was incorrect. I go back to the chart and notice the following. The Moon, co-ruler of lost objects, is 7° from the Ascendant, my mother-in-law. In seven hours she got her keys back.

The 7th house represents my father-in-law because he is the querent's spouse. At the time my wife's mother asked the question, my father-in-law was sitting on a couch against the south wall of the TV room, which was southwest of us.

The 8th house represents my father-in-law's possessions. I had not considered derivative houses in trying to locate the missing items. The keys were indeed with my father-in-law's possessions (8th house) in his pants pocket. They were also in a dark place (the pocket), and near his personal plumbing and water; the 8th house rules the body's organs of sex and elimination. In addition, Mercury (the keys) last conjoined the sun (a man, a father) and will next conjoin Uranus (sudden or unexpected discovery). The chart made sense, but only after I knew the right answer. You can't win them all!

## CHART 39: "WHERE IS NICK?"

This is a missing person chart, of sorts. I met Nick through a local computer bulletin board. He was interested in astrology and we corresponded by computer. We also met for lunch a couple of times. Nick is an excellent computer programmer and works at it free-lance. When he learned I was a psychiatrist, Nick told me he suffered from recurrent depressions that periodically impaired his ability to work. For several weeks Nick did not respond to messages I left him on the bulletin board. Finally, the sys-op deleted his name from the user list, which meant that he had not called in for some time. I became concerned and on June 4, 1989, at 7:00 A.M. EDT asked the horary question, "Where is Nick?" See Chart 39.

Saturn is in the 7th house representing the astrologer. Is this a stricture against judgment (meaning I will have difficulty reading this chart)? Or, does it describe Nick who may possibly be represented by the 7th house as a person with whom I have dealings?

If the 7th does represent Nick, he should be due west of me (7th—a western house) and at home because his ruler, Saturn, is in his own first house. Saturn has passed a conjunction with Neptune and in now retrograde and returning to conjoin Neptune again. Perhaps my worry that Nick has been depressed is correct. The retrograde significators in the 7th mean that I will be able to re-establish contact with Nick.

Later that day I telephoned Nick at his apartment. He was home (due east of me) and told me he had been depressed because his computer died and he could not afford the repairs. He said he was feeling fine now except for his broken computer. As the chart suggested, he again became depressed toward the end of the summer and was unable to work for several weeks.

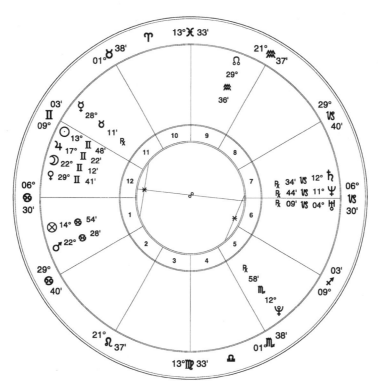

Chart 39: "Where Is Nick?"
June 4, 1989, 7:00 A.M. EDT 73W01/41N19 Koch Houses

In re-analyzing this chart for the second edition of this book, I realized that Nick was due East and not due West of my location. With a retrograde Saturn in the 7th, I must have been in error in my original interpretation. Most likely, I should have taken the 11th house for Nick, an acquaintance or friend, rather than the 7th. With a Taurus 11th cusp, Venus becomes Nick's ruler. Venus lies at the end of Gemini (in the terms of Mars) and in the unfortunate 12th house, reflecting his depressed state. Venus is close to the Ascendant, implying that Nick is due East of me, as he indeed was. Ascendant ruler, the Moon (me), will conjoin Venus (Nick), which is herself applying to conjoin the Ascendant (me). Thus, we will be reunited. Mercury retrograde in the 11th probably symbolizes Nick's broken computer at home in Nick's turned 1st house.

## CHART 40: "WHERE IS TOMMY?"

Another missing person chart. Tommy is a teenage boy I had worked with clinically. His parents were divorced and he lived with his mother. Although he had always been a good student, in the current school year he began "hanging out with a bad crowd," skipping school, and getting failing grades. His mother was concerned that he might be using drugs, which he adamantly denied.

On June 19, 1989, at 1:09 P.M. EST, his mother called me in a panic to say that Tommy had run away. The night before she had confronted him about some marijuana she found in his room. The next day he left a note that he did not like her checking up on him and he was leaving. See Chart 40.

At this time I knew both the mother and son fairly well. Although Tommy had an exterior toughness and bravado, I knew he was a frightened, dependent child underneath. I reassured the mother that I believed her son would soon return, but I told her to notify the police of the runaway for her son's safety. When I got home that evening, I cast the chart for my own edification. At the time I was using McEver's system of taking the 7th for persons specifically referred to by name. Because the mother had mentioned her son by name, I used the 7th as Tommy's primary ruler. In addition, Tommy, as one of my clients, could be represented by the Aries 7th house, and its feisty ruler Mars does represent young men. Because Tommy was her son, I also used the 5th house (children) as his ruler. The Moon naturally governs runaways.

In a sense this is a chart with two querents. Not knowing of my interest in astrology, the mother called me as her counselor to ask about the welfare of her son. I conceived the idea of asking the horary question to satisfy both myself and the mother of the answer. From my perspective the son is the 7th house client. From the mother's perspective the son is the 5th house of children.

There are no considerations before judgment present. The Part of Fortune is near the 7th cusp, so my client Tommy is safe. His ruler, Mars, is in the 10th in Leo. He probably went south to a park or place of amusement (Leo). Because Leo is on the 11th cusp, he may be with friends. Mars (the young man) will sextile the Ascendant (querent mother) in about eleven and a half degrees, suggesting that he may return in by midnight. Tommy's other rulers are Saturn, Uranus, and the Moon. Saturn and Uranus are both retrograde in Capricorn in the

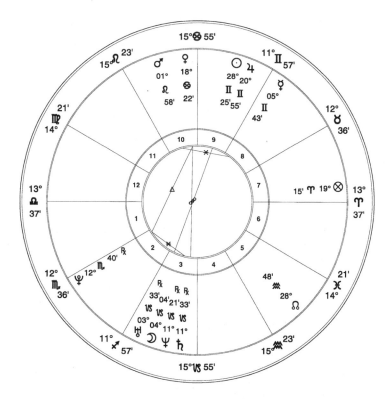

Chart 40: "Where Is Tommy?"
June 19, 1989, 1:09 P.M. EST, 72W55/41N18  Koch Houses

3rd house. Retrograde significators show that he will return. The 3rd house suggests he is in the neighborhood, and its Sagittarius cusp suggests he may be outdoors.

The Moon is also in the 3rd house in Capricorn. Luna has just left a conjunction with Uranus (breaks, running away) and is moving forward to join Neptune (drugs, deception). Immediately after joining Neptune, the Moon will go on the conjoin Saturn (loneliness, abandonment) and then will enter the 4th house (home). Furthermore, the Moon (the fugitive Tommy) is in early Capricorn in the terms of Venus (the querent mother—Libra rising) and Venus lies in Cancer, ruled by the Moon. This mutual reception suggests that the runaway Tommy will return to his mother.

I understood the chart to mean that Tommy had recently run away. He went south to a park or place of amusement with some friends. The future aspects of the Moon suggest he will do some drugs, begin to feel lonely, and return home. The mother called me the next day to report that Tommy had come home the previous evening. He indeed had gone to a park with some friends. He, of course, denied any drug use. I do not know what direction the park is from his house.

## CHART 41: "WILL I GO TO JAIL?"

In my work I come across unusual people and situations. The following chart refers to a woman who came to see me in the hospital clinic. I had read about this woman in the local newspapers. She was on trial for participating in an embezzlement and was trying to use her history of psychological problems to avoid going to jail. The sentencing was a week away and she was feeling overwhelmed with anxiety.

At one point in the interview she said, "You can't tell me if I'm going to jail." I glanced at the clock and did a chart that evening to see for myself if it would answer her question. Although she did not request a horary chart, the matter was most pressing to her when she asked the question. Chart 41 is for September 21, 1989, at 2:04 P.M. EST.

The chart appears radical. Capricorn rising reflects her serious and depressed state of mind. Her ruler, Saturn, is in the 12th house of imprisonment and self-undoing. Saturn is two degrees away from a conjunction with Neptune, the natural ruler of confinement and sorrow. As an occupant of the 12th house, Neptune is a co-ruler of imprisonment in this chart. It looks like she will go to jail.

The primary ruler of the 12th (jails) is Jupiter in Cancer in the 6th. Jupiter has recently passed an opposition to Saturn (the querent). Unfortunately, Jupiter will turn retrograde and again oppose Saturn in November. I took this to mean that within two months she will be in jail. For confirmation, I looked at the final aspect of the Moon. It is a square to the Sun in the 9th house of legal proceedings, confirming a negative outcome. The Moon is also within orb of squaring Mars, ruler of the 11th of her hopes and wishes, and of opposing Uranus, posited in the 12th of imprisonment.

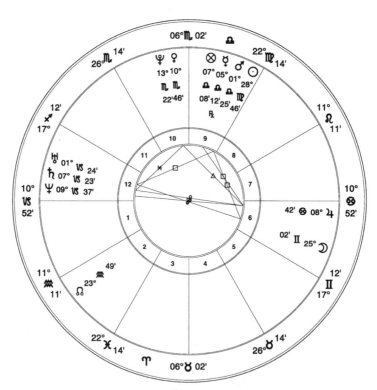

Chart 41: Will I go to jail?
September 21, 1989, 2:04 P.M. EST, 72W55, 41N18  Koch Houses

In addition, Mars co-rules the querent because he is Almuten with Saturn of the Ascendant. Mars lies in the 9th of legal matters in Libra, the sign of his detriment, and under the sunbeams. Mars is also conjunct the contrascion of the Sun (ruler of the unfortunate 8th house and posited in the 9th). This is similar to Mars square the Sun and is another indicator of misfortune. Mars (the querent) is also applying to a square of Jupiter (imprisonment).

I read in the paper the following week that she was sentenced to five years in prison.

## CHART 42: "WILL LING-LING'S BABY LIVE?"

On Friday, September 1, 1989, I heard the news that Ling-Ling, the giant panda bear at the Washington Zoo, had given birth. The zookeepers were afraid that the baby panda would not live because Ling-Ling had lost her other children born in captivity. At 5:54 P.M. EST I asked the question, "Will Ling-Ling's baby survive?" See Chart 42.

Almost 29° of Aquarius is rising. The question may be too late. The baby's fate may already be decided. The news report said that the baby had an infection. The Moon lies at the end of Virgo in the unfortunate terms of Mars. The Moon is Void of Course in the modern definition, suggesting that matters will not go handsomely forward.

I took the 12th house of large animals for Ling-Ling. To find Ling-Ling's baby, I counted to the fifth of the 12th which is the natural 4th house. Gemini is on the 4th cusp so Mercury rules the baby. The house ruling the baby's death is the eighth of the 4th or the natural

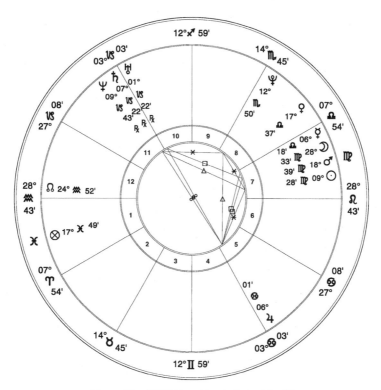

Chart 42: "Will Ling-Ling's Baby Live?"
September 1, 1989, 5:54 P.M. EST, 73W01, 41N19   Koch Houses

11th house of the chart. Capricorn is on the 11th cusp so Saturn rules the baby's death. Saturn is also a natural ruler of death. Both Saturn and Neptune occupy the 11th house, making Neptune a co-ruler of the baby's death.

Saturn, primary ruler of the baby's 8th, retrograde in the baby's 8th and approaching the cusp of the baby's house of death suggests the baby will die. Mercury (the baby) at 6° 18' Libra is applying to a square with Saturn (baby's death) at 7° 22' Capricorn. Retrograde Saturn simultaneously applies to the square with Mercury. This mutual application makes the aspect more powerful. Mercury is cardinal and angular and is a little over a degree away from squaring Saturn and then conjoining the radical Koch 8th cusp of death. Mercury also rules the 4th house end of the matter of the question. The baby will die in a little over a day.

Ling-Ling's baby died at 12:20 A.M. EDT on Sunday morning, September 3, 1989, a little over a day after I cast the chart.

## CHART 43: "WILL CICIPPIO BE HANGED?"

This chart is for another event in the news, one that deeply disturbed me. In early August, 1989, Middle Eastern terrorists murdered American hostage William Higgins and threatened to hang another hostage, Joseph Cicippio, by day's end. On August 3, 1989, at 8:32 A.M. EST, when I was feeling most upset by the new broadcast, I asked the horary question, "Will Cicippio be hanged?" See Chart 43.

There are no considerations before judgment present. The Moon occupies the 12th house of confinement fits a chart about a hostage. Mutable signs occupy all the angles, showing a volatile situation. The Part of Fortune rising in the 1st house is an encouraging sign.

I used McEvers' method of assigning the 7th house to Cicippio, the person inquired about and with whom I had no other relationship. Pisces is on the cusp. His primary ruler is Jupiter and his secondary ruler, Neptune. Jupiter is strong in the 10th house and exalted in Cancer. These are fortunate indications and would confirm a favorable outcome. Jupiter is in a critical degree, at 0° of a cardinal sign. Critical degrees signify crisis situations and, without a doubt, Cicippio faced a crisis.

The question is about Cicippio's death. His eighth house is the eighth of the 7th, or the natural 2nd house of the chart. Libra is on the 2nd cusp. Actually, 23° 21' Libra is on the 2nd cusp, Koch system. This is the ecliptic longitude of Spica (23° 41' Libra in 1989), the most benefic fixed star. Thank God! Spica will almost certainly prevent the hanging from taking place. The rulers of Cicippio's derivative eighth house are Venus (Libra on the cusp) and secondarily Pluto (in the 2nd house). Venus (primary ruler of his death) and Jupiter (primary ruler of Cicippio) make no aspect. No aspect, no action. Good news again. Jupiter (Cicippio) will eventually trine Pluto (co-ruler of his death). This trine is a long way off, ephemeris time, and is a favorable indication. Neptune (Cicippio's co-ruler) is retrograde, showing his eventual return.

I felt relieved after reading this chart. The news reports from the Middle East confirmed my interpretation. The terrorists decided to spare Cicippio's life for the time being. Unfortunately, Neptune moves toward a conjunction with Saturn in the chart, and Saturn rules Cicippio's derivative 12th house of confinement. Although the chart promises he will not

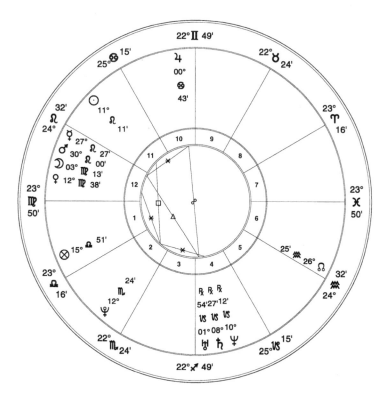

Chart 43: "Will Cicippio Be Hanged?"
August 3, 1989, 8:32 A.M. EST, 72W50, 41N27  Koch Houses

be hanged at this time, it suggests he is moving toward a prolonged period (Saturn) of confinement (12th house). When I wrote this in December, 1989, Cicippio was still a hostage. After a long period of confinement, he was eventually released by his captors.

Traditional astrologers might object to taking the 7th to represent Cicippio and use instead the 12th house. According to Lilly, captives and imprisonment are signified by planets in the 6th and 12th houses, by planets under the sunbeams, and by the cusp and planetary ruler of the 12th house (CA, pp. 463 and 470). With a Leo 12th cusp, the Sun would represent Cicippio. The Sun is dignified in Leo and in the fortunate 11th house. Jupiter, ruling the 7th, would become the significator of the 8th of death of the 12th of hostages. Sun and Jupiter make no aspect. The Sun (Cicippio) will square Pluto (a modern planet not used in traditional horary) and will also sextile the Part of Fortune.

The Moon, which occupies the 12th and therefore also signifies the hostage, is applying only to favorable aspects (trine Saturn, trine Neptune, sextile Pluto, and finally conjunct Venus). If we take Mercury at the cusp of the 12th to signify Cicippio, Mercury will perfect no aspects while in its sign. Before leaving Leo, Mercury will conjoin Regulus which Lilly considered the most beneficent of all the fixed stars. When Mercury enters Virgo, it will conjoin Mars (ruler of the 3rd = end-of-the-matter of the 12th) and then quickly sextile Jupiter (ruler of the end-of-the-matter 4th of the radical chart). By traditional methods, it does not appear that Cicippio will be hanged.

A historical note: Joseph Cicippio was taken hostage in Beirut, Lebanon, on September 12, 1986. After spending over five years in captivity, he was released on December 2, 1991.

## CHART 44: "WILL I MARRY MICHAEL?"

My friend Marie is a single parent who has the greatest difficulty in her relationships with men. For several years she has been asking horary questions about various relationships and the answer is always "no." She has a knack for inquiring when the Moon is void of course or when other strictures appear in the chart. As an aside, my experience and that of other horary astrologers, is that relationship questions frequently have "no" answers. If you think about it, the reason is obvious. People who are engaged in gratifying relationships do not ask horary questions about whether things will work out. Only when troubles arise is the querent prompted to make a horary inquiry, and by then it's usually too late.

On August 29, 1987, at 3:01 P.M. EST, Marie asked the question, "Will I marry Michael?" The man in question is the brother of one of Marie's friends. Marie had had a long-standing crush on Michael and had dated him for a while. When she heard that Michael had become engaged, she called me to ask her horary question. The reality of the situation suggested that Marie will not marry Michael. Let's see what Chart 44 shows.

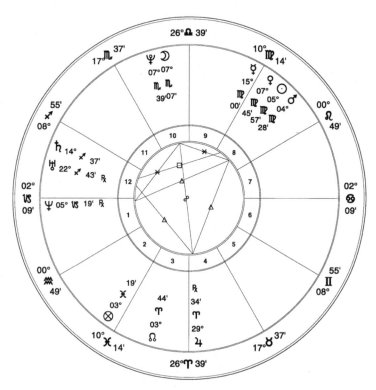

Chart 44: "Will I Marry Michael?"
August 29, 1987, 3:01 P.M. EST, 73W01, 41N19  Koch Houses

The Ascendant is 2° Capricorn. As usual, Marie's relationship question produced a chart with a classical consideration before judgment. Early degrees rising often mean a premature question. In this case, I would use the Bonatus rule that early degrees show a trivial or insincere question. Marie must realize that the situation between her and Michael is hopeless.

Neptune is retrograde in Capricorn and approaching the Ascendant. Neptune, as Marie's co-ruler, shows her state of self-deception. The thoughts about Michael are a pipe-dream (Neptune). Marie's primary ruler, Saturn, is in the 12th house of illusion, unreality, and self-undoing. Michael's ruler is the Moon because Cancer is on the Descendant. The Moon is in the Via Combusta, another classical warning. How does Marie pick these times to ask her questions? Two strictures in the same chart! This is another indication that things will not work out with Michael. The Moon (always the querent's co-ruler) is also conjunct Pluto, indicating her obsession with marrying this man.

The Moon (as ruler of the 7th or Michael) makes no major aspect to Marie's rulers Saturn and Neptune. The Moon will semi-sextile Saturn in 7° from the 12th house side of Saturn. The semi-sextile is a 2nd and 12th house aspect, and again confirms that Marie is deluding herself. Michael, of course, continued with his engagement and married someone else.

## CHART 45: "WHAT WILL BE THE OUTCOME OF MRS. B'S LIVER TRANSPLANT?"

A nurse, whom I know through work, was born with a congenital liver problem. Her condition worsened gradually into middle age. Her doctors finally decided it was time to have a liver transplant. She waited months for a liver donor. Suddenly in late July, 1989, a liver became available. I heard the news of the liver donor on July 27, 1989, at 8:16 A.M. EST and cast a chart for that time. My question was, "What will be the outcome of Mrs. B's liver transplant surgery?" See Chart 45.

This chart resembles the Cicippio chart above. According to McEvers' method of assigning the 7th cusp to Mrs. B, her primary ruler is Jupiter and her co-ruler is Neptune. The Mutable angles suggest an unstable situation. Jupiter (Mrs. B) is in a critical last degree of a sign. She is in a crisis situation and about to undergo a change of state. Jupiter, the natural ruler of the liver, is about to pass from Gemini into Cancer. At 29°, her liver (Jupiter) is "at the end of its rope." Mrs. B is about to have a liver transplant. The chart is radical and the symbolism fits the situation remarkably well.

Jupiter is strong in the 10th house, a positive indication. At the end of Gemini, Jupiter is in the terms of Mars (surgery). The natural 2nd house is Mrs. B's house of surgery because it is the eighth house of the 7th (Mrs. B). Libra is on the 2nd cusp. Venus is the primary ruler of the surgery. Pluto, in the 2nd, is the co-ruler of the surgery. Mrs. B's primary ruler, Jupiter, is void of course (modern), suggesting the matter is out of her hands. Her co-ruler, Neptune, is mutually applying to a trine with Venus (the surgery). The trine suggests a positive outcome. Her co-ruler, the Moon, is also in a critical degree at 0° 35' Gemini. This confirms her crisis state, as if we needed any confirmation. The Moon will square Venus (the surgery), suggesting obstacles or problems to be overcome. The Moon

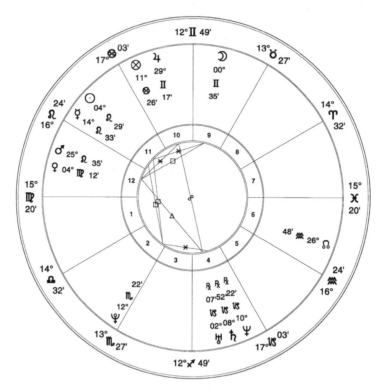

Chart 45: Mrs. B's Liver Transplant
July 27, 1989, 8:16 A.M. EST, 72W50, 41N27  Koch Houses

will quincunx Pluto, co-ruler of the surgery and natural ruler of complications, implying necessary adjustment and restructuring, apt symbolism for a liver transplant and the recovery after surgery. The last aspect of the Moon would be a conjunction with Jupiter, implying a positive outcome.

I found this chart difficult to synthesize. There were mixed indications of a favorable and a difficult outcome. The course of events fit the mixed nature of the chart. The surgery was successful, but Mrs. B developed many post-operative complications (Pluto). She needed to remain in the hospital for more than three months to receive antibiotic treatment and intensive rehabilitation. She finally went home in early November, and the liver transplant appears successful.

Traditional horary astrologers might approach this chart differently. Lilly taught that "in questions concerning sick people, give the Ascendant and his lord and the lord of the figure for significators of the sick party" (CA, p. 282). Virgo (the sign of caring for the sick) rising fits a question about a nurse and a medical problem. Mercury rules Mrs. B and is about to enter the 12th house of hospitals. The Sun has the most dignity and is "lord of the figure." The chart appears radical from this perspective.

Mercury is out of orb and thus void of course in Lilly's sense of the term. The Moon, which shows the general action in the chart, will next square Venus in the 12th (suggesting a difficult hospitalization) and then sextile the Sun in the 11th of her hopes and wishes, suggesting a positive outcome. In addition, the Sun, as most dignified "lord of the figure," represents Mrs. B. The Sun is Almuten of the 8th of surgery and of the 12th of hospitalization, thus linking the sick person with her surgery, hospitalization, and hopes and wishes. The Sun's great dignity suggests that these matters should go well.

## CHART 46: ABOUT A SMALL LION: WILL HE BE TAMED?

This is a typical fifth-century horary question analyzed by Palchus in Alexandria, Egypt, and reported in the book *Greek Horoscopes* by Neugebaur and Van Hoesen. The querent wanted to know if he could tame a young lion before spending a lot of money on a new pet. The question is dated July 8, A.D. 483 at 6:20 A.M. LMT, 29E55/31N13. See Chart 46.

Palchus, using fifth-century rules, argued that the Ascendant at 2° Leo fit a question about a young lion. Palchus thought the lion would be tamed because of the house positions of the two benefics; Venus was rising in Leo in the 1st house, and Jupiter was in the 11th house of the Good Daemon, where he rejoices. Furthermore, the Moon, co-ruler of the querent, would soon trine Jupiter, primary ruler of the querent's domestic animals (6th house). Jupiter is also the natural ruler of large or wild animals represented by the 12th house. Palchus said that the lion would go abroad on a ship because the Moon and the Lot of Fortune (by his calculations) were in the setting sign Aquarius, which is watery. Again, we see the water symbolism of Aquarius, as in Simmonite's example of the absconded mother.

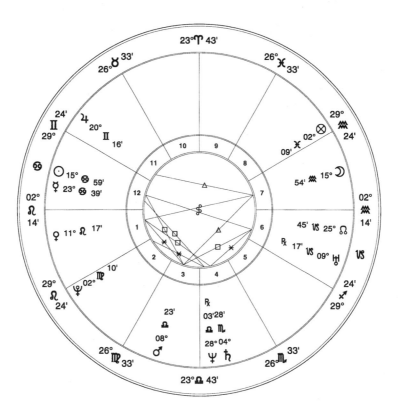

Chart 46  About a Small Lion: Will He Be Tamed?
July 8, A.D 483, 6:20 A.M. LMT, Alexandria; 29E55/31N13  Porphyry Houses

The computer chart has the Part of Fortune at 2° Pisces. Palchus calculated Pars Fortuna by hand from the tables available to him. The 5th century figures placed Pars Fortuna at 28° Aquarius. Palchus thought the lion would go abroad because the Moon had just left an opposition with Venus in the 1st (the "sender" of the Moon) and was about to trine Jupiter (the "receiver" of the Moon), natural ruler of long voyages, in Gemini (travel) in the 11th.

## CHART 47: "WHERE DID I PUT THE MEDICATION?"

The same weekend my mother-in-law lost her house keys, she asked a horary question to locate some medication she bought for her husband the week before. She remembered bringing it home but could not find it anywhere. On December 8, 1989, a Friday, at 9:39 P.M. EST she asked, "Where did I put the medication?" She knew it was in her home. See Chart 47.

The chart appears radical. Hypochondriacal Virgo on the 2nd cusp fits a question about missing medication. The 2nd ruler is Mercury which resides in Capricorn in the 5th house. McEvers would consider only the position of the 2nd ruler Mercury and tell us to look northwest (5th house) and then south (Capricorn). The missing medication may be in a dark place, low down, or on the floor (all suggested by Capricorn).

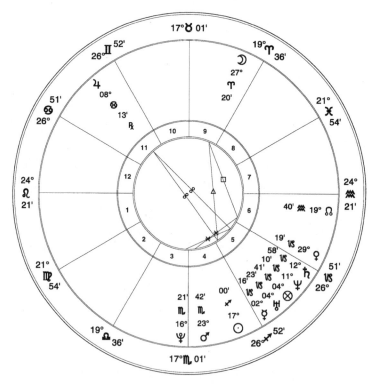

Chart 47: "Where Did I Put the Medication?"
December 8, 1989 9:39 P.M. EST, 73W01, 41N19  Koch Houses

Jacobson's list would look like this:

| Indicator | Planet | Sign | Sign Direction | House | House Direction |
|---|---|---|---|---|---|
| 2nd Ruler | Mercury | Capricorn | South | 5th | NNW |
| | Venus | Capricorn | South | 6th | WNW |
| | Moon | Aries | East | 9th | SSW |
| Dispositors of P.F. | Saturn | Capricorn | South | 5th | NNW |
| | Uranus | Capricorn | South | 5th | NNW |

Jacobson follows the houses first, then the signs. Using Jacobson's method, I told my mother-in-law to follow these directions upon her return: "First go north and west (directions taken from the mundane houses) in your condo and then go directly south (Capricorn). Look low down in a dark place (Capricorn). It may be near a heat vent (Moon in Aries; Sagittarius on 5th cusp)."

When my mother-in-law returned home after visiting us for the weekend, she followed the directions exactly as I had given them. She went north and west in her condo and this took her into the living room. From the northwest corner of the living room she turned south. This led to the entrance to her bedroom facing a closet. She opened the closet and there on a shelf, midway up, was the lost medication. She had looked for the medication in this closet several times during the previous week but did not see the missing item. In the attic above the closet is the heat pump for her condo.

Both she and I were astonished at how directly the horary instructions took her to the hidden goods. In retrospect, I realized I had not paid enough attention to the fire signs (Moon in Aries and Sagittarius on the 5th house cusp). If I had, I would have told her to look midway up because fire signs signify middle levels.

## CHART 48: WILL AN ASTROLOGY FORUM ON COMPUSERVE SUCCEED?

Ed Perrone is an excellent astrologer who writes a monthly feature for *American Astrology* magazine. I used to correspond with Ed on CompuServe, which Ed was trying to convince to start an astrology forum. One day Ed left me the following message:

*Date:* *06-June-89 23:54 EDT*          *From: Ed Perrone*
*Subject:* *Horary Question*
*Dear Tony,*
*Okay—here's a horary question that won't destroy me emotionally if the wrong answer comes up. Will the Astrologers Forum be approved by CompuServe? If so, will it go over? Also (if you can tell this from the chart), what sort of direction should I take to increase its chances of approval/success?*

See Chart 48. Here is my response:

> *Dear Ed,*
>
> *I read your question at 9:26 P.M. EDT, 73W01, 41N19 on 6/7/89. Only 2° of Capricorn are rising so it may be too early to tell if the Forum will succeed. Uranus (astrology) is on the Ascendant so it appears to be a valid chart.*
>
> *I used the 11th for the Astrologers Forum, which is a club. Scorpio is on the 11th so Mars and Pluto rule the Forum. If I use the 3rd house (Pisces cusp) for a communication network like Compuserve, there are no major aspects between Jupiter/Neptune (rulers of the 3rd represent CompuServe) and Mars/Pluto (rulers of the 11th) represent the Forum. No aspects suggests nothing will happen.*
>
> *If I use the 7th house (Cancer cusp) as other party for CompuServe, there is a square between the 7th ruler Moon and the 11th co-ruler Pluto. That's not too encouraging. It doesn't look like they will approve the Forum.*
>
> *As for increasing the chances of approval, Pars Fortuna is in the 2nd house, and Jupiter and the Sun are in the 6th. To increase the chance of success, I think you would need to convince CompuServe that it would bring them more money (2nd house) and provide a needed service (6th house). Also you would need to do a lot of detailed and tedious (6th house) work getting people to write in support of the idea.*

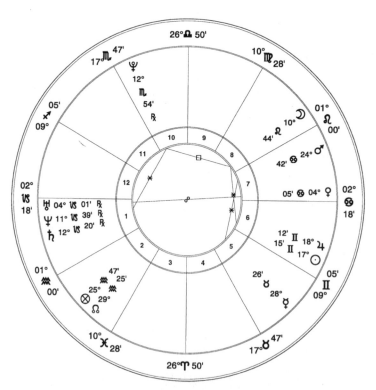

Chart 48: "Will an Astrology Forum on CompuServe Succeed?"
June 7, 1989, 9:26 P.M. EDT, 73W01, 41N19  Koch Houses

*Finally, Uranus, Neptune, and Saturn all retrograde in the 1st house suggest that at this time Compuserve is not favorably disposed to the idea. But it's very early in the project (2° rising) and anything can happen (Uranus conjunct Ascendant in 1st).*

*Best Wishes,*
*Tony*

The result was that CompuServe never approved an Astrology Forum.

## CHART 49: "WHEN WILL MY SON BE TOILET TRAINED?"

On the Friday before Christmas, 12/22/89, a good friend was visiting. In the course of the evening she mentioned how her 3 1/2 year old son was refusing to give up his diaper. He was the only child in his nursery school still requiring a diaper. His mother asked if I could do a chart to tell when her son would be fully toilet trained and no longer require a diaper. I noted the time to be 9:43 P.M. EST, coordinates 73W01/41N19. (The child was born 6/7/86 about 10:30 A.M. at 72W55/41N18.) See Chart 49.

The Moon is in the Via Combusta at 5° 9' Scorpio. Normally this consideration would concern me, but the boy's natal Pluto is almost exactly conjunct the horary Moon, and Pluto and Scorpio are both connected with bodily elimination. In addition, the Via Combusta often refers to messy situations. I thought the chart was radical and fit to judge.

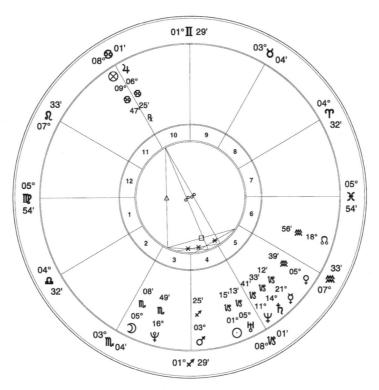

Chart 49: "When Will My Son Be Toilet Trained?"
December 22, 1989, 9:43 P.M. EST, 73W01, 41N19  Koch Houses

The 5th house rules the child in question. Capricorn is on the 5th cusp so Saturn is the primary ruler of the boy. I reasoned that the child's toilet training would be ruled by his 8th house, which is the 8th of the 5th or the 12th house of the horary chart. The 12th house has Leo on the cusp so the sun rules his toilet training.

The sun is at 1° 15' Capricorn. Sol will conjoin the 5th cusp in 7° (Koch) or 8° (Regiomontanus). The sun will conjoin Saturn (the boy) in 13°. Because the sun is angular and cardinal, I first thought the boy would be toilet trained in between 7 and 13 days. However, he had been quite stubborn about continuing to wear a diaper so I ignored the traditional rule about timing and opted to tell his mother he would stop wearing a diaper within 7 to 13 weeks. In addition, the sun would conjoin Uranus and Neptune on its way to the conjunction with Saturn. I interpreted these conjunctions to mean that the boy would have some accidents along the way, first a bowel and secondly a bladder accident.

In mid-January, 1990, I checked with my friend about her son's toilet training. She said that he stopped wearing a diaper at home on either January 5th or 6th, she couldn't remember which date. January 5th was 13 days after I did the horary chart. January 6th was the date the sun conjoined Saturn ephemeris time. On January 10th he stopped wearing a diaper to nursery school. Some time around January 6th he had a bowel accident while trying without a diaper. He ceased wearing a diaper entirely after that accident.

## Chart 50: "Will This Book Be Published?"

After studying hundreds of horary charts and doing much reading, I wanted to write a book on horary astrology. In the summer of 1989 I decided to ask a horary question before proceeding because I did not want to spend months writing something that would not see the light of day. On July 2, 1989, at 9:06 P.M. EST, I asked the horary question, "Will this book be published?" See Chart 50.

The chart appears radical. Aquarius rising fits a book about astrology. The sun, Moon, and Mercury are all in the 5th house of creative activity. Jupiter in the 5th seems to promise that creative writing will go well. With Aquarius rising, my primary ruler is Saturn and my co-ruler is Uranus. Both these planets are retrograde in Capricorn in the 11th house of astrology. The retrograde status of these planets fits with my plan to review the history of horary astrology. They do not refer to my debilitated state because I found writing this book quite invigorating. Perhaps my retrograde significators anticipate critical reviews that will call my horary thinking backward and atavistic. Time will tell.

The 3rd house rules books and the 9th house rules publishing. With Aries on the 3rd cusp, Mars signifies the book. With Libra on the 9th cusp, Venus is primary ruler of its publication. Because Pluto occupies the 9th house, Pluto is a secondary ruler of publishing.

Are there any aspects between Mars (the book) and either Venus or Pluto (publication)? In less than six degrees, Venus at 4° 36' Leo will conjoin Mars at 10° 17' Leo in the 6th house. The conjunction between the two primary rulers is a strong indication that the book will be published. Perfection in six degrees suggests it will take about six months (not six years, I hoped) to get the manuscript to the publisher. The 6th house fits the tedious work that goes into writing a manuscript.

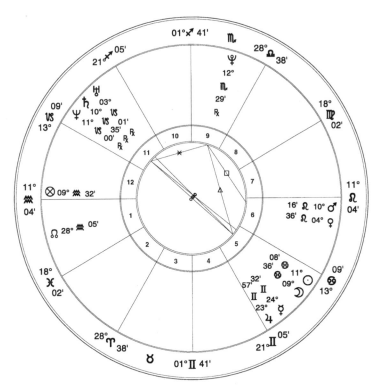

Chart 50: "Will This Book Be Published?"
July 2, 1989, 9:06 P.M., 73W01, 41N19  Koch Houses

On the other hand, Mars (the book) will square Pluto (secondary ruler of publication), and Pluto is in the Via Combusta. This aspect to a secondary ruler carries less weight but may indicate some problems along the way. Perhaps it is a foreshadowing of the theft of the manuscript which delayed my getting it to the publisher, or perhaps it indicates some other problem I am not yet aware of. The Moon is approaching a conjunction with the sun. This is a traditional malefic influence in horary which I tend to ignore. The New Moon in the 5th symbolizes a new beginning and fits my pending decision to begin work on a creative project.

The Moon's last major aspect in this chart is a trine to Pluto in the 9th. I take this to mean that in the end, after some problem shown by Mars square Pluto, the book (Moon as co-ruler) will be published (trine Pluto in 9th). The Part of Fortune having just risen and the Moon's North Node in the 1st house confirm this interpretation.

Addendum: In February 1990, I learned that a well-known horary astrologer was planning to submit a manuscript on horary to Llewellyn and I felt the Mars square Pluto signified this event. Fortunately for me, the other author did a horary chart about whether Llewellyn would publish her manuscript. The answer was negative and she submitted it elsewhere for publication. For a few weeks, however, it seemed like Llewellyn might have to choose between my manuscript and someone else's.

Having read this chart as I did above, I made a decision in July, 1989 to contact some publishers to see if any would be interested in a manuscript on horary astrology. Only three publishers responded to my many inquiries. Two of them had already commissioned other authors to do books on horary, so I found out I had competition.

Llewellyn expressed interest and asked me to send drafts of some chapters. I began writing the book in mid-summer of 1989 and sent Llewellyn drafts of the initial chapters in September. I had the good fortune to connect with Llewellyn's Tom Bridges, whose thoughtful comments helped shape the structure and content of this volume. I sent the full manuscript to the publisher before the year's end.

If you are reading this chapter, obviously the book was published and my interpretation of the chart was correct. If you are not reading this material, then I have spent hundreds of hours writing in vain and no one will ever know of my error in analyzing this horary chart.

## CHART 51: "WILL THE AD FLY?"

On June 5, 1990, at 10:52 A.M. CDT, at 93W06/44N57, Tom Bridges asked his own horary question about whether an advertisement for this book that he wanted to run in *American Astrology* magazine would be approved by his supervisors at Llewellyn. The ad was moderately expensive and Tom was concerned that his employer might not want to spend that much money on an unknown author's book. See Chart 51.

With Leo rising in the chart Tom is signified by the Sun. Tom took the 3rd house with a Libra cusp and Venus to represent the ad. Venus is quite dignified, being in her own sign, day triplicity, and term. This augured well for the success of the ad. The 10th house governs Tom's employer, Llewellyn. Taurus is on the 10th cusp, making Venus the ruler of both Tom's boss and the ad. Mercury and the Sun in the 10th are co-rulers of the employer.

The 11th house represents Tom's employer's money. Mercury rules the 11th cusp (Gemini) and Mercury's placement in the 10th shows how carefully Llewellyn guards its money.

The contract for the ad is governed by the 7th house of agreements. As the house of the other party, the 7th also rules American Astrology magazine. The question boils down to this: Will Llewellyn (10th house) or Llewellyn's money (11th house) connect favorably with American Astrology (7th house, ruled by Saturn) or their money (8th house, ruled by Jupiter)?

The answer is that Mercury (Llewellyn's money) in just about 3° will trine Saturn (American Astrology) by mutual application. Yes, Llewellyn will approve the ad in about three days. The fact that Jupiter (ruler of the 8th, American Astrology's money) is posited in the 11th, Llewellyn's income) and exalted in Cancer suggests that running the ad will ultimately profit Llewellyn.

Initially Tom did not use this interpretation of the Mercury/Saturn trine to find the answer. Instead, he used the chart to plan a strategy to insure that his boss would approve the ad. Noticing that Saturn was dignified in Capricorn and posited in the 6th, Tom enlisted the aid of a co-worker (6th house) to approach his boss (co-ruled by Mercury in the 10th). He reasoned that the trine would allow his co-worker to easily convince his employer of the ad's worth. His strategy worked and the ad was approved two days later.

The ad "flew" despite the presence of the Moon at 14° 06' Scorpio in the via Combusta. Perhaps what "saved" the Moon is a mixed mutual reception. The Moon is in the terms of

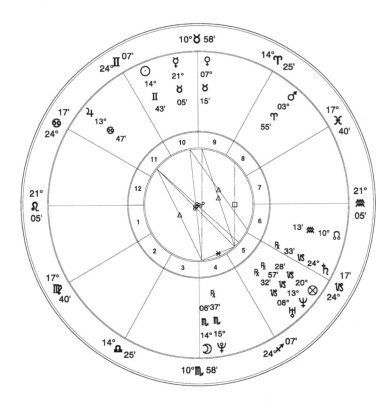

Chart 51: "Will the Ad Fly?"
June 5, 1990, 10:52 A.M. CDT, 93W16, 44N57  Koch Houses

Venus, and Venus is in the exaltation of the Moon. Marc Edmond Jones might say that the chart worked despite the Via Combust Moon because Tom was trying to bring order out of confusion.

## CHARTS 52 AND 53: A STUDY IN HORARY ASTROLOGY

On March 11, 1990, I received a phone call from a woman I hardly knew. To preserve her confidentiality I will refer to her as Rachel. She knew nothing about astrology but had been visiting my friend Sara in New York City when I gave her directions for finding her son's lost video game from a horary chart (see Chapter Fifteen, pp. 247–249). Impressed that the chart located the missing object, she had a question of her own to ask.

Rachel wondered if astrology could tell her what was happening in her marriage. I noted the exact time of the question to be 7:03 P.M. EST. I gave a brief explanation of the difference between horary and natal astrology and asked her for her birth data. Unfortunately, Rachel did not know the exact time of her birth but was certain it was around 9:00 A.M.

For reasons of confidentiality I will not give all of Rachel's birth information. She has an 11th house Sun at 16° Cancer and a 12th house Saturn at 21° Leo. Her natal chart for 9:00 A.M. has 8° Virgo rising with 8° Pisces on her 7th cusp of marriage and husband.

I noticed immediately that her husband's ruler Neptune, now transiting her 5th house in Capricorn, was approaching an opposition to her 11th house Sun. Since Neptune is slow-moving and was about to turn retrograde, she would feel the effect of this opposition for the next couple of years. Her husband's ruler opposing her Sun from her 5th house of love affairs made me wonder if Rachel's husband were having an affair which was causing marital difficulties.

In looking at her secondary progressions, I noticed that her progressed Sun and progressed Saturn were about to conjoin in the 12th house. The conjunction would become exact in the next couple of months. I took this to mean that Rachel might experience some sorrow because of an impending loss or separation.

Having examined her natal chart, transits, and secondary progressions, I next looked at the horary chart for her question "What's happening in my marriage?" See Chart 52.

In this horary chart Rachel is signified by Venus, the ruler of the 1st house. Rachel is also governed by the Moon which always co-rules the person asking the horary question. Her husband's signifier is Mars, the planet which rules the 7th house of the horary chart.

Venus is separating from a conjunction with Mars in Aquarius, and both significators are headed into the 5th house of the horary figure. The separating aspect shows Rachel and her husband pulling apart, and the repeated emphasis on the 5th house again raises the possibility of a love affair. The Moon is void of course (modern), showing that things are not functioning in the marriage and that Rachel is ineffectual in straightening things out.

Because I did not know Rachel very well, I was deliberately vague in reporting my findings to her. I explained that the chart indicated she was headed into a period of stress

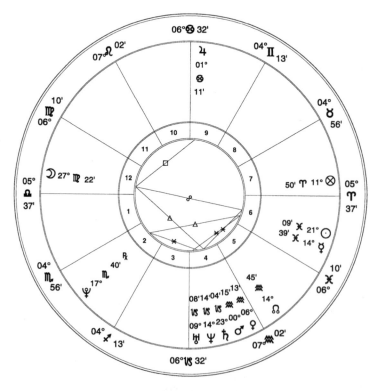

Chart 52: "What's Happening in My Marriage?"
March 11, 1990, 7:03 P.M. EST, 73W01, 41N19  Koch Houses

between herself and her husband. I mentioned nothing about the 5th house emphasis on love affairs, and I apologized for not being very specific in my answer to her.

A few weeks later, on April 8, 1990, I got a second call from Rachel. This time she sounded quite upset, almost in tears. She said her husband had just left her; she then asked two questions: "Will he return, and will I move from New York City?" I noted the time to be 1:50 P.M. EST. See Chart 53.

With Leo on the Ascendant, the Sun rules Rachel and the Moon is her co-ruler. With Aquarius on the 7th, both Uranus and Saturn, the traditional ruler of Aquarius, signify her husband. The Sun is about to square Saturn, indicating the problems between them. The Moon, which co-rules Rachel, is also about to square both Uranus and Saturn, her husband's two significators. It does not look like he will be returning any time soon.

In addition, both Uranus and Saturn are in the 5th house of the horary figure with Neptune between them. Uranus and Saturn rule her husband in the horary chart, and Neptune rules her husband in her natal chart. I asked Rachel if it was possible that her husband was seeing someone else. "Yes," she said, "an actress" (note Neptune in the 5th). Rachel had just learned her husband had been having an affair (which prompted his moving out).

Will Rachel move from New York City? The 4th house governs her current home base, and the 7th house in horary rules removals. Because Scorpio is on the 4th cusp, Mars rules her home base with Pluto as a co-ruler. The Sun (Rachel) is about to sextile Mars and makes no aspect with Pluto. The sextile indicates that it is better for her to stay in New York City.

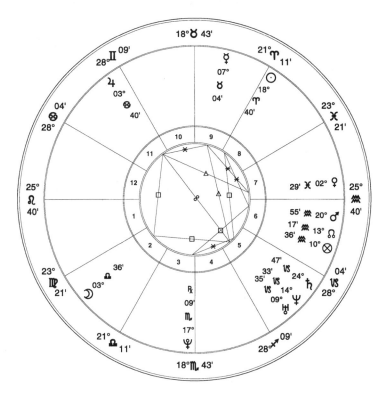

Chart 53: "Will He Return, and Will I Move from New York City?"
April 8, 1990, 1:50 P.M. EST, 73W01, 41N19 Koch Houses

Both Saturn and Uranus govern the 7th cusp of removals. We have already seen the squares these planets form to Rachel's significators. Any attempt to move from New York City would be fraught with obstacles and difficulties. On the other hand, the Sun was a little more than two degrees from the 9th house cusp and would sextile Mars, ruler of the 9th house, in a little over two degrees. I thought this meant she would be taking a trip within two weeks to two months time.

I called Rachel to give her my analysis of the horary chart. I told her that it would be difficult for her and her husband to reunite and that I did not think she would be moving from New York City. I also said I expected she would be taking a long-distance trip within the next couple of months. She then said she was planning to visit her parents in Florida to discuss what had happened in her marriage. She made plane reservations for the last week in April, about two and a half weeks away.

When I wrote this at the end of June, 1990, Rachel was separated from her husband. They went on to have an acrimonious divorce. Rachel still lives in New York City because she thought a move would be "too drastic."

## Charts 54, 55, and 56: The Case of the Missing Twin

On Saturday August 24, 1991, at 4:25 P.M., I received a call at my home from the owner of a New Age bookstore where I had recently given a talk on horary astrology. He wanted my help in finding a missing person. See Chart 55 for the time I received the call.

The young man in question was a college student who had disappeared after visiting his girlfriend in Boston for the weekend. He had called home to New Jersey at 1:00 A.M. on July 29, 1991, to let his family know he was leaving his girlfriend's house in Boston and would see them in the morning. See Chart 54 for the time of the family's last contact with the missing twin.

The young man never arrived home and the family feared the worst. His twin brother led the search. About three weeks after the missing student's last phone call to the family, the brother entered the New Age bookstore and asked if there was any occult method for locating his lost brother. The store owner noted the time of the inquiry to be 3:30 P.M. on August 23, 1992. See Chart 56 for the time of the twin brother's inquiry of the store owner.

I studied all three charts using horary methods and drew the unfortunate conclusion that the missing twin was most likely dead, either from foul play or from an accident.

Chart 54 is of primary importance because it depicts the time the college student was last heard from by his family in New Jersey. William Lilly says that, in missing person charts, the 1st house represents the missing person unless the querent bears some special relationship to the missing party.

In Chart 54 the malefic fixed star Caput Algol conjoins the Ascendant. Algol can symbolize head injuries, beheading, misfortune, and death. Venus rules the Ascendant and hence the missing twin. Venus lies in her fall in Virgo where she conjoins Mars, the natural ruler of accidents and injuries, and the accidental ruler of the 12th house of sorrow and self-undoing.

Significantly in Chart 54, the Point of Death (Mars + Saturn - MC) lies at 7° Virgo in conjunction with both Venus and Mars! The traditional Part of Death (Ascendant + 8th - Moon) lies at 27° Scorpio exactly opposite the Ascendant which symbolizes the missing person and his physical body. Pluto is quite powerful, having just turned stationary direct, and lies on the midpoint of Mercury (travel) and Saturn (death).

In Chart 56, for the time when the twin inquires about his missing brother, the querent is shown by the Ascendant and his brother by the 3rd cusp. The missing brother's rulers are Jupiter (traditional ruler of Pisces) and Neptune (modern ruler of Pisces). Neptune is retrograde in the 1st, showing that the missing person will eventually be found (retrograde implies return) but that he will return in a debilitated condition.

In Chart 56 Jupiter, the primary ruler of the missing twin, lies in the 8th house of death. The Moon rules the 8th house (Cancer cusp) and applies by opposition to Jupiter (the missing brother). These are indications that the brother is dead. In the turned chart the derived 8th death house of the 3rd house of the missing brother is the 10th of the horary chart. Venus rules the missing person's house of death (Libra cusp) and occupies the 8th house of the horary chart, another confirmation of death.

The Moon is a natural ruler of fugitives and missing persons and applies to a square of Pluto, a modern ruler of death. Remarkably, the Part of Death in this chart conjoins Caput Algol and the Ascendant of Chart 54.

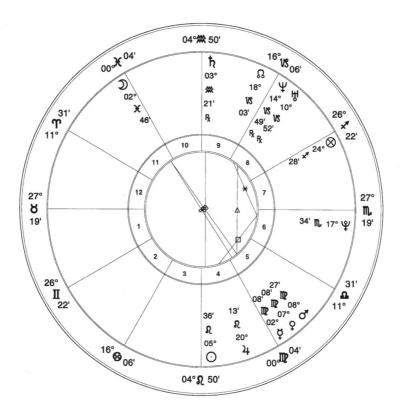

Chart 54: Brother's last call
July 29, 1991 1:00 A.M. EDT, 40N48, 74W12 Regiomontanus Houses

In Chart 55 for the time I received the inquiry, the 1st house represents the missing person because I have no natural relationship with the missing twin. Saturn retrograde in the 1st is a traditional warning in horary that "the matter of the question seldom or ever comes to good." Lilly says that Saturn retrograde in the 1st "infortunates the question, causing the querent to despair."

The planets in the 1st house in Chart 55 describe the missing twin. Three retrograde heavy planets (Saturn, Uranus, and Neptune) occupy the 1st, suggesting an accident (Uranus) due to carelessness, sleepiness, or drugs (Neptune) and resulting in death (Saturn). In addition, the 8th ruler Sun (Leo cusp) is almost exactly quincunx (150 degrees) the 1st house Saturn. The quincunx is often associated with 6th and 8th house matters like illness and death.

The surviving twin had asked the bookstore owner where his brother might be found. In Chart 56 the 3rd house ruler Jupiter lies in Leo in the 8th house. The 8th house indicates a direction south and west. This made sense because the missing twin was traveling from Boston to New Jersey in a southwest direction. Lilly described Leo as symbolizing places "where wild beasts frequent, woods, forests, desert places, steep rocky places, inaccessible places, and parks."

The young man was found dead shortly after Labor Day in a deserted wooded area alongside Route 84 East in northeastern Connecticut. He had apparently fallen asleep at the

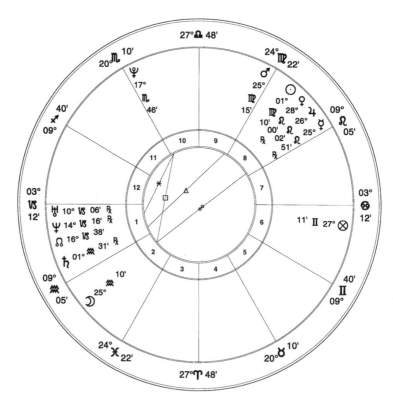

Chart 55: Help requested
August 24, 1991, 4:25:EDT, 41N17, 73W03 Regiomontanus Houses

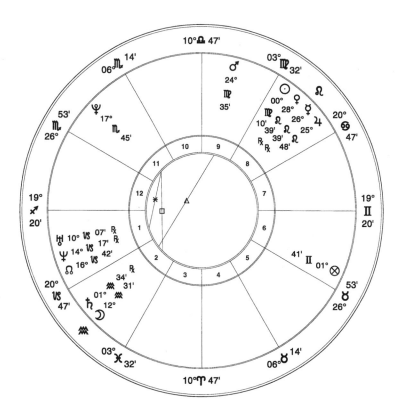

Chart 56: Twin to Bookstore
August 23, 1991, 3:30 P.M EDT,40N48, 74W12  Regiomontanus Houses

wheel, and his car went off the road in a remote, inaccessible area. The car struck a tree and the young man apparently died instantly of a head injury.

## CHART 57: THE MISSING AUDITORIUM KEYS

There is nothing more gratifying to an author than a letter from a grateful reader. In August 1992, I received such a letter from an astrologer in Indiana. The woman who wrote the letter is a teacher who was able to use the first edition of this book to help a colleague find her lost keys. Her fellow teacher was distraught because she had lost the keys to the high school auditorium. Here is an excerpt from her letter to me:

"(After school) I managed to quickly run the chart. I spent about twenty minutes on it and consulted your book about the location of objects. I called her about 6:15 P.M. and told her that according to my reading of the chart the keys would be found in her classroom at the school, not in her home or in her car, that they should be at mid-level about waist high, and near something hot or that could be hot in the SE corner of her room."

The teacher who had lost the keys drove back to the school that evening. When she entered her classroom, she noticed that her student teacher had pushed an overhead projector on its cart into the southeast corner of the room. She looked on the cart near the projector's bulb that becomes quite hot during operation. There she discovered her missing

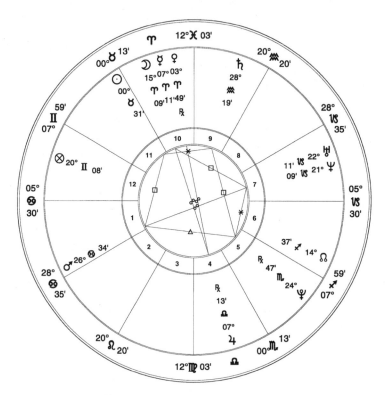

Chart 57: Missing Auditorium Keys
April 20, 1993, 9:39 A.M. EST, 85W00, 41N39  Koch Houses

keys at waist height and wedged between the projector and the top of the cart—just as the horary chart suggested they would be. Study Chart 57 and see if you too can locate the missing keys.

## CHART 58: THE MISSING ORTHODONTIST

On October 5, 1992 an orthodontist, Dr. John Susman, disappeared without a trace. Despite a continuing investigation by the East Haven Police and the FBI, he has never been found. According to the New Haven Register of Saturday October 5, 1996, at the time of Dr. Susman's disappearance he had no large debts and was not involved with drugs, gambling, or any kind of illegal activity. He had filed for divorce a year earlier and the separation was amicable. He was a model citizen described as an "easygoing and polite man" who liked wind surfing and tennis.

Dr. Susman was last seen when he left his office in Orange, CT, at 5:15 P.M. EDT on October 5, 1992. At 6:00 P.M. he telephoned his brother from his shorefront home on Long Island Sound and played his brother a message from his answering machine: "Sus, you're a dead man, it's coming soon." The police suspected that the voice on the machine might be that of Dr. Susman but the FBI was not able to confirm this theory. See Chart 58 for the brother's last contact with Dr. Susman.

The next day, October 6, 1992, Dr. Susman did not show up for work. His brother called the police who searched Dr. Susman's home where they found his four wheel drive vehicle and his Mazda still in the driveway. Inside the house the police found the doctor's keys, wallet, clothing, belongings, and $10,000 in cash. There was no sign of violence or forced entry. No one saw him leave and none of the Taxi or transportation companies had any record of giving him a ride.

Lilly advises us to use the 1st house for a missing person. With Aries rising, Mars signifies the orthodontist. Mars rules both the Ascendant and the 8th house of death and is Almuten of the 4th house of the grave. Mars lies in Cancer (oceans) in the end-of-the-matter 4th house. Mars is partile square to the Sun, ruler of the unfortunate 6th of sickness and accidents. The Sun is Almuten of both the 1st and 6th houses, connecting the physical state of Dr. Susman with the misfortune represented by the 6th house. As the 8th ruler, Mars squaring the Sun, Almuten of the 1st—the missing person's body, suggests that he may be dead. Mars applies to an opposition of Uranus/Neptune and the Sun applies to a square of both these planets. These aspects suggest some kind of sudden accident, piercing blow, or injury, perhaps due to carelessness or a state of depression or inattention.

The Sun (Almuten of the 1st and ruler of the 6th), Mars (ruler of the 1st and the 8th and Almuten of the 4th and 11th), Pluto (a natural ruler of death), and the Moon (missing persons and 4th ruler) are all in critical degrees at the cusps of the Lunar Mansions. This was

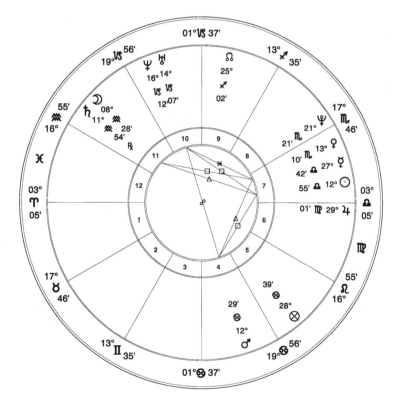

Chart 58: Missing Orthodontist
October 5, 1992, 6:00 P.M. EDT, 73W04, 41N16 Regiomontanus Houses

certainly a critical time in Dr. Susman's life. In addition the Sun and Mars, which signify the orthodontist's body, are both in their fall, indicating a debilitated state. Finally, the Sun (Almuten of the 1st, the orthodontist's body) conjoins the fixed star Algorab (at 13° 20' Libra), which is prominent in cases of loss, accidents, suicide, and injury.

The Moon is a general significator of fugitives and missing persons. Here the Moon (4th ruler—final resting place) lies in Aquarius (near water) and mutually applies to a conjunction of Saturn (dark rocky places) near the cusp of the 12th (self-undoing). This symbolism suggests that the orthodontist fell, injured his head or suffered a heart attack (Mars square Sun) in a rocky place (Saturn) near water (Mars in Cancer, Moon in Aquarius). He may have been knocked unconscious and then drowned, the body being hidden near or under rocks along the shore. The mystery remains unsolved as indicated by so many peregrine planets in the chart: the Sun (authorities), Mercury (3rd ruler, the brother), Venus (2nd and 7th ruler, the consultants on the case), Jupiter (9th and 12th ruler, the legal system and private investigators), and the Moon (4th ruler, the family). Eventually we may find out what happened.

---

### HISTORICAL INTERLUDE
### WILLIAM LILLY'S BIRTHDAYS

William Lilly, the great horary astrologer, was born in the spring of 1602 at Diseworth, seven  miles south of Derby (52N50, 01W16), when the Julian calendar was still being used in Great Britain. His birth date is listed by various authorities as either April 30 or May 1, 1602 in the Julian calendar. It happens that both dates are correct—depending on one's calendrical perspective.

At that time in England, days were regarded as beginning at Noon. Because Lilly was born at 2:08 past midnight, his birth date was originally recorded at 14:08 past Noon on April 30. This was later rewritten as 2:08 past midnight on May 1, 1602 by modern authors who considered the day to begin at midnight rather than at Noon.

To convert these dates to the Gregorian calendar, we need to add ten days. In doing so, we see that William Lilly can have four separate and valid dates of birth: April 30, May 1, May 10, and May 11, 1602.

# CHAPTER FIFTEEN

# Conclusions and Recommendations

This book grew out of the confusion I experienced while reading the existing horary literature. As I took notes to clarify horary concepts, I discovered numerous contradictions among the authors who wrote about the art. The authorities couldn't seem to agree about the meanings of many of the terms commonly used in horary practice.

To get to the bottom of some of the definitions, I found myself reading backwards in time from twentieth-century horary authors to nineteenth-century ones such as Simmonite. I discovered that almost everything written about horary after the seventeenth century was essentially derived from Lilly's 1647 masterpiece *Christian Astrology*. Lilly was a genius at horary analysis and his work is a monument to his scholarly erudition and empirical verification of the art. But even Lilly fell prey to some nonsense of the ancients, like squares that conveniently become trines and vice versa. I felt a need to understand how Lilly arrived at his system and I continued to trace his sources back in time.

My search led me to the thirteenth century works of Guido Bonatus, from whom Lilly derived much of his system. Bonatus, in turn, had learned astrology from the works of Manilius and Firmicus Maternus, and horary largely from Latin translations of the ninth-century Arabic texts by Abu Ma'Shar. Although the Arabs contributed much detail to astrology, they learned the basics from Arabic translations of the Greek texts by Ptolemy, Dorotheus of Sidon, and Antioch of Athens. The Greeks, of course, had distilled the astrological wisdom of the Babylonians and Egyptians, particularly at the great center of learning in Alexandria. The fertile crescent of the Middle East is where it all began. Astrologers will not be surprised by the symbolic connection between the fertile crescent and the phases of the Moon, the most important planet in horary.

Writing this book and studying numerous horary charts helped to clarify my thinking about the art. After trying many rules and different systems, I found myself returning to the fundamentals espoused by Dorotheus, Bonatus, and Lilly. I would like to summarize my thinking about the practice of horary astrology. A horoscope cast for the moment a baby enters the world from the womb symbolically captures some essential meanings about the nature and life of that individual. Similarly, a chart erected for the moment of birth of a pressing personal question symbolically represents the nature and ramifications of the querent's concern. Fortunately, a horary chart will warn the astrologer when the question is less than sincere or when the astrologer may have difficulty interpreting the chart or satisfying the client.

The classical method of horary analysis is simple to state but often complex to put into action. The person asking the question belongs in the first house. The matter inquired about belongs in one of the twelve mundane houses. When the question is about someone else, the astrologer uses the derivative system of houses.

Each house has a planetary ruler. The planet ruling the person asking the question and the planet ruling the matter asked about will make a major Ptolemaic aspect, or they will not. The next applying aspect between primary significators shows what will happen between the querent and the quesited. If there is no aspect, nothing will happen. An analysis of this aspect between the two significators is the essential step in horary judgment. A host of rules can modify the message given by that aspect.

In reading a horary chart, it helps to assume an anthropomorphic viewpoint. The planets become people or things that relate to one another. The aspects show how they do it. Planets can be strong or weak depending on their dignities and status in the chart. The astrological symbolism must fit the empirical situation.

The above principles are the essence of the horary method. I have covered many of the details in the earlier chapters of this text. If you are as enthusiastic about horary as I am, the next step is to analyze as many charts as you can. Silly questions will produce trivial charts with contradictory or confusing indications. The more sincere and meaningful the question, the more precisely the astrological symbolism will fit. Such charts give the astrologer an uncanny feeling and a sense of awe at the concordance between the universe and the human mind.

As you do horary charts, be sure to save them for review after you see how things turn out. All horary astrologers make mistakes. When you get wrong answers, go back to the chart and find where you went wrong. The key to success in horary is to remain firm in the conviction that, if the question is sincere, the answer lies buried in the chart. Your job as a horary practitioner is to release the meaning pent up in the astrological symbolism. Don't be afraid to consult with another astrologer if you get stuck on a particular question, especially when Saturn (the teacher) appears in the 7th house. Some charts may take months or even years to release their secrets to you.

Difficulty understanding a horary figure frequently results from a blind spot in the astrologer's world view. If you stick with a chart that gives you trouble until you comprehend it, you will grow personally, enlarge your understanding of the world, and enhance your skill as an astrologer. My friend Luis Alvarado commented that asking a horary question is like casting a stone into the water and watching how the ripples spread out into the universe.

An appreciation of horary principles will improve your ability at other branches of astrology. Skill at horary or other forms of astrology is largely a function of the practitioner's ability to think symbolically. Some people seem to do this easily and others only with great difficulty. There are many ways to enhance your appreciation of symbolism. Reading the classics of world literature, including poetry, will acquaint you with the basic themes faced by the human race. Learning a foreign language can help you see how different images are associated with human experience. I found Freud's *Interpretation of Dreams* coupled with an analysis of my own dreams to be of great assistance in understanding how the mind thinks symbolically. Freud's pupil Carl Jung further explored the universe of archetypal images.

Almost any form of meditation, including creative visualization, will be of great benefit to the horary astrologer. Pondering the great myths of humanity or meditating on archetypal symbols such as those depicted in the Tarot are powerful techniques for enhancing one's ability to think symbolically.

If you wish to learn more about the history of astrology, the books by Tester and by McIntosh are excellent sources of information. They are listed in the bibliography. Finally, if you are interested in learning more about horary astrology, you must read the seminal 1647 text by William Lilly. Carol Wiggers of Just Us & Associates (1420 N.W. Gilman Blvd., Suite 2154, Issaquah, WA 98027) has typed the entire text into her computer and made it available in modern type to twentieth century readers. She also publishes an excellent journal devoted to traditional horary astrology called *The Horary Practitioner*.

Other useful horary texts are those by Simmonite, Jones, Jacobson, DeLong, Appleby, and Barclay. The classics by Ptolemy, Dorotheus, and Bonatus provide a solid foundation in the ancient tradition of the art. Thanks to Project Hindsight, more and more of the classic sources are becoming available in English. As you read horary texts, including this one, never take the authority of the author at face value. Test the horary rules for yourself and use only those that provide consistent and reliable results. The proof of the pudding is always in the eating.

Since the first edition of this text, the world has seen the explosion of information available on the Internet. Readers with a computer will surely want to check out several excellent sites devoted to horary astrology. Carol Wiggers, Sue Ward, and Allen Edwall all have World Wide Web pages devoted to horary and traditional techniques. By the time this edition is published there will doubtless be even more available about astrology on the information superhighway.

Having given my last bit of advice, it is time to bring matters to a close. This book began with a question by my friend Sara. It is fitting that it should also end with one of Sara's questions. On Tuesday, January 16, 1990, at 10:00 P.M. EST Sara telephoned with the question, "Where is John's GameBoy?" Her seven year old son could not find one of his favorite video games and was beside himself with concern. I was feeling tired at the end of a day and was not in the mood to analyze a horary chart; but John was quite upset so I turned on the computer and brought the chart up on the screen. See Chart 59.

I warned Sara that I was sleepy and would only give her a cursory reading. My preference would have been to print out the chart, study it carefully, look up information in references, meditate on the symbolism, and then give a well-reasoned answer. In my haste to give Sara some feedback, I ignored the late Ascendant. Because Sara had asked about John's GameBoy and did not say "my son John," I used the 7th cusp to represent John. With Pisces

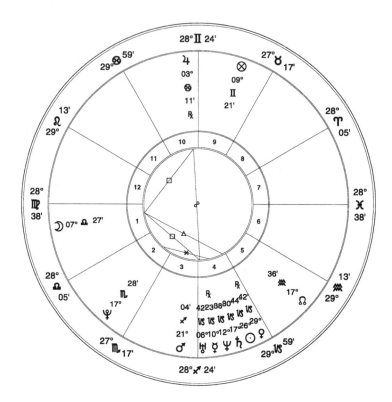

Chart 59: "Where is John's GameBoy?"
January 16, 1990, 10:00 P.M. EST, 73W01, 41N19  Koch Houses

on the 7th, John's rulers are Jupiter and Neptune. John's possessions fall in the 8th house (the 2nd of the 7th). Aries is on the 8th cusp, making Mars the ruler of his lost game. Seeing Mars in the 3rd house, I asked Sara if he could have left it in the car.

"Funny you should ask that," replied Sara. "John last remembers having the game in the car, but he insists he brought it into the house, and we searched the car and couldn't find it."

"If you're sure it's in the house," I said, "then it's hidden or secluded (Mars in 3rd house), in the Northeast part of the apartment (3rd house), near heat (Mars in Sagittarius), and also near water (Scorpio on 3rd cusp)."

Sara lives in a condo in New York. Her furnace room and laundry room are in the Northeast part of the condo, and I suggested she search that area. Using the Moon as a timing device, I interpreted its sextile to Mars in fourteen degrees to mean that Sara would find the game in about fourteen days, and that I was sure she would find it.

Glancing at Mars in Sagittarius, I got an image of airplane travel (Sagittarius, 9th house) and told her it might be high up somewhere. In my haste I ignored the traditional wisdom that fire signs (Sagittarius) are mid-level, and water signs (Scorpio on 3rd) are low.

Two weeks came and went. No GameBoy showed up. Exactly a month after the question, on February 16, Sara was looking for something in the closet next to the furnace and laundry rooms when she found the game - amidst some clothing stored toward the bottom of the closet in the Northeast part of the condo, near heat and water. I went back to the chart to find out why my timing was so far off. When I checked the ephemeris for February 16, I discovered that Mars (the game) was at 12° 46' Capricorn at 00:00 EST on that date. In other words, she found her son's game when Mars (the game) conjoined the position of Neptune (her son) in the horary chart. When Mars came together with Neptune, the game came back to her son John.

I telephoned Sara to tell her the news of this exciting "coincidence"—the Mars/Neptune conjunction. Sara wondered aloud how and why the chart could mirror the events and concerns of a small boy's life with such precision. She then remembered a phrase from her youth about God being aware of even the slightest sparrow that falls. If we could comprehend how God knows even the slightest sparrow that falls, we might understand the essence of horary astrology.

# Fixed Stars and Malefic Degrees

Below is a list of fixed stars that are referenced in the horary literature. William Lilly used about fifty fixed stars in *Christian Astrology*. In the following list, the letter **L** after the star indicates that the star was used by Lilly. The letter **R** after the name identifies that star as important according to the research of Diana Rosenberg. The planets whose names are capitalized are those cataloged by Ptolemy. Planets in parentheses describe the nature of the star according to the research of Diana K. Rosenberg. The fixed stars move forward in the zodiac about fifty seconds of arc per year. In ten years, the fixed stars advance about eight minutes and twenty-one seconds of arc. On average, every seventy-two years these stars move forward in the zodiac an entire degree (by apparent motion).

## Some Fixed Stars and Malefic Degrees (January 2000 Positions)

ALPHERATZ: 14° 18' Aries (VENUS; Jupiter, Mars) Honor, wealth, good fortune. Possible violent death. Suicide.

BATEN KAITOS: 21° 57' Aries (SATURN) Isolation. Depression. Accidents. Emigration. Sexual problems. Scholarly. Shipwrecks ("more than any other star," Rosenberg).

SHARATAN: 3° 58' Taurus (MARS, SATURN) Violence, defeat, accidents, injury, danger. Also honors & good fortune.

HAMAL: 7° 40' Taurus (MARS, SATURN) Unlucky. Violence, cruelty. Head injury. Suffering in love.

SCHEDIR: 7° 47' Taurus (SATURN, VENUS) Good for astrology, mysticism, writing.

ALMACH: 14° 14' Taurus (VENUS; Mars, Jupiter) Artistic success. Good fortune. Popularity.

CAPUT ALGOL: **L** 26° 10' Taurus (SATURN, JUPITER; Mars, Uranus, Pluto) Malefic. Decapitation; losing one's head. Damage to neck & throat. Fires. Sickness. Violence. Criminality. Murder. Horror. (Diana Rosenberg reported that Caput Algol is the fixed star most frequently active in charts of harmful fires.)

ALCYONE: **L, R** 00° 00' Gemini (MOON, JUPITER; Mars, Sun) Something to cry about. Sorrow. One of the "Weeping Sisters." Unlucky. Exile. Suffering.

HYADES (Prima Hyadum): **L, R** 5° 48' Gemini (SATURN, MERCURY; Mars, Neptune, Uranus) Scandal, violence, disgrace, imprisonment. Evil, resentful, mentally unbalanced. Murder, extremism. Shipwrecks.

NORTHERN BULL'S EYE: 8° 28' Gemini (SATURN, MERCURY; Venus) Success, good fortune. Lucky for the occult, sports, writing, arts.

ALDEBARAN: **L, R** 9° 47' Gemini (MARS; Mercury, Jupiter) A Royal Star. Courage. War-mongering. Military leadership. Danger of violence or sickness. (There are four "royal" stars: Aldebaran, Regulus, Antares, and Fomalhaut). Regulus is considered the most royal.)

RIGEL: **L, R** 16° 50' Gemini (JUPITER, SATURN; Mars)Success in technical fields. Artistic ability. Inventiveness. Ambition. Lucky.

BELLATRIX: **L** 20° 57' Gemini (MARS, MERCURY) Accidents. Sudden dishonor. Fond of power. Talkativeness. Trouble through love affairs. Jealousy. Unlucky.

CAPELLA: 21° 51' Gemini (MARS, MERCURY) Popular, successful, fond of learning. A good researcher. Talkative, eccentric. Legal or domestic problems.

PHACT: 22° 10' Gemini (Venus, Mercury; Uranus) Good luck, hope. Talent in art or science.

EL NATH: 22° 35' Gemini (MARS; Mercury) Luck, fortune, success. Quarrels. Headstrong.

ALNILAM: **L** 23° 28' Gemini (JUPITER, SATURN; Mercury) Brief fame. Quick tempered. Scandal. Good for military, sports, law, church, science. Headstrong. Studious. Possible violent death.

AL HECKA: **L** 24° 47' Gemini (MARS; Mercury, Saturn) Accidents. Quarrels. Bad temper. Depravity. Lung disease. Honors, wealth, power, aggression, greed. Sickly partner.

BETELGEUZE: **L** 28° 45' Gemini (MARS; MERCURY; Saturn, Jupiter) Good fortune, success, fame. Shrewd, rash, inventive, determined. A rebel. Fevers, acute illnesses.

SIRIUS: **L, R** 14° 05' Cancer (JUPITER, MARS; Moon) Luck. Pride, wealth, ambition, good reputation. Fame. Honors. Occult interests. Dog bites.

CANOPUS: **L** 14° 58' Cancer (SATURN, JUPITER; Moon, Mars) Voyages. Piety. Scandal. Violence. Trouble with father. Quick temper. Depression. Suicide. Stubborn.

CASTOR: **L** 20° 14' Cancer (MERCURY; Jupiter; also Mars, Venus, Saturn; Moon, Uranus) Crippling of limbs. Mental illness. Sudden fame or loss. Murder.

POLLUX: **L** 23° 13' Cancer (MARS; Moon, Uranus) Good for astrology & the occult. Danger of disgrace. Murder, rape, cruelty. Danger from large animals, women, or poisons.

PROCYON: **L** 25° 47' Cancer (MERCURY, MARS; Venus, Moon, Jupiter, Uranus) Good fortune, but sudden fall from high places. Occult interests. Wealth through violence.

PRAESAEPE: **L, R** 7° 20' Leo (MARS, MOON; Neptune) Inner drive. Reclusive. Blindness. "Exhalation of piled up corpses" (Allen). Injury, murder, tragedy, fires.

NORTH ASELLUS: **L, R** 7° 32' Leo (SUN, MARS) Military preferment. Blindness. Eye problems. Shipwreck.

SOUTH ASELLUS: **L, R** 8° 43 (SUN, MARS) Leo Same as North Asellus, with the addition of mass murder and horrors.

ACUBENS: 13° 38' Leo (SATURN, MERCURY; Mars) Good for astrology & writing. Perseverance. Domestic problems. Poison. Liars.

DUBHE: 15° 12' Leo (MARS) Good for astrology. Arrogance. Psychic. Destruction.

"OWN WORST ENEMY:" 22° Leo An unfortunate degree. One's own worst enemy and not free to act on one's own behalf.

ALPHARD: **L** 27° 17' Leo (SATURN, VENUS; Neptune, Sun, Jupiter) Sudden death by poison or drowning. Legal problems. Trouble through love affairs. Drug addiction.

AL JABHAH: **L** 27° 54' Leo (SATURN, MERCURY) Wealth, sound judgment. Clever. Prone to violence. Self-seeking. Danger, loss, scandal. Mutiny.

REGULUS: **L, R** 29° 50' Leo (MARS, JUPITER) The royal star. High office. Great power. Sudden downfall. Fortunate for matters of status and leadership. Accidents, violence. Lilly's highest "accidental dignity."

ZOSMA: 11° 19' Virgo (SATURN, VENUS) Keen intellect. Depression. Fearful. Unhappy. Feels restricted. Poisoning, accidents, intestinal problems. Suffers loss in childhood.

DENEBOLAL: 21° 37' Virgo (SATURN, VENUS; Mercury, Uranus, Mars) Honors. Undesirable associates. Distress. Happiness turns to despair. Vindictive. Mental illness. Disease. Natural disasters. Catastrophes.

COMA BERENICES: **L** 23° 52' Virgo (MOON, VENUS) Eye problems.

LABRUM: 26° 41' Virgo (Mercury, Venus) Honors, riches, ambition. Psychic. Chronic illness. Dishonest income.

VINDEMIATRIX: 9° 56' Libra (SATURN, MERCURY; Venus) Widowhood. Loss. Depression. Witch hunts. Mysticism & the occult.

ALGORAB: 13° 27' Libra (MARS, SATURN) Loss, lies, accidents, suicide, injury. Greed.

SEGINUS **L**: 17°40' Libra (MERCURY, SATURN; Venus) Good for business, astrology, law. Loss through friends. Disasters. deceitful, keen, shameless, irascible.

FORAMEN: 22° 09' Libra (SATURN, JUPITER) Prosperity. Indecision. Ear & eye problems. Leadership. Shipwreck.

SPICA: **L, R** 23° 50' Libra (VENUS, MARS; Jupiter, Mercury) Good fortune. Luck. Riches. Victory.

ARCTURUS: **L, R** 24°14' Libra (JUPITER, MARS; Venus, Mercury) Like Spica. Success through patient work.

PRINCEPS: **L** 3° 09' Scorpio (MERCURY, SATURN) Resourceful, profound, a good researcher. Good for business, government, law, science, arts. Impulsive in speech. Lies.

ALPHECCA: **L** 12° 18' Scorpio (VENUS, MERCURY; Mars) Honor, dignity. literate, inventive, brilliant, poetic. Scandals. Betrayal in love. Sorrow through children. Legal problems. Poor health. Lazy.

SOUTH SCALE: **L, R** 15° 05' Scorpio (SATURN, MARS; Venus, Mercury) Loss, theft, betrayal, abuse, venereal disease, poisoning, drowning, anguish, revenge, criminality.

SERPENTIS: 19° Scorpio According to some, a malefic degree; its possible origin is the fixed star Alpha Serpentis, also called Unukalhai (q.v.). Tragedy. Misfortune. Accursed degree of the accursed sign. (This is not too reliable.)

NORTH SCALE: **L, R** 19° 22' Scorpio (JUPITER, MERCURY; Mars) Honors, wealth, distinction, intelligence. Hasty words cause problems. Tragedy, violence. A good organizer. Success in sports, war, religion, law, writing.

UNUKALHAI (Unuk): **L** 22° 05' Scorpio (SATURN, MARS; Venus) (Also called Alpha Serpentis) Success followed by fall. Legal problems. Suicide. Insanity. Accidents. Chronic disease. Success in war, politics, writing. Problems in love. Forgery. Shipwreck.

AGENA: 23° 48' Scorpio (VENUS, JUPITER; Mars, Mercury) Honors, high status. A good organizer. Sensuality, Scandal, gossip. Sarcastic. Success with the masses. Clever.

BUNGULA: 29° 37' Scorpio (VENUS, JUPITER; Mars, Moon, Uranus) Occult interests. Self-analysis. Honors. Insensitive, stubborn, cruel.

YED PRIOR: **L** 2° 18' Sagittarius (SATURN, VENUS; Mars) Success in astrology and 9th house matters. Shrewd, conniving, sarcastic.

ANTARES: **L, R** 9° 46' Sagittarius (MARS, JUPITER; Mercury, Saturn) A Royal Star. Honors & riches but sudden loss. Good for war. Legal problems. Eye problems. Fires. Quarrels. Will marry more than once. Stubborn, suspicious. Violence.

RASTABAN: **L** 11° 58' Sagittarius (SATURN, MARS, JUPITER; Venus) Impulsive, honorable, influential. Good for astrology, government, writing, sports, finance, the arts. Accidents, wounds, blindness. Criminality.

ALGETHI: 16° 09' Sagittarius (MERCURY; Mars, Venus) Optimistic, daring, bold. Makes new discoveries. Takes risks. Shipwreck.

ACULEUS: 25° 44' Sagittarius (MARS, MOON) Blindness. Leadership ability.

ACUMEN: 28° 45' Sagittarius (MARS, MOON) Blindness. Leadership ability. Jail sentence.

SINISTRA: 29° 45' Sagittarius (SATURN, VENUS) Leadership ability. Loss. Poisoning. Callous, domineering. Self-destructive.

FACIES: 8° 18' Capricorn (SUN, MARS) Blindness. Violent death. Leadership ability. War. Cold, detached. Perfectionistic. Not close to anyone. Earthquakes.

ASCELLA: 13° 38' Capricorn (JUPITER, MERCURY) Gains, good judgment, happiness. Influential friends.

MANUBRIUM: 15° 00' Capricorn (Sun, Mars) Heroism, courage. Blindness. Legal or domestic problems. Overconfident. Good for sports & politics. Fires, explosions.

VEGA (WEGA): **L** 15° 19' Capricorn (VENUS, MERCURY; Neptune, Jupiter, Saturn) Luck in politics. Wealth through dealing with the government. Talent for art or music. Fleeting fame. Double-dealing. Problems with mother.

DENEB: 19° 48' Capricorn (Mars, Jupiter) Good fortune, success. A quick temper. Legal entanglements. Pride.

TEREBELLUM: 25° 51' Capricorn (VENUS, SATURN) ("Long ago, a scribe's error for tetrapleuron." - Rosenberg) Leadership, ambition, success. Does well in religion or politics. A doubter. Despair, regret. Terrorism, violence, mass death, murder. Racism, prejudice, anti-Semitism. (This star is prominent is the charts of the founding of modern Iraq and of its leader Saddam Hussein.)

ALTAIR L: 1° 47' Aquarius (MARS, JUPITER; Saturn, Mercury, Uranus) Accidents. Hypersensitivity & emotional imbalance. Disability. Courage, ambition. Good for astrology, writing, the public. Sudden but fleeting wealth.

OCULUS: 4° 43' Aquarius (SATURN, VENUS) Help from friends. Gains. Clever.

BOS: L 5° 10' Aquarius (SATURN; Venus) Good for business, military, analysis. Keen intellect. Shameless. Possible legal activities.

NASHIRA: L 21° 47' Aquarius (SATURN, JUPITER) Good for writing, government, religion. Legal advisor, counselor, ingenuity. Success. Hypocritical. Danger from beasts. Can overcome evil.

DENEB ALGEDI: 23° 33' Aquarius (SATURN, JUPITER; Uranus, Mercury) Fame, wealth, leadership. Sorrow. False friends. Psychic. Depression. Violent death. Domestic problems.

SADALSUUD: L 23° 49' Aquarius (SATURN, MERCURY; Uranus, Sun) Good for astrology and occult, government, sports, writing, business. Visionary, original, psychic. Leadership. Unusual in all areas. Scandal and disgrace.

FOMALHAUT: L, R 3° 52' Pisces (VENUS, MERCURY; Neptune, Jupiter, Saturn) A Royal Star. Inherited illness. Congenital defects. Magic. Fame through the occult. Infamy. Can be very good or very bad. Karma. Undesirable associates. Legal problems. May commit or suffer crime. Addiction.

DENEB ADIGE: L 5° 20' Pisces (Venus, Mercury) Intelligent, creative, original, naive. Good for astrology, writing, the public, psychism. Clever, erratic. Dog bites.

SKAT: 8° 52' Pisces (MERCURY, MARS; Jupiter, Uranus, Venus) Good fortune. Honors. Influential friends. Occult interests. Sadism. Sensitivity. Rudeness.

ACHERNAR: 15° 19' Pisces (JUPITER; Mars, Uranus) Success. Empathetic, humane, patient. Religious, philosophical.

MARKAB: L, R 23° 29' Pisces (MARS, MERCURY; Saturn, Jupiter, Venus) The star of sorrow. Emotional scars. Tragedies to loved ones. Literary ability. Legal problems. Accident prone.

SCHEAT: L, R 29° 22' Pisces (MARS, MERCURY; Saturn, Neptune, Uranus) Unlucky. Murder. Suicide. Drowning. Being condemned to death or imprisonment. Malevolence of sublime scope. Suffering. Extreme misfortune. Literary and artistic ability.

# Some Arabic Parts

The Arabic Parts in this list are taken from both modern and classical sources. The definitive text on Arabic Parts is the one by Zoller (see Bibliography). The following parts have the same basic formula: an equation of three longitude equivalents for components of the horary chart, one subtracted from the sum of two. In this table the first column lists the part. The second column is the point of origin. The third column is added to the second column, and the fourth column is subtracted from the sum of the second and third columns.

| Part | Point of Origin | Addend (+) | Subtrahend (-) |
|---|---|---|---|
| Accomplishment | Ascendant | + Sun | - Jupiter |
| Advancement | Ascendant | + Sun | - Saturn |
| Appreciation | Ascendant | + Venus | - Sun |
| Astrology | Ascendant | + Mercury | - Uranus |
| Assassination (I) | Ascendant | + 12th Cusp | - Neptune |
| Assassination (II) | Mars | + Neptune | - Uranus |
| Bereavement | 12th Cusp | + 12th Ruler | - Neptune |
| Brothers & Sisters (day) | Ascendant | + Jupiter | - Saturn |
| Brothers & Sisters (night) | Ascendant | + Saturn | - Jupiter |
| Cancer & Malignancy | Ascendant | + Neptune | - Jupiter |
| Catastrophe | Ascendant | + Uranus | - Sun |
| Catastrophe & Exile | Ascendant | + Uranus | - Saturn |
| Change | Ascendant | + Uranus | - Pluto |
| Children (*Pars Filiorum*) | Ascendant | + Jupiter | - Mars |
| Commerce; Communication | Ascendant | + Mercury | - Sun |
| Cooperation | 7th Cusp | + Moon | - Sun |
| Cucumbers & Melons | Ascendant | + Saturn | - Mercury |
| Cutting & Surgery | Ascendant | + Saturn | - Mars |
| Damage | Ascendant | + Neptune | - Mars |
| Danger, Violence, Debt | Ascendant | + Mercury | - Saturn |
| Daughters | Ascendant | + Venus | - Moon |
| Death, Disaster | Ascendant | + 8th Cusp | - Moon |

| Part | Point of Origin | Addend (+) | Subtrahend (-) |
|---|---|---|---|
| Death (medieval) | 8th Cusp | + Saturn | - Moon |
| Death of Parents | Ascendant | + Jupiter | - Saturn |
| Death of Siblings | Ascendant | + 10° Gemini | - Sun |
| Death Point | Mars | + Saturn | - MC |
| Decapitation | 8th Cusp | + Mars | - Moon |
| Deceit | Ascendant | + Venus | - Neptune |
| Disappointment | Ascendant | + Mars | - Neptune |
| Discord, lawsuits (day) | Ascendant | + Jupiter | - Mars |
| Discord, lawsuits (night) | Ascendant | + Mars | - Jupiter |
| Disputes | Ascendant | + Mercury | - Mars |
| Distress, Upset | Ascendant | + Mars | - Saturn |
| Divorce (I) | Ascendant | + Venus | - 7th Cusp |
| Divorce (II) | Venus | + 180° | [n/a, 0°] |
| False love | Ascendant | + Neptune | - Venus |
| Fame; Wisdom (day) | Ascendant | + Jupiter | - Sun |
| Fame; Wisdom (night) | Ascendant | + Sun | - Jupiter |
| Fatality | Ascendant | + Saturn | - Sun |
| Father (day) | Ascendant | + Sun | - Saturn |
| Father (night) | Ascendant | + Sun | - Saturn |
| Female Children | Ascendant | + Venus | - Moon |
| Finding lost Objects | Moon | + 4th Cusp | - ASC Ruler |
| Fortune (by day) | Ascendant | + Moon | - Sun |
| Fortune (by night) | Ascendant | + Sun | - Moon |
| Fraud | Ascendant | + Neptune | - Mercury |
| Friends | Ascendant | + Moon | - Uranus |
| Gossip | Ascendant | + Mercury | - Neptune |
| Higher Education | Ascendant | + 9th Cusp | - Mercury |
| Illness | Ascendant | + Mars | - Saturn |
| Imprisonment, Sorrow | Ascendant | + Pars Fortuna | - ASC Ruler |
| Individuality | Ascendant | + Sun | - Uranus |
| Information (true or false) | Ascendant | + Moon | - Mercury |
| Inheritance | Ascendant | + Moon | - Saturn |
| Injury to Business | Ascendant | + Pars Fortuna | - ASC Ruler |
| Insincerity | Ascendant | + Moon | - Neptune |
| Killing Planet (Anareta) (day) | Ascendant | + Moon | - ASC Ruler |
| Killing Planet (Anareta) (night) | Ascendant | + ASC ruler | - Moon |
| Lawsuits | Ascendant | + Mercury | - Mars |
| Legalizing | 9th Cusp | + 3rd Cusp | - Venus |
| Life/Death of Absent Person | Ascendant | + Mars | - Moon |
| Lost Animal (light color) | Ascendant | + Mars | - Sun |
| Lost Animal (dark color) | Ascendant | + Mars | - Saturn |
| Love | Ascendant | + Jupiter | - Venus |

| Part | Point of Origin | Addend (+) | Subtrahend (-) |
|---|---|---|---|
| Love & Marriage | Ascendant | + Jupiter | - Venus |
| Luck | Ascendant | + Moon | - Jupiter |
| Male Children (day) | Ascendant | + Jupiter | - Moon |
| Male Children (night) | Ascendant | + Moon | - Jupiter |
| Man's Marriage | Ascendant | + Venus | - Saturn |
| Marriage & Partners | Ascendant | + 7th Cusp | - Venus |
| Mind; Captivity | Ascendant | + 3rd Cusp | - Mercury |
| Mother (day) | Ascendant | + Moon | - Venus |
| Mother (night) | Ascendant | + Venus | - Moon |
| Mother & Family | Ascendant | + Jupiter | - Venus |
| Obstruction; Caution | Ascendant | + Neptune | - Saturn |
| Occultism | Ascendant | + Neptune | - Uranus |
| Passion | Ascendant | + Mars | - Sun |
| Peril (day) | Ascendant | + 8th Ruler | - Saturn |
| Peril (night) | Ascendant | + Saturn | - 8th Ruler |
| Point of Death | Mars | + Saturn | - MC |
| Popularity | Ascendant | + Venus | - Pluto |
| Profession | Ascendant | + Moon | - Saturn |
| Property (Movable) (day) | Ascendant | + 2nd Cusp | - 2nd Ruler |
| Property (Movable) (night) | Ascendant | + 2nd Ruler | - 2nd Cusp |
| Radical Change | Ascendant | + Pluto | - Uranus |
| Real Estate (day) | Ascendant | + Moon | - Saturn |
| Real Estate (night) | Ascendant | + Saturn | - Moon |
| Repression | Ascendant | + Saturn | - Pluto |
| Retribution (day) | Ascendant | + Sun | - Mars |
| Retribution (night) | Ascendant | + Mars | - Sun |
| Resigning (dismissal) | Saturn | + Jupiter | - Sun |
| Ritual Ceremonies | 9th Cusp | + 3rd Cusp | - Venus |
| Secret Enemies | Ascendant | + 12th Cusp | - 12th Ruler |
| Secrets | Ascendant | + 10th Cusp | - ASC Ruler |
| Self-Undoing | Ascendant | + 12th Cusp | - Neptune |
| Sex & love | Ascendant | + Venus | - Sun |
| Sex Drive & libido | Ascendant | + Pluto | - Venus |
| Sickness | Ascendant | + Mars | - Saturn |
| Slander | Ascendant | + Saturn | - Neptune |
| Slyness | Ascendant | + Neptune | - Pluto |
| Sons | Ascendant | + Jupiter | - Moon |
| Speculation (I) (day) | Ascendant | + 5th Cusp | - Jupiter |
| Speculation (I) (night) | Ascendant | + Jupiter | - 5th Cusp |
| Speculation (II) | Ascendant | + Jupiter | - Neptune |
| Success (day) | Ascendant | + Jupiter | - Pars Fortuna |
| Success (night) | Ascendant | + Pars Fortuna | - Jupiter |

| Part | Point of Origin | Addend (+) | Subtrahend (-) |
|---|---|---|---|
| Successful Issue | Ascendant | + Jupiter | - Sun |
| Sudden Advancement (I) (day) | Ascendant | + Pars Fortuna | - Saturn |
| Sudden Advancement (I) (night) | Pars Fortuna | + Ascendant | - Saturn |
| Sudden Advancement (II) | Ascendant | + Sun | - Saturn |
| (or if Saturn combust) | Ascendant | + Sun | - Jupiter |
| Sudden luck | Ascendant | + Jupiter | - Uranus |
| Sudden Parting | Ascendant | + Saturn | - Uranus |
| Suicide | Ascendant | + 8th Cusp | - Neptune |
| Surgery; Police; Army (day) | Ascendant | + Saturn | - Mars |
| Surgery; Police; Army (night) | Saturn | + Ascendant | - Mars |
| Surprise | Ascendant | + Mars | - Uranus |
| Sweet Foods | Ascendant | + Venus | - Sun |
| Time for Action | Ascendant | + Jupiter | - Sun |
| Torture | MC | + Saturn | - Moon |
| Tragedy, Fate, Fatality | Ascendant | + Saturn | - Sun |
| Travel by Air | Ascendant | + 9th Cusp | - Uranus |
| Travel by land | Ascendant | + 9th Cusp | - 9th Ruler |
| Travel by Water | Ascendant | + 15° Cancer | - Saturn |
| Treachery | Ascendant | + Neptune | - Sun |
| Treasure | Ascendant | + Venus | - Mercury |
| Trickery | Ascendant | + Mars | - Moon |
| Unusual Events | Ascendant | + Uranus | - Moon |
| Urgent Wish | Ascendant | + ASC Ruler | - Hour Ruler |
| Weddings | 9th Cusp | + 3rd Cusp | - Venus |
| Widowhood | Ascendant | + Vindemiatrix | - Neptune |

(Vindemiatrix = 9° 56' Libra  in year 2000)

# Data for the Charts of William Lilly

For readers who wish to read Lilly's *Christian Astrology*, I have listed below my best approximation of the data for Lilly's charts in the format from Allen Edwall's program *Horary Helper for Windows*, which I highly recommend to students of classical horary astrology. This data, however, can be entered into any chart calculation program to produce the charts found in Lilly's classic text on the subject. The dates have been adjusted to accord with the modern Gregorian calendar now in use. These computer calculations will differ slightly from those found in the seventeenth-century ephemeris used by Lilly. The page numbers refer to the pages in the Regulus edition of *Christian Astrology*. The chart numbers (Ch1, Ch2, etc.) refer to their order in Lilly's text. P means P.M. and A means A.M. Most of the charts are set for time zone 0 at coordinates 000W10 and 51N30.

Lilly: p135 Ch1, 24 Mar 1633, 2.26, P, 0, 001.10, 51.30
Lilly: p152 Ch2, 30 Jul 1638, 11.55, A, 0, 000.23, 51.22
Lilly: p162 Ch3, 07 Jan 1645, 3.32, P, 0, 000.10, 51.30
Lilly: p165 Ch4, 19 Mar 1647, 10.29, A, 00, 000.10, 51.30
Lilly: p177 Ch5, 26 Jul 1634, 11.05, A, 0, 000.10, 51.30
Lilly: p196 Ch6, 17 Nov 1645, 11.44, A, 0, 000.10, 51.30
Lilly: p200 Ch7, 21 Apr 1643, 4.29, P, 0, 000.10, 51.30
Lilly: p219 Ch8, 10 Apr 1634, 6.03, P, 0, 000.10, 51.30
Lilly: p238 Ch9, 22 Jun 1635, 9.30, A, 0, 000.10, 51.30
Lilly: p240 Ch10, 17 Apr 1645, 2.17, P, 0, 000.10, 51.30
Lilly: p286 Ch11, 18 May 1645, 6.10, P, 0, 000.10, 51.30
Lilly: p289 Ch12, 26 Jul 1645, 7.31, A, 0, 000.10, 51.30
Lilly: p385 Ch13, 27 Jun 1646, 7.35, A, 0, 000.10, 51.30
Lilly: p389 Ch14, 21 Jun 1646, 10.39, A, 0, 000.10, 51.30
Lilly: p390 Ch15, 07 Mar 1645, 10.30, A, 0, 000.10, 51.30
Lilly: p392 Ch16, 08 Sep 1646, 4.05, P, 0, 000.10, 51.30
Lilly: p395 Ch17, 03 Jun 1647, 4.54, P, 0, 000.10, 51.30
Lilly: p397 Ch18, 20 Feb 1638, 9.02, A, 0, 000.23, 51.31
Lilly: p399 Ch19, 08 Apr 1644, 10.16, A, 0, 000.10, 51.30
Lilly: p401 Ch20, 27 Apr 1643, 6.49, P, 0, 000.10, 51.30
Lilly: p415 Ch21, 16 Feb 1645, 9.22, P, 0, 000.10, 51.30
Lilly: p417 Ch22, 25 Apr 1645, 1.09, P, 0, 000.10, 51.30

Lilly: p419 Ch23, 13 Dec 1644, 2.19, P, 0, 000.10, 51.30
Lilly: p421 Ch24, 25 Jul 1634, 6.18, P, 0, 000.10, 51.30
Lilly: p436 Ch25, 05 Feb 1643, 9.43, A, 0, 000.10, 51.30
Lilly: p437 Ch26, 16 Aug 1644, 8.26, P, 0, 000.10, 51.30
Lilly: p439 Ch27, 21 Mar 1647, 4.50, P, 0, 000.10, 51.30
Lilly: p442 Ch28, 06 Jun 1647, 10.38, A, 0, 000.10, 51.30
Lilly: p452 Ch29, 08 Dec 1642, 9.20, A, 0, 000.10, 51.30
Lilly: p455 Ch30, 28 Mar 1643, 6.00, P, 0, 000.10, 51.30
Lilly: p467 Ch31, 21 Jan 1647, 3.10, P, 0, 000.10, 51.30
Lilly: p468 Ch32, 23 Mar 1647, 8.12, A, 0, 000.10, 51.30
Lilly: p470 Ch33, 16 Jun 1647, 7.57, P, 0, 000.10, 51.30
Lilly: p471 Ch34, 29 Oct 1645, 6.53, P, 0, 000.10, 51.30
Lilly: p473 Ch35, 24 May 1644, 12.25, A, 0, 000.10, 51.30
Lilly: p473 Ch35 Capr Moon, 24 May 1644, 12.37, A, 0, 000.10, 51.30 (This adjustment was needed to get the Moon in Capricorn as it appears in Lilly's text.)
William Lilly natal chart: 11 May 1602, 2.08, A, .019, 001.16, 52.38

# BIBLIOGRAPHY

Adams, Evangeline (1931). *Astrology for Everyone.* New York: Dodd, Mead, & Co., 1960.

Allen, Richard H. (1899). *Star Names: Their Lore and Meaning.* New York, New York: Dover Publications, 1963.

Alvarado, Luis. *Psychology, Astrology & Western Magic.* St. Paul, MN: Llewellyn Publications, 1991.

Appleby, Derek. *Horary Astrology.* Wellingborough, Northamptonshire: The Aquarian Press, 1985.

Barclay, Olivia. *Horary Astrology Rediscovered.* West Chester, PA: Whitford Press, 1990.

———. *"Will I Make Money at This Job?"* The Horary Practitioner, Issue 3 (October/November 1989): 27f. Issaquah, Washington: JustUs & Associates.

Barrett, Francis. *The Magus, or Celestial Intelligencer.* London, 1801.

*Benet's Reader's Encyclopedia,* Third Edition. New York: Harper & Row, Publishers, 1987.

Bills, Rex, E. *The Rulership Book.* Richmond, Virginia: Macoy Publications and Masonic Supply Company, Inc., 1971.

Bonatti (Bonatus), Guido. *Liber Astronomiae, Part IV: On Horary.* Project Hindsight Latin Track XIII.

———. *The Astrologer's Guide.* ed. William Lilly, 1675. Tempe, AZ: American Federation of Astrologers, 1970.

Boorstin, Daniel J. *The Discoverers: The History of Mankind's Search to Know His World and Himself.* New York: Vintage Books, 1985.

Bouche-leclercq, A. *L'Astrolgie Greque.* Paris: Culture et Civilisation, 1899.

Bratcher-Hill, Bobbye. *A Basic Introduction to Horary Astrology.* (Audiotape.) Aquarian-Cancerian Tapes.

Campion, Nicholas. *The Practical Astrologer.* New York: Harry N. Abrams, Publishers, 1987.

Carter, Charles E.O. *The Principles of Astrology.* Wheaton, IL: The Theosophical Publishing House, 1963.

*CCAG: Catalogus Codicum Astrologorum Graecorum.* Bruxelles, Lamertin, 1898 to 1953 in 12 volumes.

Clark, Jonathon. *Average Daily Motion of Mercury and Venus.* The Horary Practitioner, Vol. 7, #20, 1996 Special Edition, p.15.

Coley, Henry. *Clavis Astrologiae; Or a Key to the Whole Art of Astrologie: In Two Parts.* London: Printed for Joseph Coniers, 1669.

Cozzi, Steve. *Planets in Locality.* St. Paul: Llewellyn Publications, 1988.

Dariot, Claude. *A Breefe and Most Easie Introduction to the Astrological Judgement of the Starres.* Translated by Fabian Wither. London, circa 1583.

DeLong, Sylvia. *The Art of Horary Astrology in Practice.* Tempe, Arizona: American Federation of Astrologers, 1980.

DeLuce, Robert. *Horary Astrology.* New York: ASI Publishers, 1932.

De Vore, Nicholas. *Encyclopedia of Astrology.* New York: Philosophical Library, 1947.

Dorotheus Sidonius (first century). *Carmen Astrologicum.* ed., trans. David Pingree. Leipzig: BSB B.B. Teubner Verlagsgesellshaft, 1976.

Ebertin, Reinhold. *The Combination of Stellar Influences.* Tempe, AZ: The American Federation of Astrologers, 1940.

Ebertin/Hoffman. *Fixed Stars and Their Interpretations.* Tempe, AZ: American Federation of Astrologers, 1971.

Filbey, John and Peter. *The Astrologer's Companion.* Wellingborough, Northamptonshire, Great Britain: The Aquarian Press, 1986.

Freud, Sigmund. *The Interpretation of Dreams.* trans. James Strachey. New York: Avon Books, 1985.

Gadbury, John. *The Doctrine of Horary Questions, Astrologically Handled.* London: printed by John Coniers for William Larner, 1658.

Granite, Robert Hurzt. *The Fortunes of Astrology.* San Diego: ACS Publications, 1980.

Hamaker-Zondag, Karen. *Handbook of Horary Astrology.* York Beach, Maine: Samuel Weiser, 1993.

Hand, Robert. Excerpts from "Bonatti on Horary." *The Horary Practitioner,* Vol. 7, #20, 1996 Special Edition, pp.20-26.

Holden, Ralph William. *The Elements of House Division.* Essex, Great Britain: L.N. Fowler & Co., Ltd., 1977.

Hone, Margaret E. *The Modern Text-Book of Astrology.* South Hampton, Great Britain: The Camelot Press, 1978.

Ibn Ezra, Abraham. *The Beginning of Wisdom.* Edited by Raphael Levy and Francisco Cantera. Ascella.

Innes, Brian. *Fate and Fortune.* New York: Crown Publishers, 1977.

Jacobson-Goldstein, Ivy M. *Here and There in Astrology.* Pasadena: Pasadena Lithographers, 1961.

———. *Simplified Horary Astrology.* Alhambra, California: Frank Severy Publishing, 1960.

Jones, Marc Edmund. *Problem Solving by Horary Astrology.* Philadelphia: David McKay, 1946.

*Larouse World Mythology.* New Jersey: Chartwell Books. 1965.

Lavoie, Alphee. "Horary Myths," *The Ascendant: Journal of the Astrological Society of Connecticut,* Volume 13, Issue 1 (1989): 20ff.

Lehman, J. Lee. Classical Astrology for Modern Living. Atglen, PA: Whitford Press, 1996.

———. *Essential Dignities.* West Chester, PA: Whitford Press, 1989.

———. "A Note on Almutens," *The Horary Practitioner,* 1995 Special Edition, April 15, 1995, p.31.

Leo, Alan (1901). *Horary Astrology, Third Edition.* New Delhi: Sagar Publications, 1973.

Lilly, William. (1647), *An Introduction to Astrology,* ed. Zadkiel. Hollywood, California: Newcastle Publishing Company, 1972.

———. *Christian Astrology.* Copied by Carol A. Wiggers. Issaquah, WA: JustUs and Associates.

———. *Christian Astrology* Regulus edition, 1647.

Lindsay, Jack. *Origins of Astrology.* New York: Barnes & Noble, 1971.

Leoni, Edgar. *Nostradamus and His Prophecies.* Bell Publishing Company, 1982.

Louis, Anthony. "Peregrine Planets and Mutual Receptions," *The Horary Practitioner,* Issue 4 (January, 1990): 3f. Issaquah, Washington: Just Us & Associates.

Manilius, Marcus (?A.D. 15). *Astronomica,* trans. G.P. Goold. Cambridge, MA: Harvard University Press, 1977.

Maternus, Firmicus (A.D. 334). *Ancient Astrology, Theory and Practice, The Mathesis of Firmicus Maternus,* ed, trans. Jean Rhys Bram. Park Ridge, New Jersey: Noyes Press, 1975.

March, Marion, & McEvers, Joan. *The Only Way to Learn about Horary and Electional Astrology,* Volume IV. San Diego, CA: ACS Publications, 1994.

———. *The Only Way to Learn Astrology.* Volume II. San Diego, CA: ACS Publications, 1981.

Mason, Sophia. *Understanding Planetary Placements.* Parma, OH: Aquarian-Cancer Publications, 1977.

McEvers, Joan. *Hooked on Horary, Volume III.* (Audiotape.) Astroanalytics & The Arizona Federation of Astrologers, 1989.

McIntosh, Christopher. *The Astrologers and Their Creed.* New York: Frederick A. Praeger, Publishers, 1969.

Munkasey, Michael, "A Primer on Market Forecasting," *Financial Astrology for the 1990s,* ed. Joan McEvers, 18ff. St. Paul, MN: Llewellyn Publications, 1989.

Neugebaur, O. & Van Hoesen, H.B. *Greek Horoscopes.* Philadelphia: The American Philosophical Society, 1959.

Noonan, George C. *Classical Scientific Astrology*. Tempe, Arizona: American Federation of Astrologers, 1984.

Parker, Derek. *Familiar To All: William Lilly and Astrology in the Seventeenth Century*. London: Jonathan Cape, 1975.

Puotinen, C.J. "Lost & Found: The Basic Rules," *The Horary Practitioner*, Issue 1 (April, 1989): 5f. Issaquah, Washington: Just Us & Associates.

Ptolemy. *The Almagest*. trans. in 1939 by R.C. Taliaferro. Chicago, IL: Encyclopedia Britannica, Inc., 1948.

———. *Tetrabiblos*. trans. F.E. Robbins. Cambridge: Harvard University Press, 1940.

———. *Tetrabiblos & Centiloquy*. trans. J.M. Ashmand. North Hollywood, California: Symbols & Signs, 1976.

Ramsey, William. *Astrology Restored*. London, 1653.

Rosenberg, Diana K. *Fixed Star Workbook*. Diana K. Rosenberg, 100 La Salle St. #6A, New York, NY: 10027, 1981.

Rudhyar, Dane. *The Astrological Houses*. Reno, Nevada: CRCS Publications, 1972.

———. *The Practice of Astrology*. Netherlands: Servire/Wassenaar, 1968.

Scofield, Bruce. *The Timing of Events: Electional Astrology*. Orleans, MA: Astrolabe, 1985.

Simmonite, W.J. (1850). *Horary Astrology*. Tempe, AZ: American Federation of Astrologers, 1950.

Tester, Jim. *A History of Western Astrology*. New York: Ballantine Books, 1987.

Ungar, Anne & Huber, Lillian. *The Horary Reference Book*. San Diego, CA: ACS Publications, 1984.

Ward, Sue. "The Considerations Before Judgment." Sue Ward's page on Internet: http://www.horary.com/swindex.html.

———. "Traditional Horary FAQs" URL: http://www.horary.com/swindex.html.

Warren, Adrienne. *A Handbook of Physical Descriptions*. Issaquah, WA: Just Us & Associates, 1990.

Watters, Barbara. *Horary Astrology and the Judgment of Events*. Washington: Valhalla Paperbacks, 1973.

Weinstock, S. "Lunar Mansions and Early Calendars," *Journal of Hellenic Studies* LXIX (1949): 48ff.

Zain, C.C. *Horary Astrology*. Los Angeles: The Church of Light, 1931 by Elbert Benjamine

# INDEX

# LOOK FOR THE CRESCENT MOON

*Llewellyn publishes hundreds of books on your favorite subjects! To get these exciting books, including the ones on the following pages, check your local bookstore or order them directly from Llewellyn.*

## ORDER BY PHONE

- Call toll-free within the U.S. and Canada, 1-800-THE MOON
- In Minnesota, call (612) 291-1970
- We accept VISA, MasterCard, and American Express

## ORDER BY MAIL

- Send the full price of your order (MN residents add 7% sales tax) in U.S. funds, plus postage & handling to:

  Llewellyn Worldwide
  P.O. Box 64383, Dept. K401-4
  St. Paul, MN 55164–0383, U.S.A.

## POSTAGE & HANDLING

(For the U.S., Canada, and Mexico)

- $4.00 for orders $15.00 and under
- $5.00 for orders over $15.00
- No charge for orders over $100.00

We ship UPS in the continental United States. We ship standard mail to P.O. boxes. Orders shipped to Alaska, Hawaii, The Virgin Islands, and Puerto Rico are sent first-class mail. Orders shipped to Canada and Mexico are sent surface mail.

**International orders:** Airmail—add freight equal to price of each book to the total price of order, plus $5.00 for each non-book item (audio tapes, etc.).

**Surface mail**—Add $1.00 per item.

*Allow 4–6 weeks for delivery on all orders.*
*Postage and handling rates subject to change.*

## DISCOUNTS

We offer a 20% discount to group leaders or agents. You must order a minimum of 5 copies of the same book to get our special quantity price.

## FREE CATALOG

Get a free copy of our color catalog, *New Worlds of Mind and Spirit.* Subscribe for just $10.00 in the United States and Canada ($30.00 overseas, airmail). Many bookstores carry *New Worlds*— ask for it!

**Visit our web site at www.llewellyn.com for more information.**

## Tarot Plain and Simple
### Anthony Louis
### with illustrations by Robin Wood

The tarot is an excellent method for turning experience into wisdom. At its essence the Tarot deals with archetypal symbols of the human situation. By studying the Tarot, we connect ourselves with the mythical underpinnings of our lives; we contact the gods within. As a tool, the Tarot helps to awaken our intuitive self.

*Tarot Plain and Simple* presents a thoroughly tested, reliable and user-friendly self-study program for those who want to do readings for themselves and others. It is written by Anthony Louis, a psychiatrist who brings a profound understanding of human nature and psychological conflict to the study of the Tarot. Tarot enthusiasts will find that his Jungian approach to the card descriptions will transport them to an even deeper level of personal transformation.

1-56718-400-6, 336 pp., 6 x 9, illus., softcover                    $14.95

## Astrological Timing of Critical Illness
### Early Warning Patterns in the Horoscope
### Noel Tyl
#### Foreword by Mitchell Gibson, Ph.D.
#### Introduction by Jeffrey Wolf Green

Now, through master astrologer Noel Tyl's work, astrology has a thoroughly tested method with which to understand and anticipate the emergence of critical illness: from the natal horoscope, throughout development, and within the aging process. Astrologers can use Noel Tyl's discovery to work with people to extend life as much as possible, to live a full life, and to do it all with holistic understanding.

Tyl painstakingly researched more than seventy cases to test his patterning discoveries. Your analytical skill will be alerted, tested, and sharpened through these very same cases, which include notables such as Carl Sagan (bone cancer), Betty Ford (breast cancer), Larry King (heart attack), Norman Schwarzkopf (prostate cancer), and Mike Wallace (manic depression), and many, many others.

- Explore the predisposition to pathology as indicated in the horoscope

- Learn the aspect patterns natally that, with Solar Arcs and Transits, reveal extreme challenge to the life system, the onset of specific body weakness and critical illness

- Exercise your observational skills and your facility reading planetary networks and timing patterns through the study of 70 horoscopes

- Lead your clients to seek the early medical attention that could save their lives

- Learn to communicate the indications of the horoscope to the client in a sensitive manner

1-56718-738-2, 288 pp., 7 x 10, softcover          $19.95

## Prediction in Astrology
### A Master Volume of Technique and Prediction
### Noel Tyl

No matter how much you know about astrology already, no matter how much experience you've had to date, you'll be fascinated by *Prediction in Astrology*, and you'll grow as an astrologer. Using the Solar Arc theory and methods he describes in this book, the author was able to accurately predict the Gulf War, including the actual date it would begin and the timetable of tactics, two months before it began. He also predicted the overturning of Communist rule in the Eastern bloc nations nine months in advance of its actual occurrence.

Tyl teaches through example. You learn by doing astrology, not just thinking about it. Tyl introduces Solar Arc theory in terms of "rapport" measurements, which you begin to do immediately, without paper, pencil, or computer, dials, or wheels. Just with your eyes! You will never look at a horoscope the same way again!

Tyl, in his well-known, very special way, also gets personal. He presents 30 Aphorisms, the keenest of maxims, the most practical of techniques, to create predictions from any horoscope. And as if this were not enough, Tyl then presents 20 Aphorisms for Counseling. Look for Tyl's "Quick-Glance" Transit Table, 1940-2040, to which you can refer more quickly than a computer. The busy astrologer will use this Appendix every day for many years to come.

0-87542-814-2, 360 pp., 6 x 9, softcover                    $17.95

## Pluto, Vol. II
### The Soul's Evolution Through Relationships
### Jeffrey Wolf Green

From the great mass of people on the planet we all choose certain ones with whom to be intimate. Pluto, Vol II shows the evolutionary and karmic causes, reasons, and prior life background that determines whom we relate to and how.

This is the first book to explore the astrological Pluto model that embraces the evolutionary development and progression of the Soul from life to life. It offers a unique, original paradigm that allows for a total understanding of the past life dynamics that exist between two people. You will find a precise astrological methodology to determine the prior life orientation, where the relationship left off, where the relationship picked up in this lifetime, and what the current evolutionary next step is: the specific reasons or intentions for being together again.

In addition, there are chapters devoted to Mars and Venus in the signs, Mars and Venus in relationship, Mars and Pluto in relationship, and Pluto through the Composite Houses.

1-56718-333-6, 6 x 9, 432 pp., softcover                                        $17.95

## Instant Horoscope Predictor
### Find Your Future Fast
### Julia Lupton Skalka

Want to know if the planets will smile favorably upon your wedding day? Wondering when to move ahead on that new business venture? Perhaps you're curious as to why you've been so accident prone lately. It's time to look at your transits.

Transits define the relationship between where the planets are today with where they were when you were born. They are an invaluable aid for timing your actions and making decisions. With a copy of your transit chart and the book *Instant Horoscope Predictor*, you can now discover what's in store for today, next month, even a year from now. Julia Lupton Skalka delivers an easy-to-use guide that will decipher the symbols on your transit chart into clear, usable predictions. In addition, she provides chapters on astrological history, mythology, and transit analyses of four famous people: Grace Kelly, Mata Hari, Theodore Roosevelt and Ted Bundy.

**1-56718-668-8, 6 x 9, 464 pp., softcover**                                **$14.95**

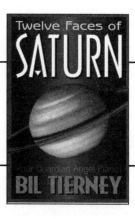

## Twelve Faces of Saturn
### Your Guardian Angel Planet
### Bil Tierney

Astrological Saturn. It's usually associated with personal limitations, material obstacles, psychological roadblocks and restriction. We observe Saturn's symbolism in our natal chart with uneasiness and anxiety, while intellectually proclaiming its higher purpose as our "wise teacher."

But now it's time to throw out the portrait of the creepy looking, scythe-wielding Saturn of centuries ago. Bil Tierney offers a refreshing new picture of a this planet as friend, not foe. Saturn is actually key to liberating us from a life handicapped by lack of clear self definition. It is indispensable to psychological maturity and material stability—it is your guardian angel planet.

Explore Saturn from the perspective of your natal sign and house. Uncover another layer of Saturnian themes at work in Saturn's aspects. Look at Saturn through each element and modality, as well as through astronomy, mythology, and metaphysics.

**1-56718-711-0, 6 x 9, 360 pp., softcover**                                        **$16.95**

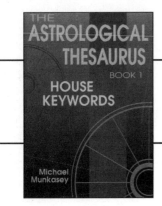

## The Astrological Thesaurus
### Book One: House Keywords
### Michael Munkasey

Keywords are crucial for astrological work. They translate astrological symbols into clear, everyday language—which is a never-ending pursuit of astrologers. For example, the Third House can be translated into the keywords "visitors," "early education" or "novelist."

*The Astrological Thesaurus, Book One: House Keywords* is a the first easy-to-use reference book and textbook on the houses, their psychologically rich meanings, and their keywords. This book also includes information on astrological quadrants and hemispheres, how to choose a house system, and the mathematical formulations for many described house systems.

Astrologer Michael Munkasey compiled almost 14,000 keywords from more than 600 sources over a 23-year period. He has organized them into 17 commonplace categories (e.g., things, occupations and psychological qualities), and cross-referenced them three ways for ease of use: alphabetically, by house, and by category. Horary users, in particular, will find this book extremely useful.

**0-87542-579-8, 434 pp., 7 x 10, illus., softcover**                    **$19.95**